Prologue

This book, like our collaboration, came about more by chance than by anything else. In 1981 I was one of three principal consultants—Wayne Booth and Maxine Hairston were the other two—at the Wyoming Conference on Freshman and Sophomore English. Each of us was to give two prepared papers and in the final session of the Conference a talk of twenty minutes "summing up" what seemed to us "the major issues of professional concern" as a week of panels, presentations, and workshops had defined them. Most of what was expected of us as consultants, in other words, we could prepare for. The final session—all that winter and early spring it loomed for me as more and more of a nightmare—we could do nothing about ahead of time.

For some reason, the last thing I did before leaving Pittsburgh for the Conference was to get from my files a copy of the same student paper I talk about in this book. I really don't know why I did that. For comfort I suppose, in some purely private totemic way. I had no conscious thought of making any use of the paper at all. It's impossible, without my supplying a good deal of context, for lots of people to hear at all. And though for years the paper has symbolized for me, just for me as an individual teacher, the most I can imagine a student's making the activity of writing mean, I had never had a way of explaining this that satisfied me, even assuming I could make what I did understand of it relevant to anything that was to go on at the Conference.

I did use the paper, of course, in my final twenty minutes of talk, relying rather heavily as I remember on a performance of high sentence that was more than a bit obtuse. The alpha and omega of the profession I made that writer's prose—linking it sonorously, if rather loosely, with time, death, God, the inevitability of certain life processes, and as much as I could recall of what I'd heard said in a week's talk about the teaching of writing. I wound up this lobster quadrille with a paraphrase of E.B. White: "Try putting *that* paper," I said, "in one of your prose analyzing machines. It may come out easy, or it may come out hard, but it will come out whole and it will live forever. And so will the writer of it. And so, as his teacher, will I. And thank you."

People were really pretty nice, all things considered—though I did overhear one woman in the foyer of the auditorium afterwards saying: "But what did he *tell* us? *What* did he tell us?"

At dinner that night with Jim Vopat, a former participant in one of my NEH Summer Seminars, I was still feeling lousy.

"Well, Bill," Jim said, "whether you can claim a control group for eternity with that paper or not, one thing you did do was to say of a particular piece of student writing: 'I like this better than any other piece of student writing I've ever read.' Flat out. Right out loud. You don't hear many people do that. Most teachers of writing would waffle—I know I would."

I said that given my afternoon I could sure as hell see why.

"No, I mean it," he said. "I was thinking what paper I'd pick if I had to. What would I use as an example of what I'd call a really excellent piece of student writing? And what would I say about it? Would I call it clear? Would I say it was vivid? It would be tough, particularly in public."

I was in a good position to know exactly what he meant.

"Wouldn't it be interesting to see what different people would pick?" Jim went on. "Suppose somebody had said to Genung: 'O.K., let me see what you think is one of the best student papers you've ever gotten. And no nonsense please about how you've read a barrelful. Just settle on one and let's see it.' What kind of paper would he have come up with, do you think?"

"And what would we think about what he did come up with? 'Oh, so that's it, is it, John? That's what you're after? That's what you want? That's what you call good writing, do you?' "

"What kind of a paper do you think Dick Young would pick?"

"Or Ohmann?" I said. "Or Winterowd?"

"Wouldn't it be interesting to see a book like that? Think what you could see about where we are as a profession with a book like that?"

"Or where we're not."

"Yes, particularly if people had to explain why they called a given piece of writing good. It might give us a whole new way of talking about the profession."

"A way of seeing what the discipline *really* is, you mean—in what senses we have one, whether we have one at all. A book like that, you know, once things shook down, might even change the way writing is taught."

"Yes. And learned. Think what students might be able to learn from a book like that, for instance."

"You might even be able to make a text of a book like that," I said.

"Want to try it?" Jim said.

So we agreed that we would.

What Makes Writing Good

What Makes Writing Good

A Multiperspective

William E. Coles, Jr.
University of Pittsburgh

James Vopat
Carroll College

D. C. Heath and Company
Lexington, Massachusetts / Toronto

Cover illustration: "Nude Descending a Staircase No. 2," 1912, by Marcel Duchamp.
Philadelphia Museum of Art: The Louise and Walter Arensberg Collection.

International Standard Book Number: 0-669-06614-1

Library of Congress Catalog Card Number: 84-80295

Preface

Though we were clear at the outset that with *What Makes Writing Good* we wanted more than an academic showpiece—more than just an anthology of prize-winning student papers, say, or a collection of distinguished essays on student writing—how to make a textbook out of the diversity we intended to assemble, a textbook that writing teachers of all sorts could teach from in all kinds of classrooms and with which students would have a chance to learn, this was by no means clear.

Assembling the Material

It would have been easier, of course, if we had selected as our contributors only those teachers of writing who approach that activity from a similar perspective or whose standards of evaluation conform to certain principles. However, we chose our contributors as deliberately for what they do not have in common as for what they do. All are highly experienced and, for the most part, widely published and nationally known figures in the field of rhetoric. But they represent a variety of theoretical commitments, standards, and pedagogical styles. They work in a variety of educational settings—from community and private colleges to large state universities. And they teach a number of different kinds of undergraduate writing courses—from basic and technical writing to courses that focus on writing about one's self, or on writing about readings.

It would have been possible also to have gathered examples of only a single kind, type, or mode of student writing for consideration: a group of five-paragraph themes, for instance, or a collection of autobiographical narratives, essays of description exclusively, or of persuasion. But in this book there are papers of fewer than five sentences as well as those of many more than five paragraphs. There are examples of biographical and autobiographical writing, but also papers in which students deliberately attempt to assume personalities different from their own. In addition to papers of description, there are papers of definition, analysis, argumentation, and comparison and contrast. There is writing here that is meant to persuade, but also writing that is used to express a dilemma or to solve a problem. There are examples of writing as different in form and purpose as the résumé, the short story, the field report, the meditation, the fifty-minute diagnostic essay, the journal.

Guidelines to Contributors

In fact, the only stipulation we imposed on the teachers represented in this book had to do with format. Each contributor was asked to supply three things:

1. An example of a piece of college student writing (limited to 1000 words of discursive prose) that for that teacher in some way demonstrates excellence, however flawed or unfinished the paper may be in other ways. Indeed, we advised people to select writings that would start conversations rather than stop them.
2. The writing assignment to which the student paper was addressed.
3. A commentary (limited to 1500 words) in which the teacher would explain to a student audience why he or she finds the paper praiseworthy.

Within those limits our contributors were free to do as they chose: to work with any piece of student writing they wished, to talk in whatever terms they thought appropriate to help other students understand in what senses a particular piece of student writing might be considered good. For it seemed to us essential that our collection make clear just how diverse the teaching of writing is as a discipline: how many different rhetorical scenes are being created for the rhetorical acts of students to take place in, how many different points of view are being taken on what the rhetorical activity of writing means. Thus *What Makes Writing Good* would be a way of dramatizing first of all what it *means* to say, as teachers continually do, that excellence in writing can come in many forms and genres, and can be understood as praiseworthy from various points of view. Secondly, and more importantly, since what is said to be an excellent piece of writing from one perspective can be said to be mediocre or even unacceptable from another, the book would also be a way of dramatizing how no judgments about writing can be taken as final or absolute.

Shaping the Material

The problem, of course, was to find a way of presenting this diversity in a form that people could use.

Our solution was to design *What Makes Writing Good* so as to provide students with two things:

1. A manageably connected learning experience based upon their own writing about writing.
2. An opportunity to develop as writers by practicing in the context of the practices of others.

The student essays and commentaries of this book, then, are not in any sense intended to supply either a definition of or a formula for producing good writing.

But they can, along with a writing class, help create a context in which students can learn to shape better and to evaluate with more discrimination whatever they write. They can help create a context in which it makes sense to say that one can learn from his or her experience with writing—whether or not students admire or agree with any of the contributions to this book. For simply to think about and practice one's own writing in relation to the thinking and practices of others, simply to become conscious of what other writers are doing (and not doing), is to become more conscious of what one can do one's self as a writer. To become aware of the different things writing means (and does not mean) to others is for students to widen their awareness of what writing can mean to them. Ultimately, all writers in all writing courses must make their own ways for themselves, but no writer finds his or her way alone. *What Makes Writing Good* is constructed to clarify as well as to vitalize this paradox for students.

The Design of the Text

The forty-eight teacher-student contributions to this text are organized into ten groups by means of twelve writing assignments, each of which, except the first and last, is to be addressed *after* students have read whatever selections an instructor assigns from a given group. The subject of each of these writing assignments derives from an important similarity shared by the student essays of a particular group, however the essays may differ in other respects. Thus all five student essays in Chapter 3, "Perceiving What Is Seen," though done for different purposes and by students at different stages in their development as writers, are essays that can help students investigate some uses of description. This grouping prepares students for Writing Assignment 3, which invites them to write a description. The five essays of Chapter 6, "Creating Lives," are either biographical or autobiographical; they lead to Writing Assignment 6, which invites students to write a paper on that subject. And so forth.

In aggregate, the assignments are devised to enable students to develop a full range of cognitive and compositional skills by giving them the opportunity to use writing in many different ways. Thus there are assignments as open as those asking students to take a stand on an issue, or to describe a time when they came to terms with something, but also assignments as focused as one in which we ask students to construct the kind of composition course they imagine would best prepare them to work with a particular teacher. We have fashioned assignments to have students speak for themselves, but also an assignment asking them to speak through a deliberately constructed persona, as someone other than themselves. Other assignments require students to revise, to make models, to attempt to solve problems, to address different audiences. The twelve writing assignments, therefore, in having students write for a variety of purposes, involve them automatically in the writing of analysis, description, argumentation, and definition; in the processes of comparing, contrasting, selecting, and arranging things in patterns.

Sequencing as Design

The assignments, however, offer more than just variety. We speak of them as *organizing* the contributions to the book in order to make clear that they are sequenced—a term that in this context refers to something the assignments are constructed to do both generally and specifically.

Generally, as in any responsibly run composition course, the writing assignments of this book are designed to provide students with the kind of writing practice that can help them become better writers. They move from relatively uncomplicated writing tasks to those that are more sophisticated, from a focus on informal discourse to a concern with problems calling for more formal modes of discourse, from having students draw broadly from their experience to having them draw from it more and more particularly. In addition, the assignments are constructed to enable students to draw from their experience with earlier assignments in such a way as to make each writing task a preparation for those that follow. Writing Assignment 5, for example, involves students in a problem of inference, a problem analogous to one that they coped with earlier but, as they are told, "a bit different from the [inferential process] . . . used in addressing writing Assignment 3." In this way students prepare themselves gradually to handle the more complicated inferential problems of Writing Assignments 8, 10, and finally 12.

Specifically, the twelve writing assignments are sequenced to help students consider step by step, and from a number of points of view, the question of what makes writing good in the context of what good writing may be said to be good *for*. The purpose of the assignments in this second sense of the term "sequence" is to help students see how getting better at writing can have something in it for them, and, for this reason, can be worth the investment of time and energy that all writing teachers must insist on.

The Sequence: Writing Assignments 1 Through 12

We begin in Writing Assignment 1 by having students write an essay addressing the issue of why anybody ought to work at learning how to write well in the first place. Why should anyone want to bother? Subsequent assignments, together with the readings of the course, provide points of view from which students are invited to rethink, in order to be able to revise or consolidate, whatever position they may take in their first papers. The Class Exercise of Chapter 2, for example, raises the question of what constitutes good writing by asking students to examine some writing that by one set of standards is Perfect but by another valueless, and some that though flawed may be argued to have value. Given such arguments, and in the light of the kinds of student papers grouped in the chapter and the way they are praised, how, we ask in Writing Assignment 2, are we to talk about what makes writing good, and in what ways does how we choose to talk about it matter?

Maybe by looking at writing that does different sorts of things we can shed some light on the questions raised by the first two assignments. In Chapter 3, therefore, we say: Here are some examples of descriptive writing, each of which, though from a different perspective, someone chooses to call good. Now, after reading them, try your hand at writing what from *your* perspective *you* would call a good description—and then use your experience as reader and writer to say how *you* think the ability to write good description might be useful to *you*. Similarly, we have students approach writing that is used to come to terms with something (Writing Assignment 4) and writing used to take a stand (Writing Assignment 5). Then students are asked to consider what a writer does in order to write well about someone's life (Writing Assignment 6). If the writer of a biography or autobiography is not Telling the Truth, then even when the writing is good, especially when the writing is good, what is such a writer doing? Telling good lies?

Or perhaps there is another way of talking, remembering our experience with what a writer does to come to terms with something, remembering our experience with what a writer does to take a stand. Maybe it will help to look at what could be called a deliberate lie in writing: at what a writer does when successfully wearing a mask, or when skillfully imitating a literary form (Writing Assignment 7). If the term "lie" seems beside the point in talking about such writing, then what terminology would be appropriate? And how might such terminology be useful in considering other kinds of writing—even such utilitarian documents as field reports, memos, and résumés (Writing Assignment 8)? What value might there be to seeing *all* written discourse as a kind of artfully (or artlessly) worn mask, and in this sense all writing as a kind of creative writing, all telling as a form of storytelling (rather than lying)? And how might focusing on what the activity of storytelling can do for the story*teller* (Writing Assignment 9) provide us with terms for addressing a more basic question: Why should anybody work at learning how to write well to begin with?

The last three assignments continue this movement to full circle by having students use their *own* writing and their *own* experience as writers to readdress the questions with which the sequence began. Where (in every sense of the term), we ask the students, did you start this sequence of assignments? Judging from that first paper you wrote on the question of why anyone should bother to write well, what did you seem to think back then that writing well consisted of, or was good for? In saying so, what kind of writer were you (Writing Assignment 10)? And what about now? How do you now define good writing (Writing Assignment 11)? Finally, given your definition, when you review your work in this course, what would you say there is in it for you to continue to work at learning to write well (Writing Assignment 12)?

That, of course, is only the most obvious way to see the structure of the sequence, and in any case is worth no more than what a teacher teaching, a student writing, can make it mean.

The Writing Assignments as Invitations to Learning

Each writing assignment is constructed on a reflexive principle as a way of putting students in a position to learn from what they do, to possess what they can come to know through their writing. Students are asked to do something.

Then they are asked to look back at what they have done, to generalize on the meaning of a certain activity, perhaps, or to isolate the principles of an activity in order to say how these principles can have significance in another context. You've written a definition, we say to students. Now, what does your having written that particular definition mean? What's it good for? What's definition good for? Or in another assignment we say: You've read examples of writing in which people talk about coming to terms with something. And you've also written a paper in which you talk about how *you* came to terms with something. What part might writing play in this process?

Most frequently, this reflexive principle involves students in considering a writing problem from three related points of view. Students are asked to do something, then to evaluate what they have done, then to develop the implications of both. Thus, though we never have students simply *imitate* the work of another, in the first part of a writing assignment we usually ask them to do in their terms something like what the student writers represented in a given chapter have done in theirs. Then in the second part of the assignment we give students the opportunity to increase their awareness of what they have done (and by implication of what they can come to do as writers) by asking them to see it in the context of other people's work. Which student, we may ask (or which teacher), represented in the chapter do you imagine would most like what you have written? Why? Or we ask students to say which teacher's commentary they found most helpful to them as writers, and why. The third question generally asks students to consider what *point* there might be in doing well whatever it is that they have taken on in the assignment. There's a way of using writing to come to terms with something. Very well. But what is there in that for *you* as a writer?

The Philosophy of the Text

The assignments of this text, like the study questions, have been carefully designed. But we must emphasize that neither constitutes an argument. We make only three assumptions: (1) that how teachers and students choose to talk about writing matters; (2) that since certain ways of talking about writing are better in certain situations than others, it is a good thing for teachers and students both to have more than one way of talking about it; and (3) that the activity of writing can have something in it for the *writer*—even when the writer does not find the process particularly enjoyable or intend to make writing an essential part of his or her life. Beyond that, there is no party line in any of the editorial apparatus of the book for a teacher to become aware of and feed to students, or for students to become aware of and feed back to a teacher. Our study questions, for example, which derive essentially from actual classroom discussion, do not in any instance play off Right Opinion against Wrong Opinion, pit Truth against Falsehood, except as an individual reader should decide this. In the student exchanges, therefore, soundly made but specious arguments are sometimes set against those that are viable but weakly articulated. Sense will be found buried in a string of fumbling irrelevancies. Demonstrable misreadings are sometimes made to sound plausible. There are examples of silly assumptions, *ad hominem* conversation, wrong-headedness of all sorts—but also many examples of solid critical stances, of finely realized judgments, depending, of course, upon who is reading them. By the same token, the questions of the assignments must be understood as invariably open, as questions to be addressed rather than answered. All of the editorial apparatus, in fact, has one primary function: to dramatize what it means to conduct an intelligent ongoing conversation in such a way as to help students develop the sort of self-consciousness they will need in order to learn from their experience as writers.

Alternative Uses of the Text

This text, then, is not in itself a composition course. It merely provides the materials for one. In form and arrangement the writing assignments, like the study questions, represent the consensus of two teachers who worked with them. These assignments have been extensively revised on the basis of our classroom experience; we are confident that any teacher anywhere can use them as the basis for a course in composition just as they are written, and with every expectation of educational success. On the other hand, this does not mean that the current form of the assignments should be considered canonical or that there is only one way to use them. Some teachers, for example, may choose to have students focus on only a single aspect of an assignment rather than work with its three-part structure as a whole, or to have students write two or even three papers on a given topic. Other teachers may wish to construct assignments to supplement those that are here, or to ask their students to address one of the study questions or one of the forty-eight writing assignments devised by our contributors. It is also quite possible to use *What Makes Writing Good* in conjunction with other texts or books on writing. And of course there will be a wide variation among teachers who use this book as to which contributions, and how many, to assign.

Since this text has been assembled to make possible a number of ways of talking about what's in it, there is no one way to use it—nothing that cannot be rearranged, rephrased, added to or deleted as the style of a teacher, the length of a term, the requirements of a course, or the character of a class dictate. And, for the same reason, the text may be used again and again by the same teacher. A book to teach from rather than just to teach is what we have tried to write, a book that will give teachers a chance to make the teaching of writing mean as much as writing can.

We wish to say one more thing.

We could not have constructed this book without the help of the members of the composition courses—two at Carroll College, two at the University of Pittsburgh—in which we taught and refined everything that is here. From our students' insistence that we earn the right to demand from them the commitment to the activity of writing we claimed to want, we learned what it means to make such a commitment. We are grateful for that, and to all of them: Louise

Adams, Shari Arduino, Timothy Bean, Pamela Bollerud, Karen Bond, Vicki Buinowski, Bruce Bulawski, Carrie Carnoske, Sue Chambers, Mary Chase, Mike Conway, Don Curtis, Olivia Dankert, Martha Ellis, Cynthia Erickson, Michael Faillaci, James Farris, Ralph Feldman, Martin Fix, Jackie Gisch, Lori Henninger, Jennifer Hitchings, Douglas Hofstetter, Sharon Hraban, Lynn Jensen, Daniel Kasper, Andrea Keller, Joyce Kettenhofen, Donald Klemp, Michael Kratochvil, John Kujawa, Daphne LaPointe, Patricia Lenius, Susan Marie Lord, Christine Lynn, Kim Maret, Jane McClure, Bonnie McElhinny, Rob McMurry, Jeffrey Mead, Chris Michaels, Geri Milinski, Sandra Miller, Christin Nader, Mark Nadzam, Susan Newcamp, Joseph Orth, Edwin Oswalt, Kathleen Otradovec, Mary Pfost, Jeanne Prisbylla, Laurie Reinke, Vicki Sadorf, Jeffrey Lee Schupper, Linda Schwabenbauer, Robert Sieber, Paul Smarra, Carrie Smith, John Speranza, Janelle Stemberger, Alisa Stolte, Bob Thacker, Pete Tucker, Kathleen Vail, Nancy Walker, and David Wilda.

Acknowledgments

I wish to thank all the contributors, who, in order to be part of this book, risked saying what they believed makes a particular piece of writing good. In addition, I am grateful to Professors Richard A. Lanham of the University of California, Los Angeles, Richard L. Larson of Herbert Lehman College, City University of New York, Ben McClelland of Rhode Island College, and John Ruszkiewicz of the University of Texas at Austin, for their tough-minded readings of the manuscript of this book.

My principal debt is to my wife Janet, who went through all of it with me and who, in the narrow time, was a lot more to me than all the king's horses and all the king's men.

W.E.C., Jr.

I am grateful for the thoughtful insights and suggestions of those writing teachers who have commented on various versions of *What Makes Writing Good:* Theresa Enos of Southern Methodist University, Cynthia Caywood of the University of San Diego, Ben McClelland of Rhode Island College, John Ruszkiewicz of the University of Texas at Austin, Richard L. Larson of Herbert Lehman College, City University of New York, and Richard Lanham of the University of California, Los Angeles.

For their professional guidance and encouragement, I am especially indebted to those who have been involved in this project at D. C. Heath: Jacqueline Unch, Holt Johnson, Judith Leet, Michelle Lauterbach, and Vicki Sawyer.

For his uncommon good sense, constructive support, and enthusiasm, our editor Paul A. Smith deserves special recognition. His advice has been timely, detailed, and substantive. I was—from beginning to end—fortunate to work with him.

To Katherine King, I express my appreciation and admiration.

J.V.

Contents

Except where indicated, the student essays of this book are unedited. We have printed all
of them just as they were submitted to us.

6 *Creating Lives*   151

11   *Locating the Self   323*

Why Work at Writing Well? 1

Writing isn't hard; no harder than ditch-digging.

Patrick Dennis

If we concentrate our attention on trying to solve a problem of geometry, and if at the end of an hour we are no nearer to doing so than at the beginning, we have nevertheless been making progress each minute of that hour in another more mysterious dimension. Without our knowing or feeling it, this apparently barren effort has brought more light into the soul. The result will one day . . . very likely be felt in some department of the intelligence in no way connected with mathematics. Perhaps he who made the unsuccessful effort will one day be able to grasp the beauty of a line of Racine more vividly on account of it. . . . Every time that a human being succeeds in making an effort of attention with the sole idea of increasing his grasp of truth, he acquires a greater aptitude for grasping it, even if his effort produces no visible fruit. An Eskimo story explains the origin of light as follows: "In the eternal darkness, the crow, unable to find any food, longed for light, and the earth was illumined." If there is a real desire, if the thing desired is really light, the desire for light produces it. There is a real desire when there is an effort of attention.

Simone Weil

BEFORE WE APPROACH THE QUESTION OF WHAT makes writing good, the subject of this book, there's a more basic question to consider. *Why* should anyone work at trying to make his or her writing good? Why should people, particularly students, be told so often that writing is important and that working at writing well is an important thing to do? In short, what is the value of good writing? What's good writing good *for*, anyway? This is the question you are asked to address in the first writing assignment.

There are two purposes for this first writing assignment, which your teacher may have you write either in class or as a prepared paper. One of these purposes is to provide you with the beginning of a record of your development as a writer, a development that you will be given a specific occasion to measure in Writing Assignment 10 if your teacher chooses to use it. But in any event, where you come out as a writer in this course will have to be measured against where you are as a writer now. For different writers this beginning place will be different, of course, but everybody begins somewhere.

Another purpose of this assignment is to start a conversation about our subject, to start it in such a way as to be able to keep it going. To have a conversation means for all of us to try to do more than talk with final pronouncements. In other words, please don't think that this first assignment poses a question to which there's a right or wrong answer. Neither should you feel in writing this paper that you have to pose as some kind of Authority, nor, if you are writing your paper out of class, that you have to run to the library for Information. You're a writer, after all. Try to start with and stay with your own working experience in dealing with whatever you think the issue is here. Try to see this paper as one in which you work at taking a position that might at some point be worth revising or refining.

Writing Assignment 1
Why Work at Writing Well?

As a student, you have no doubt been told about the importance of your learning to write well—even though you yourself may have no intention whatever of becoming a professional writer, even though you may be interested in doing something in life that doesn't involve much writing at all.

How do you explain the importance of your learning to write well? Imagine someone—not a parent or a teacher now, but a friend that you are on decent terms with—saying something like this to you:

> Look, I can understand why someone ought to be *able* to read and write, but I don't see why writing is important to work at. Oh, I know I have to do it if I want to get good grades and all that, but that doesn't answer my question. There are plenty of good jobs in which you don't have to write much at all. Besides, you can communicate just as well with the telephone or computers. So why should writing be something that's pushed so much?

Write a paper in which you give as thoughtful a response to that statement as you can. Try to stay with your own experience as a writer. Address your paper directly to your friend.

Moving Beyond Limits   2

Someone is asked a question, and he seeks to give an honest answer. It wasn't his question and probably isn't his subject, but perhaps he sees a way to make his answer his own, an expression of something he knows. What he knows is almost always a matter of the relationships he establishes, between example and generalization, between one part of a narrative and the next, between the idea and the counteridea that the writer sees is also relevant, between his experience and what he knows of the experience of others—in short, between any two parts of his knowledge. On the one hand this, on the other hand that; not this, but that; not just this, but also that; if this, then that; because this, that; that as an example of this; not this until that; yet, moreover, since, so, and: the list is potentially endless, and by inquiring into the exact relationship between things, a writer discovers what he knows, the words he wants.

Roger Sale

THIS CHAPTER CONTAINS A TWO-PART EXERCISE INTENDED to help you in several ways. Generally, the exercise is designed to enable you to develop a vocabulary for talking about writing. A shared vocabulary is necessary to productive classroom conversation and can also be useful in your developing a critical perspective of your own from which to read the essays of this book. Specifically, this exercise introduces you to some of the particular issues raised by the selections of this chapter—issues you will be considering for yourself in addressing the writing assignment at the end of it.

Exercise: Part One

Read through these two student essays that were addressed to Writing Assignment 1, "Why Work at Writing Well?"

ᴥ Paper A

1   The human race in our modern world of today is faced with a great many earth-shattering problems. The problems of our world involve everyone, wherever he or she may live. Civilization depends on how we cope with certain problems. Handling problems thoughtfully and with emotional maturity can lead us to peace, prosperity and happiness. This is something we all want. Handling them badly can lead to disease and death. So the time to take responsibility is now. We must all do our share. And no where is this more obvious than in the field of education. We all have a responsibility to write well.

2   Where would we be if everyone felt writing wasn't important? There would be no books or magazines. We would get no letters. Advertising would come to a halt. No one would know what anyone else was doing.

3   You can't write a shopping list with a telephone. You can't leave a note for a friend with a computer. Without knowing how to write you wouldn't be able to get through school or read road signs. You couldn't pay your bills. These are just some of the reasons writing is important.

4   In conclusion, writing is important because everything depends on it. And only if every man, woman and child takes responsibility for learning to write well can civilization as we know it continue to exist. Who would want to live in a wasteland? Who would not rather live in a garden?

ᴥ Paper B

1   I'm going to have a hard time here because I feel very much the same way any friend does. How can I explain something I don't understand to someone? But my teachers must have something in mind. I don't like writing much. But sometimes I'm glad I did it. I'm not sure why exactly except I remember the time in English when I knew the weakness of *Lord of the Flies* because of a paper I did in government. I hate working at writing though just the way this student does. And a lot can be done with computers and over the telephone. My teacher have something in mind

though. Maybe it has something to do with thinking. I'm not sure I don't know.

Suppose you wanted to argue that "Paper A" is better than "Paper B." Never mind right now whether you *believe* this; all you're doing at this point in this exercise is imagining an argument. What features of the two papers might you mention? What terminology do you use to describe these features? What features of the two papers might you not mention? And why might you choose not to mention them? Write out some notes from which to make the strongest argument you can that "Paper A" is better than "Paper B." Judging from your argument, what do you mean by "better" in this instance?

Suppose, however, you wanted to argue that "Paper B" is better than "Paper A." Again, write some notes from which to make the strongest argument you can think of for this position. What features of the papers do you now mention, or avoid mentioning? In what terms do you describe what you are evaluating? And what, in the case of this second argument, do you mean by "better"?

You now have two arguments that, when considered in relation to each other, pose two questions: Which paper *is* the better paper, and what does one mean in saying so?

Write an essay of about a page in which you take a stand on this matter.

Exercise: Part Two

The kind of judgment you made in Part One of this exercise is sometimes referred to as a Matter of Taste—that is, as the kind of judgment about which no further conversation is thought necessary. Or wanted. The second part of this exercise is to provide you with some perspectives on "Paper A" and "Paper B" that can help you decide what talk like "a matter of taste" is worth when it comes to evaluating writing.

Use the following to reconsider "Paper A."

1. Suppose someone wanted more details or another couple of sentences fit so smoothly into its tone and manner that no one could tell they'd been added. Show that you can do this.

2. What kinds of things did you decide to write and how did you know where to put them?

3. Suppose someone wanted some sentences cut from the first paragraph. What sentences could you cut without anyone's being likely to notice their absence?

4. How did you decide on which sentences to cut?

5. Suppose someone wanted the third paragraph of this paper to be twice as long as it now is. Show how you can do that without changing anything that's in the paragraph now.

6. If you were teaching someone how to do what you've just done, what would you tell your student to do?

7. Suppose someone asked you to change the subject of this paper from Why Work at Writing Well? to, say, Ecology. What changes do you have to make in the paper if you want to change no more of it than is absolutely necessary?

8. What principle did you follow in making such changes?

9. How well does "Paper A" address the assignment? What in the assignment does the writer deal with? What in the assignment does the writer *not* deal with?

10. Why do you suppose the writer deals with the assignment as he does?

11. Judging from what you have noticed about this paper so far, what kind of writing would you say "Paper A" is made up of?

12. What is such writing good for?

13. What is such writing not good for?

14. Suppose you wanted to talk to the writer of this paper about how to improve his writing. You're not an expert of course; but you're a writer yourself, and you know something of the difficulties of putting words on paper. Also, you've had a chance to see this student's paper from a perspective that he himself has not. What can you say that you think might be helpful to him—about this paper in particular, about how to approach the activity of writing in general?

15. After a classroom discussion of "Paper A" that followed, roughly, the order suggested by directives 1–14 above, the writer of the paper decided not to attempt to rewrite what he'd written but to scrap it and start over. Why do you suppose the writer decided to do that?

Now use what follows to reconsider "Paper B."

After a classroom discussion of what *she'd* written, the writer of "Paper B" did decide to rewrite her paper, and this is what she came up with.

୬. Paper B Revised

Part of me knows exactly what this student means. Most of the time the telephone is a lot faster and more efficient than letters, as can be proved by the expensive communication systems that most companies invest in. And computers are *surely* more efficient as a way of storing and retrieving information. Also, I have to confess I don't much like writing. In fact, I hate working at it. That is as I said part of me does. I've got a feeling the student in the assignment feels the same way.   1

But there's another part of me that knows something else and this is a result of something that happened in English—not one of my favorite classes. We were discussing Golding's *Lord of the Flies.* Someone in class suggested that the book shows how all governments, all attempts to set up laws for people to live by, are doomed. Even democracy is a sham, Golding says, because it just gives way to totalitarianism eventually. I'd done a paper for my government class, however, one that gave me a lot of trouble too, in which I'd had to examine the objections that can be made to democracy and find a way of answering them. I didn't do very well on the paper, but I did see why I thought Golding's book was wrong. It tries to make you believe that what can happen will happen in government. At first I was the only one in English to argue this, but after a while some of the class agreed with me.   2

So maybe one of the reasons writing is pushed has something to do with how it makes us think or see things. If I can be better in political science, which is what I want to major in, as a result of working at writing, then maybe it's worth working at no matter how I feel about it.   3

1. The class discussion of "Paper B" concluded with two main suggestions to the writer for revising the paper. Judging from "Paper B Revised," what do you think these were?
2. The writer of "Paper B" turned in a note with her revised paper, which said: "I'm glad I rewrote this paper. I think it's worth a higher grade than

my first one. But even if it doesn't get a higher grade, I'm still glad I rewrote the paper." What do you think the student might have meant?

Whether you have changed your evaluation of papers A and B or not, whether your understanding of "better" is any different now from what it was, how would you respond to someone who said to you, without explanation: "The preference of either of these papers to the other is purely a matter of taste."

Is it, so far as you are concerned? And what do you mean by saying it is or isn't?

None of the teachers represented in this chapter would have any difficulty seeing why a phrase like "a matter of taste" needs explanation when it comes to what makes writing good. In this chapter, in other words, there is a lot of material you can use to improve your ability to talk about writing and to see why *how* one chooses to talk about writing matters.

ROBERT HOLLAND'S Assignment

The Self-Fulfilling Prophecy

Here is a case involving naming, knowing, and valuing. Read the following essay; spend some time sorting out the questions following it; and then address the assignment following the questions.

The year was 1890 and the Hollerith tabulating machine had just been installed at the United States Census Bureau. The machine, something like a typewriter, required the clerks to learn a new skill, which the inventor, Hollerith, regarded as quite demanding. He expected that a trained worker could punch about 550 cards per day. After two weeks the workers were adequately trained and began to produce about 550 cards per day. After a while the clerks began to exceed the expected performance but only at great emotional cost. Workers became so tense trying to beat the expected limit that the Secretary of the Interior forbade the establishment of any minimum performance criterion. This was seen as a step necessary to preserve the mental health of the establishment.

Then, a new group of some 200 clerks was brought in to augment the Hollerith machine work force. These clerks knew nothing of the work, had no prior training, and had never even seen the machine. No one had told these workers what the emotional cost of the work might be nor of the upper limit of production that could be achieved. This lack of information turned out to be their greatest asset. Within three days this new group was performing at the level which was reached only after seven weeks by the earlier, "more properly" indoctrinated group. Whereas clerks from the initial group were exhausted after producing 700 cards per day, members of the new group began turning out three times that number and without ill effects.[1]

Here are some questions intended to help you clarify your response to what you have just read:

1. In what terms did the inventor see the task? What might have led him to see the task in those terms?
2. In what terms did the original group of clerks see the task? What might have led them to see the task in those terms?
3. In what terms did the Secretary of the Interior come to see the task? What might have led him to see the task in those terms?

---

[1] Robert Rosenthal and Lenore Jacobson, *Pygmalion in the Classroom* (New York: Holt, Rinehart and Winston, 1968), pp. 5–6.

ROBERT M. HOLLAND, JR. is currently Associate Professor of English and former Director of Composition at the University of Akron. He has published articles on applications of Piaget's learning theory to the teaching of writing and on subjective criticism in the teaching of writing.

4. How much of the phenomenon described in this account could be seen as a matter of language and language use? What language or languages are involved, who uses them, and how are they used?

Here is your writing assignment: Choose a moment from your own experience or from that of someone you know in which a presumed limit was found not to exist. Describe the moment of discovery. How was it learned that the "known" limit was not real? In what sense might that moment of discovery be described as a matter of language and language use?

Write a paper in which you make clear what the moment was and how you interpret the discovery in terms of language and language use.

☜ What We Don't Know
Just Might Help Us
by Sandy Heise

1   When I was a member of my junior high school's gymnastic team, I would faithfully work out on all the pieces of gymnastic apparatus available to us except for one, the vaulting horse. It was not that I hated working out on the horse, it was just that I was never able to markedly improve my technique. One must run up to the horse, jump on a springboard, and be hurled in countless ways onto and then over the horse to an awaiting crash mat. Now, I could do the running, springing and landing, however, I could not perform without placing the springboard closer than regulation distance to the horse. I was scared that if I moved the springboard further out, the more likely my chances would be of landing directly on and not on the other side of the horse. This concept of distance seemed to cloud the faith I had in my ability for I had seen many of my teammates land right on the horse because they did not have the strength necessary to compensate for the increased distance from the horse.

2   Then one day my coach had me work out on the horse as she watched. I set my springboard's distance, too close as usual, and walked back to the beginning of the runway. My coach asked me if I would like to lengthen the distance between the springboard and the horse, but I would not for I was sure that I would fail. So I went ahead with my performance, everything going smoothly. Again my coach asked if I would prefer to increase the springboard's distance, but as always I refused.

3   After about ten vaults, coach shook her head and said, "I knew that you could do it, you have been for your last round of vaults." Now I was totally baffled because I had carefully measured the distance between the board and horse. It seems that my coach had moved the springboard from

my five feet to the regulation distance of seven feet. At that moment, I realized that I was not working up to my full capacity. I had allowed my fear to act as my limiting factor for so long that I no longer had confidence in myself. Once I knew that I could do it, I was no longer scared to perform on the horse, in fact I began to like the apparatus. Once I found that I could overcome the fear complex I developed with the horse, I was able to operate with the same degree of certainty on it as well as on the rest of the gymnastics equipment.

Before, mere words were able to make a barrier between me and my ability to vault. Once these words which promoted fear and insecurity were left to the past and I simply executed each vault one at a time, I was no longer limited to doing a half-hearted job in gymnastics. 4

Robert Holland's COMMENTARY

Sometimes the quality of a piece of writing is seen in its completion of an assigned task: it provides the information called for, argues a premise, explains an idea, answers a question. Sometimes quality is assessed in terms of a paper's adherence to rules and convention, the degree to which a paper's grammar, syntax, spelling, punctuation, diction, format are correct, appropriate, effective. Sometimes quality is seen in a piece of writing's artfulness, in the ways it fits together, becomes clear, engages a reader through its design and movement. Sometimes quality is a function of approximation of an ideal: a paper could be seen as a perfect model of a paragraph, an essay, a research paper. And sometimes quality is thought of as an exemplary manifestation of efficacy, power, or fruitfulness in the process by which a piece of writing is brought into being: its conception, design, production, perfection.

For me as a teacher of writing, *all* of those ways of seeing quality can be relevant and useful. All of them can be ways of helping writers discover excellence. All offer a writing class common vocabularies in terms of which a writer can understand better what "works" and why it works, or what fails to achieve what the writer had hoped to achieve, or what produces effects the writer had never intended. But when I define myself as a teacher in a writing class, none of the kinds of quality mentioned above takes me to the heart of what makes a piece of writing specifically excellent insofar as that paper is a paper written for a writing class. None goes very far in helping anyone see what is uniquely excellent through a paper's being written in a class, on an assignment, at the invitation of a writing teacher.

An analogy might help here. When a music student "has a good lesson," the quality that makes the lesson good is not simply the expertise with which the student performs what was assigned the preceding week. One can readily imagine an excellent music lesson in which the performance is, by any musical standard, simply awful. And one can imagine an hour spent by student and teacher in which the student's performance is in all ways musically first rate, and yet the lesson as a lesson is unprofitable, misleading, even destructive. A performance within a music lesson, then, has some measure of excellence beyond correctness, completeness, dexterity, or approval. There is (I would say, there *must* be) a kind of excellence peculiar to the student's performance insofar as that performance is part of a music lesson and not part of something else (a feigned recital, an imitative interpretation, a technical exercise, and so forth).

Perhaps we should begin by agreeing that, viewed in the terms of excellence summarized above, Sandy's paper does not excel. A reader might well be distracted by what look like sentence errors or casual punctuation, or by the conversational idiom. One might argue that the paper lacks an introduction, that the conclusion lacks focus for a reader, or that there are any number of ways the narrative could be more clearly, more efficiently managed. A reader might point out that the paper does not explain its own title, or that it fails to address adequately the final direction of the assignment, "Make clear . . . how you interpret the discovery in terms of language and language use." How, then, could a paper so "flawed" be called excellent? Is not Sandy's paper better seen as an example of "doing a half-hearted job" as a writer?

Granting that there may be substance to those criticisms, it is nonetheless in Sandy's very "failure" that I claim to see this paper's excellence as a piece of writing in a writing class. And precisely because her paper does *not* represent that which is usually praiseworthy or labeled as first-rate it may better permit us to see what can be hoped for from a writer who is trying to become a better writer by taking a writing class.

"What can be hoped for" here is the way I would identify the special quality I see in Sandy's paper addressing the writing assignment, the first assignment of the course. Whatever else Sandy may have done or have failed to do, she has created on essay that enables readers (the others in the class) to see and follow the languages she used in coming to terms with the moment she writes about, both as the gymnast she was and as the writer she made herself in composing the paper. We can follow, any of us, a language of fear, for example, "I was scared," "I refused"; Sandy the gymnastics student "knew" something about herself in terms that defined who she was and who she was able to become. Sandy the writer is able to name "my fear" as something she could later claim she had created: "the fear complex I developed." We can follow a language of doubt: from her lack of confidence in her abilities ("I was never able to markedly improve my technique"), to her identification with teammates who had failed "because they did not have the strength necessary to compensate for the distance," to the critical moment's inductive leap ("I was sure that I would fail").

For Sandy the gymnast, *regulation distance* had come to mean the likelihood that she would land "directly on and not on the other side of the horse." Her "concept of distance" had become a conviction of failure. And her way of putting together what she knew about herself with what she knew about gymnastics meant not only a clouding of her faith in her own ability but a refusal even to attempt more than "a half-hearted job in gymnastics."

We can point to all that on the page. But we can also point to the way Sandy as gymnast took what the coach told her ("I knew that you could do it, you have been for your last round of vaults") and put it together with what she herself "knew" of her abilities. At the moment of discovery these did not make sense together: "I was totally baffled." Then she chose the terms in which she would interpret and resolve the paradox ("At that moment I realized . . .").

As a writer, Sandy turned directly from her narrated discovery to some analytic talk that may well baffle a reader. Which "mere words" is she referring to in her final paragraph? Her claim that thereafter she "simply executed each vault one at a time" suggests something of the ease with which she later perceived what had been an impossible feat, but she has not led up to that claim with anything specific. The last paragraph of the paper may well "fail" to address the final direction of the writing assignment. But by putting her moment and her ways of using languages into words (no one would call them "mere words"), her paper lays claim to the experience in a unique way, in a way she could not have otherwise laid claim to it.

Her paper, as a paper addressing a writing assignment within a writing class, excels in the way she has made use of the Rosenthal and Jacobson case without alluding to it. She has made a connection between that passage and her moment, and, although the making of that connection was the occasion for the paper, she has not made it the subject of her paper. Her paper excels because she has been able to see her experience as a complex function of languages, both verbal and nonverbal, both her own and her coach's. (What *was* the coach "saying" in moving that springboard?) And although Sandy is writing about a language experience she cannot yet fully explain in "mere words," she is attempting— essaying—to exceed what she is now capable of writing or saying.

What I am commending here, then, is what I perceive as the whole-heartedness of Sandy's attempt to write the best paper she can. Her paper can be uniquely useful and fruitful for a writing class *not* because "everything goes smoothly," but because it offers readers a way of seeing a barrier between effort and success that they could not see in any other way. By reading and discussing together in class what Sandy has done, we may learn something of what it means to be a writer because she chose to put herself in a position to see what it means to be a writer and, by doing that, to glimpse a truth for which she might otherwise "have forgotten to ask."

Study Questions

1. In a paper written about Sandy Heise's essay a student said,

> If this writer rewrote her paper, particularly the last paragraph of it, in terms of the final question of the writing assignment, she might have a chance of seeing something really important about the relation of her use of language to her experience. She says "mere words" had been "able to make a barrier" between her and her ability to vault. What she *doesn't* see is the other side of that, that it was "mere words," or language, as Robert Holland calls it, that made it possible for her to vault. Language imprisoned her, but language freed her too. For her to see this might make an enormous difference to her—and as more than a writer.

   How would you explain what this student means to a classmate who didn't understand him? Do you agree with his comment about Sandy Heise's paper?

2. Judging from what Robert Holland says of Sandy Heise's paper, how do you think he would respond to the question in the first writing assignment of this book: Why should people work at learning to write well?

3. Sandy Heise's paper, says Robert Holland, "does not explain its own title." Should it? If so, how? Or should the paper be retitled? If so, how?

   Judging from your answers to these questions, what would you say is the importance of a title to an essay?

WILLIAM IRMSCHER'S Assignment

[All individuals seeking admission to the University of Washington under the Educational Opportunity Program are given an opportunity to show how well they can express their thoughts in writing. They are given sixty minutes to write their response to three separate questions. The writing is therefore completely impromptu. Candidates are given no specific directions or restrictions about length or kind of writing; they are instructed merely to write in a style that makes them feel most comfortable under the circumstances. One of the three questions given to these students appears below.]

When is the last time you made an important choice about your way of life? Perhaps you decided whether or not to quit a full-time job to come back to school, whether or not you would go steady with one person, whether or not you would get married, whether you would buy some luxury you wanted or save your money, whether or not you want to try to change your self-image. Tell about some choice you have made and why you made it.

[Untitled]   *by Shawn McGinnis*

Original Version

I made an Important decition on finding out what happen when I die.   1
DEATH its a word that makes strong and rich men tremble with fear.
Why would I choose such a subject like death when people try to run
from it. Its only becouse I've seen death stalking old people. Playing hide
and go seek with young men on the battle feilds. Its also becouse death
has no mercy on its choosen victims. Children my brother my grandfather my faveriote pet a good freind. They come into my life than leave
with deaths touch. I've seen death but I never felt it, the cold touch of
death. forever I will be looking over my shoulder for death. I will never
really know what its about intel that last minute that last breath it might

WILLIAM F. IRMSCHER is currently Professor of English at the University of Washington. For twenty-three years, he served as Director of Freshman English. His best-known publications include *Ways of Writing* (1969), *The Holt Guide to English* (3rd ed., 1981), and *Teaching Expository Writing* (1979). He has served as editor of *College Composition and Communication* (1965–1973), Chair of the Conference on College Composition and Communication (1979), and president of the National Council of Teachers of English (1984).

happen next week or in fifty years. It will change my life dramaticly, yes. For now I'll only think about it.

Edited Version

[First sentence omitted.] *Death.* It's a word that makes strong and rich men tremble with fear. Why would I choose a subject like death when people try to run from it? It's only because I've seen death stalking old people, playing hide-and-go-seek with young men on the battlefields. It's also because death has no mercy on its chosen victims—children, my brother, my grandfather, my favorite pet, a good friend. They come into my life, then leave with death's touch. I've seen death, but I have never felt it, the cold touch of death. Forever I will be looking over my shoulder for death. I will never really know what it's about until that last minute, that last breath. It might happen next week or in fifty years. It will change my life dramatically, yes. For now I'll only think about it.

WILLIAM IRMSCHER'S COMMENTARY

For fifteen years I have been reading writing samples by men and women who are not regularly admissible to the University of Washington. Selected students are admissible under the Educational Opportunity Program if a reading test and writing sample show the candidate's potential for doing university work. If EOP didn't take high risks occasionally, it would be of little value in offering a chance to those whose talents are apparent, but whose skills do not yet allow them to express themselves with basic proficiency and certainly not with the refinements that more practiced writers can call upon.

I have just finished reading twenty-nine such writing samples. Twenty of them are acceptable in varying degrees, although half of them hold little promise. Of the twenty, however, only one shows a quality of perception that makes it unique among the otherwise prosaic, albeit far more orderly and correct, paragraphs. What I have come to realize is that we often recognize quality by contrast. We read many dull, boring pieces of writing. Then suddenly we are struck by something that commands our attention. Good writing is striking because there is so much bad writing. It helps, however, if we can recognize what the basic qualities of good writing are—the way we might say a child's writing is good. Obviously, a child's writing is not sophisticated; it is not polished. But it may express a simple honesty that is quite beyond the capacity of more experienced writers.

Possibly most of our differences of opinion about excellence among experienced writers revolve around stylistic differences and matters of taste. Some readers like parallel structures; others do not. Some like loosely connected, associative prose; others do not. And one might go on to list preferences. We should differentiate, however, between what we like and what we recognize as good writing, whether we like it or not. If we cannot agree about what is basically good, then we may find ourselves inextricably at odds.

What is good about Shawn's paragraph?

First, he wanted to write about his subject. He had something to say about death. He doesn't in any way answer the question he was asked: he does not describe a "decision" or "choice" at all. Instead, he describes a realization about death that has come to him. But, since the question was intended as a point of departure for writing, not as a test question, his decision to write about something that he could express with conviction was correct. Good writing results when writers are engaged with the subject they are writing about.

Second, the tone is right. It is restrained rather than overly dramatic. The diction is simple. Death is not the grim reaper or the holocaust. Death touches; it does not slaughter. Death "stalks," but also plays "hide and go seek," almost like a cat. We get a mixed tone of apprehension and attraction.

Further, the voice of the writer is direct and clear. It is marked by a kind of disarming innocence. Death is a leveler, but that is not the kind of statement Shawn makes. He lists those who have died—"children, my brother, my grandfather, my favorite pet, a good friend." They have been a part of his life. With remarkable simplicity, he says, "They come into my life, then leave with death's touch." We sense here a wonderment about this mystery—no rage, no rebellion, no philosophical probing, just quiet thought: "Now I'll only think about it." The musing about death is left unresolved.

Third, the strategy of the writing is un-self-conscious. Shawn has a fine sense of the rhythm of language. Read the passage aloud. These are not necessarily the rhythms of speech. I doubt that Shawn talks as he writes here. But the rhythms are natural. He has a good sense of structural balance, of repetition, of words in a series, of climactic order. This is prose that can be read aloud and listened to with pleasure.

If we omit the first sentence of the paragraph—the perfunctory nod to the question asked—the rest is tightly knit. The next-to-last sentence has a touch of unintended humor—death "will change my life dramatically"—but the intensity of this sentence, which contrasts with the calm of the final one, reveals its serious intention. The rhythm and the coherent structure indicate a good intuitive sense of how language works best.

Finally, he writes unconfused sentences, although the punctuation does not fully reveal their regularity. My edited version of Shawn's paper shows that the sentences are far more sophisticated structurally than the original suggests. Furthermore, almost all of the sentences have an agent in the subject position and a verb in active voice. The result is prose that is easily readable.

Thus, in terms of content, structure, diction and style, this brief passage represents qualities of good writing. Shawn obviously lacks mastery of mechanics. But a question immediately arises: Does the edited, basically repunctuated version, gain or lose in effect? If correctness is a part of effectiveness, as I happen to think, then it gains, primarily because it puts no barriers before the reader. A passage of this kind tells me that we already have a good writer who can become a better writer. But isn't that what writing courses are all about?

Study Questions

1. In an essay written about Shawn McGinnis's paper a student said,

> I like the unedited version of this paper better than the edited one. The corrections make clear that the paragraph is put together with nothing more than clichés about death. I don't mean that the original essay hides this exactly, but for some reason I forgive the writer more when I read the unedited version. The clichés don't look like clichés.
>
> My father's a carpenter—a damned good one too. Most of his letters to me look like the unedited version of this paper. But I like his letters, and not because I feel superior to him either. In fact I think I like his letters as much as I do because they *aren't* correct. I know that doesn't seem to make much sense, but I wonder if maybe the incorrectness of a piece of writing can be part of its effectiveness sometimes.

   What do you think of such an argument?

2. "We should differentiate," William Irmscher says, "between what we like and what we recognize as good writing, whether we like it or not."

   How is such a remark a way of defining what it means to be a reader?

   To what extent do you accept this definition of "reader" for yourself?

3. "Good writing results when writers are engaged with the subject they are writing about," William Irmscher says, which in this case resulted in a student's doing something other than answering "the question he was asked."

   A student seeking to learn to write well might turn such an observation into advice that could mean trouble for him or her as a student. How?

   But it is also possible for a student to turn such an observation into advice about writing that could be very helpful. How?

   Judging from your responses to the two preceding questions, what do you conclude about how to use such observations about good writing?

Janet Kotler's Assignment

[Courtney Wayshak's paper was not a direct response to an assignment but was prompted by the class's reaction to his previous paper. And yet, in another way, it *was* addressed to what might be called the underlying assignment of the whole course: that each student in the class take a stand with respect to the course as a whole. (In a sense, Courtney accepted this invitation long after most of the students had; in a more real sense, he got there way ahead of everyone else.)

The assignment for Courtney's first paper had asked him to consider these questions: "What separates a child from an adult?" Does a child experience the world because of, or through, his *naiveté*, or is it the child's consciousness (and how is that different from an adult's?) that 'opens' the world to him?" Our class had spent many weeks discussing the difference between a child and an adult in an effort to get at the issue of how a particular way of using language determines how we see things.]

☙ [Untitled]   *by Courtney Wayshak*

I have to look at this again, Ms. Kottler. When I wrote assignment 8 it had to be fake writing at it's finest. I tried to maintain the formula that seemed to bring me a little recognition, a needed pat on the back. I've been feeling good about learning. I've been feeling proud. I have a whole new outlook on the things my father calls life.   1

I've been at Goddard now for about 1 and a half semester. Which is good; because my parents said I wouldn't last this long.   2

You know I grew up on the southside of chicago, in the roughest, meanest, baddest neiborhood you ever saw. It made the south Bronks look like Disney world. I was the last white kid to graduate for both grammer school and high school. And I had something to prove to my peers and my self. I was by no means some punk ass kid fresh out of the burbs. No way ray, I was a punk long before being a punk was fasinable. I could roll dice with the best of them, I could palm cards and shot hoop, and walked with that glide in my stride. I rapped shit and got into plenty of trouble. I was *bad*. And I thought that was the only way to go. I thought if I could make it in that enviroment then I could make it in   3

JANET KOTLER has taught writing, women's studies, and social history at Goddard College in Vermont, has been Assistant Coordinator of Composition at the University of Wisconsin/Milwaukee, and currently teaches freshman English and advanced business communication at the University of Richmond in Virginia. One of her major interests is the language that English professors use in communicating with one another.

any. But the only thing that came about was that I was the victim of my own belifes. As cool as my friends were, I saw they were going noewhere, and I was going with them. I could steal and fight and all that old noise, but I could'nt add 2 and 2 and come up with 4. My reading was limited to the Playboys we stole from the crippled newstand vendor. My math apptitude was "what odds do I get on rolling stright sevens" and my writing was all the times I could write Courtney loves Cathy on the playground walls.

4   My parents had all but given up by this time. They had my brothers who were you all american mr wonderfuls and there was no hope's for Courtney they only hoped that I would'nt end up in jail. I bounced around several differant schools Being a discipline problem was easy, I was excluded from the chicago public school system when I was in 7th grade and had to attend private school intil high schools when the CPSS did'nt care who came to school. asfar as they were concerned they were in the business of prossing students reguardless of what they learned in school. I hated school, my teachers hated school, they had a look about them when they came to school every morning like "whats going to happen next?" And in my high school that was something to wonder about.

5   But my mother began to wonder why I was'nt learning like I should be. So I was tested and they found out I had a learning disibility and that I would always have trouble learning. "Wow" I thought now I have another excuse to get out of doing school work. So everytime I had'nt turned in an assignment I would say something to the effect of "I could'nt do it because of my learning disibility and the teacher would by it and I was out of another assignment.

6   But I'm a man now who has to make his own judgements. I don't fear teachers any more. But ask me if they ever inspired me. I'll laugh. Even though I have a hard time laughing now.

7   That last assignment I handed you was trash and I knew it. Last semester I handed in papers in psychology and history that I would'nt have given my eighth grade teacher, but still, they liked them. I've given you papers that I thought were good, would have been better had I taken the time to polish and retype, but I thought they were good enough to get my point across. Last week I tried to charm you guys. You could have taken the typical goddard cop-out and said "Well Courtney it was good for what it was and if you just learn to. . ." Aaaahhh, I tried to do it again! Sleazed through another assignment, learning disibility and all— the greatest crutch in the world. But James and Sharon and Bill said, "Wait a minute, we're not even going to read this."

8   I walked out because I was mad, and also embarasd.

9   I've loved being able to have some pride in myself and for once my parents are proud of me. Which by the way is very important to me at

this stage of the game, Ms Kottler. So here's assignment 8 again and I may sound Ignorant at times but I am going to try. . .

JANET KOTLER'S COMMENTARY

First, I ought to say that when I read students' papers, in the back of my mind I hear an old Sesame Street song that's supposed to teach little kids about distinguishing among things. It goes:

> One of these things is not like the others;
> One of these things just doesn't belong.
> Can you tell which thing is not like the others
> By the time I finish my song?*

I guess that's what I look for first. Is there something in this stack that's "not like the others"?

Second, and this is central to the question of judgment, is how I *feel* about student writing. When I read a paper like Courtney's, some deep part of me is engaged. I root for the paper and for the writer, all the way. I *want to teach*—and right *now*. I fantasize telephoning every student in my class and convening it *this minute*, even if it's 1:00 in the morning. When I read one of "the others," I suddenly need to count the towels in the linen closet or go get my tires rotated. I fantasize about terrible accidents that might befall the writer before the next class. I dread the next class.

Five'll get you ten that most teachers' first response to Courtney's paper would be "Oh, God!" or "Kid, if you can figure out how to get to the bookstore, buy a handbook." Even though I see their point of view, I would argue that Courtney's paper is "good" because it's "not like the others." In it, I hear a *voice*, the voice of a person who feels a responsibility to his own writing, to me, and to our work together; I see that sense of responsibility in the writer's use of specific language; I note a degree of modesty—Courtney's not trying to be A Writer here (something he's not, yet); I sense a serious attempt to respond to an important question; finally, I welcome—*and how*—the wit.

I recognize in Courtney's work what Roger Sale, who wrote a book called *On Writing*,† meant by his description of what characterizes "good" writing:

> Someone is asked a question, and he seeks to give an honest answer. It
> wasn't his question and probably isn't his subject, but perhaps he sees a

---

* "One of These Things," words and music by Joe Raposo, Jonico Music, 1970, collected in *The Sesame Street Songbook* (New York: Simon and Schuster in conjunction with the Children's Television Workshop), 1971.

† Random House (New York), 1970, p. 71.

way to make his answer his own, an expression of something he knows. What he knows is almost always a matter of the relationships he establishes . . . between the idea and the counteridea that the writer sees is also relevant, between his experience and what he knows of the experience of others—in short, between any two parts of his knowledge.

Damn right. That's one of the things I particularly admire about Courtney's paper—he was answering a "question"—an angry outburst from his colleagues, really—that wasn't his own, but that he *made* his own by taking himself, his writing, and his classmates seriously.

I should explain the circumstances of Courtney's paper. For several weeks, he had been writing very long papers that the class usually admired—his papers had a strong voice that conveyed his rather unusual viewpoint in persuasive terms. But the papers were unreadable (everyone in this class brought Xeroxed copies of their work with them for class discussion). The text, single-spaced, invariably ran from one side of the page to the other, without benefit of margins. There were *never* paragraphs, just one long saga. One word in three was misspelled; the punctuation was nonexistent. During our tenth meeting, the class blew up.

"Damn it, Courtney!" several people expostulated. "You write *better* than any of us, and a whole lot *worse*. We can't *read* this stuff—it's totally impossible. Just *forget* it!" (I, of course, smirked happily to myself; for once, others had made my criticisms for me.) Courtney, obviously furious, stalked out. After the weekend, I found the paper you've just read on my desk.

We can still find plenty of technicalities to complain about. But as depressing as the spelling and the punctuation are, they're much better than before. Courtney *tried:* the paper has margins and paragraphs; the sentences, generally, are complete and well formed. While it's impossible not to see what's *uncontrolled* in this paper, it's equally impossible to be deaf to the voice, or to be blind to Courtney's serious effort to come to terms with his own experience.

In his paper, Courtney explores the relationship between an "idea," (his experience in response to Assignment 8) and the "counteridea," which he sees for the first time is also relevant (his colleagues' insistence that he *write* that experience in a way that can be shared). His evaluation of his raw experience—his high school perceptions—in light of "what he knows of the experience of others" brings his fledgling acceptance of "the things my father calls life."

So it is, first, an honest paper. Here is a writer—just like you, probably, although you probably spell better—perplexed and annoyed and frustrated about something in his life that limits him in some way that is of immediate concern. What Courtney does here that goes far beyond just apologizing is to step back as far as his language will take him to figure out *what* this limitation is and *how* he might deal with it. Instead of maintaining what he called, in the first paragraph, the "formula" he'd been relying on (blurting out his life at the top of his lungs), he begins to look carefully at his own experience. You can see him weighing this experience against the requirements of the course, the demands of his own education. To do that, he begins to use a language other than his usual one.

Let me show you what I mean by tracing out and then commenting on what I see as the key shifts in Courtney's paper. He begins, essentially, with a judgment about himself in high school:

> I was *bad*. And I thought that was the only way to go. I thought if I could make it in that enviroment then I could make it in any. But the only thing that came about was that I was the victim of my own belifes. As cool as my friends were, I saw they were going noewhere, and I was going with them.

I think Courtney's entitled to make that observation because of the language he's already used to describe his role in his high school:

> I could roll dice with the best of them, I could palm cards and shot hoop, and walked with that glide in my stride . . . I rapped shit. . . My math apptitude was "what odds do I get on rolling stright sevens" . . .

That is, he describes concretely the things that made him "bad" *in the language that was "bad" to him at the time.* Now he can look back and reflect, "I was going nowhere."

Through a series of turning points, Courtney earns that lovely concluding sentence (concluding, though it appears in the very first paragraph): "I have a whole new outlook on the things my father calls life." That is not just an idle assertion; he "backs it up," as they say in freshman English, with sentences that show us his experience concretely, and in which he shows a change of mind about that experience:

"I don't fear teachers any more." (True: he walked out of class. If you're afraid of the teacher, you don't do that.)

"Even though I have a hard time laughing now." (Probably. He wrote *this*, after all—which is not something you'd do if you still equated "assigned work" with "education.")

"That last assignment . . . was trash and I knew it." (Yes; he *did* know it. Otherwise, he wouldn't have walked out; he'd have stuck around to defend himself. Courtney was not exactly shy.)

"Last week I tried to charm you guys." (Charm, in abundance, was what Courtney had had going for him all semester. And until Assignment 8, when the class got fed up, it had worked.)

"Aaaahhh, I tried to do it again! Sleazed through another assignment . . ." (By me, the words "again" and "sleazed through" are acknowledgments that Courtney saw himself continuing to fall back on his learning disability [which, in case this point escaped you, was real enough]. And from where he was *now*, that disgusted him: "Aaaahhh!")

"I walked out because I was mad, and also embarasd." (Yep. He was downright humiliated—but he couldn't have *been* "embarasd" if he were still doing business at the same old stand; it's only his realization that he's conned *himself* that embarrasses him. When somebody points a finger at you but you know you're right, you get mad. When you can see what that person is pointing at, it's a different story.)

I've read too many abstract papers of the "I once was blind, but now I see" variety not to be impressed when somebody really takes a stand on something. In Courtney's paper, the details of his blindness are not missing; his new vision I am not asked to take merely on faith. *This* writer is trying to include me in his new perspective, not just trying to con me into believing some change took place. *This* writer is saying, in effect, "Look. Once I saw the world, and described it to myself, in *that* language; I remember it; I can still use it. But now that I see things differently I have to use a *new* language. I could not have put it this way before; now, it seems the *only* way to describe my experience." So I believed Courtney when he said he was going to try. (He did, too.) He didn't see me as an adversary (the TEACHER) anymore, but as a participant in his discovery: what more could either of us want?

Courtney's paper demonstrates a truth that makes us teachers crazy: very little "good" *beginning* writing combines both voice and linguistic control for more than a couple of paragraphs. A *part* of what makes me a teacher wishes that Courtney could spell. A *part* of what makes me a teacher longs for the occasional comma. But not, I think, the best part. The best part of *me* as a teacher—and I think most teachers are like me—would much rather work with a student who knows where he stands and has the guts to say so than with one whose "perfect" language is politely removed from himself and from me, whose own voice he has stifled in the name of Not Making Waves.

In sum, when I read, I'm looking for some evidence of thought—for sentences like "I have a whole new outlook on the things my father calls life." I'm looking to see if you can step back from a subject until you're far enough away to see it, if you can recognize the distance, if you can see things—even for a fleeting moment—from more than your immediate perspective. To at least know where you are. To give up pretending you have the thing wrapped. Because you don't. You know you don't; I know you don't: why pretend? It scares me, and it probably scares you, and it bores both of us. I know you think it's risky, especially when you have the seaworthy five-paragraph-theme to hold onto. But I admire risk. I value writing that takes chances with itself, with its author, with its audience. Which, after all, is me. And which, after all, is finally you.

Study Questions

1. A student who read Courtney Wayshak's paper and Janet Kotler's commentary on it said,

    > Why isn't this just another way of "sleazing through an assignment"? This student must have known what his teacher liked and wanted from him, so that's what he gives her. All that stuff about the bad background and his trouble with learning and the parents who don't seem to understand him, and what dopes all his other teachers are, is a bid for sympathy really, another kind of con.

    But another student responded,

    > If it is a con job, it really isn't a very good one. He tells us too much about himself for this to be only that. Also, I don't think if he were just putting it on that he'd include all that stuff about wanting his parents to be proud of him. He sounds sincere to me.

    What position would you take in this controversy?

    What does your position enable you to say about what seems necessary in order for a reader to make a responsible judgment on the "sincerity" of a piece of writing?

2. Edit Courtney Wayshak's paper by correcting the mistakes in it, the misused marks of punctuation, the misspellings, and so on.

    Do you have in this edited version a better piece of writing than the original, or not? In either case, make clear what makes you say so and what you mean by "better."

3. "Courtney, obviously furious, stalked out. After the weekend, I found the paper you've just read on my desk."

    Suppose someone said the following about that segment of Janet Kotler's commentary:

    > If more students understood that *all* real learning has moments like that one as one of its dimensions, maybe it would make make things easier for them. And if more teachers tried to arrange more such moments for their students, they'd teach a lot better than they do.

    What would you understand this person to mean?

    Would you agree with the position he or she seems to be taking?

Susan Miller's Assignment

For a writing class to work as a group, we have to know each other better than we need to in some other classes.

This does not mean that we have to be friends, or be personal, but that we each must have a sense of what the people in the group are like. We need to know about each other's characteristics as coworkers.

The best way I know to get this sense of each other is to have stories from each person that represent an important part of the person's life. Use the same story you wrote to tell me about yourself in Assignment 1, but recast it in a public form that is suitable for the class to read.

Set a scene (time, place), identify the characters, and take the point of view of a narrator—a storyteller, not just yourself. The high point (revealing moment, resolution of conflict) should be at or near the next-to-last sentence.

✍ Put It On A Matter Of   *by Vince Dawson*

1   On November 1, 1980 was a day never to be forgotton and a day that would change the lives of many people.

2   SGT. Bill read the roll call bulletins, while SGT. Don inspected and gave each man his traffic assignment.

3   Today was a very special day because President Jimmy Carter was due to arrive at General Mitchel Field at about 7:45 p.m., in hopes to gain more support for his bid for the upcoming election.

4   The traffic bureau cycle men filed out of District #1's garage to take on their daily work before the President's plane lands. P.O. Vinc, Mel, and James rode to their beat areas together.

5   The day was cool, sunny, and dry. The traffic was heavy, everyone was rushing to and frow.

6   P.O. Vinc was dispatched to 35th and Lisbon Ave. for an Automobile-Truck accident personal injury. He turned on his siren and red lights, heading for his assignment.

7   Upon his arrival, he found 3 cars badly damaged and 1 truck with minor damages.

8   A three year old girl was the only one injuried, with multiple head injuries. She was taken to the hospital and was later listed in stable condition.

SUSAN MILLER is a member of the Department of English and Director of Writing at The University of Utah. She teaches writing, rhetoric, and composition theory. She has written *Writing: Process and Product* (1971) and revised the seventh edition of *Writing With A Purpose* (1980).

Her mother did not use the safety chair that was intended for her   9
daughter in the back seat of the car.

Before 7:00 p.m., P.O. Vinc had investigated 5 accident, 2 assist an   10
officer, 2 arrest, numerous parking violations, many contacts.

The time was about 7:05 p.m., SGT. Bill was broadcasting various   11
codes to let us know the status of Air Force 1.

The President was ahead of his schedule. P.O. Vinc was riding his   12
motorcycle southbound on Action Street when he noticed some bright
headlight coming toward his direction, then it happened. The motorcycle began to shake from the impact. The sound of metal against metal
got louder and louder. P.O. Vinc stood up on his motorcycle looked at
the car pass after it struck his motorcycle.

At that time he felt a burning sensation to his left leg, he looked down   13
and saw his left leg hanging. The cycle kept going as did the car. The
driver of the car was apprehended. The blood began to cover everything.
He finally stopped the cycle about half a block away and with the aid of
P.O. Mel a tourniquet was applied and the ambulance arrived in about
38 seconds after it was called.

P.O. Vinc was conscious but the shock from the impact was taking its   14
toll. After arriving at the hospital he remembered seeing himself lying on
a table with several doctors standing around him. They were working
very hard to try and save the left leg but the body rejected the badly
smashed limb.

During the operation all of a sudden a doctor said, "he's gone, we've   15
done all we could do." P.O. Vinc began screaming, its only my leg, my
leg but know one seem to hear him. He kept trying to fight his way back
into that body that was lying on the table, but all he could see was the
doctors shaking their heads and the nurses disconnecting the equipment.

He began shouting but the more he shouted the further away he   16
seemed to float from his body, the doctors, the nurses, the operating
room. He then went into a deep unconsciousness, his eyes began rolling
around the back of his head. He then snapped out of it, he opened his
eyes only to find himself lying on a hospital bed.

P.O. Vinc could not durning this difficult time say where he had been   17
but dispite the loss of a limb it felt good to be alive. . .

SUSAN MILLER'S COMMENTARY

This essay by Vince Dawson was written at the beginning of a new course
at the University of Wisconsin–Milwaukee, English 99, for very inexperienced writers. I usually think I write "better" than this, and most of
you probably do too. But I chose this paper as my example of good
student writing because most of us do not in fact write this well. What

the writer of this essay has achieved takes more intellectual courage than I can usually find myself or can help my students to find.

I should point out that Assignment 1 had asked the class to tell me something about themselves that would help me understand them as *learners*. Throughout this course, we discussed, read, and wrote about "teaching" and "learning"—not only school lessons, but the lessons in unplanned events, the lessons of major changes in our lives and in our learning from family and friends. This paper was, then, a revision. Its writer, Vince Dawson, recast the paper he had written for me as a story for a wider audience—his classmates.

When I read any student paper, I'm always asking two questions. First, I'm a teacher who wants to know what remains to be learned by the student writer. Here, I could see writing at a point between the day-to-day ways we speak and think and the conventional, public, documented world of texts that universities enclose and are enclosed by. For Vince, writing was a way of recording the sounds of sentences as he said them, not a standardized graphic code that we use to *represent* what we say. He wrote "frow" for "fro," "know one seem to hear him," even "Vinc" for the conventional spelling of "Vince."

My second question is always "What is this student *doing* in this writing?" Reading this essay, I could see the signs of inexperience with the conventions of public writing only *after* I sorted out my answers to this second question. This story put my assignment firmly in its place: "Tell me about yourself. Tell *us* a *story* about yourself." As I read this economic, direct account of November 1, 1980, my assignment seemed more and more trivial, about as directly related to the power of this writing as the first shots at Fort Sumter were to the Civil War. I thought of Hemingway, Capote, and Mailer piling detail on detail to make an emotional impact that no single detail ever contains. What Vince was doing was closer to these writers' powerful uses of seemingly simple de-tails than the writing I anticipated in creating this assignment. He turned a usual classroom exercise, "write a story," into a moving tragedy.

P.O. Vinc had not heard of Hemingway, Capote, or Mailer, much less imitated their techniques. To say his writing was good because it struck all of us dumb is true but not very helpful to others who also want to write well. But what he did to achieve this essay's power can be explained and transferred, even to those of us who are "better" writers.

The only writing Vince had done often before coming to the Univer-sity was as a policeman filling out reports: What happened? In what order? At what time? Where? What were the weather conditions? Who was involved? What were the results? He was a trained observer who had written in a certain way for a certain audience, in what teachers call a *genre*—the police report. He knew how to record events for later reference so that subjective feelings and judgments would not influence the responses of a more removed audience.

On one level, then, what he did when he wrote this essay was simply to answer my question. He chose an important event and reported it from a point of view that he had practiced time and time again. He was an impersonal but conscientious observer. He writes as a narrator, able to say "The driver of the car was apprehended. The blood began to cover everything." Even after the crisis of his accident, he maintains this point of view. He watches as the officer on the hospital table watches himself.

As a teacher, myself a trained observer of writing, I perceive in this essay a good technical sense of language, the necessary counterpart to a writer's courage. This writing requires us to become more aware of ordinary language and of nonacademic ways of thinking and to adjust our ideas about storytelling accordingly. This essay is not a mere police report, nor is it a personal account of "my most terrible moment." The child injured because her seat belt was unhooked foreshadows the police officer whose leg is lost to a careless, "apprehended," driver. Both events transform a day of ordinary, fragmented experience into coherence and tragic irony because the writer chose one, controlled point of view. The voice that defines this point of view allows the truth—the facts—to serve him in a new and unfamiliar context for writing: the teacher's idea of telling a story. He moved his voice, experience, and memory into the academic world of ideas about writing good stories, and his writing calls all our ideas into question. All of us in the class learned something new about the controlled and contextualized honesty that good writing always displays.

"Contextualized honesty" is a mouthful that requires more explanation if it is not to be tasteless academic sawdust. What I mean by it is that Vince's writing places his experience beyond its moment in his life and beyond the agonizing months we can imagine following. Because he *reports* himself rather than telling us about feelings that we could better imagine for ourselves, and because his report reminds us of other, similar voices and accounts, we are forced to ask what his experience means. We can see the outline and shape of significance in this writing; the ordinary way of reporting becomes extraordinarily important by virtue of the writer's controlled, authentic voice and his adherence to a particular form. Vince held a tension between flat reporting and personal anguish. His writing is powerful because it is not sentimental, and it is not sentimental because of his adherence to a commonplace form that is used for minor as well as such extraordinary events.

Vince's writing also reminds us that being able to write is not, at least not only, a matter of correctness, of well-developed paragraphs and clear syntax. Primarily, it is a matter of using a particular form to express insights and experience—a matter of conceiving and executing a purpose that writing can best accomplish, whether as story, report, explanation, or any other genre. Here was a fortunate combination of an assignment, a student's experience with a public voice, and human tragedy. As writing, Vince's piece is better than the sum of those parts. You do not need to have had his devastating experience to learn how to use an authentic voice in expressing your own experience and ideas. The power of good writing is most often the surprising combination of a need to write in a particular situation, the use of a standard form, and a personalization of that form by allowing it to convey your most honest insights.

Study Questions

1. At the end of her commentary on Vince Dawson's paper, Susan Miller speaks of "the power of good writing." Judging from what she says leading up to that comment, what would Susan Miller see this power as being good for?

2. A student responded to Vince Dawson's paper and Susan Miller's commentary on it by saying this:

   > I wonder how courageous we would find this paper if the writer of it hadn't *lost* his leg. Suppose he had just had it broken, for example, and had written about that this same way. I think I might complain more then about some things in the paper. You can't tell exactly how this man was injured, for instance. The writing really isn't very clear. In other words, maybe the people in the class found the writing of this paper powerful and technically good because of the *event*, not because of the writing about it. After all, the writer himself, without his leg, was sitting right there.

   How do you respond to this student's statement?

3. The title of Vince Dawson's paper, "Put It On A Matter Of," is taken in part from a police accident report form that is headed "A Matter Of." When told this, one member of a class discussing the paper said,

   > I don't see why Vince Dawson didn't tell us that, or why Susan Miller didn't tell us that. When you get a title that's as queer as this one you have a responsibility to explain it. This title makes no sense unless you know what it refers to.

   Another student responded,

   > I like the title just the way it is *without* any explanation. I think it's strangely effective somehow, like a play on words of some sort. It made me want to read on. And that's the primary reason for a title anyway.

   What position would you take in this controversy?

JAMES SLEDD'S Assignment

[This assignment was made at Claflin College in 1971. I have reconstructed it from correspondence with Dr. Louie Crew, who gave it. Dr. Crew is not responsible for the reconstruction.]

Write brief, imagined conversations with each of the following people: a white policeman about to arrest you, a white employer interviewing you for a job, your girl friend or boy friend, your closest friend of the same sex (late at night, as the conversation gets very serious), a child whom you have just met. Each of the five conversations should give a different answer, at least by implication, to the question, "Who are you?"

༄. Who Are You?[1]   *by Martin Roberts*

I. A cop about to arrest you—

Alright this is the police. what is you name boy, do I look like a boy to   1
you pig. Alright nigger watch your language before I beat you across you
head with this jack. Well you'll have to prove that to me, action speaks
louder than words, I wasn't doing anything to make you try to arrest me
any how my name Martin Roberts. Oh, you are the wrong guy. Next
time Be right because I'll shot the snot out of you.

II. Whitey interviewing you for a job—

Hi whats happening man do you have any job open, I am a very good   2
sales men had 7 years experience in stores carlots and factories anything
you name I've had it. What you reason for quiting all these job, see when
I get a man I won't one that is responsible of being hear. If you salary is
right, you have a responsible cat working for you today, tomorrow, and
the next days. Well you is on. Oh my name is Martin Roberts, let go
back in my office.

---

[1] Copyright © January 1973 by the National Council of Teachers of English. Reprinted with the permission of the publisher.

JAMES SLEDD is a professor of English at the University of Texas at Austin, where he is also a former director of freshman composition, and a recent director of five NEH seminars. Though he has taught composition and written about it off and on for over forty years, he doesn't pretend that he has really taught anybody how to write. Some of his students have learned, others haven't; but Sledd takes neither credit nor much blame for either outcome.

III. Your girlfriend—

3   Hell-o whats happening baby how are you feeling. Well I am feeling alright, just thinking of what was the mean of being with that Girl last night. Man I dont no what you are talking about, you no I wouldn't do nothing like that baby, But, Hell you did, Woman I'll take you mine out, and pinch it and see if it will jump if you don't believe me well you can do the next best thing. Ok honey I'll be right.

IV. Your closest friend of same sex, late at night, as conversation gets very serious—

4   Hay man I mean brother man I am in some serious trouble man I got caught steeling some potato chips, now I have to pay out 100 dollars for just one simple thing. Do you parents no about it yet, man I dont wont them to fine out about that they beat the mess out of me with my cloths on. Well we'll fine it out what we can do.

V. A child whom you have just met—

5   Hi, man, my name is Martin what is your's Old Blacks the snot catcher I catches any thing you can let loose Well thats go man because I have some Bugger in my nose that is ready to fly. Well I do other things besides that I play sports, now thats whats happening lets see what going down in the park OK man.

James Sledd's COMMENTARY

Is it psychopathic to be well-adjusted? In a quiet study at high noon on a bright spring day, the question stubbornly refuses to look absurd, and the answer comes insistently that people who accept and manipulate the world as it is are crazy already, while people who reject it had better watch for symptoms. But English teachers, if they're to be worth *anything*, must deny what their world believes and believe what their world denies.

That, I suppose, is why Dr. Louie Crew, a white Episcopalian, was teaching black freshmen in a little Methodist college in South Carolina a dozen years ago, when he assigned the paper which is here reprinted just as it was written (except that the writer's name has been changed). It's a good paper, a casual but intelligent response to an intelligent, careful assignment; yet most teachers and students of English whom I have known would read it in bewilderment or despair or even with contempt, and many eminent black Americans would say that a teacher who calls such a paper good is a sentimental and condescending paternalist, denying students the help they need in learning standard English as one means to some secure employment and maybe even to some control over their own lives. Young people who know nothing better than street talk ought not to get into college and will certainly not get on in the world of work.

It's because I think those judgments are mostly wrong—one index to the craziness of our world—that I chose to offer this paper for this volume. No language, and no variety of a language, would survive for long if it did not serve some purposes better than any other serves them, and it follows that our problem in using English is the problem of reasoned choice among purposes and among the linguistic means to accomplish them. We limit our choices unnecessarily if we refuse to learn more kinds of English than our social and personal histories give us without our effort, but our cruelty blocks the main function of language, communication, if we deny respect to other people because their different histories have not given them the kinds of English that we value. We can abuse language as grossly when we read or listen as when we speak or write.

Dr. Crew had invented his assignment to exercise his students in the art of thinking in their own language. Explicitly intended as a beginning, not an ending (Dr. Crew insists that one goal of his teaching is the mastery of standard English), the assignment asked for the kind of concretely embodied thought for which the students' own language was the best medium—better than the standardized formalities of book talk, academic English. But the assignment went beyond unthinking self-expression. Each dialogue, just because it was a dialogue, invited the students to imagine the speech of others, varieties and uses of language not their own. The invitation might be expected to deepen the realization that there are indeed many kinds of English, each with its own uses, and that one's choice among them cannot be made by considering only oneself, the speaker-writer's character and wishes. Dr. Crew hoped besides that the answers might help his students later, when he prompted their writing by other provocative or provoking questions, like whether it is possible or even desirable to be just one integrated self and not some number of different selves at once, whether honesty is relative, and whether the truth of a statement can be judged without regard to the situation where it's made.

Among English teachers, the assignment prompts the further question what English teachers ought to teach. "The means to upward mobility in the mainstream culture" is not a sane answer in the United States today, for upward mobility for Americans means the continued conspicuous waste of the biosphere's irreplaceable resources and the continued exploitation of weaker nations by the United States. The many possible sane answers include "some means to survival as human beings in a crazy world," "the art of thinking in one's own language," "other languages (or varieties) to think in," and lots of others. One good way to sort the proffered answers is the opposition between liberation and domestication. Teachers shouldn't be animal-trainers, whatever else they do.

The animal-trainer's methods anyhow wouldn't work with Martin Roberts. Pride is obviously one strong quality of his personality, and the successful representation of that personality is the strongest quality of his paper. Led by the assignment, he defines himself in his relations to hostile white authority, to his parents (his father is a minister), to friends of his own age among both sexes, and to young children. The conversations show concretely what he is, without the necessity for difficult, perhaps repugnant, abstract analysis. The analysis, if it came at all, would come later, when (as Dr. Crew had planned), this paper would provide material.

The assignment itself provided some assurance of success, some encouragement (not affront) to Martin's pride. Because Dr. Crew did play to the students' conversational strength and established a frame in which to exercise it, he offered them the satisfaction of seeing that they had made something worth making; but Martin's paper went beyond the minimal accomplishment of meeting the assignment. Though Dr. Crew provided the larger form of five short, contrasting conversations, he did not provide the form of those conversations themselves. The student's own experience within his culture provided that smaller form—the form of the verbal combat, the duel in words. In each conversation, Martin talks for victory—and never loses. Casually, without analysis, he presents an imaginative self-portrait in which language and form work together to show what he is and what he wants to be. He is, in part, his language.

The well-adjusted, intent on upward mobility and other forms of domination, might very well sneer at Martin—at his language, his paper, his teacher, and most of all at me for taking it all so seriously. To Martin, himself, English classes and English teachers were maybe a bit absurd, and no one would consider his paper more than a beginning (just as no one has ever opposed the teaching of the standard language, in right ways and for right reasons). For all that, Dr. Crew's assignment and Martin's paper remind us that both teacher and student must not just accept but must honor the student's language and culture, the only possible start for a life's learning. Of what we say and write, we can be as demanding as we wish, driving ourselves to the most careful choices among the resources of our language; but we abuse our language if, when we read or listen, we demand that others choose as we do or as the powerful tell all of us we should.

The insanity of the well-adjusted is their love for getting and spending and their contempt for those who don't have much to spend. Prompted by Louie Crew, Martin Roberts put himself on paper—a living human being. Reading such a paper (was it written without real effort?), one hopes that the writer will learn much more about himself and about the possibilities and impossibilities of his language; but if zeal for some one of the many kinds of English blocks respect for that human being, the indispensable foundation has been destroyed. Even Old Blacks knew the need for mutual respect, no matter how much we might laugh at his juvenile belligerence or he at our solemnities.

Study Questions

1. If you were teaching Martin Roberts, how would you mark and grade his paper?

   How would you explain your marking and grading if you were talking to him directly?

   How do you hope Martin Roberts would act on your explanation?

2. Edit one of Martin Roberts's dialogues by putting it into standard English, correctly spelled and punctuated. What does a comparison of your edited version with the original tell you about Martin Roberts's strengths as a writer? What does he need to learn?

   What might Martin Roberts stand to gain if he learned what you think he needs to? What might he stand to lose?

3. In a classroom discussion of Martin Roberts's paper and James Sledd's commentary on it a student said,

   > I'm not quite clear what James Sledd means when he says "English teachers, if they're to be worth *anything*, must deny what their world believes and believe what their world denies." What's this mean about what James Sledd thinks students ought to learn in a writing classroom? Should we be learning certain things, or not learning certain things, or what exactly? I don't want to be an "animal" trained by "animal trainers," but what does James Sledd think I should be and do to learn to write?

   How do you answer this student's questions?

Writing Assignment 2
Moving Beyond Limits

Imagine that someone has just said to you,

> There's no particular mystery about what makes writing good. Above all, good writing is clear, logical, coherent, and correct. Without these qualities the writing can't be taken seriously and neither can the writer.

You have just read some student writing as well as some critical commentaries which suggest that such a definition of good writing may not be the whole story. "Paper A" for example is clear, logical, coherent, and correct. And, is it enough to say that the five student writers represented in this chapter should not be taken seriously? By anybody? Under any circumstances?

On the other hand, be sure you consider very carefully whether you would be willing to say that the way a writer spells and punctuates doesn't matter or that the way a writer expresses an idea makes no difference.

Once you have considered these questions and have made some notes of your ideas, compose a response to the statement quoted above. Use whatever you find relevant in this chapter. Please don't think that you are expected here to come up with whatever the whole story may be. We are, in our class discussions and with these assignments, beginning a conversation, remember. But notice that in having some specific examples of writing and some specific critical commentaries on that writing to draw from, you do not have to stay at the level of generalization in your response. Be sure to make clear in your paper which student essays and/or which commentaries you are drawing from.

When you have finished composing your response to the statement quoted above, on a separate sheet of paper explain, in a paragraph, what makes it difficult to talk about what makes writing good.

But difficult as it may be, *how* one chooses to talk about what makes writing good matters. On still another sheet of paper write a paragraph in which you say why.

Perceiving What Is Seen   3

Nature cannot be imitated or transcribed without first being taken apart
and put together again. . . . The artist cannot copy a sunlit lawn, but he
can suggest it. Exactly how he does it in any particular instance is his
secret, but the word of power which makes this magic possible is known
to all artists—it is "relationships." [An accurate description therefore] is
not a faithful record of a visual experience but the faithful construction
of a relational model. . . . A model can be constructed to any required
degree of accuracy. What is decisive here is clearly the word "required."
The form of a representation cannot be divorced from its purpose.

E. H. Gombrich

T HE ACT OF PICTURING IN WORDS, OF giving a detailed account of something" is the way one dictionary goes about defining the word "description." Such a way of talking has its usefulness of course—in the same way
that it may be useful in certain circumstances to say good writing is clear,
logical, coherent, and correct (or alternatively to say that it is fresh or vital, that
it must be sincere or personal, or some such). But these abstractions, whatever
they may be good for, are not, all by themselves, very helpful to writers wanting
to learn how to improve their ability to write description, wanting to learn how
exactly to *give* a detailed account that is logical and correct as well as fresh and
sincere.

What *can* help?

It might be helpful for you to see your writing of a description in relation to
other students' descriptions, to see your definition of good description in relation
to other people's definitions of good description. To have this sense of your own
writing in relation to that of others and of your own definitions in relation to
those of others is to have a context.

It is the assumption not just of this chapter but of this book that thinking about and practicing writing within such a context can provide you with a fuller sense of what you can come to do as a writer, a broader perspective in which to see what your writing can mean. For to become conscious of what other writers are doing (and not doing) is to become more conscious of yourself as a writer. To become aware of the different things writing means (and does not mean) to others is to widen your awareness of what writing can mean to you. One learns to do something by doing and by trying to understand both the nature and the importance of whatever it is one is doing. One learns to practice effectively within a context of the practices of other people.

The five student essays and commentaries in this chapter are not then, either individually or as a group, intended to provide you with a formula for writing good descriptions—no more than taking a writing course automatically turns someone into a writer. But they can, along with your writing class, help create a context in which you can shape and revise, evaluate and recast what you write. They can create a context in which it is possible for you to learn from your experience with writing—and whether you admire any of the selections you will be working with or not. For just as you can sometimes learn more from classroom conflict than you can from classroom agreement, from a piece of student writing that you dislike or from a commentary with which you violently disagree it is quite possible for you to learn things you could learn in no other way. This goes not just for learning about writing. It goes for all education when looked at from any distance.

Edward Corbett's Assignment

Take one of your journal entries that describes a place that is interesting or meaningful to you and expand it into a full-fledged essay.

[When Timothy Hagood wrote the paper that appears here, he was enrolled in an advanced composition course at Texas Tech University in Lubbock, Texas. The course was taught by Nevin Laib, who gave the assignment. Tim felt that interesting places are hard to come by on the High Plains and asked if he could describe the sky instead. —E.P.J.C.]

EDWARD P. J. CORBETT is Professor of English and former Director of Freshman English at Ohio State University. He was editor of *College Composition and Communication* from 1974 to 1979 and is currently the CCCC representative to the College Section of the National Council of Teachers of English. He is the author of *Classical Rhetoric for the Modern Student* (2nd ed., 1971), *The Little English Handbook* (4th ed., 1984), and *The Little Rhetoric and Handbook with Readings* (1983).

❧ The West Texas Sky   *by Timothy Hagood*

Vain in its immensity, shameless in its ambiguity, the sky inundates the   1
consciousness of those that live in West Texas. The earth here offers no
resistance to the heaven's imperious dominance. It neither challenges
the sky with a mountain or a tree nor embraces it with a valley or a
flower. Instead, like an ignominious victim, it meets the implacable sky
in an acquiescent horizon. Consequently, one living here is forced to
look upward for his cosmographical sustenance.

For those who have travelled to West Texas from places where the   2
earth is more generous and irregular, this subjugation of the earth by the
sky is at first oppressive. They may occasionally remark about an inspiring sunrise or a magnificent sunset, but they are rarely able to transcend
the drearily predictable geography here and make the transition from
earth to sky. They quickly weary of its vertiginous expanse, and for them
the sky soon disappears into an oblivion of languid resignation.

I have experienced the same feelings as these earth-chained refugees,   3
only the circumstances were inverted. I once spent several months
travelling in the mountainous regions of Southern Mexico and the trop-
ical rain forests and jungles of Guatemala and Honduras. At first, I was
overwhelmed by the richness of the flora and fauna and awed by the vast
variety and asymmetry of the land forms there. However, I soon found
myself growing tired of all this botanical and geographical baroqueness. I
felt glutted and suffocated by the density of the foliage. The myriad
mountains and ravines became like waves on an endless sea; infinitely
changing, infinitely monotonous. But more importantly, the sky was
distracted and obstructed. I was seduced by the sky so early in life that I
had grown up consumed by it.

* * * *

The sky of West Texas is a cosmorama. It is an artist's gargantuan   4
canvas as well as the source of all dynamic natural activity for this area. It
holds darkness and light and infinite shades, hues, and colors. A summer
sky of stifling hot pearl is debilitating. A cool violet sky in winter dumps
hindering loads of snow. The same gunmetal oyster-grey sky that nur-
tures the crops with soft rain annihilates them with vindictive hail. The
West Texas sky's moods run the gamut from crystalline midnight with
piercing starscapes to vague dawns enclosed by numinous fog. Such por-
tending ostentation could have been the reason why the Indians living
here once beheld the sky and feared and worshipped it as a god.

I, too, see God in the sky. I can also feel his breath and hear his voice.   5

It is a dissatisfied wind of constant restlessness. It begins in the morning, sighing, softly singing, then whispering; inhaling, exhaling truth. As the day wears on, the wind begins to whistle and whirl with a shrillness. Gradually it builds. By mid-afternoon, it is a roaring, vindictive crescendo.

6   The wind is also the carrier of the litter of earth and sky. Dust is its all too palpable component. A sudden gust slaps your face and grates your eyes, but then stops. The wind sighs. It is mocking you. You think it is calm then it bludgeons your ears and buffets your lips. Blasting, eroding, until it finally whips you into compliancy.

. . . .

7   When I was a child, I was told that God lives in heaven. So when I wanted to talk to God, I would speak at the sky. This developed into my holding God responsible for the many happenings in the sky. I praise his glory when the sky is beautiful or when he puts on a brilliant display, such as the electrical storms of spring. Last Thursday, the sky rained, sleeted, and snowed on my parade, and I was livid! I started to think of God as the gnostic demiurge. Perhaps, I thought, Zarathustra's Ahura Mazda hit the mark in its expression of the totality of God. I shook my fists and cursed the sky out of anger.

8   A practical man might call what I have written the ruminations of a ridiculous fool. A pious man might construe as excessive hubris my attempts to decipher the arcane mysteries of an incomprehensible sphinx. The theosopher, Jacob Boehme, said, "A thing can only be revealed through another thing that resists it." Perhaps I'm thinking of a different Jacob, though. Perhaps I'm thinking of the one in Genesis that wrestled an enigmatic stranger. As I see it, I can either resist the sky or ignore it. I have chosen not to be ignorant.

EDWARD CORBETT'S COMMENTARY

In this essay, Timothy Hagood gives us his intensely personal reactions to the phenomenon of the West Texas sky. His essay not only describes that sky but presents his reflections on his experiences with that sky. I chose this essay partly because it represents a fairly successful example of a kind of writing that young, inexperienced writers usually do not handle well: a description of a place or a scene or a phenomenon. Frequently, descriptions by inexperienced writers are pieces of overwrought prose bespangled with glittering adjectives. Men especially are reputed to be inept at creating verbal pictures. Their thoughts about what they describe—if they reflect on it at all—are often a tissue of hackneyed and pious generalizations. But Tim has avoided both of those pitfalls and has composed a quite impressive combination of descriptive and meditative writing.

Before I comment on the merits of this piece, I want to point out some of its errors and weaknesses. When I reproduced Tim's essay here, I silently corrected his six spelling errors: *ignominious, baroqueness, Guatemala, Southern* (not capitalized), *dissatisfied, Boehme* (the umlauting *e* left out). I did not, however, silently correct the most shocking errors in the paper: the comma splice ("I have experienced the same feelings as these earth-chained refugees, only the circumstances were inverted"); the fused sentence ("You think it is calm then it bludgeons your ears and buffets your lips"); the sentence fragment ("Blasting, eroding, until it finally whips you into compliancy"); and two faulty uses of the semicolon in paragraphs 3 and 5 ("The myriad mountains and ravines became like waves on an endless sea; infinitely changing, infinitely monotonous" / "It begins in the morning, sighing, softly singing, then whispering; inhaling, exhaling truth"). I have called these "shocking errors" because a writer as bright and as skillful as Tim should not be making the kind of flagrant punctuation errors that remedial students routinely make. I would ride him hard about these errors because I would want to shame him into putting his mind to these matters of punctuation and to learning once and for all the boundaries of the English sentence. The sentence fragment that he wrote could be justified stylistically, but I would want to make sure that the fragment was deliberate.

One of the conspicuous merits of Tim's prose style is his extraordinary vocabulary—extraordinary for its richness and its range and often for its precision and its aptness—but here I want to point out some instances where Tim's command of language lapses. In paragraph 3, for example, there are two instances where his aptitude for precise diction fails him: "earth-chained refugees" and "myriad mountains and ravines." I wonder why he refers to the visitors to West Texas as "refugees," and "myriad" seems a bit too hyperbolic for this context. In paragraph 6, we see three phrases in which the verbs are slightly awry: "grates your eyes," "buffets your lips," and "bludgeons your ears." Tim also exhibits a tendency toward redundancy and tautology. Here are three examples of superfluous words: "arcane mysteries" (paragraph 8), "enigmatic stranger" (paragraph 8), "excessive hubris" (paragraph 8). I could cite some other instances of diction that miss the mark, but finally I would have to concede that the occasional lapses are overshadowed by the predominance of precise, apt, vivid diction throughout the essay.

Let us consider the larger dimensions of Tim's essay. He has structured his essay into three major parts:

A. Observations of how the sky dominates the scene in West Texas
B. Descriptions of the appearance and the operations of that sky
C. Reflections on the significance of that sky

He uses a typographical device—a string of asterisks—to signal the transition from part to part. I suspect that he did not consciously plot the structure of the piece. His instinct for organization, however, was sound, for the structure he used here is apt, if not inevitable.

The first sentence of the essay is remarkable not only for the felicity of its structure but also for its figurativeness. First of all, a personification is implied by attaching the adjectives *vain* and *shameless* to *sky*. Secondly, a metaphor is implicit in the verb *inundates*. The word *inundates* creates an especially startling metaphor here because it is etymologically related to the word *waves* and suggests something earthbound rather than something connected with the heavens. This opening sentence sets the tone for the entire piece and prefigures Tim's attitude toward the sky. The West Texas sky is so "real" for Tim that he cannot talk about it as a lifeless phenomenon; it is a vital presence for him, demanding and commanding his attention.

After talking in the second paragraph about how unimpressive the sky is for visitors to West Texas, Tim indicates, in the third paragraph, his empathy with the indifference of those casual visitors to West Texas by talking about his own visit to another part of the world, Central America. But what is particularly notable about this paragraph is the salient contrast it draws between the natural scene in Central America and the natural scene in West Texas. Whereas the sky dominates the environs in Texas, the earth dominates the scene in Central America. Tim implies here that all human beings are influenced mainly by that aspect of the environment which most insistently demands their attention.

Paragraph 4 presents Tim's writing at its best. Here Tim gives us his one and only *particular* description of the West Texas sky. Up to this point, he has pictured that sky for us only in a general way. Now he sketches that sky for us specifically, precisely, and vividly. He indicates by the sharpness of his diction that he has really *seen* that sky, in its various aspects. Note the startlingly accurate, sensory words that he uses to depict the sky: "stifling hot pearl," "cool violet sky," "gunmetal oyster-grey sky," "crystalline midnight with piercing starscapes," "vague dawns enclosed by numinous fog." To be able to describe a scene that precisely and vividly, one must observe keenly and command a rich vocabulary. The most startling choice of diction in this paragraph—startling for its unusualness and its aptness—is exhibited in the word *hindering* in the phrase "dumps hindering loads of snow." That phrase is good enough to take your breath away.

In the rest of the essay, Tim philosophizes about his experiences with the West Texas sky. He makes the transition to that philosophizing rather smoothly at the end of paragraph 4, where he remarks that the Indians so feared and worshipped the sky that they deified it. His ruminations about the sky become unusually lyrical in this third section of the essay. Note the unobtrusive but apt alliteration in this passage—apt because he is trying to intimate to us that he has felt the breath of God and heard His voice: "sighing, softly singing, then whispering . . . whistle and whirl with a shrillness."

In the final paragraph, Tim seems to lose the firm control that he has had throughout most of the essay. I cannot tell whether he was so overwhelmed by his recollections of the West Texas sky that he was disconcerted or whether he simply did not know how to conclude the essay. In the previous paragraph, the one false note in the entire essay was sounded: "Last Thursday, the sky rained, sleeted, and snowed on my parade, and I was livid!" That false note may be an indication that Tim *was* rattled by his recollections.

In any case, the admirable coherence that prevailed in the rest of the essay begins to unravel in this final paragraph. At the beginning of the paragraph, two beautifully structured parallel sentences set up a pattern and raise our expectations. But the third sentence not only breaks the pattern but introduces a new note that seems to be out of sync with what preceded it. The association in Tim's mind of the two Jacobs seems to be tugging the paragraph back into some semblance of coherence, but then he adds the enigmatic note about the wrestling with a stranger. What has that note got to do with Tim's relations with the West Texas sky? Certainly that sky has not become a stranger to him; it has become an intimate, reassuring presence for him. Is Tim really suggesting by the last sentence of his essay that he is now going to resist the sky? Maybe this final ambiguity is a small price for us to pay for the pleasure Tim has given us with his extraordinarily skillful handling of language in this essay.

Study Questions

1. In his commentary on Timothy Hagood's paper, Edward Corbett isolates several mistakes made by the writer, mistakes he calls "shocking errors" that he says he would "ride [the student] hard about" with the intention of "sham[ing] him into putting his mind to these matters." None of the "shocking errors" Edward Corbett lists, you will notice, causes a reader any difficulty with the writer's meaning.

From what point of view might Edward Corbett's position be called unconvincing, unsound?

From what point of view might the position be called sound, even compelling?

Where do you stand concerning these two points of view on this kind of error in writing?

2. In a classroom discussion of Timothy Hagood's essay and Edward Corbett's commentary on it, a student said,

> But the writer *doesn't* lose control at the end. Of course he's going to resist the sky, wrestle with it, the way Jacob in the Bible wrestled with the angel. The sky has always been a sort of stranger to him. Along with loving the sky he's always had to resist it. In fact he has double feelings about the sky all the way through his paper. It's never been *just* "an intimate, reassuring presence for him." I don't think ambiguity is a price we pay to read this paper. That final ambiguity is the whole point of it.

What do you think of this interpretation?

3. The following classroom exchange followed a reading of Timothy Hagood's paper. One student said of it,

> I think this guy is putting it on. He wrote this paper out of a Thesaurus, not out of anything he really knew about or saw in the sky in Texas. I don't think his use of words is very precise at all. He isn't really trying to describe anything. He's just trying to show off how smart he is. I couldn't even finish reading this thing.

Another student responded by saying,

> I think you're jealous of this writer, that he has a vocabulary that he's using to try to understand something he doesn't understand. He's not just throwing big words around. He's trying to find the right words. He's struggling.

Suppose you were to step into this exchange responsibly, that is, with some particular things in Timothy Hagood's paper to point to in defense of your position. What would your position be and what sections of the paper would you refer to in defending it?

Donald Daiker's Assignment

Take any event, however trivial it seems, that you still remember from your childhood or from elementary school. That you still remember it is one sign of its importance to you. In a paper of approximately 500 words, narrate and describe the event so that your reader comes to feel and understand why it was (is?) important.

Keep in mind that narration aims not to tell us about an event but to give us the event and that description aims not to tell us about an object but to give us the object. Because your aim in both narration and description is to show rather than tell, you will want to use specific details, especially sensory details, details that appeal to your reader's sense of taste, touch, sound, sight, and smell. Especially useful for specific details are the constructions we've practiced in our sentence-combining exercises—relative clauses, participles, appositives, and absolutes. One final suggestion: the fact or detail that you are tempted to exclude because it is too revealing or too embarrassing is likely to be a detail that adds life and individuality to your writing. When in doubt, be gutsy.

Above all, try to make your reader experience what you experienced.

❧ Memories   *by Steve Nelson*

There were many signs of summer that the gang and I looked for every year. The days and the mercury in our thermometer lengthened. Leaves and flowers appeared. Baseball season started, and school ended. All of these told us which season was approaching, but none was more dependable than Old Lady Murphy.

She came out on the first warm day of the year, and from then until the cool days of September, she became a landmark in our neighborhood. Sitting in her rocking chair, she could be seen on her porch from the earliest hours of the morning until it was nearly dark.

The surprising thing about her was that she maintained complete privacy. No one, not even the adults, could remember a time when she hadn't lived there, and still not a fact was known. Maybe that's why

DONALD A. DAIKER is Professor of English and Director of the Center for the Study of Writing at Miami University. With Andrew Kerek and Max Morenberg, he has written the monograph *Sentence Combining and College Composition* (1980) and the textbook *The Writer's Options* (1982). He is the coeditor of *Sentence Combining and the Teaching of Writing* (1979) and of *Sentence Combining: Toward a Rhetorical Perspective* (1984). He is coauthor, with Mary F. Hayes and Jack E. Wallace, of *Literature: Options for Reading and Writing* (1985).

there were so many stories. For years, I was terrified by tales of her eating worms and torturing stray dogs. We could never prove it, but we tried.

4   One day, I sat for hours behind the shrubs in front of her house with a telescope in my hands, trying to actually see her eating a nightcrawler. This is the first time that I, perhaps anyone, had seen her up close, and to my amazement she didn't look at all menacing or evil. She was thin— very thin. Her small skeleton-like hands held her familiar brown shawl in place. Worn and frayed, it had warmed her ninety-pound frame since the first day I saw her. It draped over her equally antique dress. The dress, which once shouted bright red tulips, now barely whispered the undistin- guishable pinkish forms. Her face was as white and wrinkled as a crumpled sheet of clean paper. Everything about it was bland. She wore no expression at all. If it weren't for her eyes and the constant motion of her chair, it would have been hard to tell if she were living or dead. Yes, her eyes were full of life, deep blue wells of memories. That's all she had left to do, remember—rock and remember. I don't even think that she was aware of the world around her—rocking and remembering, remem- bering and rocking.

5   That day, I watched her for quite a while. You might even say that we became friends, in a one-sided sort of way. Afterwards, I never believed another story about her. I even defended her from the gang's cruel remarks.

6   Fall came early that year. Stinging winds sent Old Lady Murphy inside during the first week of September. Fall and winter were uneventful, and no one even mentioned her until the frost began to retreat and the grass became green again. Bright, warm days returned, bringing with them the other clues of summer. The days and the mercury in our thermometer lengthened. Leaves and flowers appeared. Baseball season started, and school ended. It was a summer like all the others, but something was different.

7   A sign was missing. At first no one noticed, but soon it became clear. Old Lady Murphy would not come this year. Weeks later, we learned that she had passed away in late December, the mailman discovering her body.

8   The rocking chair remained on the porch throughout the summer. It rocked in the wind with a slow, even rhythm, just as Old Lady Murphy had rocked. Likewise, life went on for us just as it always had.

9   Soon, people stopped telling stories, and no one even mentioned her anymore. Vandals took her chair away and smashed her windows long before the first snow, and two years later her house was torn down.

10   With this, every trace of a woman that was hated by most, forgotten by all, and pitied by one was erased from the earth.

Donald Daiker's COMMENTARY

I like Steve Nelson's "Memories" more than any other freshman paper I can remember.

I like "Memories" because of its simplicity and straightforwardness. It is, on one level, a child's story, and Steve nicely captures the simplicity of a child's vision. He does so by telling the story in exact chronological order and by keeping its focus steadily on Old Lady Murphy herself. He further creates a childlike perspective by selecting boyish details—baseball and grass and worms and telescopes—and by including comments like "not even the adults" remembered when Old Lady Murphy wasn't around. Even in sentence structure Steve preserves the illusion of a childlike perspective: he frequently uses simple coordination—note how often the coordinators *and* and *but* appear—and his clauses and sentences, which tend to be short, therefore seem unsophisticated. Finally, Steve's consistent use of repetition, another hallmark of the young writer, helps create a sense of youthful simplicity.

But "Memories" only appears to be simple and childlike; it is in fact a mature and carefully crafted narrative. Steve is especially skillful in creating free modifiers—relative clauses, participial phrases, appositives, and absolutes that are set off by commas from the main clause of the sentence. Look, for example, at his fourth paragraph. There we find a series of vital, individualizing details cast in the form of free modifiers: a relative clause ("which once shouted bright red tulips"); a participial phrase ("trying to actually see her eating a nightcrawler"); an appositive ("deep blue wells of memories"); and appositive adjectives ("Worn and frayed"). Although every student in Steve's class completed sentence-level and whole-discourse combining exercises designed to help them control relative clauses, participles, appositives, and absolutes, "Memories" is exceptional in so effectively incorporating a wide range of free modifiers. I like "Memories" because of its bold and innovative sentence constructions. I like writing that takes chances.

Steve takes further chances in his consistent use of repetition. He repeats words ("She was thin—very thin"), phrases—sometimes in reversed order—("rocking and remembering, remembering and rocking"), and parallel sentence parts ("hated by most, forgotten by all, and pitied by one"). Even more impressively, Steve extends his use of repetition beyond the single sentence: "The days and the mercury in our thermometer lengthened. Leaves and flowers appeared. Baseball season started, and school ended." These three sentences repeat a structural pattern. Each of the four clauses here not only follows the same subject-verb order but also consists of a one-word predicate: *lengthened, appeared, started,* and *ended.* The repetition of similarly patterned sentences at the start of "Memories" both contributes to the coherence of its opening paragraph and helps to create a sense of cyclic movement that corresponds to the progress of the seasons of the year.

But when Steve repeats these same three sentences, word for word, in his sixth paragraph, it suggests that he is concerned with more than the seasonal cycle. Of course "Memories" calls attention to the seasonal signs that return again and again, perhaps forever—long days, warm weather, green grass, leaves, and flowers. But what "Memories" makes equally emphatic, even as the natural cycle repeats itself indefinitely, is that Old Lady Murphy will return no more. It is the human being who will, in time, be excluded from the cyclical pattern and who will one day fail to return. So the insistent use of repetition in "Memories" reminds us, by contrast, of the transience and brevity of human life. Nature repeats its return every spring, but the individual does not.

And yet the narrator of "Memories" is wrong—and I think Steve knows it—in concluding that every trace of Old Lady Murphy has been erased from the earth. He is wrong because in "Memories" Old Lady Murphy continues to live for us—in her brown shawl, her antique dress, and her blue, well-like eyes. She lives for us because Steve the child came to care for her and because Steve the adult learned how to write so as to make us care for her, too.

Looking back upon "Memories" five years after he had written it, Steve reacted this way:

> With the exception of the last line, it's far less embarrassing than I expected it to be. Certainly, there are small corrections I would make throughout. For instance—now—I would never describe her face as being "bland." And I would change "Old Lady Murphy would not come this year" to "Old Lady Murphy would not *return* this year," etc., etc., etc. As I said, the last sentence is a bit clumsy. The words "hate" and "pity" bother me especially. Today I would rewrite it something like this: "With this the final trace of a woman that was feared by some, scorned by most, then forgotten by all, passed from the earth."

With or without such changes, I like "Memories"—and I continue to be moved by it—because it gently and unpretentiously affirms that affection and art together have the power to confer at least a limited sort of immortality upon mortal men and women.

Study Questions

1. Neither Donald Daiker nor Steve Nelson finds the original ending of "Memories" wholly satisfactory.

   If you find either the original ending of "Memories" or Steve Nelson's proposed revision satisfactory, write a paragraph explaining why.

If you do not find either ending satisfactory, write one that you think might be and explain in a paragraph why yours satisfies you.

2. What would you have to do as a writer to produce what Donald Daiker defines as "writing that takes chances"?

What might be in it for you to produce such writing?

3. The following classroom exchanges took place over Steve Nelson's "Memories." One student said,

> There are certainly lots of specific details in this student's paper, some of them very nice, like the dress that once "shouted bright red tulips," for example; and there's lots of sentence variation and repetition, as Donald Daiker points out. But for some reason I *don't* come to care for Old Lady Murphy. She *doesn't* live for me. The details just don't add up to anything like the image of a person so far as I'm concerned. It's sentimental, like something out of *The Reader's Digest.*

A second student said,

> That's just a matter of taste. You can't criticize a writer just because you don't like what he's describing. Besides, the writer here is describing things the way a child sees them and children are often sentimental. This is a very human paper about a human being.

A third student said,

> Maybe we ought to look at the writing here rather than talk just about our feelings. Maybe then we'd have a way of making terms like "taste" and "sentimental" mean something.

Suppose you want to join in this discussion, but you agree that exchanges like "This is sentimental" versus "No it isn't" aren't likely to lead anywhere. How do you "look at the writing here"? What position do you take on this essay?

KENNETH DOWST'S Assignment

Your description of the street corner for Assignment 4 was, in all probability, somewhat different from your description of the same spot for Assignment 3; and this was, in all probability, somewhat different from your description of the same spot for Assignment 1. Your readers varied from one assignment to another and so did your supposed purpose for writing: sufficient cause, you thought, for varying what you noted and the language that did the noting ("bums" or "colorful local characters"?). Okay, reasonable enough. But a question arises when you make such changes in a description: Are you still being accurate? Still telling the truth? What *does* it mean, exactly, to be accurate or truthful when you write?

As a way of exploring these questions—and as a way of continuing to explore the decisions writers make as they write—try the following exercise.

Select another small portion of Iowa City—another corner, say, or a university building, a bar, a restaurant, a public square, or whatever. Compose two different descriptions of this place, each description containing nothing but true, objective, specific, factual statements relevant to the place. Both descriptions should describe the place over the same stretch of time.

Do not say anything in one description that contradicts anything you say in the other (for example, let it not be sunny in number 1 and rainy in number 2). And do not write any explicit evaluations or generalizations (for example, "Maxwell's is a depressing place on Thursday nights"). Just compose true, objective, specific, factual statements.

Let the true, factual statements of your first description imply that the place you are describing is attractive. Let the true, factual statements of your second description imply that the place is unattractive.

When you have completed these two descriptions, look back over them and reflect upon how you did what you did; try to come to terms with the significance of your having been able to do it. Then in a long paragraph or two, explore what, in general—so far as you are concerned—a true and accurate description of any person, place, or thing would be like, and how such a description could be composed. (Would this be a description that implied absolutely nothing, were such a thing possible? A description that made the subject look exactly 50 percent attractive and 50 percent unattractive? Exactly 42 percent and 58 percent? Would you say that every description is equally true and accurate, so long as it's free of blatant lies, such as "At the corner of Clinton and Iowa are nine purple buildings"? Or is there no truth or accuracy to be found anywhere? Or what?)

If perchance you are unable to come up with answers, at least try to define the exact nature of the problem as you see it.

KENNETH DOWST is Assistant Professor of English at the University of Iowa and a staff member of the NEH–Iowa Institute on Writing. He teaches courses in, and has written several articles on, rhetoric and composition, writing pedagogy, and literature. His recent publications include "The Epistemic Approach," in *Eight Approaches to Teaching Composition* (1980); and "Cognition and Composition," in *Freshman English News* (1983).

৯ৎ Two Descriptions   *by Nancy Roberts*

It is three o'clock on a Friday afternoon. A steady stream of students are 1
busily moving their way through the ornate wooden door of the Airliner
Bar on Clinton Street. Once inside, a mass of smiling and laughing
people file up and down the aisles, drinks in hand and munching on
the free popcorn. The yellow booths, besides the wear and tear over the
years, support groups of talkative girls and boys happily discussing the
latest in college gossip. The jukebox, playing the new Top 40 hit, spreads
the "boogie" throughout the room: feet tapping with the beat below on
the floor, fingers keeping time on the table tops, and those assorted
others who "jive" up and down the aisles, meeting and greeting their
friends. One walking on the sidewalk past the Airliner finds many a
smiling person seated at the front window enjoying their pitcher of beer.

It is three o'clock on a Friday afternoon. A slow, steady stream of 2
students are shuffling through the heavy, dark brown, splintering,
wooden door of the Airliner Bar on Clinton Street. Once inside, bodies
are herded through the narrow, dimly lit aisles, grasping glasses of lukewarm beer and gorging themselves on burnt, greasy, over-salted popcorn.
The floors are slick with unpopped kernels and assorted spilled alcoholic
beverages. The yellow booths are scarred with various pen markings,
cigarette burns, and slits in the vinyl patched with silver duct tape. The
room itself is full of squealing girls, boisterous boys, and the jukebox
blasting the latest Top 40 hit by the Rolling Stones. Those sitting at the
window gawk at others walking by on the sidewalk, often making rude
comments about those passersby who are physically undesirable.

As far as the accuracy of the two descriptions goes, they are both 3
accurate in that both contain true, factual statements. What differs are
the perceptions I made about the facts before me. Walking into a room,
or anyplace for that matter, one can choose what things (good or bad) to
perceive or not to perceive. Therefore, I think that any description is
"true" and "accurate" for that particular individual if he/she perceives it
as such. But that is not to say that it is "true" and "accurate" for someone
else. Thus, I believe that as long as there are no blatant lies in the
description, it should be by any means "true" and "accurate" to the exact
perceptions of the writer. The Airliner Bar could be an actual "hell-hole"
to one person and the "greatest bar in Iowa City" to someone else (based
on what they choose to see). Admittedly, some problems could arise.

What if a writer were lying to herself or so schizophrenic she really *did* see nine purple buildings? And slander and libel could be seen as individuality in description taken too far. But besides the legal issue, I really think that you have to go with your individual perceptions of things—for they are the most accurate in your own mind.

Kenneth Dowst's COMMENTARY

Even the simplest composition is complex—complex enough to be judged by dozens of standards: originality, clarity, stylistic grace, mechanical correctness, sophistication of content, and suitability to the audience, to name only six. Since any essay will be better in some areas than in others, and since different readers will think different areas the most important, overall judgments are bound to vary. Thus, while I would praise Nancy Roberts's three-part essay highly, I can imagine other readers saying it is decent but not really fine and still others praising it for what I would call the wrong reasons.

Several strengths are obvious here, and a few weaknesses. The first two parts, the two descriptions of "The Airliner," are lively, vivid, and full of closely-observed, telling details concisely reported. The meaning is clear, the style attractive, the mechanics reasonably correct, the content very specific. As for the weaknesses, the grammar goes a bit awry occasionally—the second sentence should read "A steady stream of students *is* busily moving *its* way . . .," for instance—and the third section could use some more specifics. Nonetheless, the writer has both satisfied the assignment and conveyed her message clearly and vividly.

Yet to point to these particular strengths and weaknesses is to miss the essence both of the piece and, I think, of writing in general. In my judgment, the most important purpose of writing is not to communicate (to "convey one's message clearly"); nor is it to produce works of art (products that are "lively, vivid, and full of closely-observed, telling details," like Brueghel's paintings); nor is it to show one's well-bred awareness of what is correct and what is not (it's good manners to see that subject and verb agree). Writing does indeed serve these purposes, and others besides. But as I see it, the essence of writing, and of language use in general, is the creation of understanding. For what we see and know and understand is determined not only by the shapes and colors out there but also by the particular language we compose to tell ourselves what's out there and how things work. By means of language we identify, in one way or another, what's in front of us ("bums" or "colorful local characters"?), make connections between things present and absent, group particular observations into categories, draw conclusions, solve problems, generalize, make better or worse sense of things. Words do not just communicate what we know; they are inextricably bound up with the knowledge. "Words are the meeting-points at which regions of experience which can never combine in sensation or intuition come together," writes I. A. Richards. "They are the occasion and the means of that growth which is the mind's endless endeavor to order itself."

So for me, a good essay is one that creates, out of words, a new order for experience, one that explores ways of understanding that are more comprehensive, more helpful in guiding action. In my course we write about, and thereby experiment in understanding, our extracurricular experience (of places in Iowa City, for instance) and then our experiences in composing language (for instance, our experiences in trying to write "true" and "accurate" descriptions of places in Iowa City). Nancy Roberts's essay presents two interesting ways of understanding a bar she has visited; more importantly, it presents a new, complex, and useful investigation of many of the profoundly subjective judgments involved in composing a supposedly objective form of discourse—description. The third part of the essay, explicitly addressing these larger issues, doesn't do full justice to the exploring and experimenting evident in the first two parts. To see the excellence of the investigation, we'll need to focus on the descriptions themselves.

One subjective judgment evident in Nancy's descriptions is choice of what to report and what not to report. The interesting parallels and contrasts between Nancy's two reports and the effective use of both small and large details suggest that she has faced, explored, and usefully understood the complexity of the choice. The details reported differ in the two versions, and several obvious things are reported in neither; yet all the details seem very relevant (though I guess I like the Rolling Stones better than Nancy does), and neither passage gives a sense of something important being overlooked. Are occasional pieces of duct tape more important to know about than, say, the size of the bathrooms or the price of the beer? Is the presence of corn kernels more worth noting than the pictures on the walls, which are many thousand times larger? Are the smiles of the patrons relevant but not the rude comments? The rude comments but not the smiles? The cigarette burns? The two paragraphs reveal at least an implicit understanding of the ways in which, and of the extent to which, relevance is created rather than recognized.

The descriptions show the writer playing with and exploring some of the other subjective decisions inevitably involved in description, decisions which complicate enormously the question of truth and accuracy. For example, if you choose to report something, which of its innumerable *qualities* will you note? Is it "free popcorn" or "burnt, greasy, over-salted popcorn" that's available? Do you face an "ornate wooden door" or a "heavy, dark brown, splintering, wooden door"?

The parallels and contrasts in the language of the pieces likewise show an exploration of yet a third subjective decision necessary in writing description: How do you *name* a thing or event you've decided to report? The question is a crucial one, for a way of naming amounts to a way of understanding—and of inviting a reader to understand—what you're looking at. The same movement of objects through space might be understood either as "fil[ing] up and down the aisles" or as being "herded through the . . . aisles"; ingestion of popcorn might be conceived of as either "munching" or "gorging" (or, worse yet, "ingestion"); "people [with] drinks in hand" can, alternatively, be "seen" as "bodies . . . grasping glasses of lukewarm beer." The issue here is not which phrase of each pair is the more accurate: the writer has taken care to make both very accurate (though opposite in effect). The real issue is which of the many possible set(s) of language account(s) for the goings-on at The Airliner most usefully for the writer and, secondarily, for her readers. Though Nancy has not yet addressed this issue directly and at length, she has by now put herself in a position to do so.

The assignment, you recall, asks students to compose language to make sense of two experiences: their experience of a place in Iowa City and their experience of describing that place in truthful yet opposite ways. The final questions invite students to analyze, reflect upon, and (literally) come to terms with some of the issues they had to face, if only half-consciously, in composing their descriptions. This is hard work. Even so, given the excellence of The Airliner descriptions, I find Nancy's final discussion a bit disappointing. It does make some sense of her previous experiences in composing; it does say some useful things; it does identify some of the complexities a writer of description needs to face. Still, the explicit sense she makes here of her writing experiences strikes me not as wrong but as a little too simple to be really useful to her in subsequent writing.

Nancy here latches onto a concept, "perceptions," much too vague and ambiguous to get her very far. What *exactly* is a "perception"? How does this concept relate to language, specifically the language of the two descriptions? While it is true that different people may "see" or "perceive" the same event differently, how does this observation account for two different perceptions of The Airliner by the same person? Can a person really choose which objects she will "perceive" and which she won't ("I will not notice that duct tape")? And while it makes sense to conclude that Ultimate Truth and Accuracy are unknowable and unwritable, that personal, subjective truths are all we can hope for, is the problem that simple? Would you care to live in a world in which no one even pretended that Ultimate Truth and Accuracy existed, in which all "perceptions" were considered equally true and valid? Would you care to rely on a surgeon who believed this?

To her credit, Nancy does identify some of the problems raised by such belief: "Libel," "slander," and "schizophrenia" would become meaningless terms, for example. Indeed, I'm even a little inclined to praise the "fudging" that occurs in this section, as a recognition that easy, black-or-white answers won't do. Still, having identified many of the complexities involved in trying to write the truth, Nancy settles too quickly for an answer that is too simple to be of much help to her as a writer.

Throughout the essay, nonetheless, the writer has demonstrated a real intelligence and a willingness to explore and experiment, to play with words and ponder the results. If the conclusion falls short of real usefulness, most of the piece is good enough to help the writer when she explores the important questions again; it's even good enough to raise some new questions. That's more than good enough for me. Besides, the semester is still only a month old.

Study Questions

1. In a classroom discussion of the writing assignment devised by Kenneth Dowst, one student said,

   > I don't see why Kenneth Dowst doesn't just say, write two descriptions of a place, one that makes it attractive and one that makes it unattractive. Look at how many questions the students have to keep in mind when they write. They even have to remember earlier writing assignments in this course, and earlier papers they wrote. Besides, isn't all that stuff about what's accurate the kind of thing to take up in a philosophy course rather than one in composition? It doesn't have anything to do with writing.

   How do you respond to this statement?

2. Kenneth Dowst states that one's theory of what writing is good for influences what one looks for in an essay and how one evaluates that essay. How would some of your previous composition teachers respond to Nancy Roberts's essay? What would they praise in it? What would they criticize about it? What comments would they write in its margins? What grade would they give it?

   How about you? You're under no obligation to see things the way Kenneth Dowst does. What would you say about the essay?

   What theories about what writing is good for seem to be behind these various judgments?

3. Suppose Kenneth Dowst were to ask the students of his writing class to integrate the two descriptions they had written for his assignment.

   What questions do you think Kenneth Dowst might ask the students to address about their having performed this writing task?

   What might the students have the opportunity to learn through addressing such questions?

CARL KLAUS'S Assignment

Advanced Expository Writing/Assignment #5

Now that you've had a chance to write about the Old Capitol shopping mall based on what it looks like from across the street and from inside one of its entryways, you're probably hungering to write about what it looks like from all the way inside. So, in order to get a real taste of what the Old Capitol Center is like, I suggest that you go beyond the doorway you entered last time, in fact that you go up to the second floor and roam around in the general area above the place where you entered until you have familiarized yourself with it sufficiently to write a piece describing what you find upon looking into the Old Capitol Center from this level.

❧ Street Scene/Mall Scene   *by Curtis Buhman*

1   On the second floor of the mall, above the northside entrance, a series of windows gives me a panoramic view of the university pentacrest and the opposing rows of shops along Clinton Street. Looking down on what is passing there, it strikes me that this is not at all a random array of buildings, autos, and people, but an organized place. In fact, there is a sense in which everything in this view has been produced by years of selection. The Airliner Bar, and the Iowa Book and Supply obviously fill some need in our community, as do the street lights, the fire-hydrants, the railing around the pentacrest lawn, and all the other incidentals in my view. All of them have a history, a reason for being. What I see is a place that has grown into what it is. It is a product of the community decisions we have made. It is our baby.

2   Turning my back to the windows, I move to the edge of the walkway where I lean against the railing that borders it, and I look down into the first floor level of the mall with about the same perspective I had when looking down through the windows. I find myself willing to trust this place as though it is just another part of the community. But how can this be when the mall has only existed for a few years? As I try to find specific things that make me feel at ease with it, I look down to my left

CARL H. KLAUS is Professor of English and Director of the Institute on Writing at the University of Iowa. Codeveloper of the Primary Trait System for the assessment of writing, he is editor of *Style in English Prose* (1968), coauthor of *Elements of the Essay* (1969) and *Elements of Writing* (1971), author of *Composing Adolescent Experience* (1981) and *Composing Childhood Experience* (1981), and coeditor of *Courses for Change in Writing* (1984) and *Fields of Writing* (1984).

and see a row of shops extending the length of the mall. At first glance they seem similar to the row of Clinton Street shops. But then again, these long rows of connected shops are as close to a universal characteristic of malls as anything I can think of, which leads me to wonder whether my equating the mall scene and street scene is justifiable at all.

As I try to make sense of this mall scene, my eyes skip out from the shops to an open area where the hall widens into a sort of plaza. In the middle of this is an island bordered by a short wall, filled with plants and shrubs. My first impulse is to call these outdoor things, and so to begin associating the mall with what is outside. But they were more likely planted for completely different reasons, I tell myself, perhaps just for the sake of having growing things in here—the same reason we have houseplants. I am also tempted to see the benches that are nestled around the island as similar to the benches along Washington Street at the bus interchange, but they also have a reason of their own for being there. They are a convenience for tired shoppers.

But now I begin to understand where my impulse to see the mall as something similar to the Clinton Street area is coming from. Stretching up from this island are four street lamps, and I cannot persuade myself of any reason for their being here other than to simulate a street scene. Because this is one incidental that is in no way integral to the functioning of the mall, it becomes a key for me. The whole view must be interpreted as a representation of an outdoor shopping plaza. The benches are not just a place to sit, but are a particular place to sit, one that looks rather like a park bench. And if the row of shops vaguely reminds one of Clinton Street so much the better.

My impressions having solidified, I begin to realize that this ambience has been carefully chosen. But why was the mall designed to look this way? Perhaps the answer is to gain the sort of trust from us that we willingly give to the downtown, without having to be shaped by us over the years. This is a place that has been shaped for us, not by us. It looks like our baby, but it's not ours.

Carl Klaus's COMMENTARY

When I ask my students to do descriptive writing, I want them, of course, to convey a vivid image of things in language. But whether I ask them to describe a shopping mall, a church, a court house, a hospital, or any of the other local buildings that might be featured in my assignments, I want them to convey something besides ocular reality alone. I am also concerned with ways of seeing, with point of view in its manifold senses—literal and metaphorical, physical and conceptual. For I am one of those who believes that what we see is an outcome of the conditions and ways of our seeing—that the observer is inseparable from the thing observed, the dancer inseparable from the dance. So I invariably call upon my students to write about a building such as the Old Capitol shopping mall first from one angle, then from another, and thus to experience how their understanding of something changes as they see it from different perspectives. Out of such experience, I hope at last that my students will come to use language not only to convey what they see and know, but also to define how they have come to see it and know it as they do. Fulfillment of this obligation is, I believe, the mark of responsible writing in every field of study, every profession, every aspect of life. In this respect, I consider Curt Buhman's "Street Scene/Mall Scene" to be an excellent piece of writing, for it is a rigorous study in point of view. From beginning to end, Buhman makes clear not only what he sees in the mall, but also how he has come to see it as he does.

His opening two sentences are exemplary, identifying as they do both his initial point of view and what he sees from that perspective:

> On the second floor of the mall, above the northside entrance, a series of windows gives me a panoramic view of the university pentacrest and the opposing rows of shops along Clinton Street. Looking down on what is passing there, it strikes me that this is not at all a random array of buildings, autos, and people, but an organized place.

As if to echo the pattern and process of these opening sentences, Buhman begins his second paragraph with a sequence of sentences that painstakingly identify a shift in his point of view and what he sees from his new perspective:

> Turning my back to the window, I move to the edge of the walkway where I lean against the railing that borders it, and I look down into the first floor level of the mall with about the same perspective I had when looking down through the windows. I find myself willing to trust this place as though it is just another part of the community. But how can this be when the mall has only existed for a few years? As I try to find specific things that make me feel at ease with it, I look down to my left and see a row of shops extending the length of the mall. At first glance they seem similar to the row of Clinton Street shops.

Having so carefully outlined his shifting perspective, Buhman is able not only to describe the make-believe street scene that he perceives on the first floor of the mall, but also to describe—indeed, to reenact—the process by which he discovered the arresting similarity between street scene and mall scene. In this respect, his piece is somewhat analogous in its conception and execution to the form and purpose of a scientific report. He provides, as it were, the methodology of his observation, as well as the data gathered by that methodology. It would therefore be possible for anyone in Iowa City who had read his piece to replicate his observations and test their reliability. Buhman's description thus shows a forthrightness and a sense of intellectual responsibility that I admire.

Indeed, Buhman is forthright not only in revealing the spatial and visual perspectives that led him to perceive the mall scene as a simulated street scene, but also in showing the mental processes by which he sought to verify and understand the significance of his initial impression:

> As I try to make sense of this mall scene, my eyes skip out from the shops to an open area where the hall widens into a sort of plaza. In the middle of this is an island bordered by a short wall, filled with plants and shrubs. My first impulse is to call these outdoor things, and so to begin associating the mall with what is outside. But they were more likely planted for completely different reasons, I tell myself, perhaps just for the sake of having growing things in here—the same reason we have houseplants. I am also tempted to see the benches that are nestled around the island as similar to the benches along Washington Street at the bus interchange, but they also have a reason of their own for being there. They are a convenience for tired shoppers.

Here, as elsewhere in his piece, Buhman unabashedly lets us in on the trial and error process of his reasoning, speculating as he does so about the function of the mall's various elements and noting their similarity to aspects of the outdoor scene. In the process of speculating on the mall scene, he also gives us a sense of the principal features that create its overall effect—the row of shops, the plant-bordered island, the wooden benches, and the street lamps.

But beyond these few highlights, it should be noted, Buhman offers very little descriptive information about the mall, and not even these highlights does he convey in much detail. Nor does he present them in a systematic spatial order, as would be appropriate were he interested primarily in making a descriptive record of the scene. Instead, he presents details according to the process he evidently followed in perceiving and analyzing them. And by keeping his attention focused on those few details that initially provoked his curiosity, he is able at least to perceive and define a striking concept that must have governed the interior design of the mall. His conclusion, however, as revealed in his use of the phrase "our baby," is one I would expect readers to find provocative and controversial enough to react to on their own.

Study Questions

1. Carl Klaus chooses not to comment on Curtis Buhman's use of the expression "our baby," assuming that most readers will find it "provocative and contro-

versial enough to react to on their own." In a paper written about "Street Scene/Mall Scene," a student did just that:

> The most effective thing in Curtis Buhman's essay, his playing off of the town's being "our baby" against the way the shopping mall isn't, is also its greatest weakness so far as I'm concerned. It's too easy, too pat. First of all, how can this writer be so sure that what's in the town "*is* a product of the community decisions we have made" in just the way he says it is, and that it's something we "willingly" trust for just that reason? Secondly, couldn't the people who put up the mall be said to be responding to "some need in our community" too? It's just as much a part of the town as what's outside the mall, after all, just as much something you could say was shaped by the community as the town was. Why is trust in the town good and trust in the mall bad? I think this writer is just trying to find a fancy way of saying that shopping malls are cheap and commercial and that downtown areas are real and valuable. It's too simple a distinction.

How do you respond to this statement?

2. Judging from what Carl Klaus says about "the mark of responsible writing in every field of study," what do you think he would say to having good writing defined as "clear, logical, coherent, and correct"?

   What position do you take with what you think his would be?

3. In a classroom discussion of Curtis Buhman's "Street Scene/Mall Scene" and Carl Klaus's commentary on it, the following exchange took place. One student said,

> I don't think this is a very good paper of description at all. There are very few concrete and specific details here. You don't know what kinds of shops are in the mall, for example, or anything about the kinds of plants that are in that island. In fact this writer seems more interested in describing himself than in what he's seeing. Look at all the talk he has in here about what he thinks and what he understands. He's constantly getting in the way of what he's supposed to be describing. I think he ought to let these scenes speak for themselves.

Another student responded by saying,

> There isn't any such thing as a scene that speaks for itself, for one thing; and secondly, this writer isn't doing what you're calling a "paper of description" at all. He's writing a paper about what it means to make sense of something that you look at. He's not *interested* in things like what kinds of shops are in the mall. He's interested in talking about what all of these things mean, what they add up to. If he gets rid of the talk about what he thinks and understands, he gets rid of the whole point of the paper.

What position would you take in this controversy?

Janice Lauer's Assignment

The first paper you are going to work on in this freshman English course will give you an opportunity to raise questions compelling to you about some place whose influence on you has been strong but unexamined.

For this paper you will be producing an evolving text, a paper that will take its shape gradually as you work toward a new understanding of your subject, thinking through various ways of approaching it. In class, which will be conducted as a workshop, you will receive guidance both from me and from your fellow students as you engage in various acts of the composing process, guidance on such writing tasks as: (1) devising compelling questions and possible writing situations, (2) exploring, (3) deciding on focuses and situations, (4) planning for audience and mode, and finally, (5) revising and editing. To help you with these tasks, you will learn some useful strategies to guide your work.

❧ The Cavern[1]

by Marcia Sawyer

The room draws itself into a triangle. It spreads out from the wide glass-enclosed booth that holds the guards, and runs into a long narrowing corridor, walls tucking themselves under, past the rows of bright pink and yellow doors until they meet together, in a brief green corner. The low ceiling, as well as the floor is tiled, in a dull beige. It traps the odors that rise out of the floor and holds them in the air, the disinfectant from the mop pail mingling with the sweat from graying tennis shoes. The walls are dull green concrete blocks, broken by the lines of steel doors in the corridor. Painted by a sure, hard hand, their enamel coats are smooth and shiny, unmarred by graffiti scratches and usage. They have a gaiety inappropriate to the room. A small, high window in each door out into the hall, so many eyes watching over the children.

The girls, in loose jumpers sit, tipped back in green plastic and metal chairs lined up along the hall. Muffled in cotton tennis shoes, feet bang against the concrete, the girls watch the grey metal clock set into the

---

[1] This essay, with all of its planning stages, is taken from *Four Worlds of Writing*, Janice Lauer, Gene Montagne, Andrea Lunsford, and Janet Emig. New York: Harper & Row, 1981.

JANICE M. LAUER, coauthor of *Four Worlds of Writing*, (1981) has taught composition for over twenty years. She now directs a graduate program in rhetoric and composition at Purdue University. For eight years she has conducted a national rhetoric seminar for composition instructors, "Current Theories of Teaching Composition." Many of her articles probe the relationship between theory and pedagogy, especially the nature, importance, and strategies of invention in the writing process.

wall above the guard's station. He holds back, languidly, hoarding over precious minutes, until pulled, against his will, he jerks forward with a loud click. A clattering, followed by distant shouting rises promisingly in the air, then dies down. Music from a local radio station, piped into the room, settles, mixing with the dirty disinfectant smell. Fingers drumming against the seat of the chairs, the girls watch the miser clock give up his minutes.

3   Behind the steel doors, in the dark, there is life still. There is no need of paint on this side of the door. The close walls are green-tiled and bare. It has a thick, dark odor all its own. In the corner, on the cement floor, a young girl sits in a white nightgown, rocking back and forth. She is far away, riding her horse through an English meadow, sweet yellow-green dotted with flowers.

JANICE LAUER'S COMMENTARY

Although space does not permit me to include the peer critiques of Marcia's evolving text, it is possible for me to dramatize a part of what she made writing mean to her by presenting the dialogue she and I had as writer and reader at several crucial stages of her composing process.

Marcia began her paper by selecting a place long associated with troubling feelings that she had not had the courage to investigate. To better understand her feelings about her stay in a psychiatric clinic, Marcia began composing by identifying some values and expectations she held that clashed with her experience there, and then used this opposition to form a question she wanted to investigate. She also identified some possible situations—involving audience and media—in which she could write.

1. *Subject:* My stay in a clinical institution
2. *My Values and Expectation*   *Actual Experience*
   −freedom   −sense of confinement
   −pleasant surroundings   −the smell and artificiality of the
                                                    place
3. *Question:* What impact has a stay in a clinical institution had on me?
4. *Possible Writing Situations*
   −an entry in my diary
   −an essay I'd send back to those in the institution
   −an essay I'd write for myself to keep
   −a letter to my older sister
   −an article for a magazine (which?) that features the subject of institutions for teenagers

My comment: "You have pinpointed two important elements in conflict despite your limited analysis of the dissonance between your values and the experience of the institution. Try to restate your question, reflecting more specifically the gap you noted."

Marcia then revised her question as follows:

What impact on my need for freedom and beauty has a stay in a clinical institution had?

In order to prepare herself for a possible new understanding, Marcia then explored her question, looking at it from three points of view: by seeing the clinic as *static* (with unchanging distinctive features), as *dynamic* (changing, in movement and process), as *relative* (related to other things by shared membership in larger classifications, by comparison or contrast, or by analogy).

A STATE HOME

STATIC VIEW

Sensory impressions of the home
−a loud clatter   unknown, distant voices, mingling, a low hum
−a gray clock set into the cement block wall . . . it lingers over endless minutes, then pulled reluctantly, jerks ahead with a loud flat click
−a hoarse female whine: "please miz wells"
−arid smell   disinfectant
−dirty socks
−faded tile, ceiling and floor   walls green—dull institutional green
−florescent lights, cruel   a harsh whitish glare
−bathroom darker green door with half legible obscenities scratched into it, always locked
−"Keep your hands to yourself. There are some girls who *like* to touch other girls."
−green plastic and metal chairs
−girls in faded jumpers sit, tipped back against the wall
−gray underwear   grayish tennish shoes   gray oatmeal
−"I wouldn't if I were you. They pulled a rat out of the tureen once."
−brown mats pulled out at night, lined up along the floor.
−a gray tennis shoe tapping, tapping behind the girls . . . brilliant yellow and pink seclusion rooms, pure, unscarred, unscratched paint
−hoarse female cry rising from behind the yellow door, heavy, weighted down in the air   "miz wells: Please: Oh, God help me!"
−the hands of the clock jump forward—a click

DYNAMIC VIEW

Public attitudes (Fortas) vs. present reality
−Fortas' opinion attached firmly the prevailing view that because juvenile courts were virtually therapy clinics, children who came before them did not need the protection of the Bill of Rights of the American Constitution (case of *Gault* vs. *US,* from *The Throwaway Children,* by Lisa Richette)

—a huge brick structure with long steel screens over its windows and a high brick wall which ran in waves down Fort Street and turned the block—a castle, a fortress we would pass on the way to school and laugh. "WASPS: There's the Youth Home!"

—"Witness Gerald Gault's sentence of six years for a crime which for adults carried a five-to-fifty dollar fine and a maximum sentence of two months." *The Throwaway Children.*

—By standing close to the mesh screen and craning my neck, I could see the snow falling outside. I pushed my fingers into the metal screen and pressed against it. A child pulled his sled across the snow, and two schoolgirls, in plaid skirts, hurried down the street. I could just make out the lettering on the brown metal sign facing me a hundred miles below— Wayne County Youth Home. Established 19—

—"How many Gerald Gaults had been here? How many Croziers?" *Ibid.*

—putting my own wrinkled clothes on again, throwing the faded jumper and the old socks into a hamper. I was led back up to the ward to wait for release. I went back into the room not seeing or feeling the buzz of excitement that surrounded me. "You're going home? Karen's going home! I'll miss you kid. You're going home . . ."

—"There is nothing worse than the smell of a dirty female. You will take a shower every day and clean yourselves thoroughly." God, yes, let me get the sound of you out of my pores.

—"you're going home Karen? I hope I do too soon."

—"What kind of hearing should a child receive in a juvenile court." *Ibid.*

—Waiting on a wooden bench, pink and blue jumpers, scared, tapping feet. Braids, Afros half picked out, stringly dyed hair; slept-in curls. "Don't cry, they don't feel sorry for you and it only goes worse on you."

—moving . . . but not all stagnant   trapped in their small circular environment going through the notions like the hands of the clock on the wall

RELATIVE VIEW

Analogy

—the children move about as the hands of the gray metal clock
   steady   numbly   sluggishly
   crawling about routine tasks
      routine which cannot vary
   dragging their chairs behind them down the hall.
   tipped back against the wall   fingers drumming against the metal legs
      of the chairs   feet tapping   tennis-clad   muffled   like the toneless
      noisy clicks of the clock

—day is highlighted by feedings everyone awaits eyes glancing up pushing the hands of the clock forward from breakfast   waiting for lunch from lunch waiting for dinner   after dinner waiting until the garish lights are turned off and fanciful dreams begin

—time   clicking   an endless, toneless whisper of a scream
   inside heads of the girls
   muffled by dirty cotton tennis shoes that muffle the angry
   pounding of feet against the floor

—the muted anguish of the clock   black hands jerking forward caught
suspended in its black cage
    some frightened black insect trapped under the glass face
impaled on a slender rod   its legs kicking in the air   its
    antennae jerk convulsively while the rod moves slowly in its cycle
unable to escape—impaled and waiting for death—oblivion
    blackness which hides in the corner of the brains of all the girls
—the soft whispered screams   watching the quiet anguish of the clock
—cockroach under glass

In Marcia's exploration, she created an analogy and a contrast. She
cast the contrast in a poetic form:

Contrast

do not pity
mehitabel
she is having
her own kind of
a good time
in her own way
she would not
understand any other
sort of life
but the life
she has chosen
to lead
she was predestined
to it as the
sparks fly upward
chacunad son gout
as they say in france
start her in
as a kitten
and she would
repeat the same story
and do not overlook
the fact that
mehitabel is really
proud of herself
she enjoys
her own sufferings
(archy's life of
    mehitabel—don marquis)

cindy . . . throws
back her head
her breasts, too
large for a 14 yr
old rest on her
protuding stomach
"God: you lost your
navel kid—
a bitter cry—
You're all whores.
just because I'm
the only one who
got caught."
poor mehitabel . . .
"all marriage is
is one damn
kitten after
another." (archy)
spotted
mulatis kitten
another litter
for grandma
to look after
poor baby.

My comment: "A very fine exploration which has allowed you to return
to the institution, recapturing a sense of the place from a more detached
perspective. You certainly have enough here from which a good under-

standing could emerge. Let things settle for a couple of days before turning to the problem of focus and audience."

Marcia then reviewed her exploration and formulated several answers to her original question. The answer she chose is called the "point of significance," which, together with her subject, became the focus of her paper.

Subject	*Point of Significance*
Being confined in a state home	oppressed me but could not wipe out my sense of inner freedom.

She chose the following writing situation, with herself as audience:

Writing Situation
I have selected myself as audience because although someone else might profit from it, I know that it will be most helpful to me. I am exorcising demons, trying to rid my present self of the dread and fear that hellhole imprinted on me. I'm the one who needs to understand the experience so that I can grow beyond it.

My comment: "Your focus expresses a healthy ambivalence, a mixed conclusion about the institution's influence on you. Although you are the best judge of whether the focus answers the question you posed, it seems to me that it does capture the sense of entrapment that surfaced in your exploration. You will have plenty of details to support that idea. But nothing in your exploration suggests inner freedom as yet. You'll need to find some way of communicating that important idea. Further exploring is needed. Your choice of audience is a wise but difficult one because you will have to divide yourself into writer and audience. The role you select will be critical."

Marcia next analyzed her audience to help her decide what role was appropriate for her audience to play and what mode of organization would best help her share her focus:

1. My audience: myself
2. My audience in relation to itself
   a. Background
      —lower middle class, white neighborhood
      —experience of being in a psychiatric clinic
      —my father deserted my family
      —private city high school
   b. Values
      —I value security, concern for others, ability to write, freedom from fear and confinement
      —I have a difficult time relating well to my mother but I value my relationship with my sister
3. Audience's relation to the subject

   -My two selves—the demon-tormented, fearful self vs. the free, loved
     secure self
   a. My fearful self hates the institution and dreads remembering it.
   b. My fearful self clings to that dread.
 4. Specific role the audience will play
   -My fearful self will play a student role to my more recent self, eager to
     learn and be healed.
 5. Important features of the specific role
   a. Background: Since my audience and I share the same memories, I
     should select typical experiences from the home, striking scenes
     that connote to me ugliness and fear. Then something to
     counteract.
   b. Values: Her values are identical with mine—love of freedom and
     beauty.
   c. The attitude toward the subject I want her to hold: I want her to see
     that although my/our actual time in the home was terrible, it didn't
     cripple me/us. I want her to see strength and victory in the out-
     come.
 6. The relational role (my relation with my audience) and my voice
   -My fearful self feels estranged from my free self; the two selves are
     both strangers and intimates, but I can't write as if that were true. It
     will be best to treat the audience as a stranger and to speak to her from
     a distance but as an equal. My voice should be calm and reflective and
     friendly.

My comment: "The strain of dealing with the question that led to the
focus of your paper shows through in the answers to 2; they are limited
and occasionally even hesitant. Your answers to 3 are more definite, and
your specific and relational roles are very perceptive. Your solution to put
distance between your two selves will give you a workable voice as a
writer. But you have a challenging task ahead. Your choice of mode, as I
suggested earlier, is critical. To show that a "demon" has "been exor-
cised," that your present self understands the past self, that your fearful
self is understood and accepted by your free self, a narrative mode would
be a distinct possibility. You could show the deadly round of a day in the
prison of a state home. A descriptive mode is another distinct possibility;
your exploratory list is crammed with details—parts of the institution."

For the version of the paper printed above, Marcia chose the descriptive mode of organization. My critique of the paper is as follows:

Focus

The title "The Cavern" helps your audience find your focus because it
suggests a carved-out passage with a dead end. The whole essay seems to be
saying at first that the experience of being in the "room" was oppressive,
but at the end you turn around nicely by showing your audience how the

girl escaped in her own mind. Thus, your essay is communicating that the imprisonment was oppressive but could not completely wipe out your inner freedom. Every part of your paper seems to support either one or the other of these parts of your focus.

Development

A number of things work surprisingly well here. The amount of material you have discarded from your exploration is considerable. All those impressions have come down to a short essay—but an essay with a punch. Your use of the third-person works well to give you the distance you need. In the first paragraph, you powerfully recall for your other self some of the key dismal details of her "prison." Because your "reader" was there, you don't need to include every aspect but only highly suggestive reminders. But even your secondary audience (our class) can experience the horrible sense of confinement. In the second paragraph, you also do a good job of reminding your audience of the sense of waiting—to be free. But the clock cannot release you, nor can the guards. You imply the question "If someone is not free in time or space, in what way can they be?" That question sets you up well for the final paragraph, which answers the question— behind the steel doors in the imagination, riding a horse through an English meadow.

I am impressed with the way you transmute the yellow of the imprisoning doors and the deadly institutional green into the colors of sunlight, sweetness, and growth—the colors of a meadow. You enable your audience to understand and *experience* how you can and did escape, transcending time and space.

Organization

Your choice of descriptive mode works well as your essay moves from the whole to the parts—from the total floor plan of the room to the ceiling, the walls with their windows, to the girls, and finally to the inner room behind the steel doors. But you confuse the secondary reader in the first paragraph with the description of the room as a triangle which runs into a long narrow corridor. Where is the observer exactly? What are the spatial relationships between the booth, room, and hall corridor? Your prose needs work here. You might try to separate your description of the ceiling and the walls into different paragraphs.

Style

Your use of understatement is remarkable here. The sense of something imprisoning everyone in the home, something almost suprahuman or subhuman, is conveyed in a series of dependent sentence constructions. The guards are imprisoned in their booth; the doors have been "painted by a sure, hard hand"; the girls watch the miser clock give up his minutes; the windows suggest "so many eyes watching over the children." Your concrete diction puts the secondary readers on the scene, allowing them to see, smell, and hear the oppression, the depression—and finally, allowing them to escape to the yellow-green meadow.

Conventions

The only problems you have are with punctuation, but punctuation is important here because the movement of your piece and its syntax are complex. Examine your essay carefully for mistakes, and edit your paper.

Because space does not permit, the peer critiques and revision cannot be included. But enough has been shown to indicate why I think Marcia's writing process worked for her. She raised a question compelling to her, explored it thoroughly and imaginatively, discovered an important answer, and shared it powerfully with her audience. Writing for her was an inquiry process, a way of learning, a means of discovering a new understanding worth sharing with a reader. It was a meaningful human activity for both writer and reader.

Study Questions

1. Of her writing Marcia Sawyer says, "I am exorcising demons. . . . I'm the one who needs to understand the experience so that I can grow beyond it." Janice Lauer implies that this is what happened for her student. For Marcia Sawyer, says Janice Lauer, writing was "a way of learning, a means of discovering a new understanding."

   What evidence is there in Marcia Sawyer's evolving text that the process of writing was her "means of discovering a new understanding"? Go specifically to the text to make your case. Don't deal just with generalities here.

   That Marcia Sawyer used her writing to discover a new understanding of an experience is still an assertion. Explain why you do or do not agree with it.

2. Writing teachers can *tell* students to do something other than what they have done or are doing. Writing teachers can *suggest* that students *consider* doing something other than what they have done or are doing.

   Judging from your reading of this selection, in what senses would you say that it is difficult to lay down guidelines as to when a teacher should do which?

   In what senses could you argue that, difficult or not, it is important for both teachers and students that some attempt be made to establish some guidelines anyway?

3. A student who had read both Marcia Sawyer's essay and Janice Lauer's comment on it wrote,

Maybe it's just me, but I'm not very clear what the final version of this essay is saying. Janice Lauer says she's confused by the "spatial relationships" of the first paragraph, but I'm confused by them and other things all the way through the paper. Is the "hall" in the second paragraph the same thing as the "corridor" in the first? Is the room in the first paragraph the same one being talked about in the last? It's important I think because some sort of contrast seems being set up between the girls in the hall and a single girl somewhere else, in some kind of room by herself, but I don't know what the contrast is supposed to involve. Have the girls in the hall sold out in some way, and are they because of this sicker than the girl in the white nightgown? Or is she sicker than they are, locked in her own mind, out of touch with everything except the pictures in her head? If she's "free" that's a very limited kind of freedom.

Some of my confusion I can clear up by going to earlier forms of the final version of the paper, but I don't know whether that's legitimate or not. Maybe this text evolved too far. Or maybe it's not the kind of process every writer ought to use. Or maybe it's not something to use for every paper. There are a lot of maybe's in all this I know, but there are a lot of issues here I think we ought to talk about too.

What issues do you see being raised by this student's remarks?

Where do you as a reader of both Marcia Sawyer's paper and Janice Lauer's comments on it stand on these issues?

Writing Assignment 3
Perceiving What Is Seen

Try your hand at writing a description of any person, place, or thing (not for this paper, an event or a sequence of happenings; you will have other opportunities to write a narrative). Keep your editorial comments to an absolute minimum; as much as possible, let the details you create and the way you relate them give your paper its meaning.

Your teacher may give you more specific instructions here. You may be told to hold your paper to a certain word limit or to use a certain form. You may be asked to describe a particular person, place, or thing or to make a particular point. Your teacher may have you address one of the writing assignments contained within this chapter.

When you have finished writing your description, on a separate page write a paragraph or so explaining which of the teachers represented in this chapter you think would like your description best and why. Why *that* teacher and not some other teacher in this chapter?

This is a job of inference, you'll notice. And since there's no Right Answer to the question you're going to be concerned with—which means that the quality of your argument will be everything—be sure you refer to exactly what the teacher you've chosen has to say in making your case.

Finally, on still another page, write another paragraph in which you say what good the ability to write good description might be to you. If you could write description you thought was good, you could complete certain kinds of assignments for certain English classes. That's clear. Perhaps you could please, at least in part, a particular English teacher. But chances are that you're not going to spend a large part of your life writing assignments for English classes or working with an individual teacher. So what might your ability to write good description be good *for* so far as you are concerned?

Coming to Terms 4

After I returned to prison, I took a long look at myself and, for the first time in my life, admitted that I was wrong, that I had gone astray—astray not so much from the white man's law as from being human, civilized—for I could not approve the act of rape. Even though I had some insight into my own motivations, I did not feel justified. I lost my self-respect. My pride as a man dissolved and my whole fragile moral structure seemed to collapse, completely shattered.

That is why I started to write. To save myself.

I realized that no one could save me but myself. The prison authorities were both uninterested and unable to help me. . . . I had to find out who I am and what I want to be, what type of man I should be, and what I could do to become the best of which I was capable. I understood that what had happened to me had also happened to countless other blacks and it would happen to many, many more.

Eldridge Cleaver

ALL OF US HAVE HAD THINGS IN our lives we believed it was important for us to come to terms with, things we felt we had to deal with or work out for ourselves. This working out can be done in various ways, of course, and can result in different things. Sometimes we do it alone; sometimes other people are involved. It may be a slow and gradual process, or it may seem to happen in a moment, the result of what feels like a sudden burst of understanding, a flash of insight. Similarly, our feeling that we have come to terms may be a matter of perceiving a solution to a problem or may result in the ability to ask a new question. We may act or decide to refrain from acting. But whatever shape the resolution takes and whatever the process by which it evolves, coming to terms with something always seems to carry with it the sense that one has a new way of seeing things, a kind of clarity where before there was murk or confusion.

Coming to terms seems to involve a creation of terms with which to have a way of coping with something that one did not have before.

The student essays of this chapter have been put together to suggest some of the ways in which the activity of writing can contribute to an understanding of this process.

As you will see, these essays do not at first appear to have very much in common. They are done by writers at different stages in their development and are addressed to quite different writing assignments. Some of the essays are narratives, and some are not. They range in manner from informal (entries in a journal) to formal (an essay that uses a thesis sentence containing an assertion and a "because" clause).

But in spite of their variety, all of the essays may be read as examples of writers using the process of writing to come to terms with something of importance to them. "His struggle to make sense of fiction through writing—an academic requirement—" says Toby Fulwiler of Robert Barkema's journal entries, "led him to observations about his personal life and ultimately into a conversation with the author he once pitied." In speaking of the process by which Erling Nielson discovered a subject to write about, John Gage says, "From the somewhat confusing chatter of [our classroom] discussions, Erling isolated *the* question that for him was at issue," one that he could then go on to "attempt to think through." Frank D'Angelo reads "A Symbol of Evil" as Todd Fisher's effort "to express what the experience of visiting Auschwitz meant to him." And so forth.

This chapter and the writing assignment at the end of it are intended to help you determine what the activity of writing can have to do with your own coming to terms with something of importance to you.

James Britton and Steve Seaton's Assignment

You have read and discussed, both in small groups and in our class as a whole, two short stories, D. H. Lawrence's "Odour of Chrysanthemums" and Stan Barstow's "The Fury." You have also written a critical essay or commentary on these stories.

We invite you now to write about any aspect of family relationships that concerns you at this time.

[Eds. note: This assignment was given to students in a first-year sixth form in a London Comprehensive School. The author of the following student essay was seventeen years old when she wrote it.]

JAMES BRITTON, now retired, was Goldsmiths' Professor of Education at the University of London, Director of the Schools Council Research Project on the Development of Writing Abilities, and author of *Language and Learning* (1972). Steve Seaton took his teaching qualification at the London Institute of Education, an M.A. in education at the University of Leeds, and now teaches English in a London Comprehensive School.

❧ Me, Stuart, Mum and Dad   *by Maggie Turner*

On Saturday I introduced my parents to Stuart. After he'd left I went   1
back into the kitchen to ask my parents what they thought of him.
Perhaps I'm old fashioned, or maybe just a masochist, but I always like
my parents to meet my boyfriends. I think its good for both parties, and
as far as the bloke is concerned it tells me whether I'm onto a good thing
or not.

Boys tend to divide into two categories where my parents are con-   2
cerned. They either shrink into themselves and leave me to do the
talking, or else they'll be really outgoing and confident and stand up well
to the interrogation. On the whole I like the second type best, especially
those who aren't afraid to give their own opinions. I haven't subjected
many shy ones to the torture, because I like boys who have something to
say for themselves, and anyway, its embarassing.

Stuart definitely falls into category two. He's very outspoken, offen-   3
sive even, and he'll argue about anything just for the sake of arguing. He
also criticizes, and with my parents he picked on private education. My
sister's at a private school and he challenged my parents on it. I thought
my mother was going to expire on the spot. Still, he likes his opinions to
be known and I don't think he really upset anyone.

Although he was a bit rude to my parents, I didn't feel angry with him,   4
because, as I said, I like people to be confident in that way, and also
because, for some perverse reason, I like it if my parents don't like the
people I associate with. I'm not quite sure why I feel like this, perhaps I
unconsciously try to widen the gap between my parents and me. I do, I
think, do things which I know they dissaprove of because it makes me
feel more free from them. My parents represent everything that is ordinary about life, and I want to be different from them. I'll probably grow
out of it.

I'm not saying that I'm entirely motivated by a desire to displease my   5
parents, but it does come into a lot of things, for instance I go on a lot of
political demonstrations. I don't go just to annoy them. I believe very
strongly in the causes, but it's a way of showing my parents that I can
look after myself. I like the feeling that I have a voice of my own, and
that hundreds of people share my opinions. The last march I went on was
in October, and it was the biggest ever in Britain. It'll go down in history
and I was there. That's really fantastic, a lovely feeling of power.

But I'm getting off the subject, Stuart and my mater and pater, ma and   6
pa or whatever.

They didn't actively dislike him, but they kind of warned me about   7
him. They said not to take anything he said too seriously, especially his
political views. That annoyed me because I like to feel that nobody

influences me, especially someone like Stuart. (I've always been slightly suspicious of people who are completely, lock stock and barrel, radically left-wing. I don't think they ever consider their ideas and their implications properly. I think it's better to have separate ideas about various aspects of politics, and to have really thought about them, rather than to go head over heels in favour of one concept.) Anyway, I told my parents that nobody influences me, but I know it was a lie because every person you're close to influences you in some way, especially when you're young and the other person is like Stuart, a very strong character.

8   They were careful not to be too critical. They hedged delicately and did not mention anything which I would say was irrelevant (like his appearance). Although they didn't like his views, I think, in a way, they liked *how* he talked. He's very articulate and I know he's clever.

9   So they'll let me carry on seeing him and, like everything else, he'll be an escape for me, he'll stand for what I'd like to be. I don't admire his principals and motives, but I admire his courage because I can never really break away from my comfortable, safe, boring family. If I associate with people who have broken away, do things that they do, maybe I'll convince someone that I am different. Maybe one day I'll really get away. But I'll more likely just, as I said, grow out of it. I'll probably get married, have kids, and I'll watch them and try to shelter them the way my parents do for me. But maybe they'll be all right. Perhaps they'll be the ones that change the world and all that. We've got the right ideas but we haven't got the will power. It's not important enough. Perhaps my kids'll be different. I hope so. Because I just don't care.

10   I think anyone who reads this can see that it's quite personal and I wrote it with myself in mind. I hope I'm not quite as apathetic as I seem from this. I don't think I am, I meant it to be more about everyone alive now than specifically about me.

James Britton and Steve Seaton's COMMENTARY

To comment first on the assignment, many teachers would assume that justice had been done to a piece of literature once a student's critical responses had been articulated. In England, examination requirements would certainly reinforce that view. We suggest that Maggie's teacher took a more principled view of the role of literature in our lives, and showed a fuller understanding of what writing can achieve for a writer when he went on to assign the task we have described. He could have found support from the scholarly work of Wolfgang Iser, who suggests in *The Act of Reading* that when we "emerge" from reading a piece of fiction we are likely to find out that the real world appears, for a time, more *observable.* "The significance of this process lies in the fact that image-building eliminates the subject-object division essential for all perception, so that when we 'awaken' to the real world, this division seems all the more accentuated. Suddenly we find ourselves detached from our world, to which we are inextricably tied, and able to perceive it as an object." It is as though our perceptions had been sharpened in such a way that we perceive in real-life situations an order and pattern which normally we might have overlooked. Such "stand-back" comments as those in the first paragraph of Maggie's writing ("Perhaps I'm old-fashioned . . . but I always like . . .") seem to us to indicate something of this detachment.

In our view, a principal virtue of Maggie's writing is in its *honesty;* one reads it with a continuing sense of the writer's struggle to say what she means and mean what she says; to be faithful, in fact, to the events and the motives and feelings that gave rise to them. There is evidence of this in the way she returns to amend or amplify the image of herself she is presenting. Compare, for example, "it tells me whether I'm onto a good thing or not" in the first paragraph with "for some perverse reason, I like it if my parents don't like the people I associate with" in the fourth paragraph. What must be said here is that for her to write with such honesty on the topic of family relationships betokens an unusual trust in the reader she has in mind, her teacher. Such a relationship of trust must be the outcome of successful teaching of this class over a period of time—something that must be *earned,* can't be *demanded.*

The narrative framework, very lightly sketched in a sequence of past tense verb forms ("On Saturday I introduced", "he picked on private education", "They didn't actively dislike him,") is nevertheless strong enough to hold together the loosely associated generalisations she is concerned to make. The cohesiveness is that of spoken rather than written language.

There are in fact many kinds of excellence in writing that are not represented in this piece; there is no fine writing, no flights of rhetoric, no impassioned argument; to praise what is here is not to cast doubt on those other virtues, but rather to propose a criterion appropriate in judging all forms of writing: What does the writing achieve for the writer?

We have already referred to the running adjustments made to the writer's image of herself; what the writing achieves for her becomes clear if we compare the confident generalisations of the early paragraphs with the tentative self-questioning of the conclusion. Her own life has indeed become observable, and the observation achieves something—a gain in self-understanding.

Study Questions

1. For Maggie Turner to have written as she did, James Britton and Steve Seaton say, "betokens an unusual trust in the reader she has in mind, her teacher."

   How might it be argued that the kind of trust James Britton and Steve Seaton say exists between Maggie Turner and her teacher is valuable in a writing class, for teacher and student both?

   How might it be argued that such trust can sometimes make things difficult in a writing class, for teacher and student both?

   What kind of trust do you think ought to exist between a teacher and a student in a writing class?

2. In an essay written about Maggie Turner's paper and the teachers' commentary on it, a student said,

   > I don't quite see how the writer has achieved this "gain in self-understanding" that's talked about. At the end of the paper particularly, but in other places too, she sounds more confused than anything else.

   First of all, how might such an argument be supported? What features of the paper might be used to suggest that its writer is "confused"?

   What features of the paper might be used to argue that the writer has achieved "a gain in self-understanding"?

   It is possible to argue for both sides of this question. Is one of these arguments wrong and the other right? Are both right? Or what exactly?

   Whatever position you take on the student's comment about Maggie Turner's paper, what would you say to someone who said to you, "Writing about things mixes you up"?

3. If Maggie Turner expressed a desire to rewrite her paper and asked you for your help, what exactly would you suggest that she do to improve what she wrote?

FRANK D'ANGELO'S Assignment

Shapes or patterns emerge from our everyday actions. These patterns can be discovered in the simple narratives of popular culture: in movies, TV shows, and popular fiction. One narrative form that is always satisfying is that of the journey.

Usually, when we take a trip, we discover something new about ourselves or about other people, places, and events. Sometimes the physical journey becomes an inner journey.

Write a narrative based on a personal experience. Structure it in the form of a trip or a journey. As you are telling about what you have seen or where you have been, reflect upon the meaning of the experience. Remember: it is not the narrative pattern that will be new and original in your account but the details that fill it out and the language you use.

ଅ A Symbol of Evil

by Todd Fisher

There is an ironic beauty to the place. Lush greenery, trees, ivy, and grass contrast well with the red brick buildings and rustic wood fences. The atmosphere in some parts could even be called heavenly; it is peacefully quiet, and a cool breeze gently stirs the spring air. As I walk about this place, however, there is no peace in my soul. Through the present tranquility, an almost tangible evil pervades the very ground. The land that was Auschwitz seems cursed forever. [1]

Always fascinated by the specter of the Holocaust, I had looked forward to visiting Auschwitz during my European tour. I am not Jewish, but I had just finished reading Leon Uris's *Exodus* and found the Jewish struggle enthralling. But while I had heard about the Nazi massacre all my life, seen the documentaries and read the testimonies of survivors, the gut-wrenching reality of the horror began to really hit me only as I stood at the looming entrance gate of Auschwitz. [2]

As I passed through the gate's archway, under its brutally misleading slogan "Work Brings Freedom," I could imagine an illstarred group of new prisoners standing, scared and confused, in this spot. It was here that their possessions would be taken, with promises of return, before [3]

FRANK J. D'ANGELO is Professor of English at Arizona State University. A former chair of the Conference on College Composition and Communication and member of the executive committee of the National Council of Teachers of English, he is currently on the executive committee of the writing division of the Modern Language Association and the board of directors of the Rhetoric Society of America. He has published fifty articles and two books: *A Conceptual Theory of Rhetoric* (1977) and *Process and Thought in Composition* (1985).

they were led to a disrobing area. If healthy they would be given one pair of scanty pajamas and would then be assigned to a barracks and work detail. If unable to work, such as infants or the elderly, they would be taken immediately to the false showers to be gassed.

4   As our tour group proceeded through the compound, our Polish guide pointed out some of the "living" quarters, and showed us the interiors where thousands of diseased, emaciated human beings had been packed like kittens for drowning. Guard houses joined by two and three rows of electrified barbed wire surrounded the compound, which was only the first of many here at Auschwitz. By the end of the war this camp became a huge, industrialized complex where four million died. Looking out past the barbed wire, one could see a vast forest of chimneys stretching on and on. These were the remnants of this advanced industry's many crematoriums, whose telltale pungency had disclosed the ultimate fate to many a newcomer.

5   After the newcomers disrobed, their heads were shaved, followed in many cases by a picture-taking session. The Nazis, in perversely typical Third Reich fashion, were particularly fond of photographing children and teenagers in portrait-style poses. These mocking portraits were now displayed throughout the Auschwitz buildings as another reminder of this hell's reality. Two poses of each child were shown, each equally heart-rending. Most were teary-eyed and struggling to hold together under the commands of their tormenting photographers. Some had obviously just been beaten and were breaking down completely; others already had the empty stare of the hopeless.

6   The rest of the tour easily made me understand this hopelessness. As we continued from one horror to the next, I felt like Dante visiting a terrestrial inferno. There were the shower-gas chambers, the crematoriums, and the "Wall of Death," where over 20,000 people had been executed, 10,000 by the gun of one man. There were the laboratories of Josef Mengale, which, though empty now, still seemed to echo the screams of agony caused by his "medical" experiments. Next came the evidence; packed into vast warehouses were the cold vestiges of millions of warm, thinking, caring individuals.

7   The SS itself had hoarded these remains, several full-size warehouses filled with human hair, eyeglasses, and suit cases. Prostheses and children's clothing took up two others, while toiletries and shoes were in another large storage building.

8   By the time my group left the warehouses, we were all silent, withdrawn into our own thoughts. The atrocities seemed far too terrible to contemplate as real. I was personally filled with anger as well as sadness. Millions of innocent people had died at the hands of organized demented criminals and ignorant, misinformed accomplices—and to what end?

Even our advanced world, with its mass communications and concern for fellow man, did not learn the lesson. The Holocaust had led to the heroic formation of The State of Israel, and the Jewish people were more united than ever, but for the rest of the world the determined pledges that something like this would never happen again had just been rhetoric. Is genocide allowable when it is in less organized fashion, such as in Cambodia or Laos? I was angry not only at the Nazi savages, but at all of the many and constant evils of which they have become a symbol.

Before leaving the compound I walked a distance on my own, along-   9
side one of the numerous stretches of barbed wire. Just as I was turning to rejoin the group, I noticed a rose, left by a mourner, caught and dangling from the wire. The flower, glowing bright in the light of sunset against tangled black wire and muddy gravel, was a contrast of great beauty. In that scene were the greatest aspects of humankind—the capacities for love and progress through peace—caught in and struggling against the evil of their own race.

FRANK D'ANGELO'S COMMENTARY

When I showed Todd Fisher's essay "A Symbol of Evil" to two of my colleagues and told them I was going to present it as an example of good writing, the first commented: "This is a competently written essay, but not a great one. I like the way this student describes what's going on inside him. But he does too much telling. He explains too much to the reader instead of letting the narrative do the telling. I also like some of the phrases he uses to convey his feelings, phrases such as 'ironic beauty,' 'telltale pungency,' and 'perversely typical,' but many border on cliché: for example, 'ultimate fate,' 'empty stare,' and 'gut-wrenching reality.' "

The second colleague voiced a similar opinion: "This is a solid first-year essay. But there are problems with phrasing, transitions, and para-graphing. In addition, although the figurative language and concrete detail take the reader into the world of Auschwitz, all too often the student uses language which spells out, without great subtlety, what the place signified."

After listening to these comments, I was tempted to discard this essay and to try to find one that was marked by formal perfection. But the essay had moved me deeply, and I wanted to know why.

Todd's paper has a deceptively simple narrative framework. During his European tour, he decides to visit Auschwitz. At Auschwitz, he, his Polish guide, and the tour group pass through the entrance gate. Then they proceed through the prisoners' compound, the living quarters, and the guard houses, past the barbed wire fences, the false showers, the crematoriums, the Wall of Death, and the vast warehouses and storage buildings. Before leaving the compound, Todd wanders from the group to walk alone "alongside one of the numerous stretches of barbed wire," where he notices a rose "left by a mourner, caught and dangling from the wire."

Todd's essay uses a mixture of descriptive and narrative techniques to convey to the reader the horror of Auschwitz. Aside from a sense that Todd and his tour group have entered and left the compound, the reader gets no clear sense of chronological progression. The false showers, for example, are mentioned in two different places in the narrative, as are the crematoriums. Todd seems to be relying more on the order of his memories than on a strict narrative progression. We learn more about what the tour group is seeing and what Todd is feeling through the descriptive details than we do through the narrative elements.

The point of view is curious, moving from the first person singular ("*I* had looked forward to visiting Auschwitz") in paragraph 2 to the third person plural ("*The Nazis* . . . were particularly fond of photographing children and teenagers in portrait-style poses") in paragraph 5 to the first person plural ("As *we* continued from one horror to the next") in paragraph 6. Similarly, it moves from the impersonal ("Looking out past the barbed wire, *one* could see") in paragraph 4 to the personal ("I was *personally* filled with anger") in paragraph 8. It is almost as if the atrocities of Auschwitz are too painful to recall so that the narrator has to detach himself in some way from the horrible reality. He does this not only by the use of impersonal expressions ("one could see") but also by means of the passive voice ("Two poses of each child *were shown*," "their heads *were shaved*").

To express what the experience of visiting Auschwitz meant to him, Todd uses several techniques. He tells the reader directly how he feels about what he is observing: "As I walk about this place . . . there is no peace in my soul"; "the gut-wrenching reality of the horror began to really hit me"; "the rest of the tour easily made me understand this hopelessness"; "I was angry not only at the Nazi savages, but at all of the many and constant evils of which they have become a symbol"; "I was personally filled with anger as well as sadness."

In addition, he uses concrete, specific images to convey the sense of irony he feels when he contrasts the beauty of the physical surroundings ("Lush greenery, trees, ivy, and grass," "rustic wood fences," "a cool breeze gently stirs the spring air") with the grim and terrible sights, smells, and sounds inside the compound ("thousands of diseased, emaciated human beings," "telltale pungency," "children . . . teary-eyed and struggling," "the screams of agony," "several full-size warehouses filled with human hair, eyeglasses, and suit cases").

There is some use of metaphor ("The atmosphere . . . could even be called *heavenly*," "Looking out past the barbed wire, one could see *a vast forest of chimneys*"), simile ("our Polish guide . . . showed us the interiors where thousands of diseased, emaciated human beings had been packed *like kittens for drowning*"), irony (" *'living'* quarters"), and allusion ("I felt *like Dante visiting a terrestrial inferno*"). There is also an extensive use of impressionistic diction to shape the reader's perception of the scene and to directly convey the narrator's feelings about the horrors he is witnessing ("*tangible evil*," "*heart-rending*" poses of children, "*tormenting* photographers," "the empty stare of the *hopeless*," "atrocities . . . *too terrible* to contemplate," "*demented* criminals").

I said earlier that, despite its formal imperfections, this essay moved me deeply. Only after numerous readings did I realize that, whether or not he was conscious of it, Todd had built up a pattern of expectations for the reader. This pattern consists of archetypes of experience and corresponds to a configuration of emotional tendencies deep within the reader's unconscious mind. To put the matter simply, Todd uses an archetypal pattern of images, allusions, and symbols to shape the reader's response to his narrative. The pattern derives in part from Dante's *Divine Comedy*, but it could represent any archetypal journey.

The first clue the reader gets about this pattern is the allusion to Dante in the sixth paragraph: "I felt like Dante visiting a terrestrial inferno." The next clue is the image of "a rose left by a mourner, caught and dangling from the wire." In the *Paradiso*, the rose is the celestial rose of Faith. Although the allusions to the *Divine Comedy* may, of course, be accidental, the images and figures in Todd's essay do suggest the spontaneous working of the unconscious mind. Accidental or not, what better pattern could Todd have chosen to depict the Nazi atrocities at Auschwitz than that of an allegory of the soul's journey through hell to heaven?

As the narrative begins, Todd describes what can only be called an earthly paradise. Surrounding the compound is "lush greenery, trees, ivy, and grass." It is "peacefully quiet." A "cool breeze gently stirs the spring air." As if to underscore the significance of the setting, Todd comments that "the atmosphere . . . could even be called *heavenly*."

Led by the guide, Todd stands at "the looming entrance gate of Auschwitz." As he passes through the archway, he notices the misleading slogan, "Work Brings Freedom." In the *Divine Comedy*, Dante is led by Virgil, who stands for human reason, to the gates of hell where he sees the inscription: "Abandon hope all ye who enter here."

Like Dante, Todd is led into the depths of hell where he is confronted with every kind of evil and every kind of human transgression: falsity ("the brutally misleading slogan 'Work Brings Freedom,'" the false showers where the Jews would be gassed, the "promises of return"), theft ("It was here that their possessions would be taken"), violence, brutality, and murder ("the laboratories of Joseph Mengale," "the screams of agony," the "teary-eyed" children who "had just been beaten," the "telltale pungency"), perversity ("photographing children and teenagers in portrait-style poses"), and tyranny ("the empty stare of the hopeless"). That he envisions Auschwitz as a kind of hell, there is no doubt: "These mocking portraits were now displayed throughout the Auschwitz buildings as another reminder of this hell's reality."

As in the *Divine Comedy*, we see in this narrative a movement from darkness to light. Confronted by the horror of stench ("telltale pungency") and darkness, Todd abandons spatial and sensuous terms in an attempt to convey his spiritual horror. His physical journey becomes an inner journey as he is plunged into the depths of his own being. At the end of his journey, he has a vision of humankind's redemption, symbolized by the rose "glowing bright in the light of sunset against tangled black wire and muddy gravel." "In that scene," he comments, "were the greatest aspects of humankind—the capacities for love and progress through peace—caught in and struggling against the evil of their own race." The light of the sunset becomes a reflection of God or of order in the universe. Edified and chastened by witnessing such terrifying torments, the narrator has a vision of love and unity and a renewed faith in humankind.

Thus far, I have examined Todd's essay in great detail but have said little about why I think it is an example of good writing. Implicit in my description, however, is a definition of a particular kind of good writing. *Good writing is that kind of writing that elicits in the reader a universal human response.* Todd's essay is good because it elicits that kind of response despite lapses in grammar, mechanics, and usage. Good writing, then, is not necessarily correct writing, but *effective writing*: writing that produces the desired impression or response in the reader.

Good writing represents a process of self-discovery and a search for meaning. Todd's journey, presented to the reader in the form of images, symbols, and allusions, is connected with a goal—the enrichment and expansion of consciousness, the meaning of life, the highest good. The image of the rose glowing bright in the light of the sun symbolizes a vision of that goal. The highest good can be grasped only by symbols. These symbols, because they are common to all people, release emotional forces that translate into feelings and values.

Good writing imposes some kind of human order on chaos. It organizes experience into a meaningful sequence, and it evokes in the reader a profound emotional response. It is a way of fulfilling universal emotional needs and resolving universal human problems.

Study Questions

1. Frank D'Angelo defines good writing as the kind of writing that "elicits in the reader a universal human response."

   What advantages to you as a writer can you see in defining writing in such terms? What danger can you see in emphasizing the typical, the general, and the universal as such a definition does?

   In what ways, then, is Frank D'Angelo's definition of good writing useful to you as a writer?

2. A student who had read both Todd Fisher's essay and Frank D'Angelo's commentary on it wrote a paper that reads, in part, as follows,

   > I just read an essay by someone who thinks the Jewish struggle is enthralling.
   >
   > I usually don't think much about being Jewish. I haven't been in a synagogue in years. You could say I'm an atheist. But last week I was wandering around CMU and I stumbled on a Succah (a hut symbolizing the ones built by the Israelites in their journey through the desert). It made me feel strange. I didn't even know it was Succoth (a holiday). It used to be my favorite holiday when I was a kid.
   >
   > There were two Jewish people in my class in elementary school. On Passover we used to bring in matzahs for the class. They called them Jewish crackers. We also brought in yarmulkes; everybody called them beanies.
   >
   > One day during the class play time a girl chased me to the back of the room and pinned me against the wall, fiercely demanding, "Why don't you believe in God?"
   >
   > The other Jew was a girl nobody liked much. They used to call her a dirty Jew. One time when I happened to be close by, my friend quickly explained in an embarrassed tone that he didn't mean me, just her.
   >
   > "Oh," I said.
   >
   > My family went on a trip north through New England and Canada. I met a lot of my father's family then for the first and probably last time. Father isn't so close with his family anymore. He's not a Rabbi. He's not even orthodox. His uncle wouldn't let us into the house until we got yarmulkes (beanies).
   >
   > My dad has another cousin in Montreal. She survived the holocaust but her family didn't. She has a green tattoo on her arm. She wasn't ashamed of it or afraid to look at it. She said she didn't like to cover it up. She didn't look enthralled though.

   The writer of this paper views Todd Fisher's paper from a perspective that is quite different from those of either Frank D'Angelo or his colleagues.

   What does this writer seem to be saying about Todd Fisher's paper?

   What position do you take on this perspective?

3. In a classroom discussion of Todd Fisher's paper and Frank D'Angelo's commentary on it, one student said,

Maybe all those patterns that Frank D'Angelo sees in this paper are there, but I don't think this writer felt any of what he says he felt at Auschwitz. The sentences just don't ring true, somehow. The whole account reads like a travelogue. And I don't think he really saw that rose at the end either. It's just too convenient.

Another student responded,

You can't just claim someone didn't feel what he says he felt that way. If he hadn't seen and felt Auschwitz the way he says he did, he couldn't have used the details he did. How do you know the rose wasn't caught on the wire just the way he says it was? And even if it wasn't there, what difference does it make? He's writing about what something meant, not just describing a sight. A writer has the right to invent if he needs to.

What position would you take in this controversy?

Over the course of the term you will keep a journal in which you will write about your responses to the American literature we will be reading. You will not be required to do any other writing in this course: no quizzes, tests, or term papers. I will collect your journal several times during the term, read it, and write responses back to you. In this sense, your journal is being written for both of us— as a dialogue journal—so that we may question, answer, and provoke each other.

To fulfill this assignment you will need to purchase a small (seven-by-ten-inch) looseleaf (so you can add and delete entries) notebook. I will begin each class by asking you to write for five minutes in your journal on some topic of the day; I will end each class early, allowing five minutes of time to write in your journal and to reflect on the work of the day; I will pose particular questions and ask you to write on these as homework. Finally, I will ask you to write regularly and particularly, on your own, about each work we read in this course; such self-sponsored writing can be in any voice and from any point of view you choose— just be sure to do lots of it.

At the end of the term I will ask you to prepare the journal for formal evaluation: add page numbers, a table of contents for significant entries, an introduction, and a conclusion. From this document I will assess how well you have learned American literature. This measure will be, to some extent, subjective; however, I believe I can learn a lot about your learning by such things as (1) the number of entries, (2) the length of each entry, (3) the detail in the entries, and (4) the kind and amount of speculation about our readings and about class discussions. Students who write a good journal (good = lots of serious entries) and attend class will get good grades (good = A's and B's); students who do less will get less (less = C's); students who do nothing will get nothing.

A Personal Reading of Ernest Hemingway's *In Our Time*

by Robert Barkema

4-9-83

First impressions of Ernest Hemingway: *Depressing.* He leaves me with impressions and scenes and imagery and unanswered questions—sort of like art for art's sake.

TOBY FULWILER is currently the Director of Writing at the University of Vermont. Before that he directed the Writing-Across-the-Curriculum Program at Michigan Technological University in Houghton, Michigan, where he taught the American literature course from which this journal entry emerged. Fulwiler has published articles on journal writing in various disciplines and is coeditor with Art Young of Language Connections (1982).

2   The impressions are clearly presented but as for any kind of method to his madness, I am left with a big question mark. What is he trying to say? That life and existence is bleak and meaningless? Maybe for him it was—after all, he did commit suicide—but for me life is full of meaning, good things contrasted with bad—not just one big bleak image—if he can't find any kind of meaning to life, I feel sorry for him—but I don't like reading his works.

3   . . . yes, sometimes *I* wonder what life is all about—what the torture of reading such "classics" as Crane and Hemingway is all about—what the torture of Chem Lab is all about—what the torture of being tied to the quest for money is all about—who I am—what I am—why I am—and you know, amazing as it may seem for a scientific student, I find a good deal of answers . . . in *The Bible*—no other book has ever given me any kind of comforting feeling or any kind of plausible answers to my questions as *The Bible*—funny, both Crane and Hemingway turned away from religion. They closed their eyes and found darkness and wrote about it—it doesn't make a whole lot of sense to me—I fail to understand how they could be on a higher plane of existence—of knowledge—of understanding—of wisdom—after all, they didn't know God, they didn't know their place in God's creation, they didn't know themselves. (—a pretty rough statement but I think it is true)

4   As for the rest of these naturalistic writers . . . I'll let them keep their damned depressing bleakness and I'll just keep smiling!

4-11-83

5   Just walked to class—8 a.m. calculus—and I think I have a good idea why Hemingway just doesn't do it for me right now. Before, I hypothesized that he just wasn't a good writer—but I told myself this: if the *critics* say he's good, then he must be—after all, *critics* have a reputation to uphold! Now, I have come to the conclusion that Hemingway and Houghton have a lot in common. Having just come out of a long and dreary winter season . . . I am a bit tired of dirt clotted snow banks, of muddy mixtures of dead leaves and ice, of trees stripped of life and greenery—tired of *brown*! If there is one color that could describe the way Hemingway writes, I think it would be brown—dirty brown—like the snowbanks outside.

6   I would be willing to bet that Hemingway just loved the deadness of the U.P. [Upper Peninsula of Michigan]—well, I liked Grand Rapids—it's alive more than it is dead—even the radio stations in Houghton are dead!

4-12-83

Why—if something is meaningless in my eyes, should I fling the bull   7
and write in a meaning to a story? That is meaningless.

I guess I just wonder whether or not today's society is "growing out of"   8
yesterday's classics. Could there be any link between a possible lack of
appreciation for literature and the fact that most of today's students have
grown up with the television? It seems like you have to have one heck of
an imagination in order to make some kind of meaning out of some of the
material—with the T.V. you really don't have to have an imagination—
the pictures are all there for you—therefore, if some of these "classics"
are mediocre when compared to T.V. shows (like RBC [*The Red Badge of
Courage*] compared to M.A.S.H.) then I'm not sure that trying to find a
meaning out of a seemingly meaningless "classic" is a meaningful activity.

4-13-83

The total book concept brought up in class the other day is really   9
interesting in light of the fact that I really couldn't find any meaning
behind some of the individual stories. . . .

It seems like Hemingway traced some of the hells of war back to the   10
society that produced that war . . . maybe he is trying to say something
like: society is really no better than the war it produces and fosters—ooh,
that's good. I like that idea! Maybe I've found a meaning after all!

Another idea has struck! Finding a meaning to a story and having it all   11
be meaningful are two different things—and I don't think you can really
find a meaning to a story and not have it be meaningful.

I read a book about facades a little while ago—it seems that most   12
everyone, lives at one time or another, behind a mask—a lie—and this
lie gives them security. In "Soldiers Home", I think Hemingway is trying
to attack this lie—I don't necessarily agree in thinking that God is a
lie—although the way many people practice religion seems meaningless
(e.g., Sunday morning Christians and those who can find time on Easter
and Christmas to go to church—wouldn't it be better to skip then and go
every other day? Enough preaching.) Hemingway seems to say that . . .
once society throws you into a war, there exists no rock you can hide
behind for security—no actual or contrived rock—the lies of facades are
too burdensome to live and carry around. It really sounds apathetic—
Krebs won't try a relationship because he is afraid of having to live a
lie—he is so afraid to love—he probably doesn't love himself or anyone
else for that matter—he is afraid of being hurt.

13   Anyway, back to the book as a whole. I'm having a hard time trying to link specific ideas to the "hell of war" theme that come up in the individual stories. Right now I'm just working on a feeling that I have gotten—a feeling of meaninglessness and brutality—which seems to be a common thread through the stories. By meaninglessness, I mean not that the stories are meaningless but that life as it was presented in the stories is meaningless and that a good drink heals all wounds and that it's a real feather in your cap to do a C-section with a jack knife and that meaningful relationships with women are a dream . . .

4-14-83

14   I think after more and more class discussion, I like Hemingway better and better. I'm beginning to see the "bad in society" things and now that there seems to be a glimmer of hope—as in life or the Big Two-Hearted River—I can agree with what Hemingway is saying a little bit more.

15   I think Hemingway deserves a second look—I think I'll do some rereading.

4-16-83

16   Freedoms. Spiritual—emotional—physical—social. All necessary. When they clash, war results and makes a mockery of values and of freedom—war takes prisoners. Physically—emotionally—socially—spiritually. My eldest uncle was in the South Pacific during WWII—Kamikazes imprisoned him—and hold him today. My youngest uncle was in Nam—he is tight and bottled up today. Neither could cry two years ago when my grandfather—their father—died.

17   Grandpa was dead. When we arrived at the mobile home, he was on the couch—slumped over—pale—like something out of a Poe story—my two uncles just stood there—like two twisted elms. Grandma was on a party line and one of the other parties wouldn't get off the phone. I volunteered to get my ham radio from home so she could call other relatives to tell the news. It was past dusk when I got in the car. Fog was rising off of the Grand River as I passed by—speeding a bit in the two door Subaru we had just gotten.

18   The fog was getting thicker. Then there I was, trying to keep the little car under control—I hit the 200 lb. buck full broadside. After hitching a ride back to the trailer park, no one seemed to notice me—I hollered out—my eldest uncle handed me a beer and said "Here kid. You earned it." Mom asked about the *car*. It was the night before the Chemistry final.

19   Yes, Hemingway, you hit the nail on the head with your stories about

superficiality—about brutality and triviality—about people in the height of their people-ish-ness.

20   It seems everything we have read so far has to deal with the human experience of searching for "truth." I think they try to offer some insights to the "truth" but all four books seem to say that the truth is found within—not outside in society, and that the "truth" is relative to the eyes of the beholder. They really don't tell what "truth" is.

21   I could see the search clearest through Twain's style and very clear in Wright's style. But, Hemingway somehow brought out some deep and painful memories of things I guess I haven't completely dealt with yet.

4-23-83

22   The other day I did a free write for 10 minutes—what came out was a clarification of my own search.

23   I too search for some way to redeem my life from the meaningless conformity that I am faced with in social and academic life—to over-come complacency—to find truth.

24   I ask myself "Why?", but all I seem to come up with is "Why not?"

25   I live in Grand Rapids—Kent County—a county with probably more churches per capita than any in the U.S. Kent County also has the second highest divorce rate for all counties in the U.S. My parents are divorced. They went to church.

26   Why?

27   With this background, where am I going?

28   Sometimes I feel complacent—it is my death.

TOBY FULWILER'S COMMENTARY

Bob was suspicious of Hemingway from the start. Just two weeks earlier he had finished a bout with Stephen Crane's *The Red Badge of Courage* and, without so much as breaking a sweat, had emerged victorious, with neither black eye nor bloody lip. Crane's best punches missed their mark, and Robert was left unimpressed, but wary. War stories had to be good. They had to measure up to his all-time favorite, Remarque's *All Quiet on the Western Front*, which set a high standard with simple plot, sympa-thetic characters, unambiguous morality, and rapid narrative pace. Hem-ingway wasn't making it at all. Whereas Bob had found Crane's style ponderous and pretentious, he now found Hemingway's *In Our Time* absolutely inexplicable, pointless, and "depressing": "What is he trying to say?" As far as he was concerned, American literature after Twain was not worth more than a couple rounds—or so it seemed from my selection of authors. (What *are* they trying to say?)

But Bob is a serious, disciplined student; if the professor asked him to read a book, a classic at that, he would take it on and see what stuff it was made of. Nobody, however, could make him like what he found nor accept a challenge he found unworthy: "If he can't find any kind of meaning to life, I feel sorry for him—but I don't like reading his works."

I know this about Bob because I asked him to keep a journal in which to record his struggle with class readings on a day-to-day basis. I asked the whole class to do this, of course, but few were so admittedly ill-prepared for their battle with twentieth-century thought as Bob appeared to be and few so articulate in defense of their own value system.

As you read further in that April 9 entry you find that Bob isn't upset with just Hemingway, but with a whole stream of modern "classic" writers who affront the beliefs he holds most dear: "I find a good deal of answers . . . in *The Bible*." Bob seems to know that Crane and Hemingway want him to look elsewhere for truth—but to what point? As he sees it, "They closed their eyes and found darkness and wrote about it." Anybody who would deliberately do that, he reasoned, "didn't know God" nor "their place in God's creation" nor "themselves." What emerges in his writing is not so much confusion about what Hemingway and Crane are up to, as how their dark vision could possibly relate to his life. Of what possible use is this vision? He concludes that first entry on Hemingway: "I'll let them keep their damned depressing bleakness and I'll just keep smiling."

Two days later, on April 11, Bob again takes Hemingway's measure and finds him a lightweight. He notes with glee that the fiction of Hemingway and the dirty snowbanks of springtime in Houghton have something in common—both are "brown"—and once again he affirms his personal values in bright contrast to both Houghton and Hemingway. "Well, I liked Grand Rapids"—his home several hundred miles south of Michigan's Upper Peninsula, in a warmer, more populous, and civilized part of the state. He is being funny—maybe for my benefit, as he knows I'll see the journal entry sooner or later—and he is also quite serious.

The next day, April 12, three days after beginning to read Hemingway, he compares mediocre "classical" literature (*The Red Badge of Courage*) to good television ("M*A*S*H") and laments "I'm not sure that trying to find a meaning out of a seemingly meaningless 'classic' is a meaningful activity." (Yes, Robert, you are clever, but now you are closer.) As we shall see, this is Bob's last serious volley against Hemingway and the "meaningless" literature I'm making him read. He doesn't know or admit it yet, but this time he's misjudged his adversary. His best shot—sarcasm—doesn't protect him from insight. He recognizes possibilities for meaning *other* than those he's already considered. He acknowledges, for instance, that the sixteen separate stories that comprise

In Our Time might be best understood taken as a whole—"the total book concept," as he calls it. Bob lowers his guard long enough to see more clearly what other punches Hemingway might be throwing. He adopts a more open stance, looks hard and articulates with great lucidity a new perception: "It seems like Hemingway traced some of the hells of war back to the society that produced that war." (Not bad, Robert, clearly something to build on.)

Of course, Bob realizes this before I note it retrospectively, writes "I like that idea," and probes further, adjusting his stance to gain better balance and wider vision. He seems more willing now to explore the new combinations his literary antagonist has to offer: "Right now I'm just working on a feeling that I have gotten. . ." In other words, Bob is fully aware that, through his own act of writing, he is searching for meaning; he seems ready now to enjoy the process of discovery—to go the full fifteen rounds.

In the entry of April 14, Bob admits that he likes Hemingway "better and better," explaining to himself, finally, that a writer can point out and identify what's meaningless and depressing in a society without accepting, condoning, or endorsing that depression or lack of meaning. He's made a conscious mental breakthrough, both understanding and affirming the value of perceptive writers who actually fight corruption by pointing out that corruption to perceptive readers—which he has now written his way into becoming.

In the last entry Bob makes while we as a class are actively studying Hemingway—April 16—Bob connects the academic reading of literature to something personal, private, and profound in his own life and so completes the cycle of confrontation, frustration, understanding, and growth that the liberal arts in general and literature in particular best promote. "War takes prisoners" he writes, and he remembers his eldest uncle, still "imprisoned" by his World War II prisoner-of-war experience. The rest of Bob's April 16 narrative, relating the events that happened the day his grandfather died, speaks for itself, as he admits to personal feelings and doubts he hasn't "completely dealt with yet." Here is the same writer—but not the same—who a week earlier "felt sorry" for Hemingway and vowed to ignore him and "keep smiling." His struggle to make sense of fiction through writing—an academic requirement—led him to observations about his personal life and ultimately into a conversation with the author he once pitied: "Yes, Hemingway, you hit the nail on the head with your stories about superficiality . . ."

I want to talk about the last entry, which reflects on Bob's week of reading Hemingway and was written a week later with the class now discussing Richard Wright's *Black Boy*. Bob has gone back to look at memories he once glibly glossed over: Grand Rapids—Kent County—

the church—his parents—their divorce. We know—and he knows—that these April 23 questions will never be answered easily. But I have a strong suspicion that Bob's willingness to take on tough questions is a good indicator of personal growth and of his emergent understanding of the possible role that reading and writing play in making sense of one's own life. And I am sure, after reading both what he says and how he watches himself say it, that he understands genuinely how both the reading and the writing about the reading work together.

I don't need to explain much further why this fragmented, yet sequential piece of writing captured my attention, or why I share it with you. As a teacher, my best hope remains that my students use me and the material I teach, for their own purposes. Bob is a freshman majoring in electrical engineering. He has no need now or ever to learn the esoteric and intricate paths of professional literary criticism often taught to English majors. Nor will he ever be a "professional" in the many other elective studies—biology, philosophy, music, or whatever—that he pursues on his way to being a highly educated electrical engineer. He educates himself best when he finds purpose, method, and meaning in what he reads and in what we teach him. His struggle (for truly, Robert, you fought well) with Hemingway left him a little tattered this time—even slightly wounded in some positive way that may lead, eventually, to good healing. He trusted his language throughout to lead him to purpose. It did, and we all won. That's what makes the best match of all and what makes this piece of writing good.

Study Questions

1. In a classroom exchange that followed a reading of Robert Barkema's paper and Toby Fulwiler's commentary on it, one student said,

   > It sounds to me like this teacher is seeing this student like a rat in a maze or something, one that gets to the right door for food finally. All those comments like "not bad, Robert" and "truly, Robert, you fought well" sound like put-downs to me. And the boxing stuff works the same way. Maybe this student decided the best thing for him to do was to let Hemingway win the big fight. He doesn't *show* that Hemingway has changed him. All he says is that he's changed his mind about Hemingway.

   Another student responded by saying,

   > I think Toby Fulwiler is very respectful of this student, very caring too. If he were interested in making students into rats in mazes, he wouldn't let them keep journals of what they think about what they read. And the student *does* show that Hemingway changed him. Look at all that stuff he mentions toward the end about his own life.

   How would you enter this exchange?

2. In a paper written about Robert Barkema's journal, a student said,

> Robert Barkema doesn't just change his mind about Hemingway. In changing his mind about Hemingway he changes his mind about everything: who he is, what it means for him to be alive.

How might you argue such a point of view with reference only to Robert Barkema's journal entries?

Where do you stand in relation to the argument you have made?

3. From the journal prepared "for formal evaluation," Toby Fulwiler says, he will "assess how well [a student has] learned American literature."

How might you argue that such a journal is a fair evaluation of how well a particular student has learned American literature?

How might you argue that it is not?

In light of your arguments, what would you say is the ideal function of journal writing in formal education?

---

1. Based on our class discussions of the essays by Thoreau and King, write a thesis statement which has the following parts:

    a. an *assertion*: a complete sentence which represents the idea *you* wish to argue in your essay. The assertion should answer a *question at issue*; one, that is, on which there was disagreement in our discussions.

    b. a *because clause*: the primary reason which you wish to offer in support of the truth of your assertion. This reason will identify the *burden of proof*.

(These two statements will imply a third, an assumed logical premise to which your intended reader should agree without argument. Together, these three sentences will constitute a syllogism.) Bring this thesis statement to our next class, so we can discuss it.

2. Now that you have revised your thesis statement in light of our class discussion so that it says exactly what you want it to say, write an essay based on it. The essay (2–4 pages) should develop the logic of the thesis statement, as necessary, to make that logic clear and compelling.

∾ Civil Disobedience and Patriotism
by Erling Nielsen

---

1   Practically speaking, every government in the world has the capacity to create legal injustices, whether intentionally or not. The proclamation of an evil dictator or the opportunistic votes of a self-centered public may create such a problem, with varying degrees of detriment.

2   When confronted with an unjust law, the citizen must decide either to support the government by obeying the law, or follow the dictates of conscience by breaking the law. Unfortunately, due to the nature of most legal systems, there is no safe, middle ground. The law, like the conscience, must either be respected or violated.

3   Deciding which path to follow is not always clear. Often, a guilty conscience is easier to bear than the pain of severe punishment. For example, if the legal penalty for writing derogatory remarks about government officials were death, I think that the value I place on my own

---

JOHN T. GAGE is Associate Professor of English and Director of Composition at the University of Oregon. He has published *In the Arresting Eye: The Rhetoric of Imagism* (1981), as well as essays on the rhetorical criticism of literature. His essays on composition have appeared in *College English, Rhetoric Review, Journal of Advanced Composition, Freshman English News,* and other journals. For the past three years he has served on the Executive Committee of the Conference on College Composition and Communication.

life would prevent me from breaking that law, because I honestly believe that although the law suppresses truth, preserving my life is more important to me than insulting my congressman. The decision to use civil disobedience must come from the individual, because only the individual is capable of weighing the pros and cons in such circumstances, according to his own sense of right and wrong.

At this point, it may be argued that one individual's sense of morality may be unsound, but that really should not affect anyone's decision to practice civil obedience. Suppose, for example, that I decided (in all honesty to myself) that the law forbidding derogatory remarks about government officials was immoral. Naturally, if I thought I could live with the consequences, I would consider civil disobedience as an alternative to obeying the law and defying my conscience. But more importantly, if I really had an interest in the future of my country, I might disobey the law in hopes of either pointing out the unfairness of the penalty for violating the law or inspiring others to disobey the law to make it unenforceable. If little or no interest is shown in amending that law, the effort of the conscientious law-breaker will not have been in vain, because he can be certain in his own mind that his actions were correct. If, however, others followed his example and a large number of people broke the same law, it is quite possible that the law-makers would determine the censorship law to be out of control of the enforcement agencies and feel compelled to amend it.

The main advantage of civil disobedience is that questionable laws can be brought to the attention of the public, usually through sensationalist news accounts. Once in front of the public, the action may persuade people to put pressure on the government to amend the law. By dissenting, and subsequently appealing to public opinion, the conscientious law-breaker has given his country the chance to right its wrongs, while satisfying his own sense of dignity and justice.

When used conscientiously, then, civil disobedience can be the tool of a true patriot confronted with an injustice in the country that he otherwise respects. Unquestionably, a person who loves his country would not tolerate oppression of its citizens, nor would he approve of violence against them. The results obtained from conscientious civil disobedience are impressive. Martin Luther King Jr. and Mahatma Gandhi were two of the most effective users of passive resistance, offering substantial proof of its effectiveness to change legal injustices. And history has judged them to be true patriots.

Thesis statement: Conscientious civil disobedience is an act of patriotism, because it actively attempts to improve the quality of one's government.

John Gage's COMMENTARY

Give me the student who is willing to write as if it really mattered that an idea be said and said well. Robert Frost once asked his writing students if any of them wanted their papers returned after he had read them. When none responded, he walked over to the wastebasket and chunked the papers in. "I'm no perfunctory reader of perfunctory writing," he said. Student writing cannot be good if it is perfunctory. *Perfunctory* in this case means written primarily for the purpose of practicing some form, handing in a writing assignment, getting a grade, or passing a required course. No, to be good, student writing must be written as if the primary purpose is to earn the reader's assent to ideas that the writer had to struggle to achieve.

The trouble with saying what you think is that you have to risk committing yourself, if only for the time being, to an idea. This means that there will be people who will not agree with you, since it is unlikely that any idea worth writing about will be one that everyone agrees with. If good writing strives to earn the reader's agreement, the good writer must consider the best reasons for believing something and not try to win by mere power of eloquence or by arguments which he himself does not believe. The good student writer wants to persuade, but won't be content with a sophistical argument—one that tries to win at any cost. This means that a good writer, like anyone engaged in talk for the purpose of approaching the truth, should be prepared to lose.

Confronted, then, with a range of possible answers to questions that honest and thoughtful people honestly and thoughtfully ask, a student writer should go through something like the following mental process. The first step is to ask which, of the many actual questions under consideration, is the question that matters. The purpose for writing should be to answer some specific question, not to write *about* a "topic." Good essays derive from issues, not from topics, and issues come in the form of questions. Having found a *question at issue*, one that real participants in the discussion are debating, the student should then attempt to find an adequate answer, and to state that answer in the form of a *thesis*. A thesis is an assertion that will be supported by the rest of the essay and that will form its conclusion.

The next step is to ask "Why do I expect anyone to agree with my idea?" At this point, if the student has a genuine rather than a sophistical idea, he must enter into a process of inquiry, a mental dialogue with the unpersuaded reader, in which he tests his reasons for believing his thesis against objections that the reader might raise and defend with reasons of his own. It is *reasons*, after all, that will form the substance of the writing. If earning agreement is the goal, the reader cannot be treated like a passive vessel into which any old idea can be poured. The reader is just as capable of reasoning as the writer is. To find a good reason therefore means to find one that will have some basis in *shared* belief. We can only claim confidence in our ideas, after all, when they can convince people as thoughtful as ourselves. Adopting this attitude sometimes leads to the discovery that the thesis itself is inadequate and that we must change our own minds about what we thought we knew.

These steps only take the student to the point of beginning an essay. They are mental, not compositional, steps, although they are best undertaken with pen in hand. When they are completed, though, student writers can draft an essay with a sufficient measure of confidence in what they want to say. It is knowing what you want to say that will allow you to know where to begin, what to say next, what *not* to say next, and where to end. You will not need the artificial guidance of a "model" or "format." Good structures, like good reasons, are discovered to fit the particular needs of particular cases, not copied from somebody else's model of a good essay structure.

There is one other aspect of good student writing that I must mention before I talk about Erling Nielsen's essay. Good *student* writing, unlike the published essays of most professional writers, is not necessarily finished. Even though a composition must have gone through several stages—mental stages as well as rough drafts—it will usually point to what the student needs to think about next. This includes the way in which the student should conduct inquiry as well as how he should compose and revise.

I say this because Erling's essay is by no means flawless. It is, as the origin of the term *essay* indicates, an attempt. It is an attempt to think through a question at issue and to find good reasons, as well as an attempt to express his thoughts in a correct, precise, and meaningful way. Thus, when I commented on Erling's essay, I responded to these aspects of his attempt. For instance, I pointed out the inappropriateness of some of his word choices (e.g., "detriment," "sensationalist"), the looseness of some of his sentences, and the need for more development in his discussion at the beginning of the fourth paragraph. (You may spot other infelicities.) But most importantly, I responded as a potential member of Erling's thinking audience to the case that he made, because to grow as a writer Erling must also grow as a thinker. I had an advantage here: As his writing teacher I had seen the essay evolve, knew the context of discussion from which it emerged, and could see into the stages of inquiry that finally resulted in his choice of thesis and his strategy for developing it.

Erling began his paper by being bothered. Class discussions had provoked him to see a particular issue as important because it had brought forth conflicting answers from his fellow students. From the somewhat confusing chatter of those discussions, Erling isolated *the* question that for him was at issue, namely, "Can breaking the law on purpose be considered an act of patriotism?" It was a question worth answering, for him, because he disagreed with those students in the class who had argued, and argued well, that it cannot. This decision represented only the beginning of his thinking, because with it came the obligation to give reasons for his position in a way that not only satisfied himself but might satisfy those who believed otherwise.

It was at this point that Erling had to choose among a vast array of potential reasons. Thinking about such reasons, and the objections that might be reasonably made to them, led him to clarify his thesis to himself: He added the term "conscientious," for instance, in order to overcome a problem he discovered in his logic. I don't know how many potential theses and potential reasons he may have run through before deciding on the "thesis statement" that he handed in with the essay, but I do know what guided his search for the right ones.

Erling was looking for a thesis, and a strategy, that would satisfy several criteria. He was looking for an *assertion,* first of all, that would answer a real question at issue and that could become the conclusion of his essay. He was looking in addition for a *because clause*—the central reason that he would develop to support his conclusion. Most importantly, he knew that any reason he might offer would necessarily imply a second reason, or *assumption,** that would have to be acceptable to his audience. Thus, some of the reasons that he might have offered for his assertion would not provide him with an overall logical strategy for his writing. For instance, he might have said that

> Conscientious civil disobedience is an act of patriotism because Martin Luther King, Jr. says so.

He might then have written an interesting paper full of authoritative citations from King's writing. But that essay would not have satisfied his audience, because the logical assumption behind the *because* clause (that "whatever Martin Luther King says must be true") is not necessarily a sharable truth.

Or, he might have decided to argue that

> Conscientious civil disobedience is an act of patriotism because breaking the law on purpose implies love for one's country.

His essay would then have had nothing to develop, since the assumption (in this case, that "civil disobedience = breaking the law on purpose,

---

*By "assumption" I mean the unstated second premise that would complete a syllogism. Although the syllogism should be valid, the object is not perfect symbolic logic but rhetorically adequate premises. This is what Aristotle called an *enthymeme,* or a rhetorical syllogism.

and patriotism = love for one's country") merely redefines his assertion: The logic is tautological. His essay could only have redefined the same assertion over and over allowing no opportunity for development.

Or, he might have come up with

> Conscientious civil disobedience is an act of patriotism because it is motivated by an individual sense of justice.

The assumption (that "all acts motivated by an individual sense of justice are patriotic") would have been just as much at issue for his audience as the conclusion he wished to reach, and again, his case would not have met the needs of his thinking readers.

The *because* clause that Erling finally used was chosen by testing many assumptions in this way. The assumption behind his final thesis statement is one that he believed his audience would share. By thinking through potential assumptions until he came to this one, Erling was able to find the *strategic* reason that his essay must focus on in order to lead his audience to the conclusion that he had reached. And by finding such a reason, Erling also discovered what his essay must do, namely, to develop the terms of that *because* clause in such a way that they would satisfy the logical demands of his thesis. Writing the essay, then, was a matter of expanding on the logic of his thesis statement, taking up and developing its terms, illustrating, qualifying, and explaining as necessary.

Erling's essay is good, then, because it is an attempt to find a logic and a structure adequate to the rhetorical situation that he confronted. He wanted to argue something, and he accepted the responsibility for arguing it in such a way that the needs of his audience would be met. Erling's readers could continue to disagree with him if they wished to match wits with him. There is no such thing as an argument that we cannot lose. His essay is good, though, in spite of potential disagreements, because its tone is thoughtful; he thus shows himself willing to enter that continuing debate if need be. The writer emerges not as someone who bullies or preaches but as someone who thinks: Erling treats his readers as he wishes to be treated by them.

Erling's essay also reveals what he must do in his next attempt if he wishes to grow as a writer and as a thinker. The logical problems with Erling's essay result from his choice to argue a definition, and so at the end of his argument we might well wonder whether someone who sought to break a law by *claiming* patriotic motives is necessarily to be believed or exonerated. But from this attempt at writing reasonably in defense of his best thinking, Erling can learn that he must take his thinking beyond the stage of definition, and so I advised him when it came time for him to write another thesis statement on which to base his next attempt.

Study Questions

1. From his commentary on Erling Nielsen's paper, we can infer some of John Gage's assumptions about what writing is and what it is good for.

   What does the activity of writing seem to involve for John Gage?

   What does he suggest is the value of good writing?

   Where do you stand with these assumptions?

2. As a writer, you yourself have faced and probably will face in the future a variety of writing tasks.

   What sorts of writing tasks do you think John Gage's approach to the teaching of writing could help you to learn to do well?

   What writing tasks do you think John Gage's approach might not help you to face?

   How is the approach to writing taken by John Gage valuable to you as a writer?

3. In a paper written about Erling Nielsen's essay and John Gage's commentary on it, a student said,

   > John Gage says here a couple of times that this student is honest and believes what he's saying and runs risks in saying what he does, but I don't see what makes him so sure this paper *isn't* an example of what he calls "perfunctory writing." What real risk is being run by the student? Couldn't Erling Nielsen just as easily argue the opposite of his thesis by saying something like "civil disobedience is an act of treason because it undermines faith in the authority of the government"? I think I could argue that and just this same way whether or not I believe it. How would anyone know whether I was being honest in my paper or not?

   How do you respond to these remarks?

Donald Murray's Assignment

[The assignment for which the following paper was written was to write an Op-Ed article, one of those essays that newspapers print on the page of opinion. I passed out copies of an Op-Ed article I had written about a daughter moving to New York City for the class to analyze and pointed out that a strong point of view was vital. Four weeks, three conferences, and an in-class workshop later, Dale Paul's essay was finished.]

ᑫ Without Child

by Dale Paul

The toyshop was so tiny that I had to be careful not to step on children 1 playing with the sturdy samples. Searching for a wooden train to send to my nephew, squeezing between a hobby horse and a grandmother, I found myself face to face with an infant in a backpack. Brown eyes peeped out of an absurd white ruffled bonnet and she was crowing with delight at the commotion. Smiling back at her, I was horrified to find my eyes full of tears. Where had they come from?

Although I didn't know it then, they were the tears that should have 2 been shed months earlier in the doctor's office. I hadn't wept when he informed me that I would never bear a child. I was matter of fact, brisk and sensible, and he responded with the factual information that I requested. The few family members and friends that I told also took their cue from my icy calm.

"No contraceptive worries," they rejoiced. 3

"Look how kids turn out these days. Enjoy your freedom." 4

"These are the eighties," they declared, "Lots of women are choosing 5 not to have kids."

And that, I thought, is that. But, of course, it wasn't, for here I was, 6 about to weep in the middle of the pre-Christmas toy rush. Hurrying outside—"for fresh air"—I felt for the first time what it was going to mean to be childless. The sadness surprised me and I was totally unprepared for the months to follow.

Suddenly, it seemed, the world was filled with pregnant women and 7 babies. Friends called to announce their pregnancies with disturbing

---

DONALD M. MURRAY, Professor of English at the University of New Hampshire, is the author of *A Writer Teaches Writing* (1983), *Learning by Teaching* (1982), and *Write to Learn* (1984). A Pulitzer Prize–winning journalist before becoming a teacher of writing, he has published poetry, short stories, articles, novels, and juvenile nonfiction books in addition to his articles and books on writing.

regularity. Wasn't this the eighties when women were choosing not to have babies? When I hung up, I snarled, "Just wait until the kid interrupts the first cocktail party." I knew no one that I considered fit parents-to-be. I hated Lady Di.

8   I snapped off the TV, rejecting specials on the unwed mother, the over-40 mother, the irresponsible mother, the baby in the womb. I went for coffee during commercials for diapers, baby shampoo, and Fisher-Price toys. I disparaged commercials for soft drink, insurance, and cameras that used the cooing infant to sell their products.

9   I could only get a doctor's appointment on the day of the newborn clinics and if I happened to sit at the soda fountain in the drugstore, they were sure to be having a special on pre-natal vitamins. The grocery store filled the front windows with Pampers.

10   Without discussion, I watched my husband scrap plans for two bedrooms to create an elegant adult study and bedroom. I sent an oak child's chair off to the west coast as a baby present, never mentioning the fact that I'd bought it years earlier, "in case." I sorted my collection of children's books, ruthlessly tossing them aside to be given away or sold. I made lunch dates and career plans and attended cultural events.

11   And I still didn't know what I was doing. I thought I was being childish—just wanting what I didn't have. I told myself that I just needed to get busy with my career, to do something worthwhile with my time, to stop being sentimental and self-pitying. I told myself to examine the options rationally.

12   That's what women in my generation do—select from limitless options. The first of the post-war baby boom babies, we expected to have it all. We wanted the world to be fair and just, the air and water to be clean. We planned productive, fulfilling careers. We discussed the many options in our futures: children, husbands, careers, travel, politics. All the time we were picking and choosing among the options, doors were quietly closing around us.

13   This time, a door slammed for me. I will not have a child of my own, will never experience pregnancy, will never give birth. That is a loss which needs to be mourned. I don't need to examine the options rationally. I need to feel angry and sad, to grieve. The women of my generation have not yet learned to mourn.

14   Packing away the Christmas decorations this year, I wondered what will become of them when my husband and I die. We have been collectors, makers of tradition. Of what use is a tradition if there is no generation to inherit it? I am learning to mourn.

DONALD MURRAY'S COMMENTARY

I think Dale Paul's essay is a good piece of writing for four reasons.

Significance

The writer has something important to say. She is writing about a matter of elemental significance. Through the writing of this piece she deals with a problem that is important to her—and to others. Yes, the piece is therapeutic for her, but the problem she faces has implications for others who are in the same situation and for the rest of us, and the way in which she works it out has implications for people facing other serious problems in their lives.

Too many students try to write on trivial subjects that may occasionally work under the pen of a master writer. But young writers need the energy and importance of a vital subject to put their minds and their language under pressure. Assignments that include topics usually trivialize the writing experience. I could not have assigned this topic to a class, and I could not have assigned it individually even if I had known of it, which I did not. Such an assignment would have been an invasion of privacy. Writing of this quality has to be self-assigned.

Distance

Rarely do students realize the range of distances from which they can view their subject. They zoom in too close or stand back too far. Dale Paul's voice has established the correct distance for this piece. Another student's voice (personality? turn of mind?) might demand another range of distances that would work for her on the same subject. In all cases, however, we should be close enough to care, yet far enough away to be able to deal with it. Dale Paul's piece is not embarrassing to the reader but involving, and the voice underlines the significance of the subject.

Texture

The essay is revealed as much as it's told. The writer uses anecdotes and revealing details to give the piece authority, depth, and to ignite a resonance that reminds us of the details in our own lives. The writing is not general and abstract, but concrete and specific. Yet all the details are in context. We see their implications for the author, and we see their implications for the reader. Too often students either write only in generalities or swing in the other direction and catalogue details that have no context.

Closure

Many pieces by inexperienced writers start strong and trail off. That is one reason why so many professional writers will not begin until they know the ending. A piece must have closure. The problems set up by the writer must be solved by the end of the piece. This does not mean that everything has to be tied up in a knot, or that there must be a positive ending; it does mean that the reader must experience a sense of completion or resolution at the end.

Dale Paul's essay is the product of teaching by not teaching. In brief conferences, I encouraged her struggles with the piece by nodding, smiling, and using what William Stafford calls the writing teacher's best tools: "uh huh," "mm," and "hmm." She also had the opportunity to listen to readers' reactions in a peer group workshop. I did little in a formal sense to help Dale Paul with this piece. The assignment did give her the pressure that caused the piece to be written, and revision was demanded. I also expected the article to be submitted for publication, and pointed out that it might be a good piece for the *Newsweek* "Speaking Out" column. (They have turned it down, but it is being considered by other magazines.) I expect my students to write pieces worthy of publication outside the classroom.

I find teaching exciting because I have the opportunity to observe writing evolve. I have a front-row seat at the creative process. Dale had written a six-page first draft which I did not see until I asked her for the whole file so that I could retrace the essay's history. The pre-draft had fragments of good writing, but it wandered all over the countryside after starting out, "I have never been a gusher on the subject of babies." What she passed in to me was a three-page essay marked "first draft." It starts out, "Born in 1947, at the cutting edge of the post-war baby boom, I'm one of the generation of women who thought we were going to have it all." It's crisper, tighter, than the long pre-draft. There are three clichés in one sentence, but I didn't worry about the language at that stage. I did worry that the essay started in that global way. The scene in the toy shop, incidentally, was buried in the center of a long paragraph on page two.

I don't remember what I said in conference, but I hope I gave support for the significance of the subject; I hope we discussed the importance of engaging the reader immediately. And we may have discussed the point of closure, although I probably avoided it because the problem was clearly not resolved in the writer's mind. I may have told her to take time, not to worry about getting it done for next week, because I didn't want to force her to confront the problem if she wasn't ready. I probably did indicate to her that the piece wasn't too personal or embarrassing to the reader.

A week later the next draft started with the toy shop and worked well, putting the experience in the context of her life, and then putting her life in the context of a generation. In conference I think she indicated that the end didn't work. I'm sure I agreed—it didn't—but expressed confidence that it would.

The third draft is published here. The ending worked. And I saw in her behavior and tone of voice, a calm that is reflected in the piece. Although the subject is emotional and the writing of it was therapeutic, I feel that the piece is an example of good thinking. When a piece of personal writing is brought to a conclusion, I think students have the opportunity to see that the same cognitive activity can be applied to academic writing. I do not agree with those who think we must, in the university, exclude personal writing from our nonfiction courses. To think through a personal essay of this nature the writer has to think well, and by writing a piece such as this a student can learn how to write in an academic mode if the teacher builds the bridge from one form to the other. Does anyone really think that the author of this piece could not write thoughtful academic discourse?

I have invited Dale Paul to write her own account of the writing of this piece to see how her vision of what happened compares to mine. It is, after all, her writing and her learning that are important.

DALE PAUL'S COMMENTARY

Don Murray expects student writers to come to conference prepared to speak about their writing. As a draft comes out of the typewriter, I'm already deciding what works, what needs to be changed, what questions I have.

The Op-Ed page assignment appealed to me as a manageable bit of writing. I made a quick list of six or seven possible topics which included "not having children." After several false starts on various topics, I wrote everything I could think of that related to the situation—anecdotes, questions, feelings—a pool of resources I could use to create a draft. Those were the six pages that Don Murray calls the "pre-draft."

My first draft had its usual slow beginning—a page of background information which is unnecessary in the final paper, but which seems to be a mandatory warm up for me as a writer. At the first conference, I already knew that I would cut most of that page. I also knew that the idea of mourning which had popped up on page three was the key to the paper.

I mentioned the cuts to Don Murray as he read the first page. Enough talk went on about the subject—both the inability to have children and the choosing of options—to convince me that the subject was worth writing about and that I could talk about it without too much discomfort.

His comment, "The writing really gets going on page two," confirmed my cuts and reminded me of the need for a strong lead. We did not discuss an ending at that conference, although I may have mentioned that I didn't have one yet. He did say that this draft could be used for the next class, but I was anxious to write the second draft.

That worked well until the third page. In a class workshop with four other students, they mentioned the bravery in tackling the subject, liked the lead, and made suggestions that cleared up wording on the first two pages. Their questions and suggestions about the third page were so bizarre I knew it needed a complete revision.

In conference, we agreed the ending didn't work. Don Murray suggested I use an anecdote. I tried several and brought one into conference that included the Christmas decorations and a conversation. It felt forced to me, and his reaction was a question, "Didn't you have a paragraph in there before about options?" In an attempt to clear up my readers' confusion, I'd just eliminated everything they'd questioned. We didn't discuss that at any length, but his question reopened the options for me. I didn't write anything for the paper that week, but I did think about how to write a conclusion for a paper in which the issue was unresolved. And there sat the ending. This wasn't an issue to be resolved; it was a fact to be accepted. I wrote the last three paragraphs in a half-hour.

The achievement of distance and the puzzling out of a conclusion made this a powerful learning experience for me. The distancing seemed to happen the way the Roadrunner streaks past Wily Coyote in the cartoons. By the end of the first conference, much of the therapy was over so that I was working on a piece of writing, not a personal problem.

Paragraphs, anecdotes, thesis statements and spare lines filled the wastebasket while I searched for an ending. I tried every writing option I knew to arrive at that conclusion. I was encouraged by Don Murray's expectation not just that I could, but that I would solve the problems.

It must have required great faith to let me find my own way through this piece. When I finally mentioned, almost as an aside, that I thought I had an ending for it, he all but snatched it from me. For the first time, he became really directive, "Type it and send it out."

Study Questions

1. "Does anyone really think," says Don Murray of "Without Child," "that the author of this piece could not write thoughtful academic discourse?"

How might you argue that Dale Paul in "Without Child" shows she is capable of writing what Don Murray calls "thoughtful academic discourse"?

How might you argue that there is no evidence of such a capability in "Without Child"?

How would you respond to Don Murray's rhetorical question?

2. Suppose that Dale Paul had invented the conflict she discusses in "Without Child," simply made it all up, from beginning to end.

Would this influence your response to her essay? Explain why it would or wouldn't.

What does your position on this hypothesis tell you about yourself as a reader?

3. In a discussion of Dale Paul's "Without Child" and Don Murray's commentary on it, the following classroom exchange took place. One student said,

> Maybe it's because I'm male and don't really understand the problem here, but I don't think this paper does "have closure." I don't think the ending works at all. In the next to last paragraph the writer says she needs to mourn the loss of never experiencing pregnancy, never giving birth. She doesn't need to examine the options rationally. O.K. But when she moves to the last paragraph with all that talk about there being no generation to inherit what she and her husband have to pass on, she's making not being able to *have* a child the same thing as not raising children and the two are different. She sounds self-pitying to me, not willing to see that she's slamming the door on herself. She's using this "learning to mourn" business to cover up the fact that what's really important to her is not children to raise but a child she can feel she owns.

Another student responded by saying,

> I don't think being male or female has anything to do with it. I think what you don't make allowances for is the pressure of the emotion of this writer's realization. She isn't suggesting she'll never consider adoption, only that *now* she needs "to feel angry and sad, to grieve." She's not covering up anything at all. She's bitter with grief and says so. But she also ends with a question rather than a statement of absolute fact about where she is. She says she's learning. It took her a while to know what she felt; it will take her a while to move on. But she will. I think the ending is perfect.

What position would you take in this controversy?

Writing Assignment 4
Coming to Terms

Write an account of how you came to terms with something important to you. Give as exact an account as you can, including all relevant particulars. As with Writing Assignment 3, your teacher may give you more specific instructions. You may be asked to use a particular form, for example, or you may be given a word limit. Please do not feel, however, that you must write about something you consider embarrassingly personal or that you must reveal anything about your life that you would prefer to keep private. "Importance" is a matter of how something is perceived, not what is being looked at.

Secondly, on the basis of your experience with this assignment, explain in a paragraph or so on a separate page what "coming to terms with" something seems to involve. Try to do a little more than play the synonym game. Does it help much to say that coming to terms means to bring something into focus, that coming to terms means to gain a deeper understanding or deal with a problem effectively? You have at least five student papers to refer to, and you yourself have written a paper giving an account of how you came to terms with something. You don't have to talk in generalities that can't possibly do you any good.

Finally, suppose that at some time in the future you felt you needed to come to terms with an important issue in your life. Suppose that you decided to try to make writing play a part in this activity. What part do you think you could make it play?—bearing in mind, of course, that you're probably not a professional writer, maybe not yet even the writer you can become.

In responding to this final question, be sure you draw upon whichever student essays and teachers' commentaries you read in this chapter as well as upon your experience with the first two parts of this writing assignment. Write your response to this final question on a separate page.

Taking a Stand

5

One of the worst batches of papers I ever read came out of a good idea
we had at Earlham College for getting the whole student body involved
in controversial discussion about world affairs. We required them to read
Barbara Ward's *Five Ideas That Change the World.* . . .

It is obvious what had gone wrong: though we had ostensibly given
the student a writing purpose, it had not become *his* purpose, and he was
really no better off, perhaps worse, than if we had him writing about,
say, piccolos or pizza. We might be tempted in revulsion from such
overly ambitious failures to search for controversy in the students' own
mundane lives. This may be a good move, but we should not be surprised
when the papers on "Let's clean up the campus" or "Why must we have
traffic fatalities?" turn out to be just as empty as the papers on the UN or
the Congo. They may have more exclamation points and underlined
adjectives, but they will not interest. . . . "People often fail to realize
that nearly 40,000 people are killed on our highways each year. Must
this carnage continue?" Well, I suppose it must, until people who write
about it learn to see it with their own eyes, and hearts, instead of
through a haze of cliché. The truth is that to make students assume a
controversial pose before they have any genuine substance to be controversial about is to encourage dishonesty and slovenliness, and to ensure . . .
boredom.

Wayne C. Booth

W HAT CAN HAPPEN TO A WRITER'S SENSE of a subject in the act of
writing about it is often unpredictable. Just as there is writing that we
start out using to shape things in order that we may come to understand something, so there is writing that we use to say what we think we know
already, at least at the outset of the writing process.

Such writing has a variety of designations, none of them wholly satisfactory. One hears, for example, of "expository writing," which, however careful a teacher or a textbook may be to define it, is often understood by students to mean "writing for English teachers only"; that is, writing for people who are interested in knowing only how well students have learned to state in conventional terms what everyone agrees is true about Great Ideas, but who are *not* interested in the students' experience of those ideas—let alone of any others.

The student papers and the commentaries in this chapter, all of them quite different in manner and in purpose, have been brought together partly in order to explode this misconception. Taking a stand on something in writing, expressing one's knowledge in writing, can be a sterile exercise for a writer, meaningless as well as boring, no matter what the subject. But it does not have to be, as this chapter is intended to help you understand.

Rosemary Deen's Assignment

Imagine yourself at a party or at a new job or school with people who don't know you. You have just made a remark about something that is important to you. Maybe you say something about the sports you enjoy, and someone says, "Oh, you must be a jock" or something equally thoughtless:

"You're in therapy? You don't look sick."

"It must be pretty boring growing up in a small town."

"We all know what Italians are like."

"You're from New York? How many times you been mugged?"

Write four or five such simplistic sentences of your own as imagined responses to various experiences of importance to you. Take three minutes and write nonstop—you can't do it wrong.

Now, pick the sentence that your own experience best puts you in a position to show *is* outrageous, thoughtless, or reductive. Extend this outrageous sentence by writing a paragraph of the rest of the things you imagine that a person taking such a position might say. Write it all. Give what you are seeing as ignorance its full say.

Then, write your response to this outrageous position *by recounting your own experience:* "*They* say that, but *my* experience is this." Don't bother arguing directly with the view you've heard. Let the way you talk about your own experience do the arguing for you.

ROSEMARY DEEN teaches writing and literature at Queens College in New York City. She administered and taught a student team-teaching program, and she occasionally gives workshops for student tutors and for high school and college teachers. Together with Marie Ponsot she has written *Beat Not the Poor Desk—Writing: What to Teach, How to Teach It, and Why* (1982), which won the 1982 Mina Shaughnessy Medal for research in teaching English language and literature.

⊸ Just a Mother

by Joanne Nizzo

They say, "It doesn't take much to be a mother. Any simple-minded 1
female, who is biologically equipped can be one." They say that a man is
far too busy with the important business of bread winning to raise children. They reason that men simply do not have the patience to deal with
spills, spats, and tears; and they think that women do. They suspect that
all really good middle-class mothers stay at home with their children,
tending to their needs, which they never clearly define.

Only the surface of motherhood is seen until you actually enter in. 2
You think you know beforehand how you'll have to clean and care for
your child, but it all seems easy enough.

Before I had children, I did what they call work. My jobs varied but in 3
a word they were all tedious, and in two words they were tedious and
dull. For the most part I did sales and clerical work. Narrow-mindedly, I
thought that any and all other jobs would be equally as dull. There was a
longing within me for something more than answering phones and pouring coffee.

I decided to have a family. I knew beforetime that I'd be the kind of 4
mother who stayed home with her children, like they say you should.
After all who wanted to work anyway? They say women don't work,
meaning housewives don't work: well, that suited me fine.

The unspeakable joy I felt when I found out I was pregnant was 5
accentuated by the relief I felt at the thought of never having to work
again. From all they said about motherhood I figured I knew a lot.
Judging by its title alone "just motherhood" sounded pretty easy.

They say things like there are no bad children, only bad mothers: and 6
good mothers have happy babies. Since I aimed to be a very good mother
I anticipated having a happy baby.

When my baby finally arrived I nursed her. Enjoying every moment, 7
I'd hold and hug her. I couldn't understand why she cried so much. As a
matter of fact she seemed to cry every time I put her down. Partly because
I thought something was hurting her and partly from sheer exhaustion I
started to cry with her: realizing all too soon that this being just a mother
was not as easy as they had led me to believe. Here I was at the beck and
call of this little one who indeed had stolen my heart, and I didn't know
what to do!

It was a hard time during which I questioned my ability: "Could it be 8
that I haven't the patience that they say mothers have?" I wondered.
Instead of patience being something I had, I realized how much I needed
it. My experience has shown me that patience is not inborn. Perhaps you
could say it is something that one acquires; but I think that is misleading

because it suggests permanence. My patience was born out of love for my family and a deep desire that I had to be what they needed me to be. Still though, after ten years of experience, patience sometimes without even notifying me, just flees from my side. There I'll stand yelling, realizing that with patience I could be making my point much more effectively. Well, why do you lose your patience? you might ask. Sometimes it seems like it happens over the silliest things, like a milk spill, or a spat between two of the children, but it goes deeper.

9   It's the fact that motherhood is a job. It's a job that entails the awesome responsibility for the lives of others. It's not easy as it has been said to be. It's unending work. As a mother, I work from 7 in the morning until 10 at night. Though I eat, I do so on the job. As children get older you do get breaks, but when they're babies forget it! Sometimes you don't even get a good night's sleep. Add one sleepless night to one day of cleaning, washing, feeding, etc. and you've got one tired mother. I've learned that when I'm tired I can neglect to show my love for my children. I know this is human but I also know that the effect of neglecting (for whatever the reason) to show love to our children can be devastating.

10   Our reactions to them are so important. Whether we're tired or angry, happy or sad, they're first. For many years their only concern is how we treat them. I've learned that children are egocentric. They need to be taught to think of others without being made to feel guilty about their own inclinations toward self: guilt over their nature can rob them of their self-esteem. So my experience as a mother has shown me that we have to love our children unconditionally while teaching them right from wrong. If that sounds easy it's not; at least, not as an on-going thing.

11   I've learned that mothers often have to put their feelings aside for the sake of their children. The way we treat our children determines, to a great extent, how they will be as adults. And that is very important, not only for children and mothers but to the whole world: children are its future.

12   So when I hear them say, "Oh, she's just a mother" or "I'm tired of working: I want to stay home and be just a mother," I think, "Oh, Oh! they really don't know what they're talking about. God help them."

Rosemary Deen's COMMENTARY

The art of this kind of essay is to allow the full expression of the thoughtless opinion in the beginning—enough so that the wrongness of the opinion becomes self-evident in relation to the authentic experience described in the second part.

Joanne Nizzo's paper does a variation on this essay shape because what "they" say is also what she once thought herself. She gives the other side plenty to say—almost two-thirds of the essay, which is interesting because it suggests that a wrongheaded opinion can almost build your case for you.

The fullness of this essay's first part brings out the assumption that the "opposing" view is depending on: Staying home is the opposite of working. So, being a full-time mother means being "just" a mother—not working.

Notice that her expression of the thoughtless opinion has a narrative spine. I recognize the narrative mode in the predominant past tense and in such narrative connections as *before, beforetime, when.* But there are also plenty of thoughts and feelings, and they eventually subordinate the narrative mode and prepare for the discussion of the idea. Her thoughts and ideas are expressed in present tense verbs and in connecting words that suggest mental actions like inferring and judging: *judging by, since, partly because, perhaps, though, sometimes.* In fact there are more connections for mental actions than for narrative, which accounts for my sense, as I read, that the narrative turns out to be the example of an idea.

I love the way the essay makes its turn in the eighth paragraph, which begins "It was a hard time. . . ." The opening sentence gathers together the experiences she's narrated, particularly the funny and sad picture of the young mother crying *with* the baby.

But with this paragraph, the narrative ends. It develops a key abstract word, *patience.* Patience is the theme of the paragraph, and the word is repeated seven times. This is not too much repetition because it serves to emphasize and to further develop the idea. *Patience* comes in first as one of the words "they" use. But the author makes it her word. Experience tells her it's not inborn; reasoning tells her it's not acquired: an acquirement "suggests permanence." The most distressing thing about being a mother, even after years of experience, is this idea of losing patience, and that turns the essay from what "they" say and she used to believe to what she knows now.

What she thinks turns out to be "It's the fact that motherhood is a job." That's a good example of a beautiful, plain English sentence made more beautiful by the way it picks up earlier ideas and ties them together. When "they" say that good mothers *stay home,* and that men are too *busy* to raise children, "they" imply that mothering isn't work. The speaker herself exposes her own share in that assumption in her wonderful ironic sentence "The unspeakable joy I felt when I found out I was pregnant was accentuated by the relief I felt at the thought of never having to work again." One of the pleasures of reading good writing is not having to leave a good sentence like that behind as you read on, because you know that it will be woven into the author's fullest view of her idea by the end.

Of course, what Joanne Nizzo has told us up to this point about mothering hasn't made it sound exactly like work. She doesn't make it seem easy, but holding and hugging babies doesn't seem like a job either. But now that word *job* leads the writer to her demonstration that mothering is a job. She does this nicely in paragraph 9 with sentences like, "As a mother, I work from 7 in the morning until 10 at night."

But she's going further than that. When I first read the phrase "awesome responsibility" (in paragraph 9), I was concerned at finding a big, expensive word like *awesome* in the essay. I wondered whether Mrs. Nizzo would be able to afford it. I know such words become slang, but I am a lover of words and don't like to see the big ones marked down. So I was relieved to see that the author was going to keep the promise of that word and develop the full implications of her idea, as she does in paragraph 10.

In paragraphs 10 and 11, Joanne Nizzo draws some conclusions. Most of the words here are abstract: *egocentric, self, guilt, nature, self-esteem, love, unconditionally.* But Joanne Nizzo has provided the concrete experiences and images of paragraphs 6, 7, and 8 to illustrate them. I think she's earned those words too by the honesty of a sentence like "There I'll stand yelling. . . ." The author demonstrates what she's talking about in phrases like "They need. . . ." We know that good parents are guided by what children need. The most powerful sentences in the essay are these:

> I've learned that children are egocentric. They need to be taught to think of others without being made to feel guilty about their own inclinations toward self: guilt over their nature can rob them of their self-esteem.

Her reasoning is that to be egocentric is a child's nature; and when you call something *nature,* you say that you accept it fully.

When Joanne Nizzo develops the psychological and ethical implications of her big word, *awesome,* she shows she can afford to use it. And I had to laugh at the way she glances back at it at the end of her essay when she hears people say, "I want to stay home and be just a mother." She thinks, "God help them."

Study Questions

1. A student who had read both "Just a Mother" and Rosemary Deen's commentary on it wrote a paper in which she said,

> The sentences that Rosemary Deen calls "the most powerful" in Joanne Nizzo's essay don't seem powerful to me at all, maybe because they sound so much like the kind of thing that could have come out of *Woman's Day.* It's true that the writer does say "*I've* learned," but the key pronoun to the whole conclusion of her essay is really "we," and most of the talk there is something any parent

could come up with. Much more powerful for me is the writer's saying, "Still though, after ten years of experience, patience sometimes without even notifying me, just flees from my side. There I'll stand yelling. . . ." The way she has of seeing patience as something with a mind of its own, as something that can leave her alone without notice, really is an individual way of seeing something. It's worth more than all the woman's magazine clichés in the world.

What is your position on this statement?

2. In several places in her commentary on Joanne Nizzo's paper, Rosemary Deen speaks of how the writer is "able to afford" the use of certain words. Certain words, she suggests, should not be "marked down." They need to be "paid for" or "earned" by a writer.

Judging from the position you imagine Rosemary Deen is taking on the importance of words in a piece of writing, how do you think she would respond to the assertion that "a good writer must seek to develop an extensive vocabulary"?

What is your position on what you imagine she would say?

Perhaps to address these questions you would find it helpful to write a dialogue between you and Rosemary Deen.

3. In a classroom discussion of Joanne Nizzo's paper, a student said,

> I don't know whether it's the assignment or what, but the final section of this paper seems awfully trite to me: "The way we treat our children determines, to a great extent, how they will be as adults." Children are the future of the world. That kind of thing. It seems like the essay just stops rather than concludes. It's like the writer didn't know where to take things. I'd have her rewrite those last three paragraphs.

How do you respond to this statement? In your response, make clear whether you think the final section of "Just a Mother" needs rewriting or not. If not, what makes you say so? If so, how would you advise the writer of the paper to go about it?

LARRY LEVY's Assignment

The I-Search Paper

If you weren't in school, if you weren't enrolled in this English class, what question(s) would you still be asking and seeking answers to? What would you like to know that, given roughly five weeks and your on- and off-campus resources, you can answer or begin to find out?

Perhaps you work part-time, carry a full academic load, are on the honor roll, and still want to see your friends. How do you manage your time? Perhaps, after talking with a counselor and reading several advice-giving articles, you design and follow a detailed schedule, adjusting and readjusting it during the next several weeks and learning much about your wants and needs as you go.

Perhaps you've returned to college because you were laid off from what you thought was a secure job. You're wondering how promising your new field is, so you interview the campus employment counselor, several recent graduates from the program, and several area employers, and you decide it would be best after all to continue for a four-year degree.

Perhaps you were a fine high school runner but have never run a 26-mile marathon. How do you train for it? Can you do it? You interview local experienced marathoners, read through your back issues of *Runner's World,* and design a program for yourself. You train and finally attempt the distance.

What is your question? Consider also why you're choosing to ask it and how the answer can matter to you or to other people.

Now go find answers. The library may help you, but so may a classmate, a neighbor, a relative, or some local authority you don't know yet but would like to meet. Perhaps there is a way of getting the answers firsthand, as one student did by running his own marathon. Perhaps the best way to learn is to see people doing certain things and to do these things yourself.

Keep in mind that, although your question begins with a private need, the report of your search and findings will be public and ought to be persuasive. Show the rest of us where your question came from. Show us what valuable things you see and hear as you search. Explain how you resolved your search, whether you found what you expected or were surprised by what you discovered.

LARRY LEVY is Assistant Professor of English at Delta College in University Center, Michigan. He has also taught English in junior and senior high school and as a guest in public school, library, and gifted-student programs. He has published poetry in *Virginia Quarterly Review, Poet Lore,* and *Poet and Critic* and teaching essays in *Teaching English in the Two-Year College* and *Evaluating a Theme* published by the Michigan Council of Teachers of English.

∾ Fritz

by Jean Nerio

Schnauzer: This dog is known for his fearless disposition, daredevil antics, and raw courage. But not for his common sense.

Fritz is definitely a good watchdog, but he is spoiled, headstrong, and unmanageable. The mailman maces him, the grooming lady ties him up while she trims his hair and nails, pedestrians take alternate routes to avoid our house, and joggers run. Friends no longer visit us. [1]

When I take Fritz for his walks he stampedes out the door like a buffalo. He is never walking at my side where he belongs but running around me, tripping and tangling me with his leash. Occasionally, when Fritz escapes, I chase him around the neighborhood, almost catch him, then watch him scamper away. If he tires, he simply lies down and I drag his dead weight home. [2]

The car becomes bedlam when Fritz goes on vacation. He leaps from back seat to front seat and back again, over our heads and shoulders, trying to look out all the windows at the same time. He doesn't care if someone is already sitting in the spot he has chosen. We then have to switch seats—like the game of musical chairs—and hope he'll get comfortable and fall asleep. Fritz never falls asleep. [3]

Most people go camping because they enjoy undisturbed peace and quiet. Fritz goes camping to pursue his personal interests, the most important of which is chasing. He can chase above the ground, under the ground, along the ground, in the water and in the air. He chases moles, chipmunks, turkeys, rabbits, frogs, jeeps, dirt bikes, other dogs, and little kids. When he becomes exhausted, he returns to our campsite and recuperates by the campfire. He eats a few marshmallows and then sleeps at the foot of my sleeping bag. When I get up early in the mornings to take a shower, he howls until I return. Someone usually yells, "Fritz, shut up or go home!" Some just hurl nasty words at him. [4]

Fritz is not *all* bad. Smallest of the schnauzers, the minature is as brave, alert, and intelligent as the standard and the giant. (1, p. 89) He would probably give up his life for me. He whimpers at my going; and at my coming wags himself in two—his greatest joy is to be at my side. He is also guardian of my property and a loyal companion to my children. [5]

But a dog can be a headache if it is not given proper training. A heedless dog that ignores every command tries one's patience. This is why I have enrolled Fritz in the Greater Saginaw Dog Obedience School. [6]

There were twenty dogs there that first night, and they all acted as bad as Fritz. While Joe Kelly, trainer, explained the "joy" of owning a well- [7]

trained and obedient pet, the dogs were yipping, growling, snapping at each other, emptying their bladders, and causing all kinds of disturbances. "Training is not a test of strength," Joe explained. "It is a test of will. As training goes on, things *will* get easier." (5) It was hard believing anything Joe was telling us. I was exhausted just hanging onto Fritz's leash. I think my arms got longer.

8   The next step that first evening was having our dogs measured and sized for the proper choke chain and leash. When it was Fritz's turn he snarled viciously and nipped Joe's hand. We had a hard time finding a choke chain small enough. Joe jokingly said, "Maybe you should just get a different dog." We laughed about it at the time, but after the third week of training I was thinking about buying a Dalmation.

9   During the following weeks we practiced five basic commands: heel, sit, stay, down, and come.

Week 1: Heel

10   On this command, dog should walk close to your left side, even with the left knee. If dog starts to move ahead or lag behind, give the leash a quick jerk and say, "Heel!" Fritz either flatly refused to budge and didn't care if his head came off when I yanked the leash, or once he started he was unstoppable. When we'd stop to catch our breath, I'd plead with him. "Why must you be so hostile? Is it too much to ask of you to walk around for a few minutes without trying to kill me?" Fritz was unimpressed.

Week 2: Sit

11   This command is taught while dog is heeling. He should learn to sit the moment you stop walking. This is taught by stopping and giving the command "Sit!" At the same time, you pull up on the leash and push down on the dog's hindquarters. Fritz, of course, refused to cooperate. I could pull up on the leash until he became airborne. He just looked at me like I had two heads, and I just stood there feeling very embarrassed. Joe just kept encouraging me, "Just keep practicing. He's just stubborn, but practice, repetition, and praise when he finally does something right *will* work."

12   I went to the library after class that night and checked out books on dog obedience. I was hoping to find an easier way to train a dog, but all the books agreed with Joe's methods. (2,3,4)

Week 3: Stay

13   Dog must sit without moving until given another command. Command dog to sit. Then, hold your hand up in front of his nose and in a firm

voice say, "Stay!" You should be able to walk away, and the dog should stay until called. Release the dog with an "Okay!" and praise him for a job well done. Fritz does not get much praise. To make matters worse, when he finally does sit, Joe will walk by and try to trick Fritz into breaking the command. It was after this lesson that I asked Joe if Fritz could be retarded. He laughed and explained, "The most intelligent, highly trained dog has the mind of a kindergarten child. Fritz is probably around the year-old level. But don't worry; just keep practicing. He has to get better." We were both thinking that Fritz couldn't get worse. And we were both wrong. We realized this when we moved on to the next command.

Week 4: Down

On this command, dog should lie down instantly. This is taught by   14
giving the command, "Down!" and gently lifting the dog's front legs and sliding him into the down position. Fritz does not lie down unless he thinks it's time to sleep. My best tactic was to throw myself across his back, making it impossible for him to do anything but go down. But once I stood up, Fritz would also scramble back to his feet. I was getting close to hating him. This is the point where Joe stepped in and took the leash. He yanked it to the floor hard and fast. But only Fritz's head went down. Joe said, "He really does think he's a Doberman!" He continued holding the leash down and tight, sweat dripping from his face. Fritz threw up all over Joe's shoe and finally went down. He gave me a look that, I swear, said, "OK, enough games. I give up."

From that night on, his cooperative days outnumbered his uncoopera-   15
tive ones. He walks at my side in heel position—leash no longer wrapped around my legs. Trees and fire hydrants are no longer worthy of his attention. We even go jogging without tripping over each other. Of course, his mind is still that of a child, so I have to keep reminding and correcting him; but Joe thinks we have reached a tie. Fritz is no longer in the lead, but neither am I. With further time and practice *I* might be able to win.

Week 5: Come

Dog should come to you at once and sit down facing you. Fritz does this   16
quite well. He likes to be near me, so all he has to learn is to sit facing me.

Fritz has finally graduated from his first semester of dog training. I wish   17
I had the time to take him to the advanced class but I think Joe needs a rest. He is on his way to becoming an alcoholic after having Fritz for a student.

Sources

1. *American Educator Encyclopedia* (United Educators, Inc., Illinois, 1973).
2. Martin, Leda and Barbaresi, Sara. *How to Raise and Train a Miniature Schnauzer* (New Jersey, T.F.H. Publications, Inc. Ltd., 1971).
3. McCoy, J. J. *The Complete Book of Dog Training and Care* (Toronto, Longsmans Canada Limited, 1962).
4. Pearsall, Milo and Charles, Leedham. *Dog Obedience Training* (New York, Charles Scribner's Sons, 1979).
5. Joe Kelly, trainer, Greater Saginaw Dog Obedience School, Saginaw, MI (interview).

LARRY LEVY'S COMMENTARY

In third grade "good writing" meant "good penmanship." In seventh grade it meant "correct grammar." In eleventh grade it meant "thesis supported by three supporting details."

All of these definitions are true. And yet they are, of course, incomplete.

Many of the college freshmen I meet understand these definitions even if they are not always able to write neatly, conventionally, or coherently. They are accustomed to doing exercises and handing in assignments and getting grades. Most have not learned that "having to say something and having something to say are not the same thing." They are often puzzled—attracted and scared—by references to some "greater or higher good" that may lurk in the dark waters of College Comp. They may suspect it's time to push out from the shore of the well-dotted "*i*" and the firmly punctuated sentence. But where to?

Where we voyage next is toward that "good" where one writes not to fill up an eight-by-eleven page so that no awful blank lines accuse, nor to fill an unexamined thesis with unexamined supporting detail. We move beyond the size of the paper, beyond counting words or paragraphs, and beyond deductive formulas. We write not to collect grades, ultimately, but to delight and instruct ourselves and our readers. Failing in this, it really doesn't matter how many correct commas we use or how clearly we subordinate clauses.

I knew one freshman student who could spell and capitalize with the best. But when I asked what she might like to discover more about for a researched writing, she replied she'd like to "do abortion." Pause for a long silence from the teacher: Had she had one? Was she contemplating having one? Had someone close to her had one?

"Well," I finally asked, "why would you like to 'do abortion'?"

"Well," she shrugged, "I think there might be a lot on it in the library."

How right she was. It was all there . . . almost all there . . . well, for serious purposes, maybe it was not there at all.

"Many officials, when faced with a request for a research grant," wrote Senator William Proxmire, "fail to ask themselves the simple question, 'Who really cares what the answer to this investigation is?' Sometimes the answer obviously is 'No one.'"

So Jean Nerio's essay called "Fritz'" grew out of a procedure that began with my thoughts about students "doing abortion" and about assignments I'd fulfilled in high school and college: debates on causes of the Civil War or explications of characters in Melville, topics—not questions at all, really—that had been well researched by others before me whose writings were well known to my teacher and, in fact, placed on reserve in the school library so I could go and "find my own answers" and arrange them in a coherent and correctly documented essay using no fewer than x footnotes and sources.

Yet, it wasn't until I'd assigned a few papers of the same type that I began to wonder if this was the best way to promote or encourage good writing. Had I been telling my teachers, my only other readers, anything new about slavery? And what surprising things were my students telling me about Queequeg?

As student-writers we weigh all sorts of issues, however moot, and are always maintaining the serious implications of all of them, even if we're not sure to whom they matter. We become like those precocious school debaters who can pull all sorts of file card stats and quotes out of their drawers and defend or reject any argument, always keeping the subject at arm's length from their lives and the lives of those around them.

I wanted another kind of project, a challenge to traditional notions of researched student writing. I wanted more than a college-level cut and paste, more than education in neutral gear. It seemed to me that encouraging students to ask crucial questions about the everyday situations their lives presented was a better approach, and I hoped for questions about the kind of school and work and home and society they were living in or expected to be living in. I feared that the students might at first (or at last) hear no difference between my designs for them and the designs of countless other teachers who had assigned topics they thought controversial and worthy. I suspected there was something riskier and therefore more rewarding in having students decide for themselves what sort of question was worth asking, worth seeking answers to that might be worth sharing, paying attention to, and acting on. In short, I wanted students to develop a response beyond stereotype and mass culture to their own questions. I wanted them to see in their school work and ultimately in school itself possibilities for liberation.

"Fritz" may not be what some teachers expect or require in college writing. It does not pose profound questions or explore values. It does not weigh mighty pros and cons on anything. It is not a "hot" topic like abortion or the Alaskan pipeline.

But "Fritz" for me is good writing. It is good not because it is well-edited, typed, and of appropriate length but for the following reasons:

1. *The Author's Commitment.* "Fritz" is not about what others have done or what Jean might do. It is not about dogs in the abstract, not about Platonic schnauzers. It is about one dog whose dead weight the author has dragged to training school and then dragged home. That has its funny side and its maddening side. Jean tries, really tries, to articulate both aspects of her subject.

2. *The Author's Honesty.* Jean looks steadily at the truth of Fritz, making him neither more loyal nor more heedless than he really was. At the search's end, she calls a truce: Though he walks at her side, Fritz definitely requires post-grad work.

3. *The Author's Use of Detail.* Jean understands that we do not know her dog, and therefore can't appreciate why she might enroll him in obedience class. She understands that we don't know what such classes are like or how they work, so she takes us along on her five-week journey. She does not *tell* us Fritz is "obnoxious" or "growing more polite." Instead, she attempts to *show* what it's like to live with a high-strung dog and how, after training, he begins to ignore trees and hydrants. She wants us to see and hear the important things she has seen and heard.

4. *The Author's Control of Tone.* Jean demonstrates that sound research need not be dull writing; that light writing is not necessarily lightweight. Where bad writing may affect a self-important tone ("portentous" a teacher of mine called it), as if the author had returned from the grave to tell all, Jean is witty—but without being frivolous. She opposes the formal, institutional voice of dog training theory ("On this command, dog should walk close to your left side . . .") with the all too earth-bound response of one dog ("Fritz . . . didn't care if his head came off when I yanked the leash . . ."). Jean writes not to impress but to delight as well as to inform and instruct.

When I read "Fritz" to other freshmen writers, they usually laugh in the right places, respect the visibility of the lead-in and the search, and are a bit surprised at the paper's zest and originality. Imagine doing this for a term paper! Then they see that for all its fun, Fritz has an underlying seriousness. "What do you do with a high-spirited dog?" is her question. And she ends up with a position, even if she does not end up with an answer.

Jean is not writing as Eldridge Cleaver said he was in *Soul on Ice,* "to save" himself. Her essay is not what many English teachers might call a reflection of Jean's "authentic self." She does not concern herself consciously with values, with philosophical probing and defining. Indeed, there are times when I wonder whether on The Scale of Possible Questions (not to mention The Scale of Intelligent Life Forms) "Fritz" ranks very high. Couldn't Jean have written about something more socially or politically meaningful—like teaching illiterates to read, or campaigning against the hazards of waste dumps? Surely there's no shortage of ills needing scrutiny and correction, and surely someone with Jean's skills could be a valiant soldier against them. But then I wonder whose scale of values I'm thinking of anyway.

Other teachers and students will have doubts about this writing—as I do at times myself. But I suspect my doubts rise because I still have difficulty seeing what it is my students are trying to do, perhaps because I am still trying to turn them into imitations of myself.

Study Questions

1. A student who had read both Jean Nerio's "Fritz" and Larry Levy's commentary on it said,

    > I don't think this paper really investigates anything at all. I don't think Jean Nerio has anything like a real question she's writing to find out anything about. In fact the paper is over before it starts. She enrolls a dog in training school and it doesn't work. She just plays that for laughs, paragraph after paragraph. What does this writer really take on? What does she really learn? I think she's writing just to amuse her teacher.

    Another student responded by saying,

    > I think that's unfair. Jean Nerio isn't dealing with a lot of heavy issues no, but she isn't dull either. And she does have a question she's dealing with as Larry Levy says: What do you do with a high-spirited dog? I think she learned a lot doing this paper and shows it. Look at those sources she uses. She's writing for herself, not her teacher.

    What position would you take in this controversy?

2. Suppose the tone and manner of "Fritz" were not at issue with you as a reader. You accept Jean Nerio's choice of subject and her stance with it. How do you think she might improve her paper if she were to rewrite it? What specifically would you tell her to do to make "Fritz" a stronger piece of writing?

3. A student writing about Jean Nerio's "Fritz" and Larry Levy's commentary on it said,

    > This is the only example of an I-Search paper I've ever read. But to judge just from what Jean Nerio does and the way Larry Levy explains it, it looks to me as though the I-Search paper doesn't help students learn about much more than a subject. What does it teach them about writing?

    How do you respond to this question?

JOHN MELLON'S Assignment

English Composition I Proficiency Examination

Choose one of the following topic questions and write a carefully organized, multiparagraph essay in which you discuss one or more possible answers to the question and argue its/their reasonableness. You will be judged on the quality of your writing skills and thinking processes and not on the position you take. You have two hours in which to complete your essay. Plan carefully before you begin, and edit and proofread your essay before turning it in. Here are the topic questions:

1. How do you account for the fact that the United States has the highest rate of violent crime in the world?
2. and 3. (two additional "How do you account for" topic options)

⟋ Why America Has the Highest Crime Rate [Author unknown]

1   Of all the countries in the world, America has the highest crime rate. In spite of all the so-called advancements of our modern civilization, we are still struggling with the problem of crime in the streets. Why this is and how it can be alleviated is of prime concern to us all.

2   To begin with, America's violent history plays an important part in the level of crime today. The days of Jesse James, Wyatt Earp, and the general lawlessness of "the Old West" are glorified in our history books and in the public media. Glorified too, are the gangsters from the "Roaring 20's" era of our history. Who has not heard of Al Capone, John Dillinger, or the "St Valentine's Day Massacre"? All of these things have enmeshed themselves into our way of life and our national self-image.

3   Nothing is more important in contributing to violence in our country than violence on television and in the movies. Every day, people are exposed to hundreds of "simulated" violent crimes and think of it as entertainment. Media heroes such as Kojak, Starsky and Hutch, and Baretta are always involved in murder, dope-dealing, rape, and the inevi-

---

JOHN C. MELLON is Associate Professor of English and Chairman of the Program in English Composition at the University of Illinois at Chicago. He authored the first experimental investigation of sentence combining, *Transformational Sentence-Combining,* an NCTE Research Report (1969), and recently contributed the chapter "Language Competence" to the NCTE volume *The Nature and Measurement of Competency in English* (1981). For the past ten years he has served as consultant to the Writing Assessment Group of the National Assessment of Educational Progress, an information-gathering project of the United States government.

128

table fight scene. They are portrayed as vigilante heroes that always win the day using the violence that they claim to defend us from. These things play no small part in violence in the streets.

Another important reason for the prevalence of violent crime in this country is the availability of handguns. Inexpensive pistols known as "Saturday Night Specials" have contributed significantly to murders, aggravated assaults, and armed robberies. It is by their very inexpensiveness and availability that they are such a great problem to law enforcement officials. Handguns have yet to be effectively controlled and therefore our "right to bear arms" can be translated into the "right" to be mugged, shot, and even killed by handguns.   4

Many have argued that violent crime will not be reduced until the disparity in the distribution of our economic wealth is corrected. Robberies and armed assaults would be reduced if unemployment were lower and if living conditions in certain areas of our cities were improved. It is the frustration of being jobless and living in squalor that drives many to crime in order to provide stop-gap relief from the problems they face. If we must first correct these conditions to achieve relief from crime, then eliminating violent crime is most certainly a long range goal.   5

There are those who argue that one reason for crime in the streets is the lack of sensitivity on the part of the man in the street. Kitty Genovese, a woman who lived in New York, was robbed and murdered in front of a large crowd. No one made an effort to stop the criminal and no one offered first aid as she lay dying. Lack of sensitivity and compassion was certainly evident in this rather curious case of social apathy. It may have been due to the bombardment of violence in the papers and on television, producing a desensitizing effect on the general population. People just didn't want to be involved.   6

All of the above factors contribute to the level of violence in our land. It is essential to point out these causes so we may more quickly produce a cure. The more we know about the problem the easier we can locate the steps necessary to cure it. If this is the case, the first step to take is to care.   7

JOHN MELLON'S COMMENTARY

This essay is not artistic writing, nor does it convey a strong emotional message or a strikingly new perspective on its topic. Yet I think it is good writing, even very good writing, given its circumstances. For the essay is examination writing, test writing performed on demand to demonstrate competence in written argumentation. The college underclassman* who

---

*[Eds. Note: All attempts to identify the author of this essay have been unsuccessful. The teacher selecting it has chosen to refer to the undergraduate who wrote it as male.]

wrote it did so in two hours on an assigned topic not announced ahead of time, with no compositional aids other than a dictionary, knowing that his performance would be judged as a one-time test of his writing ability. In this test setting, the writer has produced a 600-word discussion cast in seven well-developed paragraphs simply begun and just as simply ended, mechanically almost flawless, and expressed in sentences of sensible content and mature form. While all of us should be proud to write as well under similar circumstances, none of us need aim for less.

Let me comment first on the essay's idea content. Looking at paragraphs 2 through 6, we can see that the writer has structured his argument upon three issues. Paragraphs 2 and 3 discuss violence in our national past and present, specifically the Old West and the twentieth-century gangster era, and contemporary violence perpetrated in movies and television by "vigilante heroes." The first issue, then, is the historical and cultural licensing of violence—not only is it permitted in America, it is in a sense "glorified." Then paragraph 4, by rehearsing certain facts about the widespread availability of handguns, brings in the issue of the means enabling the commission of violent crime—which is what easily available handguns are. Finally, we see that paragraphs 5 and 6 discuss factors motivating violence: joblessness and economic deprivation of the criminals themselves, together with a lack of sensitivity and of moral outrage and an unwillingness among third parties to act to prevent violence. The complete argument, then, begins with the traditions permitting violence, then gives the principal means enabling it, and concludes by discussing its psychological motivations.

Now there is nothing new about these ideas, yet they seem effective. One thing making them so is the logical order the writer has imposed upon them, as just discussed. Two additional things are his use of specifics and his ability to turn the direction of his thought unexpectedly. Paragraphs 2 and 3 make commonplace ideas seem important precisely because they feature the piling up of particular specific citations. The writer doesn't just mention the Old West and the Roaring 20's, then leave it to his readers to fill in the details. Instead, he cites Jesse James, Wyatt Earp (but not Doc Holiday, Billy the Kid, or Cole Younger), Al Capone, John Dillinger, and the St. Valentine's Day Massacre. He continues, citing Kojak, Starsky and Hutch, and so on. There is something about listing specifics that unfailingly captures one's reader. Specifics can make up for failure of inspiration, and they give sparkle to ideas that, left unparticularized, might fall flat. Paragraph 6 presents a different kind of specific, not the mention of a particular person or thing, but rather the narration of a particular happening—in this case the story of a robbery and murder that fits the point of the paragraph perfectly. It is well known enough to have a name—the Kitty Genovese murder—and to be recognizable as fact, yet not so well known as to blunt a retelling, which is what the writer provides to good effect in fleshing out his point in paragraph 6.

As for the unexpected turning of ideas, we see illustrations of this technique in the final sentences of paragraphs 4, 5, and 7. The idea expressed in the "therefore" clause at the end of paragraph 4 surprises us completely: the thought that our right to own handguns actually translates into our "right"—and here the quotation marks signal irony—to be mugged, shot, and killed by these same guns. The final sentence of paragraph 5 also turns unexpectedly, more towards the sardonic than the ironic, pointing out that if the correction of economic disparity is a precondition to the elimination of street crime, then the latter suddenly becomes "most certainly a long range goal." Finally, paragraph 7 brings the discussion to closure by raising its focus from causes of violent crime to questions of a cure. Then in the final sentence the writer raises the discussion to still another level, pointing out that, just as knowledge must precede a cure, so must caring precede the quest for knowledge. The writer ends on this point, creating an effective turn—the kind of thing many teachers refer to as "ending with a new twist."

As for his beginning and ending strategies, the writer has chosen a simple, almost spare approach. Thus we cannot tell whether he knows about artful and attention-getting introductory tactics such as questions, narrative fragments, lists of key words, and remote or bizarre generalizations. But the writer is clearly in control of the writing process, and avoids the trap fallen into by many beginning writers, namely, stating one's main points, and thus giving them away, in one's introductory paragraph. Here the writer begins by recasting his topic question in declarative form. Thus, the essay introduces its subject and takes the first step towards being self-contextualizing. The second sentence contrasts the incidence of crime with advancements in other areas of modern civilization, thereby confirming the fact that America's high crime rate is indeed the topic of the essay. The third sentence then raises the issue of cause—"why this is"—in such a way as to suggest that the causes of crime will be the focus of the upcoming discussion. The phrase "how it can be alleviated" perhaps seems out of place, since we soon learn that the writer has no plans to discuss this question at all—except to use it as a tag in closing. The writer ends his discussion with the point that knowing about the causes of violent crime is a necessary first step in the search for a remedy. A fairly self-evident statement, its function is one of closure, and the "new twist" it gives signals the end of the essay.

Something else I regard highly in this essay is the writer's handling of transitional links between paragraphs. "To begin with," he says in paragraph 2, and we know exactly what is happening. The same holds for the phrase starting paragraph 4, "Another important reason." Paragraphs 5 and 6 employ a different kind of transition, in the clauses "Many have argued that . . ." and "There are those who argue that. . . ." The semantic function of these transitions is to signal the start of a new line of argument, just as their syntactic function is to provide a frame ("argued that ———") into which a summary statement introducing the argument can be inserted. Then in paragraph 7 the phrase "All of the above factors" acts as a summarizing transition collecting the writer's several lines of argument in a single phrase about which appropriate concluding statements can be made. Even in paragraph 3, which seems to lack an obvious transitional phrase, we see that the entire first sentence serves to reiterate the topic. That is, it restates the entire essay topic, more or less as a clue to the odd reader who may have missed the topic announcement the first time around. Topic reiteration is appropriate early in an essay, and is analogous to topic summarization late in an essay. Overall, the writer provides a strong line of cohesive linkage between and among paragraphs. Readers are unlikely to lose their way in anything he might write.

Finally, I admire the writer's sentence structure, vocabulary, and style. Statistically, his essay consists of 33 independent clauses averaging 18 words each, and 48 clauses of every kind averaging just over 12 words each. Both of these averages are considerably higher than those typical of expository writing in general, and result from this writer's frequent and quite proficient use of coordinated structures within his independent clause—18 times, in fact, 6 of which join three or more elements, mostly in the early paragraphs, where the writer piles up the specific detail with which he illustrates his main points. In the later paragraphs the predominant structural relationship changes from coordination to logical subordination, of which we count eight instances: two temporal (until, as), one illative (therefore), one purposive (so), and four conditional (if). The writer's vocabulary is similarly quite mature. Words like *alleviated, enmeshed, simulated, vigilante, disparity, squalor, compassion, apathy,* and *desensitize* identify their user as a person having the resources of language at his command, yet nowhere do they seem ostentatious or intended merely to "score points." Stylistically the writer is also proficient. The triadic parallels in which he repeatedly coordinates his specific illustrations ("Jesse James, Wyatt Earp, and the general lawlessness") are impressive, as is the inversion in paragraph 2, "are glorified. . . . Glorified too are . . . ," as well as the rhythmic patterns of sentences within paragraphs such as 7. All in all, the language of this essay is nicely crafted—never lame or leaden or show-offish, but competent and effective, with just a touch of class.

Study Questions

1. A classroom exchange followed a reading of this student essay and John Mellon's commentary on it. One student remarked,

> I don't see how anybody could say that writing that isn't artistic or emotional or original is "very good writing." This paper seems like it was produced by a formula. It reads like "Paper A" back in Chapter 2.

Another student responded by saying,

> John Mellon doesn't call it "very good writing" just that way. He says it's very good writing under the circumstances, given the student's situation. He doesn't say it isn't original either. I think he's saying that the originality of this paper is a matter of how well somebody can move as a writer inside very narrow limits. If this writer had tried to bare his soul in this examination, he'd have hung himself.

What seems to be at issue in this exchange? What is your position on this issue?

2. In writing about this student essay, another student wrote,

> It's strange. I didn't enjoy reading this paper on crime in America very much. I thought it was dull and obvious. But at the same time I think this writer is a very good writer and that he could write things I would like a lot. I think he'd write fiction particularly well.

Explain why you agree or disagree with that student's statement.

3. Suppose it were your responsibility to train someone to write what John Mellon calls "test writing performed on demand," test writing that would be judged "very good writing, given its circumstances." What sorts of things would you try to teach this person to do? What do you hope would be the results of your teaching?

RICHARD OHMANN's Assignment

[The assignment that my student's paper addressed was to interview someone about their job. As my essay makes clear, the interviews I had the students of my class conduct were part of a sequence of assignments in which students were developing and pursuing questions as a group. We were focusing on satisfaction and dissatisfaction at work—basically exploring issues of alienation.]

∽ [Untitled]

by Jim Varney

1   *"I want to help people on the streets. . ."*

2   Arthur Brent is a Rodney Dangerfield who seems not to worry about getting no respect. He has been around—seven years in the Air Force, unemployed for a year and a half, a bartender in several places, and, for the last seven years, involved in one of America's most enigmatic social institutions, pornography. Today he is the proprietor of an adult bookstore (*"In the phone book under 'A,' "* he'll tell you, *" 'A' for adult."*) in Brandon, Conn. He speaks in an earnest voice with an even more earnest face as if everything he told you was not only of profound importance, but entirely justifiable as well.

3   *"I've always had an interest in porn. Before I became employed here, I'd been into buying. You see I used to be a bartender and I became an alcoholic. I've been drying out for a while now and I'm better. Anyway, the guy who interviewed me for this job had been a bartender.*

4   *"I'm really not your typical person behind the counter of an adult bookstore. I enjoy satisfying people's wants and needs, my job helps me solve their problems. A guy will come up to me and say, 'I can't get it up,' and I'll help him out. It's a peer counseling sort of thing.*

5   *"I deal with a fantasy. I provide pictures for masturbation fantasies. I allow people to vent their anger and frustration, soothe sexual repression that may have occurred in childhood. You see, porn is educational for many people. For example, marriage counselors send clients to buy dildoes. Even doctors refer to me. This job is part of a community service."*

6   Arthur Brent talks in front of a table with neatly stacked dildoes that he constantly refers to as "health aids." Behind him is a kaleidoscope of pictures beckoning to his customers with lewd smiles, magazines in rows and rows glistening in plastic wrappers. In the background is the faint, incessant hum of peep show cameras ("Changed Weekly," the ad cries

RICHARD OHMANN teaches English and American studies at Wesleyan University. He has helped write two textbooks on composition. His most recent book is *English in America: A Radical View of the Profession* (1976).

outside the store). A flock of somber, almost determined looking men cluster around the lit frame telling them what is playing in what booth. New shipment mags spill out of their boxes displaying the enticing titles: ———— and ————.*

"I want to get out of here. I'm bored. I don't get turned on unless I shoot my own stuff. I can't find a challenge here, but I do like the paycheck (he informs me that he is 'very well paid'). It's just the same problems and the same people. 7

"You see, porn is really an upper middle class luxury. A good deal of my clientele are white collar. (He nods at a man in a pinstripe suit furtively glancing about trying not to use up his fifteen minute browsing limit too quickly.) 8

"Now, I want to get into social work, work that does not pay much. I'm tired of drunks. This place is an underground meeting place for gays, men that are looking for a quick, no-strings sexual contact. Most of them are married and have kids." 9

Arthur Brent, for the sixth time since the interview began, gets up and turns a man's one, or two, dollars into four, or eight, rounded, twenty-five cent satisfaction pieces. He returns to discuss his views on porn as a beneficial cog in society. 10

"I don't have any bad feelings about what I do. I think porn should be more available but controlled. Ten percent of the business is all the mob does not own. You see, if the age of consent is sixteen, then the age for legal exposure to porn should be sixteen (the law is eighteen in Conn.). 11

"What I want to do is help people on the streets. Kiddie porn? All I can say is it keeps kids off the street." 12

Arthur Brent, with an almost defiant expression, listens to a description of "Under 21," a home designed for runaways by Father Bruce Ritter, which has become a 24-hour haven for kids ravaged by New York street life. Ritter has seen teenagers, bereft of heads and hands, lying in a puddle of blood in the doorway of "Under 21's" main outpost on the butt-sprinkled, booze-and-urine-stained streets of Times Square and 42nd. Daily, he deals with sexually violated fourteen-year-olds, and sixteen-year-olds with rearranged facial designs. He watches each night when teenagers hustle themselves to survive, only to be beaten by pimp and john alike. He sees this. I've seen this. And when you think about it, so have we all. 13

"Look, first of all you've got to understand that it isn't as bad as the people against it say it is. I know this business and kiddie porn is not that bad. 14

"I met a fourteen-year-old who was in the streets. I set him up with a guy in 15

*At the publisher's request, Jim Varney and Richard Ohmann have agreed to omit the names of the magazines. The titles are obscene, and the publisher is concerned that their presence might keep *What Makes Writing Good* out of some college classrooms. —R. O.

New York who could get him hustling himself at a bar. I found that kid a channel to get money. Believe me, I didn't do it until I called his parents and found out he was a total deadbeat. They wouldn't even take him back. I helped him out. I got him a job hustling. I found someone to take care of him."

Arthur Brent, social worker. I hope to God he's lying.   16

"I know it's hard to morally justify my position . . ."   17

With a tainted notebook, I left his store. Walking up the butt-   18
sprinkled street in Brandon, I saw the sky was murky. I wanted to go home and I wanted to stay home. Arthur Brent's distorted philosophy rang in my ears . . .

"Look, if the kids can understand sexuality then they can do it. You have to   19
be sexually mature about this and if they like what they're doing, what's wrong with it?

"This fourteen-year-old I told you about? He got raped at that 'Under 21'   20
place. It was the most traumatic thing that ever happened to him."

Well, I guess that is right. Think how much better it is to be given a   21
job hustling yourself. At least it will keep you off the streets.

RICHARD OHMANN'S COMMENTARY

The editors of this book asked me to explain what makes this piece of writing good. They expected to get many different kinds of writing from students, and many different ideas from teachers about "what makes writing good." I'm all for that—I'd be glad if this book banished forever the notion of *the* essay, or of *the* five-paragraph theme with an introduction and conclusion and three supporting paragraphs in the middle, each with a topic sentence. Who needs such dogma? Maybe beginners, but how can you be a beginner when you've been in school for thirteen years?

Still, I'm cantankerous enough to balk at saying what makes Jim Varney's interview good. Wouldn't that foster the idea that somebody (me, in this case) knows what the gods have legislated about good writing? So I'll put my case a little differently: I'll say something about why *I* like Jim's effort. But I don't want to back away into a fog of relativism; I'll also say that I would bet most of you will like the piece too, and that I hope you do.

Why? Let's start with small things: deft touches like the "twenty-five cent satisfaction pieces," or like the contrast of "lewd smiles" in the "kaleidoscope of pictures" with the "somber, almost determined looking men" inspecting the bill of fare. Jim makes you see the store and feel its atmosphere; he does that quickly. He sketches Arthur Brent quickly, too—a few facts about his past, his present situation, his tone and demeanor as he speaks. Then Brent's own words do the rest, with their cool line of self-justification, their non-sequiturs, their contradictions. Jim stands back for a while, interrupting only to remind you of the social scene around this conversation, elaborating it each time he does so.

He lets his material speak for itself—or does he? It may seem that way, but actually, the presentation of images from the store and the selection from and arrangement of Brent's words are artful and economical. This is not "just" a piece of experience, rendered as it happened. We argued in class about such issues: Is it fair to choose and reorder the interviewee's words? To paraphrase when you didn't get it all down on tape or notepad? To interject comments that, inevitably, present the speaker through the screen of your interpretation? I believe that there are no fixed answers to such questions. This kind of writing bristles with ethical problems, and they are inseparable from the problems of craft that Jim handles so skillfully.

For instance, the alternation of Brent's words with Varney's is more than just efficient. Though Jim introduces pornography in a neutral way—"one of America's most enigmatic social institutions"—and doesn't really begin to let his own judgments show until he introduces the subject of "Under 21," he has, in fact, shaped the interview toward a judgment. Jim quotes Arthur Brent on "community service," and then Jim describes the stock of dildoes behind him. We move from the obscene titles of the magazines to Brent's statement that he's bored—"unless I shoot my own stuff." What kind of a guy is this?, the transitions make us ask.

Jim does not withhold an answer. That's another thing I like about this write-up. The subject is morally loaded, and Jim lets his values show plainly by the end, in disgust and irony ("With a tainted notebook"; "Arthur Brent, social worker"). I like that sort of commitment. Some in the class did not. They wished Jim and other classmates would stay more within a reporter's role: just give the news, please. This and other interviews gave us a chance to explore the vexed question of objectivity. Is there such a thing? Should someone who is writing about people aim for it? Do the writer's judgments belong in the writing, or should readers be allowed to form their own judgments?

Of course, Jim was writing about more than just one unusual person. Through the interview, he posed questions about pornography and the whole subculture of marginal and illegal sex, especially as it involves kids. I like that about Jim's write-up, too. It is beautifully concrete; it places you right in that adult book store, hearing Brent's words, feeling the tension that grows between him and Jim; but it also reaches out from this unique scene to some abstract issues of morals and social policy. I like this kind of interchange, in writing, between the particular and the general, much more than I like either without the other.

There are, naturally, things in Jim's writing that I'd question—the beginning and the end, for instance. Don't Rodney Dangerfield and his famous cliché throw out a wrong direction signal? That first sentence looks to me like a too-easy grab for the reader's attention. And the irony of the final sentence strikes me as too obvious—and as anticlimactic, since it just repeats what Brent himself has said. I could mention other things I'd red-pencil. But the main objection I'd put to Jim is that he doesn't really give an ear to Brent's argument about the social uses of porn. We may not accept the argument, but it doesn't sound stupid or contemptible to me. That is, until Brent gets to kiddie porn. Jim picks up that remark and responds with a horrendous picture of damaged street kids and the social sewer of Times Square. But he has made a big leap: Is pornography—even kiddie porn—*responsible* for all that despair and violence? I can see why Arthur Brent got defensive at this point. The interview presents Arthur's "philosophy," but puts it down too easily, I think, closing off a debate that many consider to be wide open. (I do.)

Still, I don't mind disagreeing with what I read, nor does Jim shrink from an argument. I like writing that provokes argument, not of the debating society kind, but argument that springs from moral commitments and from the real conflicts in our society. That's one reason I began encouraging this kind of writing a few years ago. It takes us—me and all the students—out of the socially homogeneous world of the college classroom (more homogeneous at Wesleyan, probably, than at some colleges) and into parts of the society where the world looks different. One advantage of doing interviews is the variety of social experience they bring, and the challenges to lightly held ideas.

It was hard to choose Jim's interview for this collection, powerful as it is. I remembered so many others: Paul Duke's interview with an educated, "new breed" rookie cop, who nonetheless spoke of "nigger problems" and said, "I won't hold it back; I'm prejudiced"; Jennifer Hilliard's series of interviews with rape victims, and one—done in prison—with a convicted rapist; Diana DeJoseph's interview with an openly and proudly gay student; David Ryan's and Anthony Jenkins's scary, two-hour interview with the leader of the Ku Klux Klan in Connecticut. We all learned from these and from the debates they provoked. There's a society outside the classroom, and writing can be a means of exploring it.

The subject of a good interview doesn't have to be a cop or a criminal. I remember a fascinating set of interviews with some of the richest and poorest students at our college. I remember many more with very ordinary people, a series about work at and around Wesleyan, for example, with secretaries and custodians and deans and security guards and (even) professors. One class did interviews while we were reading Studs Terkel's

Working and discussing the repetitiveness, pain, stupidity, and humiliation of so many jobs. Most of the workers at our college didn't feel that way. Why not? The interviews made good reading (and many of them were printed in one of the college newspapers), but just as important, they allowed the class to pursue some tough questions about work and self-respect in our society. That questioning is a source of satisfaction in this kind of writing class: Students develop ideas and questions from books and from their own experience; they go out to test, document, and elaborate these ideas through interviews; the write-ups become a pool of information for class discussion and a body of research for the writing of analytic papers; and those papers lead to new questions for new interviews. The inquiry builds.

When it works well, such a class can turn into a collaboration in which everyone contributes to and learns from a growing fund of knowledge—and from disagreements. The students can make the writing their own: not a series of assignments, but papers that address questions important to the writers, which they have themselves developed. And matters of style, organization, and logic become urgent because they affect the ways that human beings and social issues come across to one's classmates (collaborators/audience/antagonists). Of course the class doesn't always work well. But if it turns sour, at least it will have produced some pieces of writing that were interesting and that lodge in the memory, like Jim Varney's. For an English teacher, believe me, interest has much to do with which writing seems good.

[*Note:* I have changed "Arthur Brent's" name, and there is no town in Connecticut named Brandon. Jim Varney, however, is a real person, doing a senior thesis now on the German invasion of the USSR. I didn't teach him to write; he could do that quite well before I met him.]

Study Questions

1. In a classroom exchange over Jim Varney's paper and Richard Ohmann's commentary on it, one student said,

> I don't think that the writer's values in this piece show only at the end. The whole interview is rigged from the start. Jim Varney has a right to his commitments and all that, but he doesn't have a right to pretend to investigate what he really doesn't look into at all. Richard Ohmann notices some of this, but he doesn't seem to call the writer on very much of it. Is this because Jim Varney is committed in the way he is rather than just being committed? It seems to me that if you're really trying to get people to use writing to explore "a society out there," you can't praise writing that refuses to do that.

How do you respond to these remarks?

2. Suppose Jim Varney were to decide to rewrite his paper with the intention of staying more within what Richard Ohmann calls "a reporter's role."

What would he have to change?

What might be the result of his making these changes?

3. "This kind of writing," says Richard Ohmann of the interview as a mode, "bristles with ethical problems"—a number of which he lists as questions. There is, however, apparently no agreed-upon classroom policy about these "ethical problems": "I believe," Richard Ohmann says, "there are no fixed answers to such questions."

How do you respond to the position Richard Ohmann has assumed by making such a remark?

Until now you have been narrating events which you have singled out of your memory because they make good stories. For example, last week you wrote a narrative about a childhood injustice, and the week before one about a confrontation with an authority figure. Today's assignment extends your responsibilities as a writer.

I am asking you to write about a first or last experience. Since this is likely to be a memorable experience that has been of some consequence in your life, you will need to present it in the wider context of your life. Consider all of the following questions. Write answers to three of them for Tuesday. Your writing may take the form of freewriting, or it may be more structured; in any case, come to class prepared to read what you've written. The essay is not due until a week from Tuesday.

Why was this occasion the first (last) one? Was there a precipitating cause?

What was the series which was marked by this first (last) event? Did later (earlier) events remain in your mind as impressively?

What was your life like before this event? after this event? (You may not need to answer both.)

Did this first (last) event come as a surprise to you? Were you searching for something to begin? struggling for something to end? Describe that search (that struggle).

Who else figured in this memorable occasion?

Did the occasion bring you happiness? sadness? Why?

Does the occasion provide you with an opportunity to portray yourself at a particular age? to describe a special place? a particular group of people? (Write one of these descriptions.)

Can you generalize from this experience some truth that you learned which would be of value to other people? Write your generalization. Would your essay be more interesting with this generalization expressed or omitted?

❧ My First Love   by Louise Kramer

As I played with my dolls, thoughts of love danced through my mind. I   1
laid in my bed dreaming of the male would be my Sir Lancerlot or my
Robin Hood and I would be his fair maiden, the dreams that I were

SANDRA SCHOR teaches English at Queens College, where she has been Director of Composition and Director of the Queens English Project—a program in high-school/ college articulation under an award from the Fund for the Improvement of Postsecondary Education. Named a "Master Teacher" at CUNY, she is currently training colleagues from other disciplines to teach basic writing. She publishes poems, stories, and articles, is the author (with Judith Fishman) of the Random House Guide to Writing, (2nd ed., 1981), and is at work with Frederick Crews on The Borzoi Handbook for Writers.

dreaming had me wondering what kind of man I would fall in love with. Would he be a rich intelligent person sensitive enough to understand my feelings or would he be a poor honest, hard working man too tired to even think I had any needs other than eating and sleeping. Would his morals run to the underground life of crookedness or would his morals be of higher standards. I realized as the time passed that there are many different kinds of love and this confused me more than I was. Yet the dreams never stopped the searching and questioning of, "Would I ever be in love, except with love". The answer I longed for seemed to be taking forever. God! I prayed let him come before I shrivel up and die a lonely old maid. For I am but a honest hard-working girl, wanting to feel special and beautiful and fully fulfilled as a woman. I feel my body budding and blooming in area's I did not think would bloom. Each day I awake to a new discovery about myself. I keep changing within as my body changes on the outside. Gee! God? does this happen to all young people longing to find love. I find myself confused even more so as my dreams change.

2   The familer young men in my dreams are suddenly becoming older, more mature and seem to be treting me in a different way. My waking hours I suddenly find the same things happening and I being young and naieve cannot grasp what it is that I have that men are now finding attractive. I cling to Dad for protection and Mom for reassurance that I'm still a little girl in many ways. My older brother introduces me to men that are his friends and yet that yearning keeps returning. All I dream of is how I would like to run wild in the fields of the mountains I have explored as a child. I lazily drift in the colors of the butterflys as they dance in mid-air, as I watch from my tower of concrete. I wander in my dreams from men to men and hesitate to ask the question that seems the most important one to me, "Will I be loved gently and kindly that by my early twenties I still wanted only to be involved in my mind.

3   My parents by this time felt it was time I had a more meaningful relationship to where I would eventually have a marriage. I had other plans that seemed more important to a daring young romantic such as myself and I couldn't see myself so young strapped down to a family as some of my friends were at the ages of sixteen and seventeen. My world consisted of worlds I haven't even seen except in the books I have read and movies I have seen. I felt guilty not wanting to follow the norm at the time and this was to get married. Family and friends all agreed marriage would be the answer to my searching questions to the yearning.

4   Off I went scouting. The young men I liked did not stir any feelings except the feeling of liking. Older men seemed to be attracted to me but I wasn't sure about them either, yet they pampered and adored me. Being naive I could not accept these feelings for it was reserved in my mind only for mother, from father and this I would never get from Dad.

The push was on to get me out of the nest.   5

Deciding the answer to my question was just to find that 'All Ameri-   6
can Guy' with a promising future. I flirted and pretented until I found
someone whom I thought would fit into all my ideals about a man
including my dreams. He was tall, good looking, poliet, well spoken,
protective, quiet and hard working, he seemed to me the best prospect.
We married almost immediately after his return from duty in the service.
I felt this charming young man could be trusted with my tender feelings
that I held back for so long tho when he kissed me I did not hear the
wedding bells nor tingle when he touched me. The romantic description
that I would hear so much about still had not happen to me. Our need for
one another in many ways took prefence. We married at twenty-one and
by twenty-two were about to be parents.

The day came when I gave birth to our daughter, tiny, helpless and so   7
very beautiful to me. It was then that I fell in love so completely for the
first time in my life.

Sandra Schor's COMMENTARY

No narrative is a complete record of events. But good narrative gives the
illusion of completeness. A narrator's impulse to completeness is a measure of how much of the narrative must be told to satisfy a listener or
reader. Louise's narrative, imperfect though it is, outwits our need for
completeness. Furthermore, it relieves our need for another kind of
wholeness: the unflawed surface of Standard Written English. The fragmented surface of her prose (profuse misspellings, incoherent sentences,
merged structures, redundancies, failure to punctuate, mistaken verb
forms, inconsistent pronoun reference, inconsistent verb tense) takes
little away from her success in conveying that illusion of completeness.
Louise's control of narrative structure *counters the roll* of opposing
forces—in this case the sweep of substandard grammatical forms and the
passion to tell everything.

Rodin, asked once how he would make an elephant, replied, "You
start with a large block of marble and then you remove everything that is
not an elephant." You may have discovered, as Louise has, that as a
writer you exceed Rodin's method. The writer removes not only what is
not elephant but also as many features that *are* elephant as a reader can
willingly surrender without losing the illusion of completeness. Louise's
intuition about structure, reinforced by classroom work that focuses on
wholeness, means that she understands what to include and what to
omit. She understands that her piece of writing is best served by permitting certain lacunae to exist in the telling. Good narrative begins in-

stantly, by intimations of wholeness, often as early as the first clause, to render the reader incomplete; finally, methodically, despite and often because of its omissions, it renders the reader complete.

In part, Louise owes her success to the tension of her two-part structure: a dream of love (unknown/unreal/incomplete) and the fulfillment of that dream (known/real/complete). Her intuition and skill prepare the reader for the power of the brief final paragraph. All of the previous text records the failed romantic expectations of her narrator, "I." The emotion that "I" denies herself throughout the account of her search finally belongs to the reader—upon the swift realization of love in the birth of the child. We readers, having ourselves been completed, complete the text.

Like alert readers of any strong text, we are aware of an enveloping wholeness from the outset. For one thing, the title tells us that this discourse will reveal the nature of this writer's "first love." Immediately, Louise's opening sentence introduces us to the governing tension: the outer life of "I" (playing with dolls) and the inner life ("thoughts of love danced through my mind"). Icons of Sir Lancelot, Robin Hood, and "fair maiden" quickly are unmasked by her anxiety about life's unwholesomeness, against which her dreams are played: "I" wonders about her unknown beloved, "Would his morals run to the underground life of crookedness . . . ?" And later in that first paragraph, a sweeping introduction to her confusion, she adopts the less interesting language of penny-dreadful novels and TV soaps: "I am but a honest hard-working girl, wanting to feel special. . . . I keep changing within as my body changes on the outside."

By means of a deft transition at the end of paragraph 1, ". . . I find myself confused even more so as my dreams change," she moves forward in time with the sureness of a Nadine Gordimer, unwilling to waste the reader's time in getting from here to there. "The familer young men in my dreams are suddenly becoming older. . . ." Since the inner life of a romantic dominates the outer life, "I" confirms her romantic nature and uses her dream life as if it were a lens left in the heat of passion to intensify her real-life longings: "My waking hours I suddenly find the same things happening. . . ." If fiction is about "people at the end of their rope," as Alfred Kazin has said it is, then Louise is making use of the techniques of fiction. For we detect a certain fraying of the nerves. Put another way, "I" has become a patient who will either recover or die.

Louise's "I" enters an interregnum—between child and mother—a period of a confused and unfulfilled sexuality. That same sentence about her waking hours flows on, picking up strength along a riverbed of unrecognizable feelings: "My waking hours I suddenly find the same things happening and I being young and naieve cannot grasp what it is that I have that men are now finding attractive." "I" is in possession of something, a magnet that attracts pleasure and love, but she deprives herself of its usefulness by her failure to recognize "what it is that I have." Louise inexpertly weakens that plain, beautiful statement by expressing in prolix adolescent imagery the reluctance of "I" to grow up: "running wild in the fields of the mountains" and drifting "in the colors of the butterflys as they dance in mid-air." Although these excesses lack adroitness, she knows the right moment for adolescent dreaminess. Many beginning writers have exquisite timing, but need skill to express with elegance what they have intuited.

She further senses that her "butterfly" writing demands concreteness, and she appropriately balances this sort of writing with the fairy-tale grimness of "I" watching from her "tower of concrete," the tower reifying a certain morbidity. She is a Rapunzel with hair still up. She experiences guilt at being unwilling at sixteen or seventeen to be "strapped down," an interesting word choice that merges *strapped* and *trapped*—the rigid norms of her life embedding the trap of domestic duty. She is also guilty of "not wanting to follow the norm." For those of us readers whose "norm" at sixteen or seventeen has been to graduate from high school, enter college, discover Mozart or Manet, confront sex, and move past outgrown friendships, "I" adroitly leaves us to infer a context for the "norm" she rejects.

At this point of inference, Louise is preparing us for a change of tone. Towards the end of paragraph 1, she carelessly slipped into a present tense, but now she returns to her governing past, abandoning the generalized, present-tense dreaminess of adolescence that dominates the first paragraph for a program of action in the past tense. "I" hints at a more perplexing anxiety in the paragraph about "older men" and their vaguely unwholesome sexual overtures. Notice that paragraph 4 begins with an emphatic rearrangement of normal syntax, "Off I went scouting," a business-like if ironic response to what the "norm" finally requires her to do: find a husband. But older men who pamper and adore her are unable to bring her to terms with what is expected of her. "I" continues to want "only to be involved in my mind." She continues to reserve sexual feelings for that dark pair of sexually alive shadows whom she formally refers to as "mother" and "father," finally allowing her feelings to devolve solely on "father": "this I would never get from Dad."

Enabling Louise to express order amid tension, the paragraph form provides a unifying framework for her sentences. In other writings submitted during the semester, as in earlier drafts of this piece, I discover that her unit of expression is the paragraph. This is interesting to me since I have long been persuaded by the writing of both basic and practiced students that the paragraph as a convention evades the composing mind, though it engages the revising mind. Louise's early drafts exhibit paragraphs that begin with a capital letter and flow forward to a period, all the discourse along the way punctuated by commas placed where periods ought to be. In those unrevised writings, the period is a super-period. Although in the draft published here she rarely inserts commas to set off sentences, her paragraphs retain their first-draft, period-free vigor and unity. (I am always on the alert that students not drain the vigor from their writing as they revise language and punctuation.)

In fact, notice the stabilizing force of the one-sentence paragraph, "The push was on to get me out of the nest." Having restated her "I" as a more passive "me," Louise does what William Labov says all naturally gifted storytellers do: she interrupts her narrative to admit the presence of an outside force.* I recall Labov's dramatic narration of an event in the words of a man involved in a barroom brawl over a woman; the narrator suddenly finds himself on the floor, a stranger peering down at him and saying, "Don't move. Your throat's been cut." For Louise and the reader, "The push was on . . ." is equivalent to that outside voice suddenly stabilizing the narrative with "Don't move. Your throat's been cut."

Throughout her narrative Louise uses the paragraph to provide movement in time. Thus, despite errors in tense, she clearly distinguishes the essentials of her narrative in sequence and permits the lacunae of her narrative to make their effect. The penultimate paragraph carefully lists the qualifications of her chosen bridegroom, qualifications that she erroneously believes will excite her romantic feelings. Within this paragraph she concentrates her faith that he could be "trusted with my tender feelings that I held back for so long." Her trust ends badly, inevitably it seems to us—although I suggest you think about how little we needed to know of the conditions that actually yield this inevitability. We are aware of the sexuality of a young woman and a young man, but the paragraph indulges in no descriptions of personal disappointment, no account of sexual frustration, no explicit failure. Failure is limited: "I" still "did not . . . tingle when he touched me." But, she says, "our need . . . took preference," and Louise drives her text, past this interestingly evasive and elliptical acknowledgment of sexuality, precipitously towards the expected child.

Finally, the obstetrical paragraph. I call it this not to be humorous but to introduce the presence of an efficient cause delivering "I" of her dilemma. This daringly economical paragraph has two sentences. The first holds the second in consequence. First, "I," in childbirth, witnesses the infant's beautiful helplessness. Then she falls in love "completely" for the first time. At this moment the reader suddenly sees that the narrator's

---

*I heard Labov make this point during a lecture on narrative at Queens College, March 24, 1983.

earlier search for love has been distinctly passive. Although "I" "flirted and pretended," these disingenuous actions required only superficial participation. We note that the "All American Guy," the "best prospect" who was "tall, good looking, poliet, well spoken, protective, quiet and hard working" put no demands on her. In the final paragraph she repudiates her own passivity. Love shifts from a custodial duty to an active power: she reverses herself, becoming that classic dynamo of one-way love—a mother.

In all writing—even in that of a writer as untutored as Louise—conscious literary triumphs are inseparable from unconscious ones. In the seamless product, effort is indistinguishable from luck. Such successes often single out the work of a strong beginner from other beginners. In this example, an intuitive sense of structure (reinforced by classroom attention to structure) holds Louise's remembered adolescent worlds firmly in place. Just as Hawthorne in his story "Wakefield" omits the scene in which Wakefield returns to his wife after disappearing from her for seventeen years and just as Melville in *Billy Budd* does not permit us to accompany Captain Vere into Billy's chamber after the trial, so Louise astutely pulls the shade on her unhappy marriage.

I am not suggesting that Louise's writing is ready for a wider audience. I am suggesting that students serious about learning to write—as Louise appears to be—are entitled to be strengthened by their strengths as they confront the continuing labors of learning to write the standard language. I have done what I could to make my student Louise aware of her uncommon ability to hold the reader by means of narrative structure. I argue that one of the standards of literacy is the power to possess the reader.

Study Questions

1. "Students serious about learning to write," says Sandra Schor, "—as Louise appears to be—are entitled to be strengthened by their strengths as they confront the continuing labors of learning to write the standard language."

   Suppose it were your responsibility to talk to Louise Kramer about her "strengths" as a writer. How would you try to describe them to her so that she might build on them?

2. "One of the standards of literacy," Sandra Schor argues, "is the power to possess the reader." But perhaps it is possible to gain another perspective on literacy by inquiring into what the act of writing can do for a *writer*.

   Though there's no way you can know for sure, judging from your reading of Louise Kramer's paper, how do you think she might respond to the question "What did you get out of writing that paper?"

Judging from the way you imagine Louise Kramer might respond to such a question, what do you infer that an attempt to be literate can do for a writer?

3. A student in a writing class said of the writing assignment given by Sandra Schor,

> I think that the questions Sandra Schor asks her students to address in this assignment run the risk of violating a student's privacy. There's no way a student could do the assignment without writing about something very personal. Students who *want* to do that I think should, but people who don't shouldn't be forced to.

Where do you stand on this reading of Sandra Schor's writing assignment and on the generalization the reading is used to support?

Writing Assignment 5
Taking a Stand

This time try your hand at writing an essay in which you make clear your position on something that is of interest to you, some proposition, say, or some state of affairs; your attitude toward a position taken by someone else; the significance or meaning of some process. Again, your teacher may give you more specific instructions. You may be asked to write with a particular purpose in mind, or to use a specific form, or to take a particular tone, and so on.

When you have finished writing your paper, on a separate page, write a paragraph explaining which of the *students* you've read in this chapter you think would like your essay best and why. You may assume that each of the five students represented is proud of what he or she has written. This part of the assignment will require you to make two inferences, you'll notice, but the process will be a bit different from the one you used in addressing Writing Assignment 3. The students represented in this chapter did not write papers in which they *say* what their standards are or why they're proud of what they've written. You'll need to work that out. You'll also need to work out the connections between what they've done and what you've done—just as you've had to in thousands of other situations in your life, whether your guesses were good or not. However you make your case, be sure you make clear why you choose the student you do over the others.

Finally, on another sheet of paper, write another paragraph, one in which you use both your *experience* in writing the paper you have just written as well as the paper itself to speculate on the value of being able to write a paper in which you take a stand, even if your guess about who might like it turns out to be not so good, turns out in fact to be wrong. Suppose, for example, the student that you say in the second part of this assignment *would* like your essay turned out *not* to like it at all. Suppose nobody liked it very much—including , finally, even you. What would you have then besides a mess on your hands, proof that you'd done nothing but waste your time?

Creating Lives

6

We tell ourselves stories in order to live. . . . We look for the sermon in the suicide, for the social or moral lesson in the murder of five. We interpret what we see, select the most workable of the multiple choices. We live entirely, especially if we are writers, by the imposition of a narrative line upon disparate images, by the "ideas" with which we have learned to freeze the shifting phantasmagoria which is our actual experience.

Joan Didion

ONE THING THAT IS SURE TO STRIKE you after reading the student essays in this chapter is that many of the essays from the other chapters might reasonably have been placed here. But if you stop to think about it for a moment, you'll notice also that most of the student essays in *this* chapter might easily have been considered in another. Which student essay here could not be seen as someone's way of taking a stand, or does not make use of description? Who in writing about a life does not attempt to come to terms with something and *vice versa*? Writing, particularly when defined by someone as good writing, is like that: it can be considered in a number of different contexts.

This chapter is entitled "Creating Lives" rather than, say, "Writing Biography" or "Writing Autobiography" as a way of preparing you for the focus of the writing assignment at the end. As you will see, the assignment does not focus on biography or autobiography as a literary form or genre, but rather on what it means to write about a life—either one's own or another's. What exactly does a writer do to write about a life? What's in it for someone to attempt such a thing?

The student essays and commentaries of this chapter will not provide you with the answers to these questions, but they can help you see why they are important questions for you to consider as a writer—and as more than a writer.

Write a biographical narrative about someone you know well. To be interesting, the subject should be someone who is important to you. The purpose here is not to produce an elaborate apparatus of footnotes and such, nor to demonstrate research skills, but, rather, to produce a rounded portrait of a life that will speak to your fellow students as well as to yourself and the instructor. Use as much detail as possible.

ᕕ My Father

by Kristin Martin

1   Lawrence Martin, my father, was born in San Diego on March 4, 1946. The youngest of the three children of Delza and Hubert Martin, he grew up in Kensington, an upper-middle class suburb. When my father was 8 or 9 years old, his father died. I have never been able to discern the effect that this had on him.

2   Raised in a relatively liberal household, my father developed pacifist opinions and musical talent. Over the years both of these passions grew.

3   I know little of my father's teenage years, only that he attended Hoover High School for three years and completed his high school education at the Boyden school near downtown San Diego. During these years, he was a member of the Hoover High wrestling team and an avid bicyclist.

4   My father met my mother during high school. They saw each other quite often though they lived quite a distance from each other and attended different high schools. When my father was 17 and my mother was 18 (and only one month away from her high school graduation) they were married. With the knowledge that a child was on the way, they were in the same position as so many other teenage parents, and were forced to change their lives forever.

5   After their marriage, my parents moved into a small, rented house on Jackdaw Street in Mission Hills. I was born in January 1964, just two months before my father's eighteenth birthday. Soon after my birth, they moved into a new apartment.

6   By this time, my father had become a very talented drummer, playing in several groups and giving lessons in his spare time. At the new apart-

MICHAEL HOLZMAN is currently Assistant Professor of English and Chairman of the Freshman Writing Program at the University of Southern California. He has published articles on writing in such journals as *College English* and *College Composition and Communication*. He organized the U.S.C./California Writing Project, directs the U.S.C. Model Literary Project, and is a consultant on writing to school districts and to the California Conservation Corps.

ment, my father held numerous "jam sessions" and unknowingly instilled an ear for music in his daughter. I have been told that I sang before I learned to talk. Perhaps there is some truth to this, considering this early musical influence.

My parents decided to go their separate ways and were divorced in 1965. My father moved to La Jolla, where he worked in a music store. I saw him every Sunday when we would go for walks around La Jolla or down to the beach. I have many memories of these times, like the night we went to see the Beatles movie "Yellow Submarine" at a drive-in.

These Sunday visits continued until 1969, when my father was drafted to fight in the Vietnam War. Since he did not believe in fighting in any kind of war, my father had two choices. One was to refuse to go, in which case he would go to prison. The second was to leave the country, in which case he would not be able to return, even to visit his family. Knowing that this was the turning point in his life, he chose to immigrate to Canada.

As soon as he arrived in Vancouver, British Columbia, my father found he was not alone. Several draft resisters and deserters had also come to live in Vancouver and all over Canada. After he found free shelter in a resisters' hostel, my father applied for "landed immigrant" status. This is a step which many draft resisters and deserters took because it entitled one to work in Canada and to receive unemployment and health benefits. The only privileges "landed immigrant" status denies are the right to vote in certain elections, to hold some government jobs, and to carry a Canadian passport.

After receiving "landed immigrant" status, my father went to work for the Committee to Aid American War Objectors (CAAWO). He counseled many draft resisters and deserters and helped run the hostel for several years, until he found his way into social work.

My father always puts what he believes in into his work. Whether he is producing a concert, working with juvenile delinquents, or talking with draft resisters, he has applied his principles to helping others.

His first government-sponsored job was as a musical therapist for retarded and emotionally disturbed children. By teaching them how to construct and play simple musical instruments, my father helped these children to gain a valuable creative outlet. At this time, he also worked on a youth recreation project in some low-income areas of the city. I still have a picture of him that appeared in the "Vancouver Sun" and "Newsweek". It depicts him dressed up as Santa Claus at a Christmas party for local kids, complete with his long hair and beard.

I first visited my father when I was eight, in 1972. He had changed so much since I last saw him, I didn't recognize him and even mistook him for a customs official. During my visit, my dad bought me almost everything I wanted, which resulted in me eating just about every junk-food item I saw and a 15-pound weight gain.

14   On my next summer visit, in 1973, I discovered that I had a new sister, Anais. My father had remarried and moved into a big house which they shared with another draft resister and his girlfriend. Jane, my father's new wife, was a cellist with the Vancouver Symphony. Since she only worked during the Symphony's season, she was home during my stay.

15   My father had also become involved in music again, having taught himself to play alto flute, C flute, tenor saxophone, and soprano saxophone.

16   During the summer of 1974, much talk was going around about a possible amnesty for the draft resisters. The CBS network contacted my father about appearing in a story they were producing on draft resisters in Canada. He agreed and was interviewed by Richard Threlkell for the CBS Evening News. This was during my third visit, and I was overjoyed to see myself, my father, and my sister on TV with good old Walter Cronkite. That same week, my father also appeared on two local news shows.

17   Working with the CAAWO, my father got his case cleared. This was quite a while before President Carter announced the pardon of draft resisters. Now my father was free to live in the U.S. Still, he had made the decision long before to remain in Canada, and to enjoy the life he had there. I had never resented his decision, because I knew he would come down to visit, and I think Vancouver is a beautiful city.

18   In 1976, my father moved on to another government job, this time working with juvenile delinquents. At first he counseled kids between the ages of 10 and 15, who had family problems or difficulties at school, but hadn't run into any serious trouble. It was also about this time that my father and Jane separated. A few months later he moved in with Ailsa Craig, an elementary school teacher. My father and Ailsa had Anais over during the weekends and holidays, and Ailsa took quite a liking to her.

19   Continuing in social work my father took a job dealing with hardcore juvenile delinquents in a "group home". Here they had many responsibilities and privileges, if they earned them. My father would take them to concerts, to the beach, and out to movies. He also had to use discipline to make sure they kept out of trouble.

20   Unfortunately, my father didn't use enough self-discipline. Through many circumstances, he lost his job at the group home. His long-time love for beer became alcoholism. After hearing everyone warn him to cut down on drinking for so long, he finally took action. He committed himself to an alcoholics' rehabilitation hospital on Vancouver Island. After three weeks, he had given up drinking. He hasn't had a drop of

alcohol since January 1981, which is amazing, given the amount he used to consume.

As of now, my father is working for the Social Concerns Project for Nuclear Disarmament. He is also producing local concerts and is still active in the CAAWO, most recently in the case of Ben Sasway. 21

Michael Holzman's COMMENTARY

Leslie Perlman has pointed out that a composition class is a real rhetorical situation, that it is a mistake to ask students to pretend that they are writing "as if" they were newspaper columnists or George Orwell or whatever other fantasy occurs to an instructor. It is easy to agree with Les about this, easy to find other reasons to abhor fictive writing tasks, but much more difficult to keep this in mind either while reading student writing or while trying to develop a satisfactory curriculum or writing program structure. The introductory course offered by the Warren College Writing Program at the University of California, San Diego, emphasizes writing in what its Director, Brooke Neilson, has called the informal register. Instructors there seek to give their students successful writing experiences by beginning with personal narratives that are developed—within the context of that course—for their own sake, and not, as is so often the case, as warm-ups for the "real" work of formal expository essays. The effect of this emphasis is that the papers tend to be vividly personal, often dealing with somewhat unusual situations. These young people are writing stories for one another, as they might actually tell one another stories, about their lives, about their families. They are told not to bore one another. Of course, this situation is still somewhat artificial. Teenagers probably do not frequently write autobiographical sketches for the entertainment of their friends. Even so, the audience is real, its demands are real, the written product is—dare one say it?—authentic. Kristin's paper was her final assignment for that introductory composition course. It represents her best work in the informal mode. In the following quarter she will attempt to preserve its best qualities in writing of a more formal nature.

Within these limits, then, it is not surprising that the strength of Kristin's story is in the detailing. We are not merely told that Kristin's father was a musician, for instance; we are given an inventory of his preferred instruments at each stage of his career. And we are told in equal detail about his marital and quasi-marital relationships, his jobs, his role in public life. The accumulation of detail gives the reader a vivid sense of both Kristin's father's life and, by implication, Kristin's own.

A friend of mine from Watts read this essay and commented, "And I thought I had a hard life." I suppose that is one possible immediate reaction to Kristin's story—that it is an account of a hard life, her father's or her own. (A biographical narrative is often about the biographer as well as about its subject.) But if we look at her essay again, we can see that the tone runs counter to this interpretation. She writes as if she thinks this is a perfectly normal biography for the father of someone of her generation. It may be, in a way, typical if not normal. The typicality of the story is the source of its attraction for readers of her father's generation—its typicality and its view of the sixties from a novel angle: Who ever thought the children were watching?

Writing teachers can provide, on cue, many reasons (different reasons for different cues) for the necessity of writing skillfully. I tell the students in my class for high school dropouts that if they do not learn how to write well they will starve. And I tell my Dean that writing skills are necessary for success in college or some such thing. But I also believe (I almost wrote "But what I actually believe is") that writing is a good thing because it is an effective way to tell stories, and because, as the traditional Hasidic story tells us, "God created man because He loves stories." I have been thinking lately about those scenes in the Book of Job where the Messengers arrive to tell Job of his disasters. I think those messengers, and not Job, are the heroes of the tale. They are filling the necessary human function in this world into which we are thrown. There are many stories to be told. Young people of Kristin's generation have some highly unusual stories to tell. Telling these stories is a way of creating a past, a father, say, that will be tolerable, that will be a viable basis for the present. To gain the writing skills necessary to accomplish this is valuable. One can then take one's memories, including memories of other stories, and produce them as a story, as an answer to those questions— What happened? Why? Who are you?—that seem typical of adolescence only because so many of us who are no longer adolescent can no longer ask them—not, certainly not, because we have learned any significant answers. Kristin's story "My Father" creates Kristin's father for her. This is not a bad achievement for the first quarter of a composition course.

Study Questions

1. Michael Holzman says that Kristin Martin's paper "represents her best work in the informal mode," and that in a writing course to be taken right after the course for which she did "My Father," "she will attempt to preserve its best qualities in writing of a more formal nature."

   Judging from your reading of "My Father" and of Michael Holzman's commentary on it, what would you say are Kristin Martin's "best qualities," her strengths, as a writer?

What do you think Kristin Martin needs to learn as a writer?

What sort of instruction would help Kristin capitalize on her strengths as a writer in order to learn what you think she needs to?

2. Telling the kind of story Kristin Martin tells in "My Father" "is a way of making a past that will be tolerable, that will be a viable basis for the present," according to Michael Holzman.

What kind of past does Kristin Martin create for herself in her paper? What kind of present does this seem to give her?

What advantage might attend a writing teacher's reading "stories" written by students from the perspective that Michael Holzman does?

What dangers might attend a writing teacher's reading students' "stories" from this perspective?

3. The following classroom exchange followed a reading of Kristin Martin's paper. One student said,

> I don't see that this writer seems to come out anywhere in this paper. She has almost no judgment about her father at all. What has she come to *understand* about her father? Shouldn't she conclude something?

Another student responded by saying,

> Why does she have to conclude something? Why does she have to judge her father? She's doing just what she sets out to do. She's trying to stay objective and let the facts speak for themselves.

What position would you take in this controversy?

ERIKA LINDEMANN's Assignment

You have probably written descriptive papers before. Perhaps you chose as your subject an object, a place, or a person and then created a word picture. Perhaps you selected the kinds of details that evoke a dominant impression, some response on the part of your reader. This assignment asks you to write an essay that is primarily descriptive but that makes its point by comparison and contrast. For example, you might describe one scene under different circumstances, contrasting a football stadium when it is full of people with the same stadium after the fans have gone home. Or, you could describe a person, comparing your initial impression with one you developed later after you had gotten to know the individual better. Or, you could describe an object from two contrasting perspectives, a high school English classroom, for example, as seen by a high school senior and then by a college freshman returning home to visit the school. Although the paper is to be descriptive, it must have some point. What message do you want to communicate to your reader about the subject you are describing by means of comparison or contrast? Your first step, then, is to select a subject that you care about, something you can describe. Second, decide what dominant impression, message, or effect you want your reader to gain from your description; your audience for this paper is the class. Third, begin listing details that could be used to develop the comparisons or contrasts you want to explore in your subject. You will have an opportunity to discuss your plans with your classmates before you begin roughing out a draft of your paper.

❧ At the Beach   *by Norma Bennett*

1   Every summer, my parents and I spend a couple of weeks at the beach together, but this year is different. Because my parents are separated, my mom is staying in our condominium at Emerald Isle, and my dad is spending his vacation with his girlfriend and her son at Hilton Head Island. I'm staying with my mom until she goes back to Raleigh and then going to Hilton Head to see my dad.

2   At 5:00 each morning my mom's alarm clock goes off. She gets up, puts on her jeans, a tee-shirt, and her PTL jacket,* grabs her camera and her Bible, and walks out onto the beach to take pictures of the sunrise

---

*a jacket promoting the PTL (Praise the Lord) Club.

ERIKA LINDEMANN is Associate Professor of English and Director of Composition at the University of North Carolina at Chapel Hill, where she teaches freshman and advanced composition and courses for writing teachers. She has published several articles on the teaching of writing and conducted numerous workshops for teachers. Her book *A Rhetoric for Writing Teachers* was published in 1982.

158

and "Praise the Lord." As she walks across the sand, she sees a pretty, white coquina shell, picks it up, and slips it into the pocket of her bright blue wind-breaker. By the time she walks up to the pier (about a half-mile from our condominium), her pockets sag from the weight of the shells she picks up along the way. She turns and looks out at the ocean. The sky is pinkish-orange, and the sun shines in a yellow ball, rising higher and higher over the ocean—above the soaring seagulls and away from the crashing waves. My mom, a forty-nine year old woman with streaks of gray peaking out from under the last coloring she had put in her hair, takes the camera from around her neck, praises God for his magnificent creation, and photographs her favorite sanctuary. When she gets back, I hear the sliding glass door open and the seashells clink in her pocket as she walks through the den and into the kitchen to wash her shells and lay them out to dry on paper towels. I stumble down the stairs to say good morning and help fix breakfast. Her eyes are watery, her cheeks are red, and her nose is runny. I'm not sure if it's because of the cold wind outside or if she's crying about my dad again or if she's been overwhelmed by the presence of the Lord. Maybe it's all three. I give her a hug and grumble about getting up. She laughs and teases me about being lazy. My mom won't go out on the beach in the middle of the day. She goes back to bed while I go lie out with my friends. Late every afternoon, just before dinner, we go out to the beach together, carrying sand buckets and shovels. Like a couple of kids, we sink down in the sand and start building a castle. My mom won't build it near the shoreline. She makes me go down to the water and bring wet sand up on the powdery beach. This year, for the first time, I realize why she won't build our castle nearer to the water. My mom doesn't want it to wash away; her life is a castle on a solid foundation, and she's trying to teach me to build my castle so it will never wash away. When I think of my dad, I realize why my mom comes back from her walks with tears in her eyes. It's high tide for my dad, and his castle is dangerously near the shoreline.

At Hilton Head my dad wakes up to the sound of his girlfriend's son, David, screaming to go out on the beach. Dad gets up, gripes about his hangover, puts on his velour bathrobe, and goes to David, who is sitting in the living room watching re-runs of "Gilligan's Island" and yelling, "I wanna go on the beach. I wanna go swimming. I wanna go on the beach. I wanna go swimming. . . ." Dad tells the six-year-old to shut up or else he'll get a spanking. David stops yelling and turns his attention back to the T.V. It's about 10:00, so I'm up and getting ready to go out on the beach. I walk into the kitchen just in time to see my father pouring rum into a glass and adding Coke. I try not to act surprised. Before long, Susan, my dad's girlfriend, comes prancing down the stairs in a skimpy black night gown. I don't do a good job of hiding that I'm shocked to see her dressed like that because my dad notices and tells her to go put some clothes on. Naturally, she gets upset and won't speak to anyone, so I end up babysitting her son. By noon my dad is drunk again. He and Susan come out on the beach and lie out underneath their giant umbrella. Dad's stomach hangs over the top of his madras swimming trunks, and his white legs blister quickly in the sun. He covers his bald head with a Hilton Head Golf Club baseball cap, and his gray beard shades his face. He's fifty years old, and he still doesn't know what he wants to be when he grows up. Susan is twenty-five, and she catches the attention of everyone walking by, but her only goal is to keep my dad's attention turned away from my mom and me. She wears a white string bikini and pulls her long brown hair back with a pink bandana head-band. Dad and Susan drink daiquiries until they both pass out in the sun, leaving me to watch David as he splashes around in the surf. Knowing I'm not a good swimmer, I convince David to come out of the water and help me build a sand castle. I head up to the soft sand, but David screams at me. He says that he doesn't like carrying sand that far, and his mom never makes him do it that way. I try to tell him that it will wash away, but he starts crying, and I give in. After we finish building the castle, I go to wake my dad and Susan. They stagger back inside, leaving me to bring in the cooler, the towels, the blanket, the lounge chairs, and the umbrella while they get ready to go out to dinner. Later, when I walk back out on the beach, I notice the castle is being washed away as the tide comes in. The sky is bright red, and the sun sets across the sound. The waves crash against the castle until it's finally level with the sand. My dad yells and says for me to look after David; they'll be back late. Tears come to my eyes. Dad has lost his sobriety, his family, and his God. I wonder how long it will be before his foundation is washed away, and his castle is level with the sand.

4   I love my mom and dad both. My dad has many friends and many good times, but he is too miserable to enjoy them. My mom is a loner. She has quiet times and peace of mind. As I look at my own life, I search for a castle—up high, away from the shoreline—far away from the destruction of the tide.

ERIKA LINDEMANN'S COMMENTARY

Good writing doesn't begin with grammar or with rules found in hand-books. Good writing begins with you. You know the story of your own life better than anyone else. You have spent a lifetime discovering who you are, exploring questions you think are important, developing attitudes toward the people around you, and reexamining what you know in light of new information. Good writing results from watching yourself grow up, from listening to yourself debate subjects that matter to you. What makes such writing interesting for a reader is that all of us have had some growing up to do. Although we haven't all experienced life in the same ways, we can appreciate the similarities of our experiences and learn from the differences. Good writing is most effective when we tell the truth about who we are and what we think.

What makes Norma's paper, "At the Beach," so powerful is that she is honest about her feelings toward her parents. Although their separation has certainly changed her life, she has responded to the experience by deciding what kind of person she would like to be. She has been watching herself grow up and wants to tell you what she has learned about herself. That takes courage. When we tell the truth, we risk the possibility that people may not like us. But writing truthfully is the only way to discover what we know about ourselves and our world.

"What I wanted to do," Norma explained in discussing her paper, "was to tell what I have learned. I love my parents, and I write to understand what I'm feeling. I don't care if it's good. What's important is how I feel. If I feel better after I've written it, it's good."

Norma's paper also represents hard work. An only child, Norma had been examining how she felt about her parents' separation since her junior year in high school. She had written about it in her journal, which she had begun in the eighth grade. She had explored the theme of sandcastles in a paper she wrote during her senior year, a paper she likes even more than "At the Beach." By the time she tackled the subject again as a first-semester freshman in college, she had not only thought it through carefully, but she had also given herself enough distance from it to avoid being sentimental or full of self-pity.

Like almost all good writing, "At the Beach" is not a first draft. It is a substantial reworking of an earlier version that describes a scene at the beach: a middle-aged businessman staring at a young, tanned body in a white string bikini, two boys building sandcastles, an athlete sprinting down the beach. Although the details Norma used created a clear picture of the scene, the people in it were anonymous, flat figures. Norma didn't put herself into the picture at all, and she didn't think the paper was well organized: "It jumped here, there, and everywhere." Furthermore, the paper ended with a tacked-on moral about sandcastles:

> Perhaps people live entire lives in vain because they never build their castles far enough up on the shore. Most will only gaze at the surface of the castle; few will ever care to inspect the depths; but when the tide comes in, the castle will either stand steadfast and strong, or it will be swept away to become part of an unsettled ocean floor.

The language of these two sentences is pretentious. Norma is pretending to be a philosopher; she is not telling her own truths in her own words.

But good writers are willing to judge their work harshly. They rewrite their drafts, not by substituting a word here and there, but by testing all the choices they made. They ask tough questions about their purpose, message, supporting evidence, and organization. In working out answers to these questions, Norma has changed the earlier version significantly. She puts herself and her mother into "At the Beach," omitting people who appeared in the earlier version but who aren't relevant to her purpose. She tells us honestly that the middle-aged businessman of the earlier version is her father, that the young woman in the white bikini is his girlfriend. She selects carefully the details and actions that help us see her parents and develop our own attitudes toward them. But she is also careful to create honest portraits of her mother and father. Like most people, neither parent is absolutely saintly or completely contemptible.

"At the Beach" is also carefully organized. Norma gives each paragraph a job to do and leaves clues near the end of each paragraph to help us move easily to the next one. The first paragraph announces the subject of the essay, sets the scene, introduces the major characters, and, in the last sentence, offers a blueprint for what follows. We can expect to hear about "staying with my mom" before we find out more about her dad. Paragraphs 2 and 3 focus on Norma's mother and father respectively. In both paragraphs Norma combines description and narration to let us see her parents as she sees them. These two paragraphs, the heart of her paper, are especially effective because Norma doesn't just *tell* us about her parents. She *shows* us. Instead of saying "Being a Christian is important to my mother," Norma dresses her mother in a PTL jacket, gives her a Bible to take with her as she walks on the beach, and suggests that her mother's tears may result from being "overwhelmed by the presence of the Lord." Similarly, although Norma tells us, "Dad has lost his sobriety," she also lets his actions show us who he is. He gripes about his hangover, pours a rum and Coke at ten in the morning, passes out on the beach, and leaves the cooler behind for Norma to haul back to the house. Norma persuades us to see her parents the way she does by selecting physical features, words, actions, and motives for us to interpret. She holds these two paragraphs together chronologically, with references to the time of day, and postpones the material on building sandcastles until she has drawn the portraits of her parents.

Norma's message, the point she wants to make, begins with her discussion of a simple activity: building sandcastles on different parts of the beach. The sandcastles, however, become a metaphor for living. Norma believes that people must make choices about the kind of foundation they want to build their lives on. Although Norma may not accept all of her mother's values, they will serve Norma better in difficult situations than her father's values will. Resisting the temptation to preach, Norma devotes only a few sentences in paragraphs 2 and 3 and a short concluding paragraph to explaining what she has learned about sandcastles and life. Because she has already shown us what she admires and regrets about the lives her parents lead, perhaps Norma could have omitted the last paragraph. But she keeps it short, using it to pull the two portraits together and to speak to us directly about herself.

What Norma has done is difficult. She has created in relatively few words several compact character sketches; she has told the story of two days she spent at the beach; she has developed an extended metaphor comparing sandcastles and living. "At the Beach" is an effective paper not because Norma has some special genius for writing, but because she cared enough about her subject to wrestle with the choices she needed to make. She was willing to write several drafts. She planned carefully what she wanted to say, what details to select, what order to arrange them in, and how to convey her message without sounding too sentimental, too egotistical, or too strident. Most important, she tried to tell the truth.

Study Questions

1. A student who had read both "At the Beach" and Erika Lindemann's commentary on it said,

> The more I read this paper the more I wonder whether some things are being left out or changed. Is little David as much of a brat as he's being shown to be? Is that all he is? Is Susan that much of a hooker type? She does have her son with her after all, and she gets upset when the father tells her to change her clothes. Would somebody whose "only goal is to keep my dad's attention turned away from my mom and me" be upset that way, or have her son along with her? And then I begin to wonder if the father is as much of a loser really as he's being made out to be—and if the mother really has it together the way she's said to. Maybe she isn't trying to teach her daughter "to build [a] castle so it will never wash away" at all. Maybe she's just childish. Why does she sleep all day? To avoid people? Why do we hear only *about* what these main characters are said to have said? We never hear them talk for themselves. It's as though the writer here were dealing with people she tries to make into stereotypes without quite being able to do that.

Another student responded by saying,

> Things are always left out or changed when they're written about. That's what writing is. The issue here is whether the writer is true to what *she* sees, not to what somebody else thinks she ought to see. Maybe the father isn't a loser as you put it, but maybe he is too, and even if he isn't, that's the writer's version of what she's writing about, and I don't see why she isn't entitled to it. All we

have here is somebody's words on the page. You can't talk about what they do to people we don't know and can't see.

What position would you take in this argument?

2. The sandcastles of "At the Beach," says Erika Lindemann, "become a metaphor for living."

How would you argue that this metaphor, as Norma Bennett develops it, is adequate for "the point she wants to make"?

How would you argue that it is inadequate?

Which argument do you favor?

3. Norma Bennett has already done several versions of "At the Beach." If she were to express the desire to do another, what advice would you give to help her with her revision?

IRA SHOR'S Assignment

Write about the worst job you ever had.

[A note from Ira Shor: This student essay by Michael Canlon is a good paper with some mistakes. Mike wrote it in a freshman remedial class soon after he left the Air Force, and his essay is his second draft of that paper.

Before you read the essay, I'd like you to try two exercises. You can use what you already know about good writing and about the military for these preliminary exercises. Then read the paper, and my commentary, and compare the way you and I have evaluated this student writing.

The first exercise is to list the qualities you expect to find in a piece of good writing. If you are in a class, you might want to exchange lists with someone else and compare the items each of you came up with. Hold on to your own list until you complete the exercise described in the next paragraph.

The second exercise concerns the theme of Mike's story: military service. Make a second list for yourself, this time writing down what you know about the military. Are you a veteran? Have any of your friends or relatives or neighbors been in the service? Have you seen or heard the military's recruitment ads on TV, radio, and in magazines? Have you ever thought of enlisting? Have you or has anyone you know marched in an antiwar, antinuclear, or peace demonstration? Did a military recruiter ever come to your high school? Is the military a good career for young men and women?

With your two itemized lists, "good writing" and "the military," you are a better-informed reader of the essay.]

✎ A Great Way of Life   *by Michael Canlon*

The Air Force promises many things to it's eager recruits. The biggest   1
and most laughable is the promise that the Air Force is "a great way of
life." Maybe I expected too much from this organization. I didn't think
that I was expecting too much to be received well, treated well, and
trained well. They didn't even have to feed me well if they didn't want
to. Well, they didn't. If living with people who have bad attitudes, and
living in cramped, dirty surroundings is a great way of life, then I'll take
something else, anything else!

The Air Force seems very thrilling and glamorous to a young seven-   2

IRA SHOR is Associate Professor of English at the College of Staten Island, City University of New York. His book *Critical Teaching and Everyday Life* (1980), now in its second printing, offers classroom methods from a Paulo Freire approach to literacy and awareness. Professor Shor has published and lectured widely on pedagogy; mass culture, and education policy. He recently won a Guggenheim Fellowship and is working on a critique of conservative school reforms in the 1970s and 1980s.

teen-year-old boy who thinks he is ready to take on the world. My high expectations of the Air Force were short-lived. I found out the hard way that things are not the way they seem. The Air Force was anything but a great way of life. All the signs of trouble were right in front of me every time I arrived in Fort Hamilton army base in Brooklyn for processing.

3   I always used to think about the way the recruiters did their job. They always seemed to take the long way around everything. They couldn't do the paperwork on you in one day. They had to make you come back six or seven times. These things are not easily seen by a boy who is trying to break out of a shell he has been in for seventeen years. It was time to be a man. There was no time to be second guessing yourself.

4   It didn't take much longer for me to wake up. I think the key that unlocked my blindness was the realization that I was going away from home. Everything that was familiar and comfortable to me was going to be left behind. This was when I began to realize that even seventeen-year-old men get scared. To this day I have not forgotten the look on my mom's face when we said goodbye that September morning.

5   In keeping with their tradition, the people at Fort Hamilton kept us in paperwork from seven in the morning until four in the afternoon. It was then that we finally boarded a bus to the airport. There were fifty-two of us, fifty-two frightened, confused people. Our tickets were to San Antonio, Texas.

6   We arrived in San Antonio at about midnight. From midnight until five in the morning we were introduced to our training instructors who seemed to take pleasure in scaring the hell out of everybody by letting us know that they were in charge. Anybody who got out of line was going to get an "ass-kicking." You would be safe in assuming that nobody got out of line. This was just a small indication of what was to come.

7   This was basic training. I had expected some garbage, but what I didn't expect was the treatment I received when I graduated from the Air Force technical training school in Wichita Falls, Texas in January of '82. Everybody from the school was telling us how different it was when you got to your permanent base. It was different alright. The nightmare begins this way. While in technical training school, I had received orders to report to Fort Meade, in Maryland after I graduated from school.

8   This had made me very happy. I would be able to visit my family and friends who I no longer desired to break away from. The day before I was to graduate from technical training school I received a letter informing me that my orders had been changed from Fort Meade to Kelly Air Force base. You guessed it, it's in San Antonio, Texas. Ah yes, folks, come join the Air Force and see Texas for four years.

9   I arrived at Kelly Air Force base on a Sunday evening in February. Nobody was around to show me where to sleep or get something to eat. It

took me 2½ hours to find someone who was in charge. Maybe I should say someone who thought he was in charge. It took him one hour to just find me a room to sleep in. Suddenly I felt a great urge to see my family. Was this being babyish, or was I finally being an adult?

My next day was even worse. It was time to see where I would be working. Kelly Air Force base is a security base. In the Air Force, security is a short way of saying that it takes them twice as long to do anything simple. It took my new boss forty-five minutes just to get me past the guards at the front gate. The guards were not familiar with my face. After a few phone calls by the guards, I was allowed to pass. If I had known what was to come I would not have even tried to get through the front gate.   10

After spending nine weeks in technical training school to be a tele-communications operator, I was now being informed by my new supervisor that I would not be doing this job because they needed me in a different area. The different area they were speaking of was pushing papers behind the machine I was supposed to be working on. They also informed me that I would be doing this job for most of my four-year enlistment, and that there was very little chance of getting a transfer. I even took that in stride. After pushing papers for 8½ hours I had the pleasure of going back to my beautiful sixteen by twelve foot cubicle that they had the nerve to call a room, and my distinctly filthy roommate.   11

Kelly Air Force base is on top of a hill in the middle of nowhere. If you didn't have an automobile, you were stuck on this dreary little hill with nothing to do but look at your filthy roommate and listen to the never-ending noise from the blaring stereos, which continued to vibrate the walls through all hours of the evening. Lucky me. I joined the Air Force and got sent to Devils Island.   12

One thing that Kelly Air Force base and Devils Island truly have in common is the quality of food that both serve. All meat was mostly fat, all vegetables were hard and bland, the milk was often sour. It made me glad that our supervisor gave us only twenty minutes to eat lunch. It made it that much easier to leave on time. Even if you decided to buy your own food, there wasn't a place where you could cook it. Most of us didn't have enough money to eat out every night. Without an automobile there wasn't anywhere I could go anyway.   13

I promised myself that when I got out of that dirty, miserable place I would never be unhappy again. Maybe it just wasn't for me, but from what I have seen, it shouldn't be for anybody. I often tell people of my experience in the Air Force. Many people don't believe that it could have been that bad. I always tell those people that I'm not the type of person who gets depressed easily, but I can't remember a day going by when I didn't feel out of place or confused or lost. One good thing did come out of it all. I have kept a very important promise to myself.   14

[Now that you have finished Mike's paper, decide if it is a good piece of writing according to the standards on your list. Also, ask yourself if this story corresponds to your own knowledge of military life, or if it challenges your opinions on the service. Once you've done these two evaluations, read my thoughts on the essay, which follow.—I.S.]

Ira Shor's COMMENTARY

I want my writing classes to provide broad learning experiences for me and the students, no narrow, back-to-basics drill in grammar, punctuation, and spelling. I like my students to use writing, revising, reading, speaking, listening, and discussion to learn more about themselves and their society. Another of my goals is to have students write in real voices rather than in a stiff language they invent for the teacher. In my classes, students write and discuss material from their daily lives so that they gain critical awareness of themselves as individuals connected to a larger social picture. When students communicate to each other and to the teacher about issues they care about, they tend to write with more commitment. If you write with more commitment, you put in the time needed to master the difficult act of writing. If the classroom is an irrelevant or boring prison of teacher-talk, students will merely learn how to get by. But, if the classroom is built around students' own language, problems, and ideas, they are more likely to develop strong writing skills and critical habits of mind. With strong critical literacy, you can better use your intelligence in and out of school, in the classroom and in the society, to make the kind of life and world you want.

The first thing I'd like to praise in Mike's paper is his seriousness. He picked a subject that really mattered to him and used the assignment to figure out an important episode in his life. The episode is not isolated from the lives of other people, which makes it even more valuable. Mass advertising by the military makes life in the service look exciting and rewarding and a step towards the future. The glamor of uniforms, guns, and world travel strongly appeals to many teenage boys. Many are bored with school or family life, as well as unable to find work. Many want to get away to grow up and see the world. We've had ten years of hard times, which makes military life even more attractive to unemployed young men and women. It may be a quick solution at a restless moment, promising job training and income hard to find after high school or after dropping out. The job appeal of the service is even stronger for minorities than it is for young whites like Mike. Blacks and Hispanics often find the civilian job market less open than the military one because of racism in training and hiring. Mike's story is a communication from one student to another that might help others think over more carefully the choices they are making.

Besides presenting an individual experience with larger social connections, Mike tried to work on paragraphing and illustrative detail. His first and last paragraphs help introduce and then sum up the experience. Further, his body paragraphs usually focus on single topics. In addition, many of the paragraphs employ examples to illustrate his point. The opening paragraph lists the key repulsive qualities of his time in the service—cramped living quarters, bad food, poor treatment. Mike also reveals the waste in the long processing before he entered the Air Force, as well as in the long, slow trip to Texas on induction day. Ironically, he has great difficulty entering a base that he soon wishes to leave. The awful food and the tiny room he shares are also made visible in his writing. These details lead to his analogy comparing Kelly Air Force base to Devil's Island. Without supporting details, he could not make such an extravagant claim. By summarizing it all in the Devil's Island analogy, he communicates well the trapped feeling that made the experience difficult for him. Supporting his use of details and paragraphing is a good command of vocabulary, punctuation, spelling, and sentencing.

Mike could capitalize on his strengths by taking his paper through a third draft. The introductory paragraph could mention that he was trained for a job he was not asked to do since this was one of his major grievances against the Air Force. Also, notice that in the first paragraph the word "well" is used in two different and distracting ways. The fourth and fifth sentences repeat "well" as modifiers for emphasis, while the sixth sentence uses it as a conversational expression to bridge two statements. The transition between sentences is also a problem in paragraph 2. The first sentence makes a statement that is contradicted in the next sentence: The thrilling promise of the Air Force was not to be fulfilled. Because sentence two will argue the opposite of sentence one, the writer might well signal to the reader that the paragraph is now moving in an opposite direction with a word like "however," "yet," or "unfortunately" at the start of the new sentence. In fact, paying more attention to transitions between sentences and paragraphs in general might help improve the next draft. In paragraph 7, can you find the place where the topic shifts and a new paragraph should be started? The writer might well attach the sentence that follows the breaking point to the top of paragraph 8. Lastly, mechanical errors should be corrected; commas should be added, for example, around the names of cities and states in paragraph 7 ("Wichita Falls, Texas," and "Fort Meade, in Maryland,"), and the word "alright" in the same paragraph should be written as "all right."

Because this story is a story that matters to the writer and is of value to others, Mike might consider saying more about some of his material. Was he as a teenager drawn to the military more than his friends were? He sounds more critical now than those he talks to, and the shift in his attitude could add more irony to the story. Do other veterans agree with his evaluation of the service, or do they challenge him? Should the military be subject to a truth-in-advertising law the way commercial advertisers are?

Study Questions

1. In a classroom discussion of "A Great Way of Life" and Ira Shor's commentary on it, one student said,

   > I don't think this writer is doing much more than griping, just feeling sorry for himself. I spent four years in the service, and it wasn't any picnic I'll admit, but I didn't go in expecting a great way of life either. I was buying some time for myself and I wanted to have a shot at a paid-for college education. I got both. I also had a lot of good times in the service, which this guy never mentions. Everything that went wrong he sees as somebody else's fault, never his. But he never has to look at that when he does things like call the Air Force Devil's Island.

   Another student responded by saying,

   > You weren't seventeen when you went in the service the way this writer was, for one thing. I don't have any trouble believing somebody seventeen can be taken in by the ads on the service. Also, he isn't just feeling sorry for himself. He says he did his job, even though it was one that he wasn't trained for and that he had little hope of being transferred out of. He also says that maybe the service "just wasn't for [him]." And I don't see why he has to talk about the good times he had. That's not his point in this paper. For him the service *was* Devil's Island and he has a right to see it that way. It's *his* experience he's talking about.

   How would you enter into this exchange?

2. "I like my students," says Ira Shor, "to use writing, revising, reading, speaking, listening, and discussion to learn about themselves and their society."

   Judging from Michael Canlon's paper, do you think that the experience of writing and revising it enabled him to learn more about himself and his society? What makes you say so?

3. Ira Shor says that the writer of "A Great Way of Life" could "[take] his paper through a third draft," and then he goes on to suggest a number of things that might be done to improve the paper in this third writing.

   What would you suggest, either instead of or in addition to the changes mentioned by Ira Shor, that Michael Canlon could do to improve "A Great Way of Life"?

Stephen Tchudi's Assignment

Write a paper on any topic of your choice related to the theme of freedom and human dignity. You may want to look back through the study questions and supplementary writing topics of the past several weeks.

Additional Ideas

1. Write a chapter of your family history showing how your personal history has come to influence your way of operating in the world. If you have collected letters from family members the past two weeks, include them as an appendix to your paper. Focus the paper as much as possible on individual anecdotes and stories, not broad generalizations.

2. Write about one of the elements in your "life space" diagram that you identified as important in either restricting or enhancing your individual freedom:

Home	Special Interests	Personal Strengths
Parents	Mistakes	Personal Weaknesses
Relatives	Religion	Literature/Art
Lovers	Authority	Science

Again, *show*, don't *tell*. Use stories and descriptions rather than abstractions.

3. Write about one of the factors we identified as strongly influencing freedom and human dignity in these United States:

Defense	Terrorism	The Economy
TV	Racism	Nuclear War
Media	Computers	
Newspapers	Reaganomics	

4. Compare your personal freedom this year and last.

5. Write about any aspect of freedom and human dignity that you have observed at MSU.

6. Money has come up in many of our discussions. Write about individual freedom and money. Or write about the way money or the lack of it can shape people or even distort them from what they could be.

7. Future engineers: Write about the accusation that engineers nowadays

---

STEPHEN TCHUDI is Professor of English and of American Thought and Language at Michigan State University, where he also directs the English Education Program. He has published several books on the teaching and learning of composition, including *The Creative Word* (1973–74); *Writing in Reality* (with James E. Miller, Jr., 1978); *An Introduction to Teaching Writing* (with Susan Tchudi, 1982); and *Gifts of Writing* (1980), *Putting on a Play* (1982), and *The Young Writer's Handbook* (1984) (all three with Susan Tchudi). He has conducted writing workshops for teachers from Virginia to Alaska and from Massachusetts to Hawaii. He is President of the National Council of Teachers of English (1983–84).

design for sales and attractiveness, not for individual human needs. Is it true? Debate it. If it is true, what could be done about it . . . by you?

8. Analyze your possible career from the point of view of human freedom and individual dignity, both yours and that of the people you will come in contact with.

9. Reread one of the pieces in *Conscious Reader* that you responded to very positively or very negatively. Write an analysis or critique of it.

✍ Nanette and the Purple Crayon
by Nanette L. Shields

1   I can still hear my professor's words as he told the class our first paper was to be on the theme "freedom". I panicked! All I could think of was, "How can he assign a paper on a subject that I have no opinion on?" The English class that I once considered to be enjoyable was now beginning to annoy me—especially when I sat in my dorm room on my first Saturday night trying to write my paper. Monday came and I still hadn't finished my first draft, which was due that day. I skipped class that Monday hoping that I would have two drafts done by Tuesday. Finally, I asked my roommate what "freedom" meant to her. She thought about it for a minute and then replied, "Being at Michigan State". I had never really considered being at M.S.U. a freedom, but it was. Her reply acted as a catalyst towards my thinking of freedom. I came to the conclusion that one cannot define "freedom" in exact terms. It is a personal opinion. This paper portrays how I recognize freedom in terms of art, children and individuality.

2   At the age of three, I remember taking my box of twenty-four assorted colored Crayola crayons and scribbling all over the basement walls. This purple crayon covering the walls freely expressed that purple was my favorite color. At that age, I did not care whether I was going to get in trouble or not. Purple was my favorite color and I wanted everyone to know it.

3   People express themselves in many different ways. One way which I express myself is with my art. I love art because I am able to be free with it. In art, there are no restrictions or conformities, whether it be painting, drawing, photography or scribbling. One of my favorite mediums in art is water color because the paint flows freely with the water. The colors run into each other, forming oceans of new and exciting colors. They reflect the mood of the artist whether he/she is happy or sad. With art, I express myself without any mental blocks. It is my way of freely communicating my thoughts.

Another medium I enjoy is photography. With photography, I never 4
know exactly how the image will turn out. Every Sunday I remember
traveling around Southwest Michigan taking pictures of everything in
sight. Each day we went through rolls and rolls of film. What I like most
about photography today is viewing something and reacting to it when it
comes out on film, making a statement for all to see. Have you ever seen
close-up, out of focus, bird's-eye view, or worm's-eye view photography?
These photographs express the way the artist views the environment at
the time. For example, I may see a huge door with a brass door knob and
key hole. Because I am curious to see what lies behind the door, I will
focus in on it. The door knob and the key hole represent ways of opening
my thoughts by photographing them. In this, I am suggesting that there
may be something behind the door which awaits my curiousity. Photography is a way of communicating a statement in which one often cannot
do verbally. Art is important because one can voice ideas without limitation. Art is freedom of expression.

One of my favorite periods in my life was when I was between the ages 5
of two and four. The reason why this period of my life was so special is
that it was the closest I ever felt to freedom. I was free from the many
restrictions and conformities of society. I was not concerned with the
everyday things in life; such as what I will be wearing today; what time I
will get up; looking presentable. When I was three or four, I had no
obligations. At that age, I lived each day concerned only with my own
happiness. For example, my purple crayon and I. At that time, I did not
care how much trouble I was going to get into. I was concerned about
what was making me happy at that time. Sure, mom and dad scolded me,
but what's a little yelling compared to all the limitations we face in
today's society; such as social acceptance, what clothes one wears, one's
general appearance, personality, the amount of money one has, obligations, going to college, obtaining a job and supporting a family. I am not
stating that I am not concerned with the problems in my environment
now that I am older, but one should value his/her childhood because it is
probably the most freedom that one will ever have.

In college, I found that being an individual is also a freedom. A friend 6
of mine called me one Thursday night and asked me to go to a party with
free beer. I said, "Sure". She then told me there was one catch; it was a
Theta Chi Little Sister Rush party. I knew that a party with free beer was
too good to be true. Because I lived in Kalamazoo, a college town, I have
always held a pessimistic viewpoint of the "Greek" system. Trying to be
open minded, I decided to go. Arriving at the fraternity house, Michelle
and I walked into the entry way and were soon surrounded by many
males, dressed in New England style preppy clothing. One of the guys
asked if he could take our coats. We replied, "No", indicating that we

did not want to stay long. A few minutes later, another guy in the same circle asked us the same question. At the time, it seemed to be of great importance to them, so we allowed them to take our coats. As we entered the living room, I felt uneasy—as If I was on display in a department store. That's exactly how it was. Michelle and I stood near the doorway as the boys inspected the merchandise, seeing if it was worth the cost. They looked first at our physical appearance and then determined whether they should talk to us or not. I felt that Michelle and I were on display to humor them. Appearance played an important part in the decision of them choosing us, the merchandise. Michelle and I left the party knowing that we were happy being ourselves, just the way we had been before the fraternity party. By being an individual, one is freeing him/herself from the conformities and restrictions of the social society. One should not have to conform his/her personality to fit into the mold of others.

7   At age three, I was capable of expressing myself with art, of being free from conformity and restrictions, and of being more of an individual than I am at eighteen. At age three, I was more concerned with my own identity. With my purple crayon, I expressed my individuality. At age eighteen it's ironic that I often feel like an object resulting from the conformities and restrictions of society. I hope that someday I can retrieve the attitudes that I had at that early age. My purple crayon still remains on the wall, but unfortunately it doesn't look the same as it did when I was three.

Stephen Tchudi's COMMENTARY

The piece of writing I chose to share grew out of a freshman course in "American Thought and Language," a required freshman English course taught at Michigan State University. "ATL" includes wide reading in American literature, plus frequent journal writings and three or four longer papers per quarter. ATL 1154, for which this paper was written, was a "developmental" section, meaning that the students had done poorly on a writing assessment given to all freshmen and had been assigned to lab and classroom sections that would provide extra work on their writing problems.

    I began the course with a thematic unit on a broad theme of "Freedom and Human Dignity," using writers from our anthology, who ranged from Martin Luther King to H. L. Mencken. Students wrote a half dozen short journal assignments to explore their responses to the literature and to help me promote class discussion. After two weeks, we moved to our first long paper for the course, based on the assignment that precedes Nanette's essay.

The assignment, with its multiple options and emphasis on making abstract themes personal, is characteristic of those I give. By suggesting a variety of ways to approach a topic, I hope to engage the students in writing from their own experience. I also want to push my freshmen away from writing the standard "five paragraph" freshman theme, with its canned openings, wooden organizational structures, obligatory endings. Following discussion of the assignment, students began planning, drafting, and revising, and I used a week of class time—as a developmental section we met five days per week—for workshops, with the students bringing in and discussing their writing, working their way toward final polished copy.

But not Nanette. Nanette skipped the class twice, and when she was present, she tried to avoid me, hiding out in the peer revision groups. When I caught up with her, she told me she was "doing something on photography." But she only had some notes and jottings to show me, no drafts, no revisions. She appeared to have a fairly typical freshman writing block. However, Nanette did attend class the day the papers were due, and she submitted "Nanette and the Purple Crayon."

My first reaction, perhaps predictably, was to be concerned and—to myself only—indignant. I had worked hard to make the writing assignment personal and enjoyable, and here was a student who made me sound like the tyrannical theme-giver of old, grinding down students by giving them impossible assignments.

However, as I read on, I became more and more pleased with Nanette's work. After that first paragraph—itself not poorly written—she had done a fascinating job of exploring her idea of personal freedom. She described the freedom of drawing on walls when she was young (paragraph 2), contrasted it with her adult conception of art (paragraph 3), and shifted into the discussion of the artistic freedom permitted by her current love, photography (paragraph 4).

With paragraph 5 she moved away from art and broadened the discussion to encompass not only artistic, but personal freedom, first as she experienced it in her childhood (drawing on the walls with her purple crayon), then as she found it restricted as a young adult (at a frat party where the women were treated as cattle). In the final paragraph she drew together her themes of art and life, childhood and adulthood, closing with a nostalgic look back ("My purple crayon still remains on the wall, but unfortunately it doesn't look the same as it did when I was three.").

I read Nanette's paper aloud to my class. I realized that despite her fussing at me in the opening paragraph, she had done precisely what I wanted the students to do with this assignment: She had taken the abstraction of "freedom and human dignity" and made it concrete, richly illustrated with her own experiences. Further, it seemed to me that those

experiences had led her to discover a useful and complex writing structure, far more complicated than the usual freshman theme structure.

There are flaws in the paper, of course, flaws in writing style as well as
structure. At the same time, I feel that "Nanette and the Purple Crayon"
works as a piece of writing, and I was pleased to celebrate its accomplish-
ments with my students and with Nanette. Later, when we put together
an anthology of everyone's self-selected best writing for the term,
Nanette chose her "purple crayon paper."

Study Questions

1. A student writing about "Nanette and the Purple Crayon" and Stephen
   Tchudi's commentary on it said,

   > I don't understand what Stephen Tchudi means by saying that the writer's
   > "experiences had led her to discover a useful and complex writing structure, far
   > more complicated than the usual freshman theme structure." How can any-
   > body's *experiences* lead to the discovery of a writing structure? Also, I can't see
   > that this paper is any more complicated than the usual freshman theme struc-
   > ture at all. The writer's opening paragraph announces that she's going to look at
   > freedom in three areas. Then she looks at freedom in three areas. Then she
   > writes a sum-up. How is that any different from the old five-paragraph theme?
   > What is this useful and complex new structure the writer is supposed to have
   > discovered anyway?

   How do you respond to this statement?

2. In a classroom discussion of "Nanette and the Purple Crayon" and Stephen
   Tchudi's commentary on it, one student said,

   > Stephen Tchudi says that there are "flaws in writing style as well as structure" in
   > this paper. But I think there are more serious flaws than that. Shouldn't it be
   > suggested to Nanette Shields that in talking about things the way she does she
   > oversimplifies such things as art, childhood, and therefore what it *means* to be
   > an individual, to be free?

   Another student responded by saying,

   > I think you're forgetting that Nanette Shields was in a developmental section,
   > that she was an inexperienced rather than an experienced writer. The main
   > thing I think is for her to get used to seeing abstractions in terms of her own
   > experience. How she does that isn't all that important. People have to be
   > praised for what they do, not criticized for what they don't.

   How would you enter this discussion?

3. Suppose Nanette Shields came to you and said something like this:

   > I want this paper to be as good as I can make it. I'm willing to rethink and
   > rewrite it completely to do that. What suggestions do you have for how I ought
   > to go about doing so?

   Respond to this writer, trying to be of as much help to her as you can.

[In "The Literature of Fact," a junior-senior level course offered in Fall semester, 1982, we read several kinds of texts: history, biography, historical novel, new journalism, and autobiography. The students in the class were expected by the end of the semester to have written a version of one of the kinds of things we were reading, along with a more conventional interpretive paper. Each week the students were to hand in some writing that tended toward satisfaction of these end-of-the-semester requirements. I conferred each week with each student about the writing handed in.]

Autobiographical Sketch   *by Teri Cor*

I don't know whether Catholic classrooms inherently wield more power   1
to influence a child's mind, or whether my imagination would have been just as easily activated in a public school. But I remember one nun who was intrinsically aware of the extreme impressionability of very young children, and of the unquestioning credence which we would lend to authority figures, particularly nuns; Sister Mary Margaret exploited this knowledge skillfully and unmercifully.

I don't know whether Sister Mary Margaret had ever heard of Con-   2
rad's theory of "the fascination with the abomination," but she understood the principle, and she understood as well how avidly children operated on it. Sister Mary never held the attention of her students so intensely and so single-mindedly as when she described physical tortures. Sometimes she would spend fifteen minutes dwelling on the tortures of the rack, or how it felt to be slowly broiled over hot coals like Saint Paul had been. She described the exquisite agony of the Chinese water torture, or the practice (she said) of slowly boiling Christians in hot oil, lowered inch by agonizing inch into a huge vat of the liquid until all the skin is boiled off the bones.

"They suspend you over the cauldron for days and days," Sister Mary   3
explained, the cynosure of all our wide, unblinking eyes. We tried to keep our breathing quiet and still the thumping of our hearts so we would not miss any syllable, any nuance, of Sister Mary's description. "You are never allowed to die, not until the oil boils away your guts." Despite our efforts at silence, an involuntary groan of horror and disgust escaped our

JOHN WARNOCK is Associate Professor of English and Law and former Director of Freshman English at the University of Wyoming. He codirects the Wyoming and the New Jersey Writing Projects, has published fiction, poetry, and articles on teaching writing, and in 1984, will direct an NEH Summer Seminar entitled "The Writing Process: A Humanistic View."

lips, while in the next classroom the first-graders began practicing hymns for the May Crowning of Mary, Mother of Mercy.

4   "In seven years," Sister Mary would then intone with sacerdotal certainty, "the blood of all the Christian martyrs will be running down the streets." That was how we would know the Communists were coming. First the river of blood, then the invincible soldiers, jeering with unholy glee, and finally the tortures.

5   I had been proud that I was never afraid of the dark, like some of my other classmates. But under the draconic influence of Sister Mary's horror stories I came to dread darkness, and the nightmares it would bring. They were all variations on the same theme: The howling hordes of Communists had come, and we had to pick our way carefully along the streets to avoid slipping in the little rivulets of blood that were already beginning their viscous trek down the streets. We heard maniacal laughter as they drove us like resigned cattle to the slaughter.

6   I was young and therefore resilient. As the years passed my apprehension of the coming holocaust faded into obscurity and assumed ludicrous overtones. But I could not erase from my memory the feeling uppermost in my emotional maelstrom when I would awake from those gruesome nightmares: not regret that this should happen so early in my life, nor even sympathy for the much greater suffering my parents and family would endure.

7   The worst factor of all these imaginings of my febrile brain was the knowledge that everyone else I knew would go under the scourge or the hot iron willingly—go enthusiastically, even gratefully, in order to prove to our most loving and benign Prince of Peace their love for Him and their fidelity to His One, True, Holy, and Apostolic Church. And I, coward that I was, pusillanimous cowering wretch that I was, would die shamefully and in disgrace.

8   I could see in my mind, with exquisite and unmerciful clarity, myself renouncing Christ, The Pope, the Church, all my patron saints, and—most heinous and unforgivable of all—the Virgin Mary herself, as soon as I was shown the hideous instruments of torture. It might take me a little longer to spit on the Crucifix, but I would surely do that too, long before I died.

9   The Communists never arrived. They remain entrenched in the Eastern Bloc, seemingly content to practice their unspeakable rites among members of their satellite countries. For years after the nightmare had receded, however, I experienced the impact of Sister Mary's horror stories. Whenever newscasters or religious speakers on television mentioned Russia, communism, or martyrdom in any time or country, I had to leave the room. I did not want to be reminded that torture was still going on, in any form or for any reason. The thought of anyone undergo-

ing unnecessary pain became increasingly abhorrent to me. My sensitiv-
'ity to pain did not confine itself to humanity. All mammals, eventually,
all living things even remotely capable of sentience or physical vulnera-
bility, became objects of my sympathy. I could not kill an ant in the
kitchen, an annoying housefly, the spider in my bath tub, because I did
not know how much agony I might be inadvertently causing them in
slapping them into insensibility with a dish towel or squishing them flat
with my heel.

When I entered high school I decided to grow up and grow out of such   10
childish strictures. In spite of my efforts, always in the back of my
thoughts, behind my eyes and in my throat, I felt a vague disquiet. I was
dutifully conforming to the adult world, not wishing to become "weird"
or have my friends and family wonder at my peculiarities. But I still did
not like myself much.

I liked myself even less when, for various reasons, some not clear even   11
to myself, I began to drift away from the Church. Still, this was the
legacy Sister Mary had left me: making pain and torture a delight to be
embraced, not avoided. There was something pathetically, masochisti-
cally sad about that attitude; and yet it did have a kind of pragmatic
appeal. It implied a stoic acceptance of the way the universe operated,
and an attempt by the Church I grew up with to make the best of a
wretched situation, and like it.

Perhaps Sister Mary made me turn out kinder or less selfish than I   12
might otherwise have been. That period in my life, although it might
have precipitated certain neurotic tendencies, putting me under a sort of
geis* never to be another splinter in someone else's cross, opened me up
on the inside, made me more receptive. If I could be so responsive to
pain in other things, perhaps I could also learn to become more sensitive
to positive values in them, to their beauty, perhaps, or their capacity for
love, for instance. And for that possibility, Sister Mary, for all the angst
you caused me, I am grateful.

JOHN WARNOCK'S COMMENTARY

I think there are not many English teachers who would judge this writing
by Teri Cor to be anything but excellent.

In fact this paper almost dares an English teacher not to call it excellent. Insofar as you are an English teacher, you have to say, early on:
This is good stuff. Look how the second paragraph starts with a *grabber*

---

*A Celtic word referring to a personal taboo that an Irish hero could break only on pain of death—
but that he could not help breaking.

that is also a *literary allusion*: "I don't know whether Sister Mary . . . had ever heard of Conrad's theory of 'the fascination with the abomination'. . . ." Look at the *detail*: "lowered inch by agonizing inch into a huge vat of the liquid until all the skin is boiled off the bones." And the *vocabulary* and *phrasing*: "the cynosure of all our wide, unblinking eyes," "sacerdotal certainty," "febrile brain." All these words are used correctly; none seems applied as ornament.

And the *sentences*—how *mature*, how *complex* in their structure, and not just complex either, but *dramatic* in their complexity: "Despite our efforts at silence an involuntary groan of horror and disgust escaped our lips, while in the next classroom the first-graders began practicing hymns for the May Crowning of Mary, Mother of Mercy." Of course we are *amused* at the picture of the young girls being both horrified and tickled, as Sister Mary warms to her task. And we feel *interested* in how the narrator will come to terms with such experiences: We are confident that we will not get in the end some sentimental revenge fantasy in which Sister Mary is discomposed by a spit-ball, or some such. We will willingly, as they say, read on.

The problem with the observations I have just made is that the features indicated do not, individually or together, amount to good writing. They might amount to a good grade in those situations where quality in writing is reduced to such terms. But we can all imagine a piece that manifested all of the above and wasn't excellent, wasn't even okay.

But this piece by Teri Cor *is* excellent, I think, excellent in the way one wants excellence in the writing class, excellent, that is, as a draft, as a basis for conversation about how it might be made better. Not all writing, by any means, welcomes such conversation. But Teri Cor has brought this piece of writing to the point where we can begin to say how it might be made better, and where we are encouraged to try to do so.

Teri Cor has not had a chance to speak to this draft. She wrote almost all of it between our last conference and the due date. She might be able to tell me better than I could tell her how this draft might be improved. Certainly she could tell me better than I could tell her how *she* might make it better. Here I can only try to show some possibilities. I hope we all know how much more there might be in this game than that.

Reading the first part of Teri Cor's essay, we feel what she calls a sense of "vague disquiet." We laugh with a sense of laughing off, and of laughing off something more serious than a nun who seems herself to have been a pretty good storyteller and who seems to have been one of those folks who enjoy tormenting children in the name of saving the children's souls. All the lightness and word play notwithstanding, the first part of the paper gives us, or perhaps it would be better to say it invites in us, a sense of the abomination.

The last paragraph then tells us what all the disquiet amounts to. It tells us that Teri Cor is "grateful" in the last analysis because, although Sister Mary's lies "might have precipitated certain neurotic tendencies," they might also have been responsible for making her more sensitive and receptive to the "positive values" in "things." For me, the result of this explanation is a new disquiet, this time one that I don't give the writer credit for having recognized. I don't see the reason for the gratitude. I don't see the sensitivity or receptivity. I'm not at all confident that I know what these "positive values" are, nor what are the "things" that these values are "in." And somehow I feel that those "neurotic tendencies" the writer dismisses as insignificant are not as domesticated as we are being asked to believe. If this is indeed the sum total of the abomination as I have to this point been experiencing it, then I feel a little foolish for getting so exercised: The abomination turns out to be the shadow cast by a warm puppy.

Looking back into the text, I recall that I felt a similar disquiet at several points which, I now see, are precisely those points where the "good stuff" was most apparent. To look at one kind of thing, the phrasing: Consider "the cynosure of all our wide, unblinking eyes," "inch by agonizing inch," "unspeakable rites," "vague disquiet." There is rightness about such phrasing, but it is, we might say, a "literary" rightness, the rightness of ritual, the rightness of a good "English" paper. Of course, there is nothing necessarily wrong with literary language. If such language is used to distract us from something else—the unspeakable, for example—we may need such distraction. Kurtz, in *Heart of Darkness*, from which Teri Cor's initial allusion comes, needed it. What we don't want is to be cajoled into thinking that this strategem for not speaking the unspeakable has in fact allowed us to speak it.

By contrast, Teri Cor uses two words early on that seem to me good not just in a literary way but in a writerly way because they reveal this writer's predicament. One is the word *activated* in "I don't know . . . whether my imagination would have been just as easily activated in a public school." The other is *operated* in "she understood the principle [of the fascination with the abomination], and she understood as well how avidly children operated on it." At these points, Teri Cor has found words that express the abomination as it can appear to a child in school, that is, to a still impressionable person being treated, and treating herself, as an object to be manipulated for institutional purposes. These words make us smile, but they do not invite us to see the abomination as "just" a joke, or as "just" a mental condition that we may learn about from psychology textbooks.

So I would say to Teri Cor: It is clear that you have taken up this problem with attention, with a serious playfulness, and with courage. My guess would be that you don't like your ending any more than I do, that you put it on—and thus closed down what you had opened up earlier—partly because you thought an English paper called for such a wrap-up. But it's too late: You have made something that doesn't want to be dismissed like that. You are good. Lest you be too good, try not to forget what, as writers, we want to be good for.

Study Questions

1. John Warnock begins his commentary with a list of praiseworthy features in Teri Cor's paper, but then goes on to say that the problem with talking about writing in those terms is that such features "do not, individually or together, amount to good writing. They might amount to a good grade in those situations where quality in writing is reduced to such terms. But we can all imagine a piece that manifested [such features] and wasn't excellent, wasn't even okay."

   What does John Warnock seem to think produces excellence in a piece of student writing? Is it something *other* than the features he lists? something *in addition to* such features? or what exactly?

   What is your opinion of the standard for excellence that John Warnock is using?

2. A student who had read both Teri Cor's paper and John Warnock's commentary on it said,

   > I understand what John Warnock means by suggesting that the end of this paper feels wrong, like a "wrap-up" as he says that doesn't square with the direction the paper seems to be moving in up to the end. But maybe it isn't the *last* quarter of the paper that needs to be rewritten to make it fit the first three-quarters; maybe the *first* three quarters needs to be rewritten to make the end believable. Couldn't the writer just by writing the paper have come by the end to realize she hadn't talked about her early experience with Sister Mary fairly?

   How do you respond to this statement?

3. John Warnock concludes his commentary with what he would say to Teri Cor about the paper she has written. His remarks are those of a teacher talking to a student about a particular piece of writing.

   Judging from these remarks, how is John Warnock defining himself as a teacher of writing? How is he defining a student? How is he defining writing?

Writing Assignment 6
Creating Lives

In order to write this paper you will need an example of what you consider good biographical or autobiographical writing to work with. If, in addressing Writing Assignment 4, you wrote a paper that you are proud of, you could easily use that (indeed, your teacher may suggest that you do so). Or you may be asked to choose one of the student essays in this chapter to work with. Or you may be assigned some other way of finding a piece of biographical or autobiographical writing that you admire.

The following is not a statement, you will notice, that restricts itself to assertions about what one does to *write* about someone. It is, however, a statement about our relationship to the past that is particularly relevant to an understanding of the process involved in doing so.

> What we, or at any rate what I, refer to confidently as memory—meaning a moment, a scene, a fact that has been subjected to a fixative and thereby rescued from oblivion—is really a form of storytelling that goes on continually in the mind and often changes with the telling. Too many conflicting emotional interests are involved for life ever to be wholly acceptable, and possibly it is the work of the storyteller to rearrange things so that they conform to this end. In any case, in talking about the past we lie with every breath we draw.
>
> William Maxwell

Show how you could argue that the piece of biographical or autobiographical writing that you have chosen is, as Maxwell says, "really a form of storytelling," a kind of "lie" being told in order to make life "acceptable."

Since you admire this piece of writing, to see it as a "lie," "a form of storytelling" *only*, doesn't seem to be the whole story, does it? Something else needs to be said. Some other way of talking seems to be called for. That it is "the work of the storyteller to rearrange things" in order to make life "acceptable," can have another side, can't it? Write out what else you think needs to be said about the piece of writing you are considering. Use a separate page.

Finally, on still another page, speculate on what you do in writing about someone's life. Given the problems in attempting such a thing, what do you see in it for you even to try it, let alone to try to do it well? Suppose you could come up with what you'd call a good piece of writing about a life—your own or someone else's. What then would you have? What might such good writing be good for so far as you are concerned?

Masks

7

We may think of the self as both a dynamic and a static entity. It is static when we think of ourselves as having central, fixed selves independent of our surroundings, an "I" we can remove from society without damage, a central self inside our head. But it becomes dynamic when we think of ourselves as actors playing social roles, a series of roles which vary with the social situation in which we find ourselves. Such a social self amounts to the sum of all the public roles we play. Our complex identity comes from the constant interplay of these two kinds of self. Our final identity is usually a mixed one, few of us being completely the same in all situations or, conversely, social chameleons who change with every context. What allows the self to grow and develop is the free interplay between these two kinds of self. If we were completely sincere, we would always say exactly what we think—and cause social chaos. If we were always acting an appropriate role, we would be certifiably insane. Reality, for each of us, presents itself as constant oscillation between these two extremes.

Richard Lanham

T HE STUDENT ESSAYS OF THIS CHAPTER MAY strike you in some ways as strange: as contrived (and contrived they are), as imitative (which they also are), as artificial or even unnatural (and in the root senses of these words they certainly are both of these too). And yet having students shape an essay according to the principles of a traditional literary form and having them deliberately assume the voice and manner of someone other than themselves are both approaches to the teaching of writing that have been taken for years—and to the teaching of rhetoric for centuries.

From the following essays and commentaries and your writing in connection with them, you may be able to discover some of the reasons why teachers have valued these approaches for so long.

Walker Gibson's Assignment

For the past few weeks we have been considering the question of Clarity in writing, and we have found it no simple matter. It is not enough, we have discovered, to have one's grammar right and one's sentences orderly. One person's Clarity, we have found, is another person's muddy prose. To decide whether a particular passage is Clear, we have to go beyond the language itself and look at the situation, the audience, some sort of goal. What are we trying to do, and for whom?

Now, with these complications about Clarity in mind, we are going to address a familiar subject: college experience.

It's often said that life will never be so free and independent as it is during one's college years. On the other hand, it's often said that college life is regimented and dominated by social conventions and orthodoxy. After a semester at UMass, you're in no position to solve this apparent contradiction, but you have had a number of experiences here, and you can say something about them.

Write a paper in which you address the question of whether your experience of college so far has been one of "freedom" or of "regimentation." Use whatever recent incidents you can recall that seem significant in relation to this question. Use whatever form for your paper you think will enable you to say what you have to say Clearly.

∾ A Paper Without a Name   by David Kopack

1   Where the hell is this guy? I've been waiting for the head honcho for more than an hour. I can feel the sweat in the palms of my hands. Is he going to notice when I shake his hand? Dave, you just have to be confident. Finally a door opened and it wasn't the flaky receptionist. It was the flaky secretary. "Dave, you can come in now." I replied "Thank you" as sarcastically as possible, but it didn't really sound sarcastic. Anyway good old graceful Dave with his sweaty palms walked right in there and got himself a job! This is where it all started. This is where the tobagadung (cow manure in some indian language) hit the fan. Ever since getting that job I've been living life in the fast lane, always having to be in the express line at the market. I often find myself sitting on top

WALKER GIBSON is Professor of English at the University of Massachusetts in Amherst. He has published a variety of verse and prose over a long career, including several works on writing and style: *The Limits of Language* (1962); *Tough, Sweet and Stuffy* (1967); *Persona* (1969); *Seeing and Writing* (1974). During the 1970s he directed a number of NEH seminars for college teachers of writing. He has held Ford and Guggenheim Fellowships, and is a past president of the National Council of Teachers of English.

of the clothes washer at two in the morn engaging in some homework that was supposed to be handed in the week before. As I was sitting in a pile of (cow manure in some indian language) I realized how I would like walking to the bus instead of running all the time. I have no choice being a fastlaner. I either run the fifty yds. or I walk five miles. Time is very important to us fastlaners, therefore we must learn to put up with a few frontwards summersalts in the mud. As I came to my feet and looked out of the corner of my eye I saw a few of those walkers that I envy so. They were laughing! My palms were the only thing on my body not covered with mud. Oh! by the way, my sweaty palms are a nervous condition. Well, I entered the bus with my tail between my legs, took on a few stares and sat down. Then I just decided that hey! Who cares! Big deal! But positive thinking did not help my sweaty palms any. And then a fastlaner thought passed before me. I caught up to it in no time. The thought said: Dave are you hungry? Can you make it before the dining common closes? Yes! I replied. And I left the bus in full sprint and made it without falling in any mud, but as I was waiting in line for my food I smelled the pleasant odor of what I was going to eat. I am not really into eating tobagadung but I refused to starve. What gets me about cafeteria food, though, is all the little nicknames they give the socalled food. The Diplomat Sandwich is nothing more than old tuna on a bulky roll. I sure wouldn't feed that to Yasar Arofat. I'd throw in a little tomato or something. How about the famous Frank Reuben? You assume that some guy named Frank got a sandwich named after him.—good for Frank—but all a Frank Reuben is, is a hotdog (alias Frank) with sauerkraut on it. The average fastlaner doesn't care about the Frank Reuben stuff. We just like the good old fast food that isn't made in the cafe. As a fastlaner, running all over the place, I decided I had to buy either a Ronco super duper jetpack that even slices and dices potatoes or a pair of good running shoes. I couldn't afford the jetpack. EXAMS! EXAMS! EXAMS! PAPER! All of this on top of working nights? Yes. I work better under pressure because I see it as a challenge. Making a deadline on a paper, preparing for an exam, running all over the place. I seldom make a deadline on a paper, but I do manage to fall in the mud from time to time. Being a fastlaner I feel that I am more a part of things. I belong. By the way my peers run around, they look like molecules in one of those chem experiments. You would think that some of these people had middle names of ion (POSITIVELY CHARGED). This university has such a wide range of characters and characteristics, in which all these characters have built characteristically, with all their liberal, conservative, radical characters. My most favorite group of people here at the zoo are the anti's. They don't like anything or anyone. The anti that I most believe in is the anti-Frank-Reuben campaign. Anti's can be fun to watch. When they approach you, I find that the best thing to do is just relax and shoot them the old peace sign and say "NO NUKES, NO NUKES!" and then they leave you alone. Mind you, I have nothing against the anti's. Being an anti is hard work. I even know this woman that is going all the way to Albany for some kind of anti-rally. Frank and I have both got to go. If you're a fastlaner like me, my advice is to work on your balance and do not let some NASA used-jetpack salesman sell you, just buy a good pair of running shoes.

Walker Gibson's COMMENTARY

Our freshman students write, at their best, serious respectable prose with a faintly academic flavor. It is important, of course, for them to be able to produce such prose efficiently, and we encourage this facility and reward it. They will be writing tests and term papers for the next three years, and they will be writing who-knows-what thereafter; for these tasks some mastery of the appropriate conventions is necessary, and that's what, generally speaking, this course and most freshman writing courses are all about. But David Kopack's title suggests that he is about to try something else. The piece reproduced here is not only unique in its style among his classmates' productions, but it is also just about the only thing of its kind that he himself attempted during the semester. I choose it because it suggests that writing decent conventional prose is not the only thing to do all the time, and that Clarity is relative. For me this is an essential message to dramatize in any writing course. I choose this essay, too, because it expresses with some vividness and good humor the frenzy of undergraduate life, all in one breathless paragraph.

   Furthermore, and in spite of its obvious shortcomings, I am struck by a kind of integrity in this piece, for I know that its anti-logic and its disorganization do not represent a neophyte's attempt to imitate some fashionable literary mode. On the contrary, these mannerisms come from the heart—they were freshly invented for the occasion. David has never heard of Barth or Barthelme, though he says he has read some Vonnegut and a little Salinger. (David's Verbal SAT score, 480, is about average for our students; he looks forward to majoring in computer technology.) Having given some thought to the complications of Clarity, David evidently felt that he now had to have his say in *this* way. And so he did, and it's revealing to see a nonliterary nineteen-year-old decide that the pressures and absurdities of his immediate life are to be most appropriately expressed in a prose that echoes, however amateurishly, the cinematic styles of some of our most honored contemporary writers.

(David's fellow students, by the way, were not taken by this piece, finding it weird, wild, or silly, and of course they have a point.)

But there is organization here, of a kind. Our author has put things together with key phrases that reappear in new situations: "the fast lane," "sweaty palms," "tobagadung." The language is consistently late-twentieth-century colloquial: "honcho," "flaky," "jetpack," "shoot them the old peace sign." And perhaps most admirable, to me, is the avoidance of self-pity or sentimentality. The voice here manages to accept the turmoils of daily life as comic rather than pitiful. Even the complaints about the cafeteria food—a dreary undergraduate ritual—are expressed with some good humor. Politically too the voice remains unaffiliated, for all the jocular praise of the "anti's." "Shoot them the old peace sign," that will get them off your back. This paper contrasts sharply with a classmate's well-meant essay on the anti-nuclear movement, filled with simplistic, pious outrage and nothing new.

I did not encourage David to continue in this style for the remaining weeks of the course. He was expected to respond to my assignments, some of them thoroughly pedestrian, in a sober and workmanlike manner, just like everybody else. Nevertheless he knows, if only because I have chosen this piece for publication, that I respect and honor his effort to break away for once. And his classmates may have learned something too, for they all shared in this process of selection, however undemocratically. From a little Xeroxed anthology of essays composed by the entire class, students were invited to choose the one they felt might most appropriately appear in a published book on Good Writing. Only one out of the twenty chose David's. But the prof disagreed! If this experience has widened for them the limits of acceptable expression, so much the better. On the other hand, they may simply have written it off, as they have to do with so much, as one more manifestation of professorial unpredictability. What does Teacher want? Well, to vary the famous aphorism, how do I know till I see what I get?

Study Questions

1. In a classroom discussion of "A Paper Without a Name" and Walker Gibson's commentary on it, one student said,

> I'm sorry, but I guess this is my "muddy prose," and I'm afraid I agree with the findings of the writer's fellow students. I can see that some of the phrases are repeated, but I don't think you can put things together just by repeating phrases. I can see the paper isn't self-pitying either, but if you make everything a joke, does that make it mean something? Maybe the paper doesn't have a name because the writer didn't know what he wanted it to say exactly, I mean beyond "college is frantic." I think this writer just makes a pass at the assignment. What he does isn't controlled enough to really deal with it.

Another student responded by saying,

> Look, the students were asked to say whether their experience of college was one of freedom or regimentation and they were told they could use any form they wanted to say it in. This writer wants to show he's free in spite of all the pressures of regimentation. The form he chooses shows how many pressures there are in college and how they keep coming and so how hard he has to work to stay on top of things. He *does* deal with the assignment, and I think very well, with a lot of control.

What position would you take in this controversy?

2. Walker Gibson says that "A Paper Without a Name" has "obvious shortcomings," though he does not specify them.

    Suppose David Kopack came to you for advice on how to rewrite his paper. Has the paper any "obvious shortcomings" you would want to mention? If so, how would you describe them, and what would you tell him to do about them? If not, what would you say to this writer in order to help him improve his paper?

3. "Writing decent conventional prose is not the only thing to do all the time," says Walker Gibson, "and . . . Clarity is relative. For me this is an essential message to dramatize in any writing course."

    What benefits could attend a teacher's dramatizing such a "message" in a writing class?

    What dangers might attend the dramatizing of such a "message"?

    What stance, then, do you think a writing teacher ought to take on "writing decent conventional prose" and on "Clarity"?

Linda Robertson's Assignment

[This assignment was used in a course called "Knowledge and Discourse," which surveyed writers from Socrates to Montaigne. One of the main purposes of the course was to enable students to improve as writers by practicing in their own writing the various modes of reasoning employed by the authors we read.]

The meditations of John Donne use a mode of reasoning called *analogy*, a kind of comparison. Analogy explains something hard to understand by comparing it with something familiar. Donne practices the kind of meditation that examines the self—the most difficult thing of all to understand—by comparing ideas, attitudes, responses, or emotions with some familiar action, event, or object.

Your assignment is to write a meditation using analogy as the main mode of reasoning. You can either begin with yourself, deciding what it is you wish to clarify through analogy; or you can choose an event, action, or object and see if by following the structure of the meditation, you discover something about your own understanding or responses you had not fully realized before.

ॐ Meditation

by Randy Byers

Winter is coming, and outside my window there stands a tree preparing to sleep through the cold storms of the year's final season. When the winds come howling and tearing, when the ice lays down its heavy grip, the tree will not know or care. It will rest in dormant slumber until spring's wakening call. If then the tree stirs from its hibernation to find that it has lost a limb, it will heal without pain. If it has contracted a disease, or if the soil has become somehow unfertile, it will not agonize over its impending death. Nor will it agonize over life. When spring arrives, the tree will change. It will not be a violent change. Slowly, the sap will start to run again. The roots will take in the nutrients of the soil—the good minerals and water that are necessary for the tree to grow. The bark on the slender branches and twigs will lose their grey-brown hue and turn to a lively green. Buds will burgeon on the branches and unfold under the glowing touch of the sun. The tree will clothe itself with verdant leaves, dressing for the lazy afternoons of summer. Now the

LINDA R. ROBERTSON, formerly Composition Adviser in the Honors College, University of Oregon, is now Director of Composition at Wichita State University. While at Oregon, she developed a writing-across-the-curriculum program and, with the aid of an NEH grant, helped organize the Pacific Northwest Writing Consortium, an organization of six Pacific Northwest colleges and universities concerned with developing writing-across-the-curriculum programs. Her most recent article, "Assignments in the Humanities: Writing-Intensive Course Design," appears in the *Journal of Advanced Composition* (1982).

tree will be fully alive. The roots will pry further into the ground, seeking the hidden wealths of food, and the leaves will capture the fleeting elements of the air and soak up the energies of the sun. Yes, the tree will transform this nourishment to flesh, and it will stretch and grow, in planet of earth and toward planet of sun. It will grow and change, not by violent struggle, but by careful, steady process. Mindless and painless, the tree will not know its own slow beauty. It will bask in the summer's warmth; it will bow firmly beneath the life-giving rains; it will stand tall through starry nights and cloudless days. When autumn descends with its deathless sleep, the leaves will blaze into fiery colors; the roots will doze. Winter will strip the tree of its garments, but the tree will not care. It will sleep outside my window.

2   There is something appealing about the life of a tree. True, a tree has no mind and has no motivation, but neither must it worry about what it should think nor what purpose or direction it should have in moving. A tree cannot communicate or share its hopes and fears, but, having no hopes or fears, it has no need to share them. Trees cannot consciously or unconsciously hurt anyone's feelings. They cannot experience faith, but, also, they cannot feel despair. There are advantages to having no mind.

3   But I do have a mind. That does not mean there is nothing to be learned from a tree. One thing to learn is an attitude toward change. Change is a slow process in a tree. There is no way for a tree to avoid change; change is a part of a tree's growth. With every season, the tree changes form. Each change meets the need of the specific season, whether it be the dormant stage of winter or the expanding stage of spring. In each case, the tree is reacting to its environment and using the resources available to fit into the environment. The seasons are a cycle of change, and the tree has evolved so as to work with, rather than against, that cycle. I, too, am a product of evolution and a participant in the cycles of life. In addition, I have been given a conscious will and an ability to reason. Like the tree, I should move with the changes of life, instead of trying to avoid them or move against them, as I sometimes will consciously or unconsciously do. There is nothing inherently wrong with change. It is a natural part of life. My reasoning faculties are a resource to deal with change, just as the tree's ability to use the energies of the sun is a resource. Let me learn from the tree, then, to use my reason to fit and grow with life's seasons. If I am the victim of some bad luck, let my reason show me how to recover painlessly by taking advantage of some other opportunity.

4   Another related lesson to be learned from the tree is the lesson of growth by process. The tree does not grow by wishing it had another limb. Again, it uses its resources—minerals, water, air, and sun—takes them into itself, and transforms them into the cells of growth. The tree

builds itself by making the resources into a part of itself. Likewise, I must take the resources available to me—knowledge and experience—and attempt to use them to grow. Understanding is a process of growth. By using reason to analyze and synthesize the information around me, I am able to apply that information to my own life. If I can analyze and synthesize the lessons of change and growth to be learned from the tree, then I can apply those lessons to other areas of change and growth in myself, such as the change and growth involved in learning to love someone.

Gautama Buddha achieved nirvana beneath a tree. Christ was cruci-   5
fied on the Calvary tree and went to God. Rooted in the ground and reaching to the sky, trees are the integration of Earth and Heaven. The integration is a unity of growth and change. Let me seek that integration. Let me move with the cyclical seasons of life and grow from the soil of knowledge and experience and from the fiery forge of reason.

LINDA ROBERTSON'S COMMENTARY

Randy does some things with language here that I normally criticize. The first paragraph, for instance, shows him straining after beautiful images:

"It will rest in dormant slumber until spring's wakening call."
"Buds will burgeon on the branches and unfold under the glowing touch of the sun."
"The tree will clothe itself with verdant leaves, dressing for the lazy afternoons of summer."

Randy assumes, as do many novice writers, that arcane or unusual words lend an aethereal beauty to description. But he forgets that if a word is rare—like "burgeon" or "verdant"—it is unlikely to evoke a very clear image in the mind of the reader precisely because it is not used very often; hence, readers do not have much in their experience to associate with the term.

Moreover, by reaching for such diction, Randy presents a series of cloying redundancies: *dormant* in this context is synonymous with *slumber; burgeon* with *unfold; wakening* with *call.* This kind of tautology reflects a thoughtlessness, an inattentiveness to meaning. When a writer seems inattentive to language, I as a reader become impatient: "If *he* doesn't care about what he says," I ask myself, "why should I?"

Another kind of inattentiveness is signaled by imprecision, as in the embarrassing sentence in the first paragraph, "Yes, the tree will transform this nourishment to flesh, and it will stretch and grow, in planet of earth toward planet of sun." We've got two tautologies there as well as the suggestion that trees have flesh and that the sun is a planet, a combination of redundancy and error that is especially jarring because Randy is, after all, describing something very familiar—a tree in springtime. His baroque elaboration seems false and strained.

I act generally like every other vulturous English teacher you may have known when I spot carelessness in language. But I forgive or overlook these weaknesses in this particular paper because the strengths of the opening paragraph compensate for them. For one thing, Randy enacts with language the meaning he seeks to convey. He is describing the repetitive order of seasons. But he does more than tell about them. Randy's language imitates the thought because his paragraph, like the cyclical pattern he describes, ends where it begins, that is, with winter, the window, and the tree, and his attention to rhythm, sound, and sentence structure all contribute to our understanding of what this means. Take the following sentence:

When the winds come howling and tearing, when the ice lays down its heavy grip, the tree will not know or care.

The rhythm of this sentence moves us along from one element to another just as the words describe the coming of events, and the sounds of the words work with that rhythm. Randy repeats the "ow" sound of the onomatopoetic "howling" with the word "down," for example, in such a way as to make us feel the grip of the ice as an irresistible force. Similarly, the alliterated, parallel, subordinate clauses ("when the winds. . ."/ "when the ice. . .") not only force us to see winds and ice as working together, they move us to the climactic dependent clause ("the tree will not know or care"), just as the winds and ice finally overwhelm the tree in winter.

Like any other human being, I derive pleasure from rhythmic sounds, imagery, and ordered patterns—particularly when they work together. So when I read language using all three, I'm pleased by it—drawn to it. Randy's language both pleases and convinces me because he brings me a fresh vision of something I already know—the seasonal changes of a tree. And he manages this not only through his care with language, but because in that care he provides me with a clear vision of himself. He defines himself by his response to nature. Consider, for instance, these two sentences: "If it has contracted a disease, or if the soil has become somehow unfertile, it will not agonize over its impending death. Nor will it agonize over life."

I had not previously thought very much about a tree being unconscious of death, but I'm willing to entertain the idea on the basis of that sentence. The greater revelation, however, comes when Randy says, "Nor will it agonize over life." We would all agree that death is something humans agonize over; but how often would we think that agonizing over life also defines us as humans? The sentence forces me to think: "Of course, we agonize over life even more often than we agonize over death."

Notice, too, that Randy adds to the impact of this insight by setting it off as a separate sentence even though it is a fragment. He persuades me then, even if momentarily, that there is something appealing about the life of a tree—not because it is beautiful to look at, or an elegantly arranged system for converting chemicals to life—but because it is spared the consciousness of life.

It is not easy for any of us to admit that we fear or resist this essential element of our humanity—our consciousness. Not only does Randy admit it but the power of his language—which I envy and respect—forces me to admit it to myself. And I respect also his relentless pursuit of the insight at the end of the second paragraph, where his balanced sentence weighs the advantages and disadvantages of consciousness: "They cannot experience faith, but, also, they cannot feel despair." He then moves to the stark conclusion: "There are advantages to having no mind."

Having demonstrated the attractiveness of unconsciousness, Randy goes on to wrestle with the problem, trying to find a way out by considering what he might learn about his own change and growth from the unconscious change and growth of a tree. He poses himself some very tough questions, and like all the tough questions we pose ourselves, they are tough questions for others, too. I, too, fear change. I, too, feel frightened by the notion that I cannot know what I am shaping myself to become. When I returned this essay to Randy, my written comment contained a quotation from the English psychologist Joanna Field: "I began to have an idea of my life, not as the slow shaping of achievement to fit my preconceived purposes, but as the gradual discovery and growth of a purpose I did not know." Randy Byers, Joanna Field, and I were brought together by the alchemy of Randy's struggle with certain elements of himself. One reason for writing surely is that kind of coming together.

Randy could not have drawn us together unless he had made a conscious commitment to the challenge presented by the assignment, a highly structured assignment that he could have chosen to address petulantly or begrudgingly or just as a matter of routine—as all of us too often do in response to the constraints imposed on us by another. Submitting to the constraints of the assignment, however, enabled Randy to discover connections among change, rationality, and nature, connections that he might not have discovered without a form to be responsible to. In deciding to see the assignment not as a task set by a teacher but as a challenge for himself, he became what Donald Murray calls "a magnet" for his subject. He drew himself toward himself; he became composed. Or to say it another way, his composing became a way of his composing himself.

When we talk about a musical *composition*, or the *composition* of a picture or photograph, or the *composition* of an essay, we mean that each presents us with an ordering principle, one to which we respond because it orders experience in a way that makes it possible for us to apprehend ourselves. Randy agreed to accept the rules of an assignment as a challenge to order his experience and to understand himself. By so doing he discovered what cannot be taught, only learned. Further, by making the commitment that he did, Randy became a magnet for more than himself. He drew together Joanna Field and me. To set one's perceptions in order—that is what real composing is—helps others to order their perceptions, too.

Study Questions

1. A student writing about Randy Byers's "Meditation" and Linda Robertson's commentary on it said,

   > Linda Robertson's analysis of the section of Randy Byers' essay [her paragraph 5] where "attention to rhythm, sound, and sentence structure" all work together makes clear also where these things *don't* work together in the essay (such as at the opening of the third paragraph) and provides a guide as to how they may.

   Pick a sentence from Randy Byers's essay in which you think "attention to rhythm, sound, and sentence structure" do not "work together." Rewrite the sentence so as to make these things work together. Use whatever you can from Linda Robertson's analysis in paragraph 5 of her commentary to do this.

   Judging from your experience with what you have just done, how would you say a close analysis of writing can be helpful to a writer?

2. Linda Robertson refers to the writing assignment to which Randy Byers addressed his paper as "a highly structured assignment," one that involves certain "constraints," one that has "rules."

   Judging from your reading of Randy Byers's paper and Linda Robertson's commentary on it, what argument can be made for the use of highly structured assignments in writing classes? How might they be helpful to people learning to write well?

   Explain why you think highly structured assignments could or could not help *you* as a writer.

3. In a classroom discussion of Randy Byers's "Meditation" and Linda Robertson's commentary on it, a student said,

> Is it really fair for teachers to expect students to write papers that will bring the teachers "a fresh vision" of what they "already know" or that will help them "order their perceptions"? I don't see how teachers can demand that student writing magnetize them this way. Isn't that first of all to ask students to do what a lot of them just can't do? And second, it makes an awfully big deal out of writing, doesn't it?

How would you respond to these remarks?

LEO ROCKAS'S Assignment

Choose someone you know (or can imagine) who speaks in some remarkably revealing way. Recall (or imagine) a situation in which the speaker was free to go on revealing all of her or his peculiarities. Try to become the ideal listener (or writer) who can arouse (or create) such revelations.

❧ The Coach

by Annie Beraquit

1   I would have to be passionately in love with someone, in order for me to compromise my flippant behavior. Life is good! Yup! Life is good!

2   I like work! I want to be a famous photographer, and I know I'm going to be one. Last summer *Time* magazine bought one of my photographs for $100. But they didn't give me a byline. Now, ten million *Newsweek* readers are going to see a group shot with my byline. Yeah!

3   You see, I'm like my father. He can live anywhere in the world, yet he's living in that small house in Teaneck. You saw the house, didn't you? Didn't I take you there last summer? You remember! It's a convenient place to stop at when you want to go to the city.

4   Oh, please don't mind me if I move around while talking to you. I've got work to do. It runs in the family. My brother and I practically had to tie mother down just to get her attention. "Mom, put the broom away for a second and listen." Yup! She did at times. And I have work to do.

5   Anyway . . . my father. Yeah. You know, he can also take off any time he wants to and travel. But he doesn't. That vacation he took with my mother to Paris last summer was the first one in years. And they stayed only a week, because they had to go back to work. If I was going to Paris, I'd stay for a month! And he can drive any car of his choice, but he's riding around in that old Ford. He just gets a kick out seeing his bank account grow. He buys clothes about twice a year. And I want to be a famous photographer. And I need sleep.

6   I have to be up early tomorrow, 'cause I have to go to Greenwich. I'll be making $400 in two hours. Last night I made $200 in just two hours of printing. I'm the best printer they've got here. They know it, too.

7   What? What did you ask me? Whether or not I consider myself an artist or a career person? What do you think? First of all, you don't consider yourself as something or someone!

8   But I do love art. Art is something, be it printing, sculpture, or

LEO ROCKAS is Professor of English at the University of Hartford. He is the author of *Modes of Rhetoric* (1964), *Ways In: Analyzing and Responding to Literature* (1983), and articles on rhetoric and Shakespeare.

whatever, that proves the interest of a viewer or spurs the ambition of an artist. Art is a recording of the world to make sense of chaos, to bring order where it did not exist before, or to discover the truth that is latent in a series of seemingly disconnected events. Art is merely an individual's projection of himself into anything which stimulates his fancy.

I love surrealistic art. My favorite is Giorgio de Chirico. I admire the patterned structure in his imagery. And I dig Duchamp. Do you remember that thing he did with the snow shovel, bottle rack, and urinal? What exclaimed madness! Surrealism is the art of supreme objectivity. And because it's defined as a school of thought, discipline is not relative. Or is it? Hmmmm . . . Do you think that story about Vincent Van Gogh shooting himself in the groin is true? Was he really insane, or was he just ahead of his time? Art is. . . .

The New York Yankees! I love to watch the New York Yankees on television! There's nothing like seeing Reggie Jackson on the field. Man, he was George Steinbrenner's money-player. Thirty-nine home-runs last year! He was one of the catalysts that led the Yankees to a league division championship. Steinbrenner is an asshole for replacing Jackson! The man was great with the A's, he was great with the Yankees, and he's still great!

Where are you going? Don't go! It's going to be a long night. I could use some moral support.

How's the emotional weather? I've been doing some socializing. I had a girlfriend who broke up with me last year. Now she says she wants to be hurt, because she hurt me. I don't know. I don't know. I can't sleep with anyone, if I'm not in love with her. I wish it was like in the South. I was born in Atlanta, you see, although I don't remember much, since my parents lost all of my baby pictures. In the South, you hold hands . . . then you kiss . . . then maybe in a year or two . . . Ah, sex isn't that big with me. I'm very quiet when I'm making love.

I want to be a boring person. I've been working on it, you know. I don't want to be exciting anymore. I was exciting when I was a kid. There's a difference between being 24 and being 22, you know. I even sold the very first picture I ever took. It was of President Ford, when he came to Teaneck. I was top-seeded in my high school tennis team. The girls nicknamed me "Legs," because of my calf muscles. In my senior year, I took summer classes at Harvard University with a group of pseudo-intellectuals. Then off to Europe for eight weeks. That was fun. My friends and I did drugs, ran, and did more drugs. I think I tripped out on acid once.

Anyway, my parents sent me to Wesleyan, because they thought it was the best preppie school in the East. They did. Hmmm. . . . I wonder how much it costs to go there now. You know, I worked very hard at being a Jewish American Prince. I know I'm arrogant. But I've got two people working on me to change me. And I was the one who introduced Ultimate Frisbee to Wesleyan. I was the captain, you know. I helped organize teams all over New England. You see, I was endowed with such an acuity, that it doesn't bother me if I get stoned three or four times a day, and I do. God gave me that gift! I had a very lucky life. And my father always told me that it was because I was Jewish. I don't even think twice about going out with a non-Jewish girl. I want to be a boring person. Many people think I'm a loner, because I like to think, you know. But I'm not really. I'm a happy person. Life is good. You should try transforming whatever negative energy you may have into something positive. Life is good, and life is short. Try meditation.

15   Look at this newspaper! You know, even though it's got five sections, it seems very insubstantial. Why? It seems so insubstantial! But I did have two front-page layouts. Look! "Sports" and "Friday!" Yeah! Look at that! Nice!

16   My career's doing all right. But I'm not on staff. I work more than forty hours a week, but I'm not on STAFF. My full-time position does not pay for my teeth! As well as all the other fringe benefits the other STAFFERS have, like expense-paid transportation, one-month vacations, insurance . . . I had to shoot this picture on my own time!

17   I want to go to New York. I hitch-hike to New York all the time. There's an art to hitch-hiking, you see. I've hitch-hiked my way across the country and over in Europe plenty of times. They always picked me up.

18   But there are no jobs in New York. I don't want to be waiting on tables.

19   I'm debating whether or not I should smoke a joint. What do you think? But I'm sick. I have a cough.

20   Look at this work! I'm gonna die! I need sleep! I don't even have time to be nice to those who love me and those I love! I'm doing all of this, because I just happened to be here at this time of night.

21   What are you doing tomorrow? We have to talk about this. We have to deal with this. I like ya. I want to see ya. Give me a call, and we'll have lunch. What do I have tomorrow? I have to pick up an antenna for my car, so I can get some tunes when I go to the Cape next week. I'm going on a vacation for ten days, you know. And then, I need pants . . . yeah, I need clothes. I need to do my laundry. I haven't worn any underwear for two days. Oh, and the post office. I have to go there too. And practice. We have practice tomorrow night. Well, call me, ok? I have to go back to work now. See ya.

LEO ROCKAS'S COMMENTARY

Anyone who has been teaching for any length of time is often asked, "What are students like today? How do you find them different from students ten or twenty years ago?" Oddly enough, the teachers I most respect are looking for the answers to those very questions in the writing their students submit. Deciding among the answers isn't any easier than deciding which movie or novel or play of the year or the decade seems to have hit the prevailing tone of the time.

For me, no student writing is duller than the kind students imagine their teacher wants to read. They are trying to figure me out while I am trying to figure them out. Most good teachers are put off by the conference-question "What do you want?" precisely because they fear that, in many classes, the teacher's easy answers to the question, put in practice by the student, insure a higher grade. Most students wouldn't believe me if I were to tell them the truth, to say, "I want to see in blazing clarity what you and your friends want most today, and if you can tell me I won't care too much how you get it down, and I'll reward you with the highest grade."

All this concern about what's really burning in the student's breast is based on the assumption that the best writing comes from the nondictated, the self-initiated. Only you can tell—if you are keen enough to watch your anxieties while you are having them—what's really happening to you and to others like yourself.

The essay many teachers say they are looking for, with an overall thesis and a topic in each paragraph, is oftener than not a straitjacket for what the student thinks the teacher wants. There is something to be said, of course—and it's usually said till students are weary of hearing it—for getting ideas down in orderly fashion. What isn't said so often—and it needs to be proclaimed—is that the original, the memorable, the powerful sentence or essay can't be laid down in advance.

Unlike many teachers, I am not very worried about the difference between "expository" and "creative" writing. The best creative writing (think of your own examples) is also, and may be more effectively, a *setting-forth* or expository writing.

Annie Beraquit listened to one voice that seems especially authentic. Her scene is apparently a late-night session between part-time workers in a newspaper office, the speaker nominally "coaching" the listener. Annie was responding to the hint of doing a "dramatic monologue," that is, a single voice talking on uninterrupted and in an especially revealing situation to a supremely receptive listener, in this case, a writer with all her faculties tuned to the art of letting a speaker tell all, letting him *set forth* himself.

Maybe Annie's speaker will strike you as an individual, maybe as a type. But I think Annie was trying to capture his individuality, his oddity and distinctiveness. If, in working up a monologue of your own, you begin by thinking of a type—let's say the Jewish American Prince—you may end up with nothing, or almost nothing: a list of clichés.

I hesitate to classify Annie's speaker, because any label would be a restriction. But he gives himself several labels: tennis star, Wesleyan grad, Jewish American Prince, Yankee fan, "the best printer they've got," "the one who introduced Ultimate Frisbee," and so on. I find perhaps most revealing or ingenious, his desire to become boring: "I don't want to be exciting anymore," he says, as if being exciting is something he has grown out of. But in his rambling, he expresses what he considers exciting about himself. His bid for the listener's attention seems to depend heavily on his being "the best" at whatever he's talking about. This urge to excel—at sports, studies, art, drugs, lovemaking—seems a major concern of the speaker and perhaps of many other young people today. What do you suppose his SAT scores were?

My enthusiasm for this monologue would remain high whether Annie had taken it down verbatim—taped it, let's say—or had made it all up, or had done any combination of those extremes. All of us see and hear remarkable hints and let them pass us by. The *writer* is not so much someone who gets her verbs and sentences right as someone who can recognize and assemble her perceptions and lay them out for us. What does it matter if there was a boy who talked exactly like Huckleberry Finn (even if he was Mark Twain) or a prince who talked exactly like Hamlet in Shakespeare's play? Those artists caught their subjects just right and so did Annie.

I suspect (but don't know for sure) that Annie herself fashioned or heightened much of the monologue, primarily because the speaker so tellingly reveals his foibles. Or, to put it the other way around, the writer cleverly, satirically exposes his follies. We usually don't give ourselves away quite so neatly. Though we can be sure of a satiric result, we can't be sure of a satiric intent. Direct transcripts from life, when set forth for cool contemplation, may often be read as satire.

If you want to look at some earlier examples of the monologues of self-satirists, I'd suggest those of Robert Browning (1812–1889), especially "My Last Duchess" and "Fra Lippo Lippi"; the soliloquies of Richard in *Richard III* by William Shakespeare (1564–1616); and the speeches of the main speaker in *Rameau's Nephew* by Denis Diderot (1713–1784).

Study Questions

1. In a paper written about Annie Beraquit's "The Coach," a student said,

> The trouble I have with this paper is trying to decide whether it's a kind of trick writing or whether I'm missing something. I can't put all the tones of this voice

into the same character, for example, but I'm not sure if this is my fault or the writer's. The main character says of de Chirico, "I admire the patterned structure in his imagery," as though he were an art critic for the *Times* or something. But then in the very next sentence he says "And I dig Duchamp." Is there some point to that I'm missing? Then he breaks off in mid-sentence in his talk about art and switches to the Yankees. Why? And what's it mean that the listener *then* starts to leave—and that he stops her with his talk about lovemaking—in which he doesn't really seem all that interested. Who's coaching who here? Is the writer saying this guy has a starved emotional life because he's been living in a fast lane he doesn't want to live in or what exactly? I don't want the speaker put in a pigeonhole, but I'd like to be a little surer than I am whether the writer is in control of this paper or not and what she means with what she's written. I can't honestly tell whether this paper is very carefully or very carelessly done. HELP.

Making specific reference to Annie Beraquit's paper, do the best you can to help settle this student's mind with this piece of writing.

2. "I find perhaps most revealing or ingenious," says Leo Rockas of the character Annie Beraquit has created, "his desire to become boring."

   How do you explain what Leo Rockas might mean here? In what way might such a detail be called "revealing"? Revealing of what? How might this use of the detail be said to express the writer's ingenuity?

   Explain why you agree or disagree with Leo Rockas's assessment of the function of this detail in "The Coach."

3. "Most students wouldn't believe me," Leo Rockas says of what he wants as a writing teacher, "if I were to tell them the truth, to say, 'I want to see in blazing clarity what you and your friends want most today, and if you can tell me I won't care too much how you get it down, and I'll reward you with the highest grade.' "

   Explain why you think a writing teacher who believes what Leo Rockas says he does should or should not express such a view to students.

For this assignment I will ask you to be a twentieth-century Gulliver. You have been shipwrecked and now find yourself forced by circumstances to live in a strange land, one which calls itself Illinois. Specifically, you are living in an urban center named Champaign-Urbana. While you are in this strange city, you take time to observe the customs and rituals of a unique group of persons in the society, a group identified as "college students." Now, in the hope that someday you will return to your native land and report your observations of these "college students" to your countrymen, you prepare written accounts of the activities of this group. One of your most interesting papers describes a custom (or activity or ritual) associated with an event the students call "Homecoming." Unfortunately, none of the students will interpret the custom for you. All your report contains is a description of the custom together with your interpretation of what it means. (You may assume that you have sufficient facility in the language to communicate with natives. But remember, none will *interpret* Homecoming for you.)

Clearly, your assignment is to prepare that report. However, let me emphasize one point. If you merely describe Homecoming, or any part of it, without careful consideration of the way in which you are to do it, you will not have fulfilled the assignment. You must play the role I have prescribed. To get yourself in the frame of mind necessary to do this, I suggest that you read some pages of Jonathan Swift's *Gulliver's Travels* or Samuel Butler's *Erewhon*.

❧ The Triumph of Isaac *by Michael Gianturco*

1   In the course of my first three days here I made only two significant observations, and those were very superficial. I noticed that the town had been laid out with scrupulous attention to geometric order, and that the natives seemed to venerate one man especially. The man is Abraham Lincoln, and there are streets, buildings, and business establishments named in his honor. In the evening of the fourth day, it occurred to me that I should question some of the natives about Lincoln. If I could discover why the man was so highly regarded, I might gain some insight into the culture of the people who honored him.

2   Out of a sense of consistency, I was conducting my researches on

---

DONALD C. STEWART is Professor of English at Kansas State University in Manhattan. The author of *The Authentic Voice* (1972) and numerous articles on composition theory, practice, and history in such magazines as *College Composition and Communication, College English, English Education, Research in the Teaching of English, The English Journal, Rhetoric Review,* and *Change,* Professor Stewart was also 1983 Chair of the Conference on College Composition and Communication.

Lincoln Avenue. Although it was quite late, the sidewalks were thronged, and the street was crowded with motor vehicles. I walked opposite to the drift of the crowd, occasionally singling out a native for questioning. A female informed me that Lincoln was a "president," and that a "president" was a man who represented the people.

At the end of two "blocks" I came upon, startlingly, a giant orange and green temple. I went closer, and discovered that what I had believed to be the front of the temple was a false facade, erected somewhat forward of the real front of the building. I say "temple," for that was my first impression of the place. I have decided since then that it is, in fact, a center of religious activity.

A scene had been painted on the front of the temple. There were two figures in the immediate foreground, one standing, the other kneeling in supplication. The standing man was dressed in a hideously grotesque costume, a costume bearing no resemblance to the everyday garments of the natives. The kneeling figure, too, was somewhat grotesque, with greatly exaggerated shoulders and the numerals, 27, painted on his back. In his right hand, the standing man was grasping the hair of the kneeling man. In his left hand, poised in the air, was a short, vicious-looking knife.

There was a rectangular, green field in the background, with white stripes spaced at measured intervals along its length. Looking closely, I perceived yet another figure, standing near the geometric center of the field. From time to time I could discern a brown dot, apparently flying from the hand of this figure. The dot, no doubt mechanically animated, moved rapidly across the face of the green rectangle, describing a parabola, and came to rest in the arms of a fourth figure, who was standing near the extreme left hand edge of the field. At the very top of the temple, captioning the scene, were the words, "The Illini Will Scalp 'Em." The verb, "to scalp," is not in my vocabulary at present, but I have assumed that the caption is of religious import. The phrase has probably been handed down from an earlier time, along with the mythology of the religion. That might account for the peculiar, probably obsolescent wording.

I asked a passing native about the temple and he, in turn, asked me whether I were a "foreign student." Then he explained that the structure had been erected in celebration of "Homecoming." The term meant nothing to me. I resolved to continue my researches about Lincoln, and return to the temple at a later date. The next native I spoke with provided me with some truly pertinent information, and I have reproduced his remarks below:

"Abraham who? Are you drunk? Listen, I'm drunk. Abraham, eh? Now lemme think. Abraham . . . yah, listen, he was the guy in the

Bible. Yeah, I remember it now. He was an old man who took his son, Isaac, out on the mountaintop. And he was going to put a knife into him, a sacrifice. You understand what I'm saying to you? He was going to put a knife into him, a sacrifice. You understand what I'm saying to you? He was going to put a knife into him and then . . . and then . . ."

8   The native was crudely interrupted by his female, who admonished him to "come away from that Foreigner."

9   I called after him. "And then what? What happened to Abraham and Isaac?"

10   "Nothing," he cried, "He didn't have to stab him after all. They went home."

11   His parting words struck me. They went home, I thought. Of course! Homecoming. I rushed back down the sidewalk and arrived, panting, before the temple. There could be but little doubt that the two men in the foreground, the knife-wielder and his victim, were Abraham Lincoln and his son, Isaac. I seized a young native by the arm and demanded confirmation.

12   "Lincoln?" he said. He peered into the stream of passing motor vehicles. "Yeah, I guess you're right. What of it?"

13   I was so excited by my discovery that I began to change colors, and it was necessary to hide myself for a time. I ducked down a side street and hid behind a tree. There I remained for half an hour, thinking. The question, it seemed, centered around Isaac. What was his role in this complex and bizarre mythology? When I returned to Lincoln Avenue the vehicle traffic had dwindled, and there were few people on the sidewalk. A native, male and bearded, came walking along with some books under his arm. I approached him.

14   "Who was Isaac?" I asked.

15   "Isaac? Isaac who? Isaac Newton?"

16   "Yes, yes," I breathed, "Isaac!"

17   "Well, Isaac Newton is the guy that invented calculus."

18   "And what, friend, is calculus?"

19   "Calculus is . . . It's like . . . It's where you have a moving point, see? And as it moves across, it defines an equation, that is, mathematically speaking."

20   "The point moves across *what* to define an equation?" I was eyeing the giant, green rectangle. The strange, brown dot was moving across its surface, describing a parabola.

21   "Oh," said the native, "Yeah, it moves across a system of rectangular coordinates."

22   "Rectangular coordinates?"

23   The native went on his way and left me standing, deep in thought,

before his temple. There and then, I began to develop an hypothesis about his religion.

The ritual of Homecoming celebrates Abraham's forbearance. The   24
father stayed his hand and did not destroy his son. The execution did not take place. They went home. Despite the ferocity of the knife-wielder, Isaac was triumphant.

It is known that Abraham Lincoln, the "president," is the symbolic   25
representative of the people. It would seem that at one time, here in this place, a religion flourished around the figure of Abraham. This religion must have held the people themselves to be a deity. If one worships Abraham, one worships the people. Let us suppose that a new religion grew out of the religion of the people, much as Isaac grew out of Abraham. The new religion glorified numbers, and mathematical order superseded the people as a deity. One might postulate three stages of transition from the old god to the new. First, perhaps because there were so many people, it became necessary to *number* them. Second, over a period of time, a tendency grew to divorce the symbol from the substance, to worship the numbers directly and without reference to their antecedents. Third and finally, the devout began to revere the order of the number system above the numbers themselves. Isaac Newton, the inventor of calculus, symbolizes the new deity. The numerals on his back emphasize his role. The panorama in the background is a projection of Isaac's vision, and demonstrates the mechanics of his calculus. Significantly, the great, green rectangle dwarfs the figures in the foreground, manifesting the supremacy of the vision over both men as men. Homecoming, then, celebrates the ascendant New Truth, a truth so imposing that it has displaced the old truth, Abraham Lincoln, without so much as a stabbing. Abraham leaves the field in good order—mathematical order. One has only to glance at a map of the streets, or at the precisely geometric architecture of the houses, to appreciate the triumph of Isaac.

Donald Stewart's COMMENTARY

"The Triumph of Isaac" belongs to a period during which I was still assigning single general topics for an entire class. (My preference in recent years has been to give students more and more responsibility for generating and shaping their own topics.) At that time I was beginning to be concerned with a concept with which I have been subsequently identified: the development of an authentic voice in student writing. I had noted the ease with which my students reproduced the concepts and the words of their culture, without any evidence of independent thinking. And so I created an assignment which would, I believed, tell me whether or not they were capable of freeing themselves imaginatively from ways of perceiving given by their culture, and of demonstrating imaginatively an intellectual independence which I considered highly desirable.

Most students who wrote on this subject, however, were unable to escape the limits of their own perceptions and cultural "givens." But Michael Gianturco was able to more fully realize the role he was to assume than any of his classmates, and the product was, in my judgment, a brilliant and imaginative fulfillment of the assignment. Consider, in detail, what he has done in this paper. He has fully taken on the role of a space alien who can only put together what his observation and experience give him. In this report, what has he seen? An apparent temple, with a false facade, the figures, their gestures, their costumes, and the background behind them which he describes in great detail. Very early in the paper, we, the readers, begin to enjoy the contrast between what *we* know and what the alien created by Michael does not. Imaginatively, Michael is drawing us into the world he is creating and making us forget that we are reading a student "essay." This alien, we learn, is collecting material on Abraham Lincoln, apparently a deity of some sort whose significance is not clear to him. He has already noted the streets and buildings named after Lincoln and the statues which venerate him.

Probably the most stunning examples of Michael's ingenuity are the clever mixing of Abraham Lincoln and the Biblical Abraham, and the confusion between the biblical Isaac and Isaac Newton, the inventor of the calculus, which Michael cleverly ties to the rectangular grid on the false facade of the temple. In short, we find here a completely credible assembling of data. Michael's brilliance is in making it all cohere and thus provide a basis for the conclusion to his alien's report in which the alien notes that the older deity, one representing the people, has been progressively supplanted by a more abstract mathematical concept. We have to conclude that, given the data Michael's alien obtains and the reasonable connections he makes between the pieces of information he has, his conclusions about Homecoming follow perfectly. In our modern composition class, therefore, Michael gets high marks for invention, for the discovery of material for his paper, and for his creative manipulation of it.

There is a fundamental philosophical profundity in this paper, also: its revelation that our reason, in which we in the industrialized and technological west have put so much faith and trust, may on occasion be a distorting mirror of reality. Anthropologists, especially, know that interpreting other cultures through the lens of one's own often leads to false conclusions. And there is, of course, the apocryphal story of Sir Walter

Raleigh who, when imprisoned in the Tower of London, burned a manuscript on the history of the world when he discovered that he had observed a street brawl but had interpreted what happened completely incorrectly.

The organization of this essay deserves high marks, also. Too often, I suspect, you have been given mechanical forms with which to organize your material: the five-paragraph essay; the beginning, middle, and end pattern; even the pattern coming down from classical rhetoric—introduction, background argument, refutation, and conclusion. Much to be preferred, in my judgment, is organic form. It occurs in a piece of discourse that develops like a growing plant and gradually assimilates all of the materials of the essay into a perfectly realized whole. It works by engaging the interest of the reader and holding it. Now, did you notice that the reader of Michael's essay cannot anticipate its conclusion from its beginning? We begin inside the mind of the alien who has begun to research a particular problem in our culture but who is quickly deflected from his original purpose when he encounters a festival whose rites and symbols intrigue him. I have already commented on the accumulation of information by the alien and the remarkable way in which Michael has him put it together step by step. The conclusion to the alien's report is logically defensible. The conclusions follow from the evidence accumulated, and they grow out of the material. At the end Michael's alien has put together a plausible absurdity, a logical but astonishingly incorrect explanation of Homecoming, arrived at inductively. That interpretation of Homecoming, strange as it is, must not cause us to forget, however, how carefully this essay has been constructed: its mixing of narrative and description, its sections of exposition given to interpretation, and the beautiful summary of the meaning of Homecoming. As an example of organic form, it is excellent: The material is suited to the subject, and the entire essay develops stage by stage, as does a living thing.

Even the style of the paper is distinguished by two things: (1) Michael's ease in handling sharply contrasting levels of usage; (2) the quality of its vocabulary. You should have noticed the contrast between the careful, scholarly reportorial language of the alien and the crude and informal speech of the natives. Michael's alien assumes a tone of perplexity and slight distance as he reports the speech of the natives: "The verb, 'to scalp,' is not in my vocabulary at present . . ."

The last paragraph, especially, reveals Michael's easy command of a large vocabulary and the concepts it presents. "The *panorama* in the background is a *projection* of Isaac's vision, and demonstrates the *mechanics* of his calculus. Significantly, the great, green rectangle dwarfs the figures in the foreground, manifesting the *supremacy* of the vision over both men as men. Homecoming, then, celebrates the *ascendant* New Truth, a truth so imposing that it has displaced the old truth, Abraham Lincoln, without so much as a stabbing." And the final sentence is a very sophisticated example of compression, balance, and prose rhythm: "One has only to glance at a map of the streets, or at the precisely geometric architecture of the house, to appreciate the triumph of Isaac."

Thus in invention, arrangement, and style, this paper is exceptional. And when one couples those qualities with the degree to which Michael has fulfilled the assignment and, in so doing, offered yet one more example of the compelling proof that our perceptions of reality are more distorted than we think they are, one has to conclude, as I did many years ago, that this is a most remarkable student paper.

The full recognition of the paper's quality came not from me, however, but from Michael's classmates. The day after this paper was handed in I made copies of it for class discussion. I remember very well the usual buzzing which went on at the start of the hour as my students settled into the task of reading and evaluating this paper. Very quickly, however, the room became deathly silent. You must remember that everyone in the class had attempted this assignment, so all were aware of the difficulties in it. After five minutes, the first student to finish reading the paper looked up at me, anguish and bewilderment written all over his face, and said slowly, "Someone in *this* class wrote *this* paper?" I nodded yes. He shook his head slowly and looked down at his desk. For the rest of the semester I do not recall a single student in that class asking me what an "A" paper was.

Study Questions

1. In a classroom discussion of "The Triumph of Isaac," one student said,

> I can see how this paper goes together and everything, but I don't see where it's got the "philosophical profundity" that Donald Stewart talks about. "Our reason" is a "distorting mirror of reality." That's the kind of hidden meaning English teachers are always saying is in things. This writer was just having a good time. I don't think he was trying to make any deep meaning with his writing at all.

Another student responded by saying,

> I don't think it matters what the student intended when he wrote the paper. He was obviously having a good time, yes, but being as careful as he was to bring everything together results in a creation that *has* meaning, maybe a number of different meanings. Donald Stewart calls it an example of one meaning. But it could also be seen as an example of others. That's why it's good writing.

What position would you take in this controversy?

2. A student writing about "The Triumph of Isaac" and Donald Stewart's commentary on it said,

> I guess I don't understand why Donald Stewart says that the five paragraph essay and the pattern that comes down from classical rhetoric are "mechanical forms." Couldn't a five paragraph essay gather things into a "perfectly realized whole" and wouldn't it then be an example of "organic form"? Is it being suggested that the patterns of classical rhetoric are always mechanical? And if so, what exactly is "organic form"?

How do you respond to the questions this student is raising?

3. "I created an assignment," Donald Stewart says of the one to which "The Triumph of Issac" was addressed, that would "tell me whether or not [the students] were capable of freeing themselves imaginatively from ways of perceiving given by their cultures, and of demonstrating imaginatively an intellectual independence which I considered highly desirable." Though students are told clearly what to do in addressing Donald Stewart's assignment, the intention or purpose of the assignment as stated above is not mentioned in it.

What sort of argument might be developed to support the claim that Donald Stewart should have stated his purpose in his assignment just as he phrases it above?

What sort of argument might be developed to support the claim that Donald Stewart would have lost something by stating his purpose in his assignment as he does above?

You have just constructed two arguments about a particular writing assignment. Use your experience in having done so to respond to this assertion: Writing assignments should always make clear what students are to do and why.

Using the members of the class as an audience, assume the stance of an expert explaining an unfamiliar concept, process, or idea to intelligent laypeople.

✍ A Baby Biography   *by Lillibeth E. Navarro*

1   The delightful experience of having a two-year-old niece has sparked my interest in developmental psychology, a wide field of study that deals with the child's perceptual capabilities, social development, emerging personality, learning abilities and cognitive capabilities.

2   Charles Darwin was one of the earliest scholars who pioneered the study of children. After the publication of his theory on the evolution of the species, the child became the object of his interest. He wrote a detailed account of the development of his own son, a child-study technique we now know as the baby biography.

3   Baby biographies were more or less detailed accounts written by parents concerning the early growth of one or more of their children. Early writers of baby biographies concentrated on describing the emergence and changes of specific abilities of children in an attempt to explain some phenomenon.

4   In this paper, I shall write about my niece, Rhona Marguerite D. Go, who is two years and six months old. Specifically, I will concentrate my observations on her during the last six months and share with you the little that I know about child psychology.

5   When Rhona and her parents moved to California from Hawaii in September, 1982, she was still wearing Pampers and drinking milk from a bottle. We were introduced to her as her new relatives, and she eyed us with interest. Although she was extremely quiet in our presence, it did not take long for us to win her confidence. Rhona is an extremely affectionate child. She was brought up in a loving atmosphere with her parents taking equal responsibility for her care. At bedtime, both her father and mother put her to sleep. Until she had one hand on her mother's breast and the other on her father's ear, she used to be unable to

W. ROSS WINTEROWD, Bruce R. McElderry Professor at the University of Southern California, founded and directs that institution's graduate program in rhetoric, linguistics, and literature. Realizing that problems of literacy do not begin at grade thirteen, Professor Winterowd has worked extensively with the public schools. He has directed three NEH summer seminars in "Literature and Literacy" as well as a year-long seminar in the same subject. He is the author of numerous articles and a number of books, including *Rhetoric: A Synthesis* (1968) and *Contemporary Rhetoric: A Conceptual Background with Readings* (1975).

sleep. Rhona is sensitive to even the slightest hint of disagreement between her parents. She gets very upset when she sees them unfriendly toward each other even only in pretense. Hostility disturbs her equilibrium. Little as she is, she knows how to be the vital link of love between her parents. She literally brings them close to one another. She compels them to make up after a quarrel and unless they do, she is not satisfied.

"Papa, kiss Mama now!" she commands with authority.   6

The family showers Rhona with profuse love—it is the atmosphere   7
that she breathes. Because we kiss, embrace, and fondle her, she shows a spontaneity of positive emotion. We make it a point to praise her for virtue and encourage her to be good after her naughty spells.

When my cousins (Rhona's parents) started going to work, I had to   8
baby-sit, and the first thing I learned was to talk to the baby in correct English. We do not use baby talk with Rhona; we talk to her in grown up speech until she acquires the correct pronunciation of words. It is therefore not surprising that she speaks English far better than other children of her age. She has a wide range of vocabulary and is able to express herself in grammatical sentences. For instance, when she wants to be left alone, she says, "I'll do it myself!" She denies any offer of assistance if she knows she can manage by herself. What is even more remarkable is Rhona's attitude toward possessions. When she knows she has something of the kind that you offer to give her—a toy or candy perhaps, she will not take it but will say, "I have already."

When upset, Rhona tells you straight, "Don't bother me. We're not   9
friends any more. I'm mad now!" In her more tender moments, when she sees you worried, she asks, "What happened? Are you hurt? I'll kiss you so it won't hurt anymore, okey?" Last week, when our refrigerator broke down and we could not store food for some days, she was very worried at lunch. Seeing the frige empty, she wailed in dismay, "We have no food! We're poor now!"

Children need adults to explain things to them. You just do not say,   10
"Don't do this, don't do that, or Don't touch this, don't touch that." Orders do not make sense to them until you explain why. Rhona, for instance, plays with almost anything within her reach. When tired of playing with her toys, she goes around exploring the rooms. She likes to play with the ceramics, the baskets and glassware on display, the silverware, the cosmetics on the dresser. With a little guidance, she is allowed to touch and experience a thing to sate her curiosity and then we explain why she cannot play with them like ordinary toys.

"These are Mama's toys, sweetheart. Mama keeps them here to make   11
the room nice and beautiful. Don't touch them so that when visitors come, they will see them here and say, 'Oh, what a beautiful house Rhona has!'"

12   As long as Rhona understands the explanation, she usually complies and very seldom does she disobey. With the same technique, we explain why she has to drink her medicine, why her parents have to go to work, or why she cannot eat too much candy.

13   Rhona has outgrown her fondness for stuffed toys. She is very good in what developmental psychologists call mastery play, i.e., play that involves the exercises of new skill through repetition and the manipulation of objects and exploration. Rhona easily recognizes shapes, sizes and colors. She has an incredible knack for doing jigsaw puzzles. First, we show her how the complete picture looks; then we point out how the parts fit, how the shapes differ and how the colors match. We let Rhona try doing them by herself and now, she can already complete a seven-piece puzzle in just a few seconds. In addition, she knows her alphabet, can recite her numbers and name an infinite number of things. She has an insatiable interest in children's books and the best way to entertain her is to switch on the television to Sesame Street.

14   Since Rhona is an only child, she needed an imaginary friend to serve a social function. Patty is that imaginary friend—a little girl about Rhona's age who serves as her alter-ego. Patty is a convenient partner in everything. We need her to sit beside Rhona at mealtime to make Rhona eat more than she ordinarily does. To stop Rhona from mischief, we extol Patty's virtues. For Rhona to emulate, Patty has to be consistently good. At nap time, Rhona needs Patty to accompany her to Sleepy Town, the imaginary substitute to the snugly comfort of Mama's breast and the touch of Papa's ear when they are both at work. This fantasy play as developmental psychologists call it, helps Rhona overcome her fears and anxiety. When Rhona's parents arrive from work at the end of the day, Patty makes a graceful exit in order to make way for an eager exchange of love between a delightful baby and her wonderful parents.

Ross Winterowd's COMMENTARY

"A Baby Biography," by Lillibeth E. Navarro, is a competent piece of writing, even an excellent piece, but it is *not* in any sense extraordinary. Ms. Navarro is not Superwriter, whose abilities seem God-given or genetically endowed and hence beyond the attainment of ordinary mortals. Certainly Ms. Navarro is intelligent, lively, and interesting, but her general level of skill as a writer is not beyond that attainable by most students. Anyone who has the ability to negotiate the complexities of modern society and the agility to run the gauntlet of a college or university also has the potential to produce informative, well-written expository essays.

Another point should be made about Ms. Navarro: Her native language is Tagalog, not English. During her semester in my class, she made enormous gains in her ability to produce standard, idiomatic English with virtually all of the mechanical details (such as punctuation, verb agreement, and pronoun reference) in order.

What, then, is excellent about "A Baby Biography"? To answer that question, I must take the long way around, speaking first about English composition in relation to a liberal education. A liberal education prepares one to deal with ideas fairly and penetratingly, to view experience as a series of lessons to be learned, to realize that living is a continual process of recognizing and attempting to solve problems, an ongoing passionate effort to "make sense" and understand. In my composition classes, we view writing as an instrument of thought, as a way to make sense of the human situation and to convey one's perceptions to others who are engaged in the endless process of becoming liberally educated. For me, composition and liberal education are virtually synonymous.

In "A Baby Biography," we see a writer who is fascinated by an episode from her own experience and who probes that episode to find its meaning. In the essay, we encounter a mind at work and a likeable personality.

A negative virtue is one that earns no praise when it is present, but arouses severe criticism when it is absent. In discussing "A Baby Biography," we can look first at one great negative virtue: It is clearly written. Ms. Navarro does not force the reader to extricate her thoughts from a snarled tangle of syntax; the prose style is like a clear pane of glass through which we see meaning, not like frosted glass, through which we can perceive only vague outlines.

I would like to stress the following point: *Clarity is not an absolute value in writing;* but no one should make a bad trade, giving up clarity merely to seem profound and to bamboozle readers. There are times, of course, when writers sacrifice the ultimate in clarity for other legitimate purposes.

Another strength of "A Baby Biography" is its specificity. We do not, of course, get a physical description of Rhona—and perhaps such detail would strengthen the essay—but we do learn what Rhona does and what she says: "She has a wide range of vocabulary and is able to express herself in grammatical sentences. For instance, when she wants to be left alone, she says, 'I'll do it myself!' "

It is from specific details that the interested reader can draw conclusions about Rhona's development and can infer generalities about the process of early development in all children. (Examples of Rhona's extensive vocabulary would strengthen the essay at this point.)

In written comments about "A Baby Biography," Ms. Navarro said:

"This paper was written particularly for my classmates in English 400 and my English professor, Dr. Ross Winterowd. I also wrote the paper for my family, my cousins, and my niece. The paper might be of interest, too, to the real experts in developmental psychology and to a generally literate audience."

The diversity of this intended audience may explain one problem with the essay. It is not really a social scientific case study, nor is it simply a report of personal experience; therefore, one cannot exactly determine how to take the author. In her comments, she said, "In this paper, the writer was to take the position of an expert explaining something complex to a lay person. I chose to explain what developmental psychologists call the baby biography and as an example, wrote part of the baby biography of my niece." The paper would have been more successful, I think, if her stance had been something like this: "I've been interested in the language and cognitive development of my niece, and I'm going to report what I've observed." That is, her stance should have been that of one interested layperson to others.

I will conclude my remarks with a bit of useful doctrine. The expository essay should be the main focus of a composition class, just as composition itself is central to the ideal of a liberal education: creating people who can think cogently about the world around them and communicate these thoughts to others, who see life as a series of problems to be understood and perhaps solved, who are intellectuals in the sense that they choose to live in the world of ideas.

Lillibeth Navarro's essay, one which she completed toward the end of the semester, shows that she has opted for the tradition of the liberal education.

It shows also that subject matter for writing is always at hand. Students taking classes in economics, history, psychology, and so on are novices writing for experts—their professors—and their papers are more like tests than real essays. But in composition classes, intelligent, inquiring students draw on their own resources and thus, in terms of resources at least, are the equals of their professors.

In a sense, the composition class is—or should be—a marvelous intellectual democracy, where a group who believe in liberal education get together to deal with writing as both an instrument of thought and a means of communication.

Study Questions

1. In Lillibeth Navarro's paper, says Ross Winterowd, "we encounter a mind at work," one that is "fascinated by an episode from her own experience" and that "probes that episode to find its meaning."

How do you describe the mind that is at work in "A Baby Biography"? What sorts of things does this mind assume? What sorts of questions does it raise? How does it go about putting things together? What meaning does it find in the episode it probes?

"Composition itself is central to the ideal of a liberal education," Ross Winterowd says later in his commentary, "creating people who can think cogently about the world around them and communicate these thoughts to others."

You have just described a mind at work. How well does it exemplify what Ross Winterowd sees as "the ideal of a liberal education"?

2. Suppose that Lillibeth Navarro indicated her intention to rewrite "A Baby Biography" along the lines suggested by Ross Winterowd. She wishes in her revision to assume the stance of someone saying, "I've been interested in the language and cognitive development of my niece, and I'm going to report what I've observed." What would you suggest to her that she do in her revision?

3. A student writing about "A Baby Biography" said,

> I know what Ross Winterowd means by saying that there's a problem with this essay because "it is not really a social scientific case study, nor is it simply a report of personal experience." But in another way isn't it the attempt of the writer to bring those two areas of her life together that makes the piece interesting to talk about? Maybe the greatest weakness of the essay is also the source of its greatest strength. Wouldn't just the case study have been awfully dry? But just the personal might have become sentimental.

What position do you take on this observation?

Writing Assignment 7
Masks

Imagine a friend coming to you, puzzled about the student essays and commentaries in this chapter. This person is not in your course and couldn't have participated in the conversations you've been having about writing in your class. But you may assume that she has read everything in your course that you have read. Your friend says something like this to you:

> A lot of the comments on the student essays so far have praised writing for its honesty, the writers for being sincere, authentic. But here's a group of papers most of which are addressed to what seem to me to be assignments that ask for the very opposite, and these papers are praised too. Donald Stewart tells his students to become little green men. Ross Winterowd makes his class pretend to be experts. Leo Rockas as much as has his class imitate the way somebody else talks. Linda Robertson wants students to write a seventeenth-century meditation. And though Walker Gibson doesn't ask his students to assume a special personality or use an artificial form, to judge from what he praises David Kopack for, he may as well have.
>
> First of all, I don't see the value of asking students to do what most of the teachers here are asking them to do. It seems to me that there are enough problems connected with honesty for a writer writing just as herself. How can somebody be honest or authentic if they're pretending to be a Martian?
>
> Secondly, I'll admit that some of these students are very successful in doing what they do. But what's the point of it? What's the value of it? What have the students gained or learned from having done it?

Your friend may have misinterpreted what the teachers here are asking their students to do, but she's raising an issue worth considering—one you have already been doing some thinking about, particularly if you wrote a paper addressing Writing Assignment 6.

You may not have had as yet a specific invitation to write in a voice or manner other than your own. For the purposes of this paper, consider the invitation extended. Write an essay—a paper with a point of some kind—either in an assumed voice, that is, by speaking through a persona of some sort, or in a particular literary form or writing style. Who or what you are imitating—and why—ought either to be stated directly or to be clear from the context of your paper.

Now, on a separate page, respond to your friend's statement. You have five student essays and the teachers' commentaries to draw upon. You yourself have written a paper in which you've imitated someone else's style or voice. And, for five or six weeks now you've been considering some of the things that make good writing good, as well as attempting to determine the value of good writing—with the help of others who have been doing the same thing. You don't have All The Answers, of course, but your writing and classroom experiences in working with the material in this book have given you a perspective different from that of your friend. Do what you can in this paper to make this difference into something helpful to her.

Public Worlds

8

A spoken or a written word was spoken or written by someone, and part of the recognition of the word as activity is a recognition of who it was that said it or wrote it. When I make a statement, even as coldly and impersonal a statement as a proposition of Euclid, it is I that am making the statement, and the fact that it is I that am making the statement is part of the picture of the activity. In the same way, when you quote a proposition of Euclid the fact that it is you who quote it is part of the picture which is not to be discarded. And when I quote you it is I that am doing the quoting. Attention to the activity aspect of all our communication inevitably forces mention of the maker of the communication.

P. W. Bridgman

THE WRITING THAT CERTAIN PEOPLE MUST KNOW how to do well in the course of conducting their professional lives, writing for or in a public world, is most often, and quite understandably, taught in courses that are especially constructed to focus on it: courses called business writing, technical writing, science writing, professional writing, industrial communication, and so forth. This is not to say that ordinary freshman English courses *never* give students practice in writing business letters, reports, or memos, but that they do not usually focus exclusively on this form of writing. Courses that do are usually taken by upperclassmen, by students who have already completed some coursework in writing and who feel the need to develop special skills.

This chapter is intended to help you understand two things about writing in a public world. The first is how such writing may be considered in some senses special. The second is how such writing in another way is *not* special, how what makes it good is a matter of what makes all good writing good. The writing assignment at the end of the chapter is designed to give you an opportunity to make sense of this apparent contradiction.

219

PAUL ANDERSON'S Assignment

Project 3: Unrequested Recommendation

This assignment is your chance to improve the world—or, at least, one small corner of it. You are to write a letter of 300 to 900 words in which you make an unrequested recommendation for improving the operation of some organization with which you have personal contact—perhaps the company that employed you last summer, or a club you belong to, or your sorority or fraternity.

There are four important restrictions on the recommendation you make.

1. Your recommendation must concern a *real* situation in which your letter can *really* bring about change. As you consider possible topics, focus on situations that can be improved by the modest sort of measures that you can argue for effectively in a relatively brief letter. It is not necessary, however, that your letter aim to bring about the complete solution. In your letter, you might aim to persuade *one* of the key people in the organization that your recommendation will serve the organization's best interests.
2. Your recommendation must be unrequested; that is, it must be addressed to someone who has not asked for your advice.
3. Your recommendation must concern the way an organization operates, not just the way one or more individuals think or behave.
4. Your recommendation may *not* involve a problem that would be decided in an essentially political manner. Thus, you are not to write on a problem that would be decided by elected officials (such as members of Congress or City Council), and you should not address a problem that would be raised in a political campaign.

Of course, you will have to write to an *actual* person, someone who, in fact, has the power to help make the change you recommend. You may have to investigate to learn who that person is. Try to learn also how that person feels about the situation you hope to improve. Keep in mind that most people are inclined to reject advice they haven't asked for; that's part of the challenge of this assignment. From time to time throughout your career, you will find that you want to make recommendations your reader hasn't requested.

In the past, students have completed this assignment by writing on such matters as the following:

a no-cost way that the student's summer employer could improve the efficiency of procedures for handling merchandise on the loading dock,

---

PAUL V. ANDERSON, a faculty member at Miami University (Ohio), has published several articles and chapters on technical writing and its teaching. He has edited *Teaching Audience Analysis and Adaptation* (1981) and has coedited *New Essays in Technical Writing and Communication: Research, Theory, Practice* (1983). He also works as a consultant in writing to business and industry, and directs Miami University's master's degree program in technical and scientific communication.

a detailed strategy for increasing attendance at the meetings of a club the student belonged to,

a proposal that the Office of the Dean of Students establish a self-supporting legal aid service for students.

Bear in mind that one essential feature of a recommendation is that it compares two alternatives: keeping things the way they are now and changing them to the way you think they should be. You will have to make the change seem to be the better alternative *from your reader's point of view*. To do that, you will find it helpful to understand why the organization does things in the present way. By understanding the goals of the present method, you will probably gain insight into the criteria your reader will apply when comparing the present method with the method you recommend.

Because I do not want you to undertake a project that is too complex or otherwise unsuited for this assignment, I ask you to tell me about your topic and audience before you begin writing.

∿ Unrequested Recommendation   *by Scott Houck*

Scott Houck
616 S. College #84
Oxford, Ohio 45056

April 28, 1983

Georgiana Stroh
Executive Vice-President
Thompson Textiles Incorporated
1010 Notea Ave.
Cincinnati, Ohio 45014

Dear Mrs. Stroh:

As my junior year is drawing to a close I am growing more and more   1
anxious to return to our company where I can apply my new-found knowledge and skills. Since our recent talk about the stiff competition mounting in the textile industry I have thought quite a bit about what I can do to help Thompson continue to prosper. As I was going over some

notes I was making on the subject, I was struck by how many of the ideas stemmed directly from the courses I have taken here at Miami.

2   Almost all of the notes featured suggestions or thoughts I simply didn't have the knowledge to consider without college! Before I enrolled, I, like many people, presumed that operating a business required only a certain measure of common-sense ability. That almost anyone could learn to guide a business down the right path with a little experience. However, I have come to realize that this belief is far from the truth. It is true that many decisions are common-sense, but often decisions only appear to be simple because the entire scope of the problem or the full ramifications of a particular alternative are not understood. A path is always chosen, but how often is it the BEST path for the company as a whole?

3   In retrospect, I appreciate the year I spent supervising the Eaton Avenue Plant because the experience has been an impetus to actually learn from my classes instead of just receiving grades. But I look back in embarrassment upon some of the decisions I made and the methods I used then. I now see that my previous work in our factories and my military experience did not prepare me as well for that position as I thought they did. My mistakes were not so often a poor selection among known alternatives, but were usually sins of omission. For example, you may remember that we were constantly running low on packing cartons, and we sometimes ran completely out causing the entire line to shut down. Now I know that instead of haphazardly placing orders for a different amount every time, we should have used a forecasting model to determine demand and establish a reorder point and reorder quantity. But I was simply unaware of many of the sophisticated techniques available to me as a manager.

4   I respectfully submit that many of our supervisory personnel are in a similar situation. This is not to downplay the many contributions they have made to the company. Thompson can directly attribute its prominent position in the industry to the devotion and hard work of these people. But very few of them have more than a high school education or have even read a single text on management skills. We have always counted on our supervisors to pick up their management skills on the job without any additional training. While I recognize that I owe my own opportunities to this approach, this comes too close to the common-sense theory I mentioned earlier.

5   The success of Thompson depends on the abilities of our managers relative to the abilities of our competitors. In the past, EVERY company used this common-sense approach and Thompson prospered because of the natural talent of people like yourself. But in the last decade many new managerial techniques have been developed that are too complex for the average employee to just "figure out" on his own. For example, it

has taken several thousand years to develop the Linear Programming Model for transportation and resource allocation problem solving. It is not reasonable to expect a high school graduate to recognize that his particular distribution problem could be solved by a mathematical model and then to develop the LP model from scratch. But as our world grows more technically complex, competition will stiffen as others take advantage of these innovations. I fear that what has worked in the past will not necessarily work in the future: we may find that what our managers DON'T know, CAN hurt us. Our managers must be made aware of advances in computer technology, management theory, and operations innovations and must be able to use them to transform our business as changing market conditions demand.

I would like to suggest that you consider the value of investing in an 6 in-house training program dealing with relevant topics to augment the practical experience our employees are gaining. In addition, when management or other fast-track administrative positions must be filled, it may be worth the investment to hire college graduates whose coursework has prepared them to use state-of-the-art techniques to help us remain competitive. Of course, these programs will initially show up on the bottom line as increased expenses, but it is reasonable to expect that, in the long run, profits will be boosted by new-found efficiencies. Most importantly, we must recognize the danger of adopting a wait-and-see attitude; our competitors are now making this same decision and hesitation on our part may leave us playing catch-up.

In conclusion, I would like to say that I believe I will be a valuable 7 asset to the company, in large part, because of the education I am now receiving. I hope you agree that a higher education level in our employees is a cause worthy of our most sincere efforts. I will contact your office next week to find out if you are interested in meeting to discuss questions you may have or to review possible implementation strategies.

Sincerely,

Scott Houck

PAUL ANDERSON'S COMMENTARY

In his letter to Mrs. Stroh, Scott Houck offers an unrequested recommendation to Thompson Textiles, a company that employed him before he came to college. In college, Scott has learned things that make him think that Thompson would benefit if its managers were better educated in modern management techniques. Thompson could enjoy that benefit, Scott believes, if it offered courses in management to its employees and if it began to fill job openings at the managerial level with college graduates. However, if Thompson were to follow Scott's recommendations, it would be changing its current practices considerably. Thompson has never offered courses for its employees, and it has long sought to keep payroll expenses low by employing people without a college education, even in management positions. (In a rare exception to this practice, the company has guaranteed Scott a position after he graduates.)

To attempt to change the company's policies, Scott has decided to write a persuasive letter to one of the most influential people on its staff, Mrs. Stroh. Unfortunately for Scott, throughout the three decades that Mrs. Stroh has served as an executive officer at Thompson, she has consistently opposed company-sponsored education, and she has energetically supported the current policy against hiring college graduates.

Thus, in his letter Scott faces one of the most challenging of all writing situations, one in which the writer—without being asked for advice—tries to persuade the reader to change his or her beliefs, policies, or behavior. Most readers, when presented with advice they haven't requested, instinctively reject it. Mrs. Stroh would have an especially strong motive for rejecting Scott's advice: She is likely to feel that if she were to agree that Thompson's educational and hiring policies should be changed, she would be admitting publicly that she had been wrong all those years to support the current policies.

People usually fend off unwelcome or threatening advice by compulsively defending their present positions and by aggressively searching for flaws in the advice. Good arguments rarely receive objective consideration from defensive readers.

Thus, to argue persuasively on behalf of unrequested advice, a writer must arouse as little defensiveness as possible and argue effectively in the face of the objections the reader is likely to raise. Four features of Scott's letter illustrate how masterfully he anticipates and deals with the thoughts and feelings Mrs. Stroh is likely to experience while reading his communication.

1. *Scott opens his letter in a way designed to make Mrs. Stroh feel receptive to what he is about to say.* Like the smile or frown with which we greet someone, the opening words of a communication can affect the other person's openness to what we will say next. In his opening, Scott presents himself as Mrs. Stroh's partner. He reminds her that they have talked together about the future of Thompson Textiles. This letter, he hints, is an extension of that conversation and of that partnership. Mrs. Stroh is likely to view this relationship with Scott as friendly and to feel

open, after reading the first paragraph, to what Scott might say next in his letter.

2. *Scott has organized his letter so that Mrs. Stroh will read his main argument before her defensiveness is aroused.* Scott's main argument, the very foundation of his recommendation, is that if Thompson's managers study current management techniques, they will learn to solve problems that stymie them now, when the only solutions that will occur to them are those suggested by common sense and their practical experience. Although Scott's argument seems reasonable, he can expect that if Mrs. Stroh feels defensive when she reads it, she will look with great determination for faults in it. Therefore, to increase the probability that Mrs. Stroh will read his argument objectively, Scott places it early in the letter (paragraphs 2 and 3), *before* the first statement that is likely to arouse her defensiveness (first sentence, paragraph 4).

Similarly, Scott withholds his two recommendations almost to the end of the letter (paragraph 6). In business, writers usually organize their communications in the opposite way, placing their recommendations near the beginning. They do this because they are usually writing to people who have asked for the writer's advice. The writers know that when readers pick up requested letters, memos, or reports, they want, more than anything else, to find out what the writers think should be done. If the writers postpone their recommendations until late in their communications, they risk irritating their readers.

In contrast, Scott's reader, Mrs. Stroh, is more likely to be irritated by the recommendation itself than by Scott's withholding it. Scott certainly wants to postpone triggering that irritation until he has been able to present all his arguments, in the hope that the less irritated Mrs. Stroh is when she reads the arguments, the more objectively she will consider their merits. Thus, by thinking about his reader's likely reactions, Scott was able to choose the best organization for this particular communication.

3. *Scott selects evidence that, while being appropriate and persuasive, is unlikely to inspire objections from his reader.* Scott would probably have aroused strong objections from Mrs. Stroh early in his letter if he had been less skillful in selecting the example he presents in paragraph 3. There, he argues that a manager who has studied modern management techniques can readily solve a problem that bewilders a manager who has not. If Scott had chosen to illustrate this point by talking about the blunders he saw *other* managers making at Thompson, he would probably have inspired Mrs. Stroh, out of her sense of fairness, to defend the other managers, who would not be present during her reading to defend themselves. Her defense would have led her to reject Scott's evidence. Scott avoids this undesirable reaction by using the example of a situation *he* handled poorly (but could handle effectively now that he has been to college).

4. *Scott explicitly addresses the major objections he believes Mrs. Stroh will raise.* A defensive reader is going to raise objections to the arguments the writer presents. If the writer does not anticipate these objections, the reader is likely to dismiss the arguments by saying, "This communication is fine so far as it goes, but the writer ignores this or that important point. Therefore, I reject the writer's recommendations." Scott seeks to avoid this outcome by explicitly addressing the objections he expects Mrs. Stroh to raise. His close attention to Mrs. Stroh's probable objections is illustrated in paragraph 4. As already mentioned, the opening sentence of that paragraph is likely to be the first statement that arouses any negative reaction from Mrs. Stroh. In the very next sentence, Scott deals with the reaction he expects her to have by assuring her that he knows that the present managers, hired without a college education, have nevertheless done excellent work for Thompson.

Later in his letter, Scott addresses what he predicts will be, overall, Mrs. Stroh's two major objections to his recommendations. In paragraph 5, he anticipates the first objection, which might be stated this way: "Our company has prospered under the current policies; we would be foolish to tinker with something that works." Scott responds by arguing that the situation in business has changed so that what worked in the past won't work in the future. (By casting his argument in this way, Scott adroitly avoids suggesting that Mrs. Stroh was wrong to have supported the current policies in the past.) In paragraph 6, Scott addresses the second possible objection: "Offering courses in management and changing the current hiring policy would cost the company too much money." Scott replies by comparing the prospect of increased profits if the company changes its policies with the threat of reduced profits if it does not (because competitors who *are* educating their managers and hiring college graduates would have an advantage).

Scott's skillful efforts, throughout his letter, to postpone, reduce, and deal with Mrs. Stroh's anticipated defensiveness should not be confused with a manipulative approach to writing. To manipulate someone is to trick them into making a decision based upon inappropriate or irrelevant considerations. A manipulative argument to Mrs. Stroh would be "A person who is as charming and intelligent as you, Mrs. Stroh, really ought to be surrounded by well-educated employees who can fully appreciate your sophistication and skill as a business leader." Like most manipulative arguments, this one appeals to the reader's self-interested emotions, in this case vanity. In contrast, Scott's arguments involve an appropriate and relevant criterion: the extent to which the changes he suggests will contribute to the prosperity of the company.

In praising Scott's letter, I do not mean to indicate that it is perfect. He misspells "newfound," for example, and he omits many commas. The sentence fragment near the beginning of paragraph 2 trips me up, and the mention of the "several thousand years" it took to develop the Linear Programming Model sounds a little absurd to me. Other phrasings might also be improved. Overall, however, Scott's careful work in anticipating and shaping his reader's probable reactions to his letter is skillful enough to render those blemishes relatively insignificant. Such attention to the reader's likely thoughts and feelings is one of the major characteristics of good writing.

Study Questions

1. A student writing about Scott Houck's letter and Paul Anderson's commentary on it said,

   > Paul Anderson mentions some "phrasings" that he thinks Scott Houck might change to improve his paper, but says that, given the student's accomplishment, such "blemishes [are] relatively insignificant." I agree. But I wonder whether the move at the opening of the fifth paragraph is maybe a "blemish" of a different sort. Is it going to have the effect it's supposed to? When you tell somebody like Mrs. Stroh that she has plenty of "natural talent" might that not be laying it on a little thick—particularly when you go on to say how there are new techniques that may be too complicated for people like her to figure out? Might she not hear Scott Houck saying she doesn't keep up with the times?

   What position do you take regarding this criticism?

2. In a classroom discussion of Scott Houck's letter and Paul Anderson's commentary on it, a student said,

   > Isn't this a pretty complicated assignment to ask students in a technical writing course to take on? And it doesn't seem to me to give them much practice in writing the kinds of things they'll have to be writing in the business world very often. Even Paul Anderson admits that the way this kind of letter has to be organized is different from the way most letters and memos and reports are organized. So why have students write things that are this tricky? What's the point of it?

   How would you respond to this statement?

3. In his commentary on Scott Houck's letter, Paul Anderson suggests a way of distinguishing between persuasive and manipulative writing.

   How might it be argued that the distinction as Paul Anderson draws it is in some ways valid and useful to a writer?

   How might it be argued that in other ways the distinction is neither valid nor useful to a writer?

   What do the two arguments you have developed enable you to say about the importance of knowing how we can or cannot distinguish between persuasive and manipulative writing?

Linda Flower's Assignment

A Brief Problem Analysis

Find a problematic situation you know well—a real problem—and a reader who might benefit from your analysis of the problem. In your role as a professional consultant (that is, a knowledgeable advisor) write a brief analysis that defines the key issues in this problem and suggests a reasonable action.

Remember that writing an effective analysis involves two key tasks: (1) understanding and defining the problem and (2) designing your written analysis for a reader.

1. Problems arise because two important things are in conflict. Try to define the central issues here; it often takes detective work and hard thinking to discover and define the conflict at the heart of a real problem. Then try to name for yourself the two, three, four, or more key issues (the causes, questions, or implications) that make up the problem as *you* see it.

2. A professional analysis needs to be more than a written record of your thinking process; it needs to be designed with a reader in mind. Such readers have some reasonable expectations: they want to know as soon as possible what the problem is, as you define it; they want to see the main subpoints or issues distinctly (rather than find them buried in a story about the situation); and they want to know what you propose to do. As you can see, trying to structure the report in this way will also help you articulate your own understanding of the problem itself.

✑ Problem Analysis   *by Stephen Pfeiffer*

Background

My problem-situation is fictional, or at least, I hope it is. But, the facts it is based on are real. Public mental health care facilities are woefully inadequate. Most, like the Washington D.C. system, which I know a little bit about, have been swamped. Unemployment is extremely stressful, can bring out underlying mental illness, and has been linked to all sorts of mental, behavioral and physiological problems, from depression to child abuse to ulcers. So, the only fictional aspect of my situation is my

---

LINDA FLOWER is Associate Professor of English and former Director of the Business and Professional Communications Program at Carnegie-Mellon University. She has conducted research projects sponsored by the National Institute of Education and the National Science Foundation on cognitive processes in writing. This research has led to various articles on planning, revision, and the writer's thinking processes and to a textbook, *Problem-Solving Strategies for Writing* (1981).

postulate that unemployment has produced a sudden, noticeable surge in mental health problems in Allegheny County. [The Homestead area is the site of a major, recently closed U.S. Steel plant.—L.F.]

TO: Dr. Carl Rogers, Administrator
           Allegheny County Mental Health Services
FROM: Stephen Pfeiffer, Director
           Homestead Unit
SUBJECT: Emergency Expansion of Services

In your memo of October 8, 1981, you requested that unit directors report periodically on the effect high unemployment is having on community mental health care needs, and the ability of health care services—both public and private—to meet those needs.   1

I regret to report that we are facing a very serious mental health care problem in Homestead. Since my last report to you in April, the number of people seeking mental health care in the Homestead service area has increased substantially, and the demand for health care is beginning to exceed the capacity of the Homestead Unit and other low-cost health care services in the area.   2

Because of the seriousness of the situation we are facing, I am recommending that we take emergency action to expand the Homestead Unit's services. Specifically, I am requesting authorization to ask private psychiatrists in Homestead and student psychiatrists at area universities and institutions for volunteer assistance in meeting the client overload. I am also recommending that consideration be given to more permanent solutions, such as reallocating funds to purchase part-time professional services for the Homestead unit, or permanently increasing the number of professionals on staff.   3

A more detailed analysis of our mental health care problem and my recommendations follows.   4

The Mental Health Services Overload

The unemployment crisis has been producing steady increases in the number of people seeking counseling for many months now, and the MHS has responded by asking unit directors to monitor unemployment-related mental health care needs, and by setting up special therapy groups for the unemployed. But the problem we now are facing in Homestead is that there has been a relatively sharp, short-term increase in demand for mental health care which threatens to overwhelm the health care system. I will review the status of the Homestead Unit and the other   5 low-cost services, to which most of these new clients are turning, and then briefly review the reasons we fear that demand may continue to be high over the longer term.

6   As you can see from the table below, the number of new clients requesting help from the Homestead Unit has increased by more than 50% since the beginning of May:

New Clients: May–August

May	June	July	August
73	105	98	121

7   Even though we refer patients who need intensive or long-term care to institutions or private psychiatrists (as all MHS units do), the wait for individual counseling has grown to about three and one-half weeks, and the wait for placement in one of the T-groups for the unemployed now exceeds four weeks. These response times are already close to the limits recommended in MHS regulations.

8   Other agencies tell of similar pressures. The Methodist Union of Social Services (MUSA, which is coordinating assistance to unemployed steel workers), the Homestead Health Clinic (a non-profit facility), area pastoral counselors, and social workers at the Pennsylvania welfare and unemployment offices all report that requests for referrals or assistance are up sharply. Private psychiatrists also indicate that their client loads have increased.

9   The surge in demand for mental health care is unexpected and needs further explanation. We believe that the surge reflects the cumulative effect of the prolonged unemployment in our area; a substantial number of Homestead's unemployed have now been out of work for 20 months or more. As you know, research has shown strong links between high unemployment and increased incidence of mental illness. Relatively little is known about the effects of prolonged unemployment, (as opposed to *high* unemployment), but we believe that the incidence of many of the psychological problems linked to high unemployment, such as depression, will continue to build as the period of unemployment lengthens. Certainly, the unemployed make up most of the new clients we are seeing, and it is reasonable to assume that prolonged stress will have cumulative effects.

10   The next few months will show whether our assumptions are correct, but in my view, there is good reason to fear that our increase in demand for mental health care this summer is not a seasonal variation or a fluke. In any case, I think our planning will have to reflect the possibility that demand will remain high and that we will have to provide additional capacity at the Homestead Unit.

Recommendation

I am requesting authorization to ask private psychiatrists in the Homestead area and student psychiatrists at local institutions for help in meeting the client overload. I recognize that this is at best a temporary measure, but I see two major reasons for considering it.   11

First, primary responsibility for addressing the demand problem appears to rest with the Homestead Unit. We unfortunately cannot rely on the private sector in this emergency because most of the unemployed receive only minimal insurance benefits for mental health care and cannot afford private counseling. Most of them indeed have been turning to the Homestead Unit and other low-cost services for help, and of these services, only the Homestead Unit can expand to meet the demand.   12

Second, the only way we can rapidly expand our services to meet demand is to appeal to private psychiatrists. While private psychiatrists are reporting increased client loads, many may continue to have time available for donation, or for part-time reimbursed service.   13

I would also recommend that we look at more permanent measures for expanding the Homestead Unit's services. These might include (1) reallocating MHS funds to pay for part-time professional services; or (2) permanently increasing the number of professional staffers at the unit.   14

The MHS has never actively sought help from private psychiatrists in the past, though most units are assisted by volunteer professionals. The mental health emergency facing us, however, is also unprecedented, and I believe a rapid response is necessary on our part to prevent the situation from worsening.   15

Linda Flower's COMMENTARY

This paper surprised me. For one thing, the writer, Stephen Pfeiffer, chose to play the role of a clinic administrator instead of to write in his own voice, so I was a little skeptical—could he really write a responsible and well-supported analysis of such a large problem? The second surprise came when I realized how much he had taught me about this problem. That, for me, is the mark of a good analysis.

A *Time* magazine article on Homestead might have tried to capture the flavor of the situation through human interest stories and anecdotes. Such stories make interesting reading, but the goal of this writer was to do more than recreate the feel of a complex situation. In writing an analysis, he was trying to define those two or three key issues at the heart of the problem—as he saw it. In effect, he is making a claim that says if we are going to deal with this problem, these are the issues we must face, namely: There is a genuine crisis in Homestead. Furthermore, (1) it will not go away soon; (2) it reflects a problem we know only a little about—the effect of prolonged unemployment; and (3) there are some untried measures we could take to deal directly with unemployment counseling. For me this sort of clear and focused analysis is at the heart of good professional writing, so let me say what I mean by professionalism, in the best sense of the word, and how this paper tries to achieve it.

To begin with, the writer takes his problem seriously. It would have been easier to simply describe the situation, to make a good story, or to rely on the emotional appeal of a case history to define the problem. It is often hard to know what the central issues really are. On the other hand, you will only solve that problem you define for yourself. And if Stephen Pfeiffer is right, if the people in Homestead are facing the cumulative effect of prolonged unemployment, then this problem requires a special set of long-term plans.

Notice too that in defining a problem, you put yourself on the line, saying this is what is at stake. This writer is in fact a little cautious; he leads up to the problem in his discussion (paragraph 9) and only alludes to it in his introduction. For me this paper would have been better if he had been a little more forthright in the introduction. His strategy of building the case more slowly probably reflects an awareness that his assumptions are still open to proof.

The writer also takes his reader seriously. First, he realizes that his reader needs to make informed decisions to do his own job well. Mere assertions and generalizations are not enough if the County Director needs to justify taking money from one area and giving it to another. So Stephen tries to provide data and arguments to back up his recommendations where he can, and he tries to outline the implications of his own suggestions. He tries to make his report genuinely useful—not just a demand.

Also, this report is designed for the reader—as a reader. Notice some of the ways it lets you find (and refer back to) the key ideas while it leads you through the argument. First, the headings and topic sentences are almost a synopsis of the report. One argument for such overviews in professional writing is that readers are busy people, they need concise writing, and so on. I think a more psychologically relevant argument is that the writer as a professional is often trying to teach or persuade someone else. The chief goal of a problem analysis is often to impose a new order and meaning to a complicated situation. And people understand and remember more when they have a clear context for the ideas (through previewing), when they can grasp the overall structure, and when they can easily refer back to main points as they read.

Second, the introduction tries to set the stage by finding a mutual concern the writer and reader already share. (The writer could have created a different context, such as "why my unit needs more money.") However, I also find the introduction a little stuffy and slow at getting to the point. The voice is rather official and the prologue a bit wordy—a common side effect of trying to provide background information. Nevertheless, the paragraph does deliver: You learn why you are reading; what the problem is; and what the writer would like to do about it.

Third, the prose regularly alternates between previewing and summing up. It is as though the writer can step outside his discussion from time to time and say, "In essence, this is my *point.*" Paragraph 3, for instance, tells you what is coming; paragraph 6 tells you how to interpret the data. Paragraph 8 starts by summing up the discussion with a summary noun and a prediction of the topic to come: "similar pressures." Paragraph 9 draws a conclusion (this result was unexpected) and lets you know what the paragraph will give you.

Finally, the writer seems to anticipate responses and questions the reader might have and tries to answer them in the text. For instance, he recognizes possible criticisms of his conclusions (maybe this is just a fluke, and these are, after all, only temporary measures). In answering those criticisms he shows he has thought the problem through and that he is alert to his reader's reasonable response. His report, despite its rather formal voice and business-like format, is also a dialogue with the reader.

To sum up my comments, I found this a good example of a problem analysis, and of professional writing in general, for three reasons. First, it taught me something: The writer made the best case he could for a new way to see a complex problem. Secondly, the report tried to be genuinely useful. The writer worked to imagine what a real reader would need to know and to imagine and respond to the limitations and implications of his own position from another person's point of view. And finally, the text itself, the format, organization, and sentence structure were all tailored to support the writer's purpose. There is a kind of craftsmanship here that is done in the service of both the reader's needs and the writer's ideas.

Study Questions

1. In a paper discussing Stephen Pfeiffer's report to Carl Rogers, a student said,

> I understand that this report is a request too, and that it's written to a superior, but in a couple of places I wonder if maybe the writer loses more than he gains by that cautiousness Linda Flower mentions. I can see it's maybe justified in leading up to the statement of the problem, but for me it becomes really troublesome when he states the problem. In the next to last paragraph of *The*

Mental Health Services Overload section, for example, does the writer do his image any good by saying "the surge in demand is . . . unexpected"? He's seen 20 months of what he's earlier called "an unemployment crisis," after all, and later he shows he knows the research that links high unemployment with the increase of mental illness. Couldn't he say that he's got an obviously bad, a doubly bad, situation on his hands? Does he have to be so academic with his conclusions: We can't be really sure yet; time will tell? I'm not saying he ought to sound pushy or hysterical, but I think he sounds a lot more indecisive than he should if he wants action.

How do you respond to this reading of Stephen Pfeiffer's paper?

2. "I found this a good example of a problem analysis, and of professional writing in general," says Linda Flower of Stephen Pfeiffer's report to Carl Rogers.

Make a list of the things Linda Flower finds specifically praiseworthy about Stephen Pfeiffer's report. Next, make a list of the things you find specifically praiseworthy about a poem you admire.

What generalizations does a comparison of your two lists enable you to make about the similarities and differences of poetry and professional writing?

3. "This paper surprised me," Linda Flower says of the student paper she commented on. "For one thing, the writer, Stephen Pfeiffer, chose to play the role of a clinic administrator instead of to write in his own voice, so I was a little skeptical." Judging from Linda Flower's assignment as well as from what she says in her commentary, what kinds of distinctions does she make between playing a role and writing in one's own voice?

How useful do you find these distinctions to you as a writer?

Letter of Application and Resume

The Situation: Select a specific job opening (or potential opening) for which you are actually qualified and would like to be considered. The job should be related to your eventual career plans; it should not be just a stop-gap way to make ends meet. Your inquiry should be in response to some specific knowledge you gain about the organization to which you are applying: a want-ad in the newspaper or in a trade journal, a notice in the Placement Office on campus, some communication with an employee or an acquaintance in a similar line of work, even a news item about the company. Your readers should be actual persons in actual organizations that have specific needs.

Write as yourself, including only factual information and assuming only valid personal preferences and objectives. You may project yourself one semester into the future if you will be graduating next spring; otherwise, apply for part-time or summer work, if you are not ready to apply for full-time employment.

The Assignment: Write a one-page letter of application for the position you have selected. Your specific purpose will be to obtain an interview visit, not to get the job offer. Your letter must accomplish the following tasks:

- capture the attention of the busy reader
- explain specifically what you (as distinct from your competition) can do for the employer and how your experience and education qualify you for the position
- make a clear request for an interview, indicating how you may be contacted
- direct the reader's attention to the accompanying resume or data sheet.

Prepare a one- or two-page resume summarizing and displaying in convenient and coherent chunks your educational and employment record, abilities, skills, honors, publications, interests and activities, and personal data, as appropriate for the kind of position you are seeking. Submit for my evaluation the letter, resume, and a copy of the notice or information that is the basis for your application. My evaluation will be guided by the "Evaluation Form for Application Letter and Resume."

CAROLYN RAE MILLER is Associate Professor of English at North Carolina State University, where she teaches technical writing, advanced composition, and editing; she also directs the undergraduate program in writing and editing. She has served on the executive committees of the Conference on College Composition and Communication and the Association of Teachers of Technical Writing and on the editorial boards of *College Composition and Communication* and *The Technical Writing Teacher*. She has published essays on the application of rhetorical theory to technical and scientific discourse.

235

Evaluation Form for Application Letter and Resume

	yes	no

1. Your opening paragraph

   a. clearly identifies you and your purpose   _____   _____
   b. indicates the specific job for which you are
      applying   _____   _____
   c. summarizes your qualifications for the job   _____   _____
   d. leads into the rest of the letter   _____   _____

2. The body of your letter

   a. organizes information about your education
      and experience effectively   _____   _____
   b. provides sufficient information about your
      education   _____   _____
   c. provides sufficient information about your
      experience   _____   _____
   d. conveys enthusiasm for the profession or
      for the specific position for which you are
      applying   _____   _____
   e. indicates that you've learned something
      about the prospective employer before
      writing the letter   _____   _____
   f. focuses on benefits to employer, not to you   _____   _____
   g. relates work and education to the *specific*
      requirements of the job for which you are
      applying   _____   _____
   h. draws selectively from the information on
      your resume   _____   _____
   i. refers to the attached resume   _____   _____

3. The closing paragraph

   a. asks for action and makes it convenient   _____   _____
   b. is neither too aggressive nor too
      subservient   _____   _____
   c. avoids clichés   _____   _____
   d. reinforces your interest and enthusiasm   _____   _____

4. The form of the letter

   a. is neatly typed   _____   _____
   b. follows a standard letter format   _____   _____

    c. includes an appropriate salutation and
       closing   _____   _____

    d. uses standard grammar, punctuation, and
       spelling   _____   _____

    e. avoids awkward, wordy, or imprecise
       phrasing   _____   _____

5. Your resume

    a. puts information in order of importance to
       job   _____   _____

    b. includes all essential identifying informa-
       tion about past employment, education,
       and references   _____   _____

    c. presents information concisely (no long
       sentences and paragraphs)   _____   _____

    d. provides adequate visual separation of
       sections   _____   _____

    e. has adequate margins and neat alignments   _____   _____

    f. identifies second page   _____   _____

    g. begins second page with a new section   _____   _____

☙ Letter of Application and Resume

by Clifton A. McDonald

20 February 1983

Mr. Jay L. Allen, Employment Manager
IBM
P. O. Box 12195
Research Triangle Park, NC 27709

Dear Mr. Allen:

    Through conversations with Jim Rogers, a co-op student working for IBM in downtown Raleigh, I learned that IBM would be hiring some students for summer internships. I am currently a second semester junior in mechanical engineering and would be interested in working for IBM as a summer intern.   1

    The enclosed resume covers my educational qualifications and work experience. In the resume you will find that my education includes courses in machine component design and solid mechanics, material that   2 would enable me to do stress calculations and predict lifetimes of mechanical components. I have also had hands on experience with machines, working in mill maintenance at a local sawmill in my hometown in western North Carolina.

3   Along with my education, I have been actively involved with the student section of the American Society of Mechanical Engineers, serving as chairman this year. In conjunction with the local senior section of ASME, our section has participated in a program in which student engineers can spend a day with a practicing engineer, learning about life as an engineer. Organizing programs such as this, as well as our weekly student luncheons, has given me experience in working with others and has improved my skills of communication. These assets could be put to use at IBM.

4   After completion of my junior year early in May of this year, I would be available for employment until August. I would appreciate your consideration of my qualifications and would welcome a personal interview. I can be reached by phone any afternoon, or if you prefer, I can also be reached by mail.

Sincerely yours,

Clifton A. McDonald
4111 Deep Hollow Dr. #252
Raleigh, NC 27612

RESUME

Clifton A. McDonald

ADDRESS

4111 Deep Hollow Drive #252
Raleigh, NC 27612
Telephone: (919) 781-1254

PERSONAL

Born: 10/17/61   Single   6'0"   170 lbs.

EDUCATION

Junior, Mechanical Engineering
North Carolina State University,
  Raleigh, NC
GPA overall: 3.18   GPA in Major: 3.05

Courses of interest
Machine Component Design
Solid Mechanics
Dynamics of Machines
Thermodynamics
Engineering Economics
Technical Writing

WORK EXPERIENCE

Summer 1982	Worked at odd jobs; no fulltime employment.
Summer 1981	*Mill maintenance,* Hennessee Lumber Co., Sylva, NC Worked on maintenance of entire mill. Had experience with repair and replacement of bearings, motors, and air cylinders. The average work week was 55 hours.
Summers 1979 & 1980	*Lumber stacker,* Hennessee Lumber Co. Worked stacking green lumber as it came from the mill. The average work week was 50 hours.
Oct. '79- April '80	*Woodstove installer,* Mr. Eddie Greer, Sylva, NC Installed forced air woodstoves part time during my senior year of high school.

HONORS AND ACTIVITIES

Chairman of N. C. State ASME, '82-'83
Secretary of N. C. State ASME, '81-'82
Member of Pi Tau Sigma, mechanical engineering honor fraternity
Member of N. C. State Engineer's Council, spring '82

REFERENCES

Available on request

CAROLYN MILLER'S COMMENTARY

Most people find writing job application letters uncomfortable, if not downright threatening. For one thing, unlike most writing you may have done, the job application letter has results that seem real, more real and more important than the grade you get on a classroom assignment. A negative response to a job application letter is not just a rejection of your writing, it is a rejection of you. In addition, the application letter requires you to do something that is usually considered rude—talk about yourself. Furthermore, you have to talk about yourself to an employer whom you probably don't know at all, a stranger who has an important power of decision over you. It's natural to feel tongue-tied and inadequate in a situation like that.

The job application letter is a common assignment in courses in technical writing, business writing, and professional writing. In my technical writing course, which I teach to college juniors and seniors, I like to use the job letter as the first writing assignment in the semester, for several reasons. First, it gives students the chance to write about something familiar—themselves and their career goals. Second, it helps them build a bridge from where they are now and *who* they are now to where they want to go and what they want to do when they graduate. Because the purpose of the technical writing course is to give students experience in the kinds of writing they will do as professionals in business or industry, creating this bridge is an important part of the course. The job letter helps them begin to imagine themselves not as students but as engineers, managers, staff assistants, accountants, and the like. Third, the job letter assignment provides a reader who can be easily identified—the employer. This also helps students move out of the classroom in imagination because I, as the teacher, am not the most important person who will be reading the letter. And fourth, the job letter is like a miniature technical report—it introduces most of the principles that will be discussed in more detail throughout the course.

What makes for excellence in a job application letter? There's a kind of paradox here, because anyone who is not the employer addressed will find a job letter, even an excellent one, to be fairly dull and routine. A good job letter will not bedazzle you with its wit or imagery. But it does require efforts of imagination, empathy, and diligence from the writer.

It's perhaps easy to appreciate excellence in a letter describing a person with outstanding qualifications—a perfect grade average, high-level professional experience, relevant research and publications. However, it's possible (although probably more difficult) to have average qualifications and still write an excellent letter. I chose Clifton McDonald's letter partly for that reason. He has qualifications and experience that are pretty typical for a college junior—in other words, he doesn't have any unusual advantages. This makes his achievement in the letter more commendable. The letter and accompanying resume you see here represent the third draft.

A good job application letter, like this one, has to do two things at once—it must both *fit in* and *stand out*. Let's discuss fitting in first. The job letter is trying to convince someone that you would fit into an environment you don't yet belong in; you need to prove that you can play a role that you don't normally play. When you go to a job interview, you dress not as a student but as someone who already has the job you want, to prove that you could fit in. The same with the letter. Mr. McDonald has shown that he's acquainted with and respectful of a world that he's not part of yet. He does this in part by making the letter *look* like a business letter, by putting on a set of conventions and wearing them properly. It bothers some students, for example, to address someone they don't know as "dear," but that is a custom that no one takes literally except those new to it. Mr. McDonald closed the first draft of his letter with the phrase "Yours, Clifton A. McDonald." I pointed out to him that "yours" is an informal, familiar closing that presumes an intimacy that just didn't exist in this case. So these matters of business "etiquette"—of observing standard letter format, careful grammar and punctuation, and phrasing that keeps a polite distance from the reader—are important in a negative way. Their presence will hardly be noticed, but their absence will count against you, sometimes heavily.

I like to do a "worst case" analysis with my students, asking them to imagine everything that could go wrong with their job application. Suppose, for example, that 100 other people have applied for the same job that you have, and all 100 letters are in a pile on the employer's desk, with yours number 68 in the pile. How do you get noticed? You get noticed in a negative way if you violate the conventions—if you use garish green paper or draw cartoons on your letter. You get noticed in a negative way if your qualifications clearly don't match the job or if you haven't given enough information about yourself. A good resume can prevent these negative impressions. But to get noticed in a *positive* way, to *stand out*, as well as to fit in, your letter needs to do some things a resume *can't* do. The letter represents your voice speaking, and it can make you sound inept, uncertain, uninformed, self-centered, pushy, presumptuous, immature, and so on. Or it can make you sound, as Mr. McDonald's voice does, businesslike, responsible, enthusiastic, thoughtful, and good-natured. The employer is looking not only for someone with certain technical qualifications but also for someone who would be pleasant to work with. The person who reads your letter is going to form an impression about what kind of person you are from the voice that you've created on paper.

One of the things Mr. McDonald's letter does to help create a voice worth listening to is to discuss his qualifications in some detail without sounding either shy or pushy. The letter is trying to lead the reader to some conclusions, but it doesn't force them—it respects the social distance between employer and applicant. Obviously, an applicant for a job is biased, like anyone who's trying to sell something. The reader doesn't *have* to accept any conclusions and is going to reserve the right to make his or her own judgment. What the writer has to do, and what Mr. McDonald has done in paragraphs 2 and 3, is to select and present evidence that will lead the employer to the conclusion the writer wants (hire me!). Selecting and presenting evidence requires empathy with that stranger the employer, an understanding of the work to be done, and an imaginative reading of the resume to see it from the employer's point of view.

For example, in the first version of this letter, the third paragraph read like this:

> Along with my engineering education, I have been actively involved with the student section of ASME, serving as an officer for two years. From my experiences with ASME, I have developed improved skills of communicating and working with others. These skills would be an asset in any position.

This original version is the hard sell, because it makes a claim without offering any evidence. It tries to force the reader to agree, but, as we noted above, the reader is entitled to be quite skeptical. In his revision Mr. McDonald has added detail that provides evidence for his ability to communicate and work with others. He has also distanced himself from his own life (or a small part of it) in order to select details that will persuade the reader of that point. Similarly, in paragraph 2, Mr. McDonald added some details about his academic work. Saying that you have taken certain courses means something to people in the university, but employers don't think in terms of courses and credits; they think in terms of what you learned in those courses: What do you *know*? What can you *do*? You have to project yourself into the job, imagining how you can transfer what you've learned in a classroom to the work situation. The more you know about the work situation, the better you can do this; here's where some research can pay off. Actually, I think Mr. McDonald could have done some more projecting in paragraph 2, if he'd found out exactly how these kinds of calculations and tests are used at the IBM location where he wanted to work.

Another way this letter takes the reader's point of view is by following a clear pattern, paragraph by paragraph, based on the questions that will be in the reader's mind as he or she reads. Paragraph 1: Who is this guy and what does he want? Paragraphs 2 and 3: What could he do for me and why would he be better at it than someone else? Paragraph 4 and resume: ok, maybe I'm interested—how do I follow up?

Throughout, this letter shows respect for the reader's point of view, and it shows Mr. McDonald's ability to take that perspective, to see himself from a distance. He has *interpreted* his education, his work experience, and his extracurricular activities from the employer's point of view. He has learned to speak with a public, professional voice. And those acts of imagination are what make this a good letter.

(Incidentally, Mr. McDonald did not get the internship at IBM, but he did get a similar job in machine design at another company.)

Study Questions

1. In a classroom discussion of Carolyn Miller's writing assignment, a student said,

> I don't understand why Carolyn Miller uses this checklist to evaluate the application letters and resumes her students write. Does she really have to go over things item by item the way she does? The application letter is only for an interview and it isn't supposed to be very long. Maybe students would be confused if they had to think about all these separate things when they were doing their projects.

How would you respond to such a statement?

2. A student writing a paper about Carolyn Miller's commentary on Clifton McDonald's work said,

> It's not just that Carolyn Miller's observations about what makes a good letter of application apply to other kinds of writing too. I can't think of a kind of writing—and I'm serious about writing poetry—to which they *wouldn't* apply.

What specifically in Carolyn Miller's commentary might be used to explain and support the position taken by this student?

Do you agree with the argument you have made?

3. "You have to project yourself into the job," says Carolyn Miller in speaking of an ideally constructed letter of application, "imagining how you can transfer what you've learned in a classroom to the work situation." Clifton McDonald, for example, might have learned more about how certain tests and calculations were used where he wanted to work, according to Carolyn Miller, to better project himself in paragraph 2.

If Clifton McDonald were to ask you if there were other places in his letter where he might better project himself, and, if so, what he would have to learn to do that, what would you respond?

NELL ANN PICKETT'S Assignment

A Field Report

Purpose: The field report gives the results of a visit to a particular location or site. Major sources of information for the field report are personal observation, experience, and knowledgeable people.

Uses: Field reports are used in many ways. For example, they are important in estimating the value of real estate or the cost of repairing a house; estimating insurance claims for damage from a tornado or blizzard; improving production methods in a department or a firm; choosing a desirable site for a building, a highway, a lake; or serving as an educational experience for a prospective employee or interested layperson. The field report gives an accurate, objective explanation and analysis of a situation so that appropriate action can be taken.

Main Parts: Since the field report has a variety of uses and includes various kinds of information, it has no established divisions or format. The report may include a review of background information, an account of the investigation, an analysis and commentary, and conclusions and recommendations. For a student (or any other interested person), a field report on a visit to a company might include a description and explanation of its physical layout; the personnel, materials, and equipment involved; the individual activities that comprise the major function of the company; and comments.

Organization: At the beginning of the report, state the purpose of the report, the specific site or facility or division observed, and the aspects of the subject to be presented. Then give the results of the investigation, followed by conclusions and recommendations. If the report is more than a paragraph or two, use headings. Include sketches, diagrams, charts, and other visual materials when they make explanation and description simpler or clearer.

NELL ANN PICKETT, Professor of English at the Raymond Campus of the Hinds Junior College District in Mississippi, chairs the NCTE Committee on Technical and Scientific Communication, serves as Executive Secretary/Treasurer of the Association of Teachers of Technical Writing, and directs the annual Summer Institute in Technical Communication (Mississippi Gulf Coast). In addition to articles, pamphlets, and study guides, she has written *Practical Communication* (1975); coauthored *Handbook for Student Writing* (1972), *Occupational English* (3rd ed., 1981), and *Technical English* (4th ed., 1984); and coedited *Technical and Business Communication in Two-Year Programs* (1983).

244

ॐ Planning a Color Processing Laboratory for the Commercial Design and Advertising Department

by Robert Crawford

Summary

Through interviews and reading, I collected information concerning the   1
planning of a color processing laboratory for the Commercial Design and
Advertising Department, Raymond Campus, Hinds Junior College District. Such a lab should accommodate 10 to 12 students. With minor
remodeling, the space formerly occupied by the barbering department
would be ideal for teaching color print processing. Once the minor
physical conversions were made, five processing stations, with two students to a station, could be set up for less than $8,300.

Purpose

The purpose of this investigation was to explore the possibility of setting   2
up a laboratory to teach color print processing to 10–12 students in the
Commercial Design and Advertising Department. It was necessary (1) to
determine whether the space formerly occupied by the barbering department would be practical for the color print laboratory, and, if so, how to
best use the space, and (2) to determine what equipment would be
needed.

Description of Available Space

The space available consists of two connecting rooms: a large room, 26′   3
× 45′, and a smaller room, 18′ × 26′. (See Figure 1.) The rooms are in
good condition and are equipped with running hot and cold water. The
floors are asphalt tile, which resists chemical stains. The walls and ceil-
ings are off-white, which gives good general illumination under safe-
lights. There are also a number of cabinets which can be used for bench
and storage units.

Construction Considerations

Only minor changes need to be made to divide this space into four work   4
areas for studio/lecture, loading, developing, and printing.

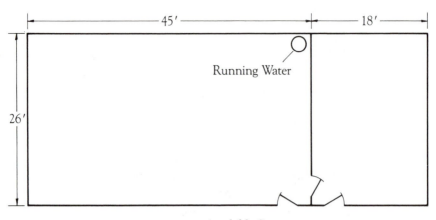

FIGURE 1   *Available Space*

- Walls (non-loadbearing) must be erected, as shown in Figure 2.
- The galvanized drains and pipes must be replaced with PVC plastic, due to strong chemicals to be used. Line sinks should be installed with mixing faucets as well as an automatic temperature controller.
- The darkrooms must be light-tight with both "safe" and regular incandescent or fluorescent lighting.

5   Consideration should be given to the installation of an electrostatic air cleaner in the darkroom. This will help dissipate processing solutions and minimize problems from dust.

Layout of Lab

6   Recommended use of the available space is shown in Figure 3. The smaller room would provide ample storage for supplies. The larger room, with the added partitions, would provide a studio/lecture room and a lab

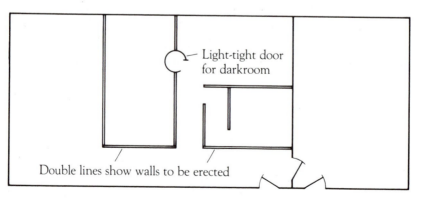

FIGURE 2   *Recommended Construction*

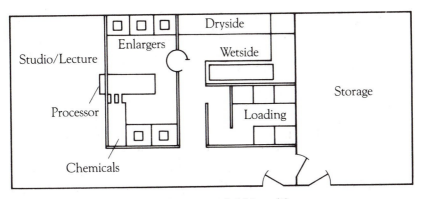

FIGURE 3   *Recommended Use of Space*

area, designed for the various steps in processing film: loading, developing, and printing.

Equipment Needs and Costs

For 10 students to gain a good, working knowledge of color processing, five complete sets of processing equipment are required. The needed equipment (with costs) to develop color film and hand produce prints up to 8″ × 10″ is given in Table 1.

Much can be learned from printing color by hand but it is a long,

TABLE 1   Equipment Needs and Costs*

Quantity	Description	Unit Price	Amount
5	Chromega D5 enlarger	$1,021.95	$5,109.75
5	Enlarging easels	21.95	109.75
1	Omega analyzer/timer	1,349.95	1,349.95
5	8 × 10 drum processors	17.95	89.75
3	Darkroom ventilators	114.95	344.85
5	Paper safes	21.95	109.75
10	Safelights	11.95	119.50
5	Developing tanks	22.95	114.75
1	Fiberglass line sink	475.00	475.00
1	Temperature control valve	279.95	279.95
	Graduates, funnels, trays, thermometers, etc.		150.00
		TOTAL	$8,253.00
Optional	Durst RCP 40 automatic processor		2,679.95
		TOTAL	$10,932.95

*Cost quotations from Standard Photo, Inc., Jackson, Mississippi, 5 November 1982.

tedious process. To process one 8″ × 10″ color print takes about an hour and almost $5.00 in chemicals and paper. It is also common to process several prints before getting the quality expected. For this reason, an automatic processor should be considered.

Conclusions

9

1. The former barbering department space would be ideal for teaching color processing.
2. Very little carpentry, plumbing, and wiring would be needed to convert the space to a lab.
3. The necessary equipment cost would start at $8,253.00 and get higher, depending on the quality desired.

Sources of Information

INTERVIEWS

Dorsett, Ray. Sales Manager, Standard Photo, Inc., Jackson, Mississippi. Equipment needs and costs. 5 November 1982.
Koelzer, Jay. Educator, former photography instructor, Jackson, Mississippi. Course feasibility. 3 November 1982.
Wann, Phillip. Production Control Manager, School Pictures, Jackson, Mississippi. Effective use of space. 1 November 1982.

BOOKLET

Printing Color Negatives. Kodak Publication No. E-66, 1978, pp. 14–25.

Nell Ann Pickett's COMMENTARY

I call this paper a well-written student report because of its

- Attention to audience (reader) analysis and adaptation
- Clearly stated purpose
- Readily apparent organization
- Accurate, sufficient data
- Effective layout and design
- Appropriate use of visuals
- Observance of conventional standards in such matters as grammar, usage, spelling, and punctuation
- Reflection of thinking that is critical, objective, thorough, and creative

Attention to Audience (Reader) Analysis and Adaptation

The technical writer asks: Who will read this report? Why? What kind of data does the intended audience need? How will the data be used? What approach to the data and what order in presenting the data are needed for the audience's purpose? How should word choice and terminology be adapted to the knowledge level and interest level of the audience?

In the report on planning a color processing laboratory, the writer indicated on the plan sheet that the report was intended for the chairman of the Commercial Design and Advertising Department. Sections of the report would be used in the department chairman's more inclusive report to his supervisor requesting a course-with-lab in color processing. The writer—the student helper in the Commercial Design and Advertising Department—analyzed the situation and then set about writing the report.

Clearly Stated Purpose

Why was this report requested? What information is needed? What kinds of decisions will be made on the basis of this information? What purpose will the report serve? The answers to these questions direct the writer in formulating a specific statement of purpose in preparing a report.

The student paper lets the reader know at the outset that the purpose is "to explore the possibility of setting up a laboratory to teach color print processing. . . ." The writer then goes on to specify that the investigation concerns analyzing the physical space available and determining needed equipment.

Readily Apparent Organization

In a report, the introductory section includes a statement of purpose or a statement indicating the major aspects of the topic to be covered. Headings and subheadings throughout the paper signal movement from one aspect to another.

After the "Summary," the student report on color processing begins with a section headed "Purpose" and alerts the reader that two major determinations (space use and needed equipment) are to be examined. Subsequent headings in the report reflect divisions of those two major concerns.

Accurate, Sufficient Data

A report should follow through on what it promises in the stated purpose. Accurate, sufficient data must be collected, analyzed, and interpreted. Then conclusions can be drawn and recommendations made.

The student report contains data that is presumably accurate. The writer uses as sources of information, in addition to the on-site inspection, a pamphlet put out by a highly reputable photography company, and three knowledgeable persons. Each person was interviewed for a particular aspect of the overall problem of planning the color processing lab. (Complete bibliographical information is given in "Sources of Information," at the end of the report.) The writer has organized, analyzed, and interpreted the data, and, on the basis of his investigation, arrived at conclusions.

Effective Layout and Design

Thoughtful layout and care in design are an integral part of a report. Layout includes such matters as spacing (paragraphing, vertical listing, ample white space), use of headings, the placement of material on the page—all for optimum readability. Design includes such overall considerations as format, sizes and kinds of typefaces, color, use of visuals, and such composition elements as balance, unity, and emphasis.

Layout and design in the student report are effective. Headings are used to good advantage. Numbers are used as emphasis markers in the "Purpose" and the "Conclusions" sections, and bullets are used to emphasize the vertical listing of minor changes in the "Construction Considerations" section.

Appropriate Use of Visuals

Such visuals as drawings, charts, graphs, tables, photographs, and the like are often as important as the written material in a report. Visuals are important because they can convey some kinds of material better than words can, they can simplify or considerably reduce textual explanation, and they can add interest and can focus attention.

The student report underscores all the preceding ways in which visuals are important. The report appropriately uses two kinds of visuals: line drawings and a table. The three drawings—in their depiction of the physical space available, the recommended placement of partition walls, and a floor plan for the lab—help the reader "see" the situations, and help the writer economize on words. Likewise with the table showing equipment needs and costs. The table gives a great deal of information in a concise, easily comprehensible form.

Observance of Conventional Mechanics

A well-written report uses conventional standards in such matters as grammar, usage, spelling, and punctuation. Deviation from conventional standards diverts the reader's attention and thus interferes with the message of the communication. The student report observes conventional standards in the mechanics of writing, and so the reader's attention is rightly focused on the content of the report.

Reflection of Sound Thinking

Good technical writing emerges from thinking that is critical, objective, thorough, and creative. Good technical writing is based on sound thinking applied to problem solving. The writer must solve such problems as audience analysis and adaptation, choice of format, decisions as to organization and layout and design, creation of appropriate visuals, and formulation of a report so clear that the reader knows exactly what the writer means.

Sound thinking is reflected in the student report in various ways, such as choice of topic, collection of data, organization, layout, construction of visuals. The student was especially astute in selecting a topic for research that could serve double duty: an assignment in Technical Writing and a request from his employer, chairman of the Commercial Design and Advertising Department, to provide a specific needs assessment for a color processing laboratory.

Study Questions

1. A student writing about Robert Crawford's field report said,

   I question how adequate the audience analysis of this report is on the basis of a personal experience I had with a situation like the one this writer is in. Last summer I worked in a camp for retarded children. We had this idea to turn an old screened-in veranda into a craft area for the kids. The director told us to work out how much it would cost and that he'd see what he could do with the trustees. We planned it all right down the line just the way this writer does. Workbenches. Lanyard making sets. We had it all on paper. The first thing the director asked me when he read our list was how much it was going to cost to make the porch into a room, to build some walls where the screens had been and things like that. Like this writer, we'd figured "only minor changes" would have to be made, that "very little carpentry, plumbing, and wiring would be needed." When the director said he couldn't begin to talk to the trustees without that figure, we got it. Those "minor changes" were going to cost almost as much as the craft equipment we'd planned to buy! So given who this writer's report is for and how it's going to be used, I don't think he's got enough information yet.

   How do you respond to this student's argument?

2. After reading Robert Crawford's field report and Nell Pickett's commentary on it, a student remarked,

   "It almost seems that to do a good field report you have to know as much about psychology as you do about writing."

How might such a remark be explained and justified?

Do you agree with the justification you have come up with?

3. In a classroom discussion of Robert Crawford's field report and Nell Pickett's commentary on it, one student said,

> I don't know anything about photography, but I build things, and I know something about plans, and I'm telling you I'd have trouble putting this lab together. Where do the sinks go, for example, and how many are there? In the written report it sounds like there is to be more than one, but only one "fiberglass line sink" is listed in the budget. Figure 3 doesn't show them any-where. Same with the air cleaner in the darkroom. It isn't listed on the budget page at all, not even optionally the way the automatic processor is. And where's it to go? In the darkroom? And where is *that* in figure 3? This kind of stuff may not seem to matter much, but it does when you've got tools in your hands and a lot of equipment spread around that there's no place for.

Another student responded by saying,

> I don't think you understand what a field report is. This guy isn't designing for a builder. He just wants to give an idea of what's possible. He's not making a blueprint or anything like that. He's writing for the chairman of the Commer-cial Design and Advertising Department after all. *He'd* know perfectly well where the darkroom is in Figure 3, because he knows photography. What's important is whether there's *room* for sinks. Exactly how many there are to be and where to put them can be worked out later. It's total concept a field report is concerned with.

What position would you take in this controversy?

Writing Assignment 8
Public Worlds

Choose a teacher represented in this chapter whose commentary you think makes usefully clear to you what good writing for or in a public world seems to involve. Imagine yourself planning to take a writing course with this teacher some time toward the end of your years in college, a course that has as its prerequisite your having taken an earlier writing course.

Write a paper in which you explain what kind of writing course you think would prepare you to work most successfully with this teacher. If you had your say in the matter, what sort of writing would this preparatory course give you practice in? Specifically, what kinds of writing tasks would you like to see yourself faced with? What would you have the teacher do in this ideal course that you are setting up for yourself? What would you have the teacher expect you to do? In what terms would you have your writing evaluated? To what purpose? In other words, what would you like to see yourself getting better at doing?

Conclude your paper with a paragraph in which you speculate on how you'd like this ideal course to prepare you to work with the teacher you have in mind. Make clear in your paragraph exactly what you think the teacher considers good writing for or in a public world to involve. Make clear also exactly what you hope to have learned in your preparatory course that you think will help you to create such writing.

Telling Stories

9

Writing a story or a novel is one way of discovering *sequence* in experience. . . . Connections slowly emerge. Like distant landmarks you are approaching, cause and effect begin to align themselves, draw closer together. Experiences too indefinite of outline in themselves to be recognized for themselves connect and are identified as a larger shape. And suddenly a light is thrown back, as when your train makes a curve, showing that there has been a mountain of meaning rising behind you on the way you've come, is rising there still, proven now through retrospect.

It seems to me, writing of my parents now in my seventies, that I see continuities in their lives that weren't visible to me when they were living. . . . Could it be because I can better see their lives—or any lives I know—today because I'm a fiction writer? See them not as fiction, certainly—see them, perhaps, as even greater mysteries than I knew. Writing fiction has developed in me an abiding respect for the unknown in a human lifetime and a sense of where to look for the threads, how to follow, how to connect, find in the thick of the tangle what clear line persists. The strands are all there: to the memory nothing is ever really lost.

Eudora Welty

JUST AS IN MANY COLLEGES AND UNIVERSITIES special courses often exist to teach writing for or in a public world, so in many schools there are courses devoted exclusively to the writing of poems, plays, and short stories. This, too, is in some senses a particular kind of writing, writing it is sometimes supposed that only a particular sort of student is equipped for or interested in. "Creative writing," a phrase you have surely heard, is the way it is most often referred to.

The writing assignment at the end of this chapter—an assignment that will involve you in the process of revision—is to enable you to have a look at what "creative writing" seems to be a matter of. It will also give you a chance to say what sort of student you think is equipped to write "creatively," or could have any interest in doing so.

The student writings and the teachers' commentaries in this chapter are offered to help you decide on a point of view from which to write your paper.

HARVEY DANIELS'S Assignment

Student Teaching—High School English

One of the maxims you've repeatedly heard in your various courses and text-books is that beginning teachers ought to carefully plan out, in writing, every single thing they intend to teach to a class. Some methods books even prescribe complex formats into which each of these lesson plans, unit plans, and year plans is to be slotted.

Now that you are only a couple of weeks away from actually starting student teaching yourself, it seems an opportune time to reopen the planning question.

Write a position paper of about 1,000 words in which you explain where you stand on the importance of instructional planning. Is it more or less important than the standard texts claim? Do you see yourself preparing detailed plans for your own classes? Why or why not? When? What problems can you see yourself encountering if you don't plan adequately? How can planning enrich your teach-ing? Are there dangers associated with over-planning? And so forth.

You'll read this paper aloud to the class; we'll discuss it for ten or fifteen minutes; and then you'll also hand it in.

ᴥ L.P.N. Strikes Again   *by Barbara M. Whalen*

1   Biff Skinner, student teacher, feels that he has things pretty well under control. Biff stands in the doorway of his seventh-period Dramatic Liter-ature class and greets each student as he or she enters. He is an easy-going fellow who deeply enjoys student teaching and gets along swim-mingly with the entire faculty of John Wilkes Booth High School. Just yesterday, his supervising teacher, Ms. Pia J. Smith, the chairperson of

HARVEY DANIELS is Associate Professor of Education at Rosary College and codirector of the Illinois Writing Project. He has published widely in academic journals and in the popular press, and his book *Famous Last Words: The American Language Crisis Reconsidered* was published in 1983. He is cochair and editor for the Conference on Language Attitudes and Composition, a national association of writing teachers.

the English Department, told Biff that he was "quality teaching material." Yes, things seem to be going pretty smoothly for Biff. However, things are not always as they seem.

The sophomores have just finished reading *Our Feet Have Tender Corns*, Biff's all-time favorite example of Dramatic Literature. Biff has dreamed about teaching this monumental work since he first read it in high school. Why, he had his lesson plan all written out even before student teaching began, and he relishes this chance to share his knowledge with the students. Good planning on Biff's part. However, things do not always go as planned.

Biff's third period class had a wonderful time discussing the play, and as he watches the seventh-period group settle into their seats, Biff is quite confident that another fifty-four minutes of stimulating discussion is about to occur. The imagery! The profound symbolism! The bold, cerebral humor! It is 1:45 PM.

Biff begins. He asks the class how they feel about the play. The room becomes strangely silent. Biff looks out across a sea of emotionless faces. This is going to be tough, he thinks to himself as a few tiny beads of perspiration appear on his upper lip.

"Aw, c'mon, gang," he cajoles winningly, drawing on the boyish charm (they really can relate to it).

After an eternity, a young man in the front of the room raises his hand.

"Yes, Brad," Biff cries.

"I have something to say about how I felt about the play," Brad offers.

"Please share it with us, Brad," Biff says expansively, heaving an internal sigh of relief.

"Well," Brad muses, "I thought it was good."

Biff's eyes jerkily scan the room. "Anyone else?" he asks.

Silence.

A pony-tailed girl behind Brad raises a hand timidly.

"Steffie!" Biff exclaims, struggling to keep his voice from cracking.

"Well," Steffie ponders, "it was okay, I guess."

"Would you like to expand on that?" Biff urges, a drop of perspiration dribbling down his temple.

"Well . . ."

She's just thinking it over, Biff reassures himself, just thinking. She's one of the good ones, one of the talkers.

"Well . . ." Steffie begins again, "it was kinda, you know, long."

Biff is now sweating profusely. "Anyone else?" he chokes, wiping large drops of perspiration out of his eyes.

Silence.

In desperation, Biff reaches for his ace in the hole. There, sitting prettily in the back row is Jennifer Grant, the brightest, most reliable, most trustworthy student in the classroom.

23   "Jennifer," Biff says urgently as his knees begin to buckle beneath him, "what did *you* think of the play?"

24   Jennifer tucks her gum to one side, lowers her eyes and moans quietly, "I didn't read it, Mr. Skinner."

25   These are the last words that Biff will remember. It is 1:49 PM.

26   Biff's supervising teacher, Pia J. Smith, came to his hospital room just as he was regaining consciousness.

27   "Wha . . . wha . . . what happened?" Biff mumbled.

28   "There now, Biff," Miss Smith said gently. "What happened to you has happened to many in our profession."

29   "What is it?" asked Biff.

30   "It's called Lesson Plan Negligence, Biff. And yes, even the most experienced teacher can be struck down by L.P.N."

31   Biff emitted a small but audible groan.

32   "Now Biff, don't take it so hard," murmured Miss Smith. "There are ways to prevent this tragic affliction."

33   "Please tell me, Miss Smith. Please!" Biff cried.

34   Miss Smith began. "It is always important to make general unit plans ahead of time, Biff. But as the school year progresses, the plans may need to be altered. Once you become familiar with your classes, you must adapt your plans accordingly. We must never depend upon routine . . ."

35   "Tell me more," said Biff, the light returning to his eyes. "Tell me everything!"

36   "Attempt to fill the class period with a variety of activities. A full period of lecture or discussion can sometimes wreak havoc with adolescent attention spans."

37   Biff rolled over laboriously. "In other words, there is more than one way to teach a subject! We must always have something to fall back on!"

38   "See, Biff, you're getting better already. What works well for one class may be a disaster in the next. We as teachers must always be prepared."

39   The color had returned to Biff's cheeks. "Thank you, Miss Smith," he said. "I feel like a new man. I can once again go out into the world and do what I was born to do!" There was a smile on Pia J. Smith's face. It was a proud smile. Biff would be all right.

40   Unfortunately, three weeks later Biff was run over by a double-decker bus during his tour of "Shakespeaere's England." Never assume the obvious. Remember Biff Skinner. Learn from his mistakes. Biff would have wanted it that way.

HARVEY DANIELS'S COMMENTARY

As an undergraduate I repeatedly heard an apocryphal story about essay-writing, a story customarily recited while a group of us were enduring ("pulling," I think was the term) another last-ditch, all-night, pre-exam study session. Since then, I've discovered that the same story also circulates among writing teachers. According to the tale, there is, at a certain university, a professor (of philosophy or psychology—the details vary) who sometimes gives a final examination on which the sole question is "Why?" Students who address this assignment in conventional terms—say, by layering material from course readings and lectures into a five paragraph theme—flunk the test. Only those with the courage to simply answer "Why not?" get A's, so the story goes.

Clearly, this tale is college composition's version of the cat in the microwave: an unsettling, distasteful, yet oddly seductive emblem of depravity. Probably it is just an academic folk tale, and no such diabolically arbitrary professor ever really existed. But like most folk tales, this one undoubtedly contains a grain of truth that we ought to examine whether we like it or not.

The grain of truth is that students who turn a writing assignment sideways and do something "creative" or "original" with it are often rewarded, while those who hew more closely to the official terms of the task join the mediocre mainstream and risk getting grades to match. Barbara Whalen's paper about Biff Skinner and L.P.N. syndrome is a good example of the former alternative. Given a fairly pedestrian assignment—to write a short persuasive essay about the importance of lesson-planning in student teaching—Barbara decided to make her case through the story of Biff rather than by reeling out the expected string of claims, arguments, proofs, and appeals. I welcomed the Skinner saga as creative and original, feeling that the spirit of my assignment had been well enough satisfied. In fact, Barbara's paper exemplified some advice I've often found myself giving (or wanting to give) to students: "The single most important thing you can do to improve your grades on writing assignments is to see those assignments more openly, more loosely—to revise, rework, or rearrange the teacher's prescribed structures in favor of your own."

The problem with this advice, of course, is that it depends. What worked for Barbara (1) with me as the teacher, (2) on that particular assignment, (3) at Rosary College in 1981, wouldn't always have such a happy ending. For other teachers, other courses, other times (even for me, under other circumstances), Barbara's tinkering with the assignment might have seemed more like simple disobedience or an attempt to camouflage ignorance. But how is a student to know? What will play in

English 101? When is it safe—when is it smart—to recast the task in some way that helps you make the writing more your own, to fulfill the assignment while simultaneously violating some of its terms?

Before I try to answer any of these questions or offer any further comments about Barbara's paper, I probably ought to say something about my own perspective on the teaching of writing. Unlike many of the other professors contributing to this book, I do not make my living by teaching college writing classes. Instead, I mostly work at training writing teachers, giving courses and institutes in which teachers from all levels, from elementary school through college, seek to improve their instruction in writing. Thus I am accustomed to studying not just writing but how it is taught, and I am in the habit of thinking about how it must feel to be a student in a writing course as well as the teacher of one.

All this experience enables me to offer immediately one reason why papers like Barbara's are always so popular with teachers: They provide a welcome burst of enjoyment amid the often dreary and endless process of evaluating student work. If this sounds harsh, consider first the students' age-old complaint against writing instructors: You teachers have no conception of the misery you cause with your horrendous writing assignments—the hours of disorientation in the library, the sleepless nights hunched over a silent typewriter, the countless missed social opportunities. Really, you are cruel to make us suffer like this.

But there is a complementary (and uncomplimentary) complaint from the teachers' side: You students have no conception of the misery you cause us when we limp home under a stack of your horrendous essays; as we slave by the hour in our drafty studies over dozens of lifeless, interchangeable essays on "Abortion: Pro or Con?"; as we turn aside the piteous cries of our spouses and children for companionship; as we scribble earnestly in your margins while the clock marches into the wee, dark, hopeless hours of the night.

Well, both sides tend to exaggerate their own nobility. But this exchange of stereotypes does dramatize the peculiar situation that student-writers and teacher-readers face. In the real world outside of schools, people write because they want to share some idea, view, or information with someone else for some real reason. Readers, in turn, read to get ideas, views, or information that will be significant or pleasant to them. Notice that these conditions pertain to memos to a boss, articles for a magazine, letters to Mom, or just about any real writing situation you can think of. In school, however, the communication situation is often distorted. Frequently, students are compelled to write on topics of no significance to them, to adopt an alien style, tone, or format, and to submit the results to a reader who already knows everything they could possibly say. And then these teacher-readers do something that no real reader would ever do: They slog through stacks and stacks of essays on the same subject, none of which contain any ideas, views, or information that is new to them. In the real world, young adults would not spontaneously draft twenty-five page formal academic research papers on the Burmese parliamentary elections of 1938—and in the real world, professors wouldn't settle down to devour thirty or forty of them at a sitting, either.

Papers like Barbara's, then, sidestep these traps of school writing. By changing the assignment into something of genuine personal challenge, Barbara equips herself with a real communicative purpose beyond (and much stronger than) merely "fulfilling the assignment." Because Barb dares herself to do her paper as a story-scenario, she has a chance to write something fresh and entertaining, if not necessarily original, and the opportunity motivates her. It's almost like real writing. There are benefits for the reader, too. Though most serious-minded teachers will never admit it publicly, most of us are delighted to come across something funny, different, original, or diverting when we're two-thirds of the way through a tall pile of look-alike papers. Sure, this is a highly subjective reaction—rather like that of a person who is doing some real-world reading and comes across something enjoyable.

Don't overlook the deeper meaning here. This is not just a matter of beating the college system—of students shrewdly selecting offbeat angles and of professors being lenient enough to reward showmanship as richly as they reward synthesis. What happened with Barbara, what happens whenever a student takes a writing assignment away from a teacher and makes it her own, is that the writer has a priceless opportunity to find and use and strengthen her own voice. And nothing is more central to all good writing than this authentic personal voice, this sound of a genuine, deeply engaged author at work finding out what she thinks. This authenticity naturally pays off at the end of a writing project, when the strong, unique voice draws the reader into the piece and propels him along. But even from the beginning, the excitement that comes from real commitment to a job of thinking and writing moves the work along, makes the writer want to get it right, motivates close revision and editing, instills care and pride in the whole process.

This authentic voice is what I immediately heard and appreciated in Barbara's piece about Biff, the student teacher. It wasn't the best paper that I've ever seen or that Barbara ever wrote, even within the span of that one course. But she really owned that story, and she refused to let me use the assignment as a check on her reading and note-taking. In the two years since Barbara handed in that paper, our paths have repeatedly crossed: I've supervised her teaching internship; she's worked as an aide in two of my summer institutes; we've collaborated on work for the Illinois Writing Project; and just recently, Barbara finally handed over her secret recipe for Irish soda bread. The better I know my friend Barb, the more familiar her special voice becomes, that voice that spoke through old Biff a couple of years ago: the persistent, sometimes dark humor; the suspicion of all authorities; the distaste for platitudes, even mine; the hint of annoyance at having to do any uncalled-for work; the deep love of kids; the strong and well-justified streak of self-confidence.

So I am saying that, at least partly because Biff is a true and coherent expression of Barbara's unique voice, this paper is good writing. But that authenticity was there in the beginning, and I didn't need any of this after-the-fact knowledge to help me recognize the strength and energy in the work. And I am also noticing with some pleasure that Barbara's insistence on remaking my assignments (she did it every time back then), her dedication to writing only the papers she wanted to write, her willingness to take risks in her studies, engendered my respect and opened the way to our becoming friends. When I think about it, this is one of the nicest results any teacher might hope for.

Study Questions

1. In a classroom discussion of "L.P.N. Strikes Again" and Harvey Daniels's commentary on it, one student said,

> I think this paper *is* an example of somebody shooting an angle and being rewarded for just showmanship. I don't see that Barbara Whalen is "creative" in her handling of this assignment at all. The paper sounds juvenile to me: *Our Feet Have Tender Corns* and Biff ending up in the hospital, that kind of stuff. That's right out of the comic strips. Where is this "deeply engaged author at work finding out what she thinks"? All she says is that lesson plans can be overdone. Who doesn't know that? Talk about platitudes. That's a tough set of questions being asked in that assignment. If I'd been in that course and had tried to deal with them and then saw this kind of cop-out being praised, I'd be damned sore.

Another student responded by saying,

> What you sound sore at is that this writer saw a way of dealing with the assignment you wouldn't have thought of. Harvey Daniels says he advises his students to see his assignments openly, to "rearrange the teacher's prescribed structures in favor of [their] own." How can you call what she does a cop-out when she does exactly what she's been advised to do? And just because you find Biff juvenile doesn't mean everybody else has to. You need types like this if you're going to write a satire and I think this is a pretty clever satire. I too find it "fresh and entertaining." What makes you right and everybody else wrong?

What position would you take in this exchange?

2. Harvey Daniels speaks repeatedly of the voice of "L.P.N. Strikes Again," calling it by turns "strong," "unique," "genuine," "special" and several times

"authentic." He mentions an "authentic voice" that he "immediately heard and appreciated" in Barbara's piece about Biff.

Using both Barbara Whalen's paper and Harvey Daniels's commentary on it as your examples, explain what advantages attend the use of the concept "authentic voice" in a writing classroom.

What dangers are there to the use of this concept in a writing classroom?

Where do you stand on the use of the concept "authentic voice" in a writing classroom?

3. A student writing about "L.P.N. Strikes Again" and Harvey Daniels's commentary on it said,

> I wonder if a student *has* to violate the terms of a writing assignment in order to be creative and original in responding to it. That is, does the choice have to be made that way? Wouldn't it be possible for a teacher to insist that students be creative and original in staying with "the official terms of the task" rather than moving outside them—and wouldn't this do more for them than suggesting that the only way to be creative is to do whatever you feel like doing? The trouble with Barbara Whalen's paper now is not that she violates the terms of the assignment, but that she deals with only part of it. Suppose she were asked to rewrite her paper keeping what she has but including what would make it clear that planning can enrich teaching too. Would that force her to become less creative or more?

How do you respond to the position this student takes?

PAUL ESCHHOLZ'S Assignment

Identify an experience that has been especially important to you, one perhaps that taught you something about yourself, and then write an essay in which you narrate that experience. In preparing to write your narrative, you may find it helpful to ask yourself the following questions: Why is the experience important to me? What is my purpose in telling the story? What details are necessary for me to recreate the experience in an interesting and engaging way? How can my narrative be most effectively organized?

ꜱᴠ Where the Heart Should Be   *by David Leith*

1   The boy made his way up the grassy slope to the chicken house. Cackles of restless chickens floated past his closed ears. As he pushed open the wooden door he could smell the stench of manure mixing with the aroma of chicken feed.

2   Taking the lid off the feed can, he reached in and scooped up a canful of cracked corn. Mechanically the boy pushed open the dusty screen door leading into the coop. The screen snapped back with a slam and the chickens scattered, the boy kicking at one by his foot. He broadcast the corn as if planting buckwheat and retreated to the feedroom for a scoop of laying mash. He filled both troughs then cleaned and changed the water bucket.

3   During the extent of his chore the boy worked diligently, yet unaware of the chickens' behavior. They were skittish and unsettled; many of them huddled in the far corner of the coop. Noticing none of this, the boy continued working. He had only to pick the eggs and his job would be finished. Armed with his egg basket he made sport of it. The first laying box was opened to reveal eighteen eggs and a hen setting on some more unseen. He picked these eighteen, then scooped up the hen and dropped her in the corner, sending frantic hens hopping and squawking. Ten more eggs, fresh and warm to the touch. He smiled as he placed them in his basket.

4   Opening the other laying box the boy started as he saw a large raccoon

PAUL ESCHHOLZ is Professor of English at the University of Vermont, where he teaches courses in writing and American literature. He has written articles on the teaching of writing and several textbooks for college composition courses: *Subject and Strategy: A Rhetoric Reader* (2nd ed., 1981); *Language Awareness* (3rd ed., 1982); *Models for Writers: Short Essays for Composition* (1982); and *Outlooks and Insights: A Reader for Writers* (1983). From 1977 through 1982, he directed The Vermont Writing Program, an NEH project.

eating eggs. It was a greasy mass of brown fur, its glassy eyes set into a black mask. A large raccoon about three feet long, it must have weighed over forty-five pounds. Without blinking, the raccoon, still clutching an eggshell in its front paws, looked up and hissed, snapping his jaw to reveal two rows of moist, yellow teeth. Without hestitation the boy slammed down the laying box lid.

Before ten minutes had passed, the boy returned to the hen house. His parents were away for the evening and this time the boy was armed with his dad's twenty-two rifle and five longs. His father had taught him how to load and shoot the gun, but he had never shot at an animal. The boy slid a bullet into the chamber and locked the bolt. Again he pushed the dusty screen door open. Peering in at the chickens, huddled cackling in the corner, the boy walked through the doorway. He hesitated a moment, checking to make sure the safety was off, then slowly opened the lid of the laying box. The raccoon looked up this time into a rifle barrel and in a split second the boy fired, point blank.   5

The raccoon just stared and continued eating. Again the boy loaded the gun and again he fired, this time into the animal's chest or where its heart should be. Another hiss from the raccoon angered the boy. He loaded and shot again, careful to take aim right between the eyes.   6

The boy slammed the lid shut with a satisfied finality and walked into the feedroom. He looked out the window toward the sunset. He looked at his feet. There was a sound from the next room. A thump as if a weight had been dropped. Scrambling back into the chicken coop, the boy caught sight of the raccoon's brown form where it had crawled from the laying box and fallen to the floor. He reached in his pocket and pulled out the two remaining bullets.   7

Again the bolt was locked and the trigger pulled. It was as if the raccoon had no heart. The boy stared at the last round of ammunition before nursing it into the rifle. He placed the rifle barrel against the top of the coon's head. His finger squeezed the trigger. Turning he yanked the screen door open and flung himself into the feedroom.   8

The sun was waning behind clouds, and orange light burned through cobwebs hanging over the window. The boy picked up an egg from the basket. It was still warm. Placing the egg back in the basket, he returned to the coop.   9

The boy's jaw dropped, his eyes darted around the floor. The raccoon wasn't where it had been left lying. Hearing a scratching sound from behind the roost, the boy investigated to find the raccoon trying to crawl to freedom. It was writhing in the sawdust seeking an escape. The boy dashed out of the chicken house.   10

He returned this time armed with his Louisville Slugger All-Star   11

Willie Mays autographed baseball bat. Inside the chicken coop the raccoon was still scratching the wall. The boy swung with deliberation, tears streaming down his hot pink cheeks.

12   The boy dropped the limp carcass into a garbage can in the feedroom. He secured the cover on so the dogs wouldn't disturb it. By this time it was dark. He picked up the egg basket, leaving the rifle and bat leaning in the corner by a broom. He pulled the door shut behind him.

PAUL ESCHHOLZ'S COMMENTARY

While I might be tempted to argue with David about some minor stylistic choices he made in his essay, I believe that "Where the Heart Should Be" is an exemplary piece of narrative writing. David has recorded a complete action for us, and he has a point to make in telling his story. David is careful to tell us when the action happened, where it happened, and to whom it happened. He has made every attempt to make the experience real for us by showing us what happened wherever possible instead of telling us what happened. David has thoughtfully selected his details, giving us enough so that we know what is happening but not so much that we are overwhelmed or confused. He has organized his narrative chronologically, placing the events in the order in which they occurred. And he has chosen and maintained a consistent point of view throughout his essay. We should not forget, however, that David's essay didn't just happen. David worked hard on this essay, made a number of important decisions about this writing, and wrote a series of drafts before he was satisfied with what he had written.

Several days after receiving the assignment in class David dropped by my office to chat about the topic he had chosen. He thought that he would write about the time he shot a raccoon that was stealing eggs from his family's chicken coop. He told me that it was the first thing that he'd ever killed and that it had made quite an impression on him at the time. David recounted the incident in some detail. In fact, he was a little surprised by just how much he did remember about the episode. He recalled that he was angry when he first discovered the raccoon; after all, the raccoon was eating his eggs and, perhaps more importantly, was going to delay the completion of his chores because he would have to do something with the animal. He felt justified in killing the pesky intruder. As he observed the wounded raccoon's desire to live, however, David became disgusted with himself and what he was doing. David knew that he had learned something from the experience, and he wanted to share that experience with others. Although he seemed to be fairly confident about what he wanted to say in his essay—especially after telling me all about the event, I remember that David expressed some uncertainty about how the essay would turn out. Something didn't feel right to him.

The next time I saw David he had written his rough draft and was ready for a conference. I could tell by the look on his face that the writing was frustrating him. I asked him to have a seat and to tell me about his writing. David confirmed what I had seen on his face; he wasn't satisfied with his essay, but he couldn't pinpoint the difficulty. I suggested that he read his essay aloud while I listened. I could tell that David was an authority on his subject from the sheer amount of information in his essay. Unfortunately, he had included too much information. The essence or meaning of the experience that we had talked about earlier was lost in a deluge of detail. David had written a blow-by-blow chronological account of the killing—nothing was left out. But these matters did not seem important at the time. I was more interested in David himself as he read the draft. He was obviously ill at ease.

When he finished reading the draft, I asked him how he liked it. David confessed that it was too immediate, too personal. He discovered that it was difficult to write about himself as a "killer." What were the alternatives? He wondered if it would be okay to write the essay in the third person. After a brief discussion in which we explored the advantages of such a change, David decided to give it a try and left.

In a few days David returned. He was smiling. He told me that he had solved his problem. He thought that the use of the third-person point of view gave him the distance from his experience that he needed in order to sift out the meaningful details from those that added nothing to his narrative. He had cut his rough draft by more than a third, eliminating such things as a description of the outside of the chicken house, a statement about where his parents had gone that evening, and an account of his looking for the gun and ammunition in the house. The result was that the narrative now focused on the killing and the boy's feelings about it. I asked David if he had considered putting the story back in the first person, but he seemed reluctant to even talk about it so I didn't press the issue.

David was visibly pleased with the changes that he had made in his draft and wanted to talk about them. But he still wasn't happy with the way he was expressing the boy's feelings. He knew that he was telling his readers that the boy was mad, that the raccoon was a vicious thief, and that the killing disgusted the boy. We talked briefly about the difference between *telling* people something and *showing* them the same thing, and he set off to see what he could do. The changes David made improved his essay tremendously. In the opening paragraphs he shows us that the boy's mind was elsewhere as he was doing his chores, and later in the essay he shows the boy's initial anger with the raccoon and how that anger changes to disgust with himself as the killing takes place. David even changed his title, substituting a pointed phrase from his essay for the rather dull "A Painful Experience."

David made yet other changes; most of them, although relatively minor, helped make the essay better. At several points he substituted new words for ones that he thought were inappropriate. In addition, he recast several sentences so as to eliminate wordiness and to gain emphasis. Before submitting his final draft, David edited his essay, carefully checking matters of grammar, punctuation, usage, and spelling.

No one would argue that David didn't struggle with his essay, but the struggle was worthwhile because David learned many things about the process of writing and about himself as a writer. David started where all good writing must start, with his content. He had something to say and a reason for saying it. Initially, David's material seemed to control him, but once he decided to use the third-person point of view, he took charge of the writing and delighted in the way the narrative developed. David experienced the satisfaction that writers get when their words not only say what they want them to say but also say it well.

Study Questions

1. A student writing about David Leith's essay said,

   > I thought if writing was going to be good it had to be authentic and that if it was going to be authentic it had to be honest. But is the writer of this piece honest? I don't mean he doesn't have a right to cut things like telling us where his parents were that night. But Paul Eschholz says the writer said he was angry when he *first* discovered the raccoon. That's not in the paper. He doesn't make it clear in his paper that he was angry about having to work longer either. And when he makes the whole story into something that happened to somebody else just because he doesn't want to see himself as a killer, isn't he copping out? He doesn't even want to talk about that change with his teacher it seems. I don't see how writing that doesn't tell the truth this way can be called good.

   How do you respond to this statement?

2. Imagine David Leith's writing a paper addressed to an assignment that reads as follows:

   > Suppose someone asked you what was in it for you to have written the narrative you just completed. How would you respond to this question?

   How do you think David Leith might respond to such an assignment?

   What makes you say so?

3. In a classroom discussion of "Where the Heart Should Be" and of Paul Eschholz's commentary on it, one student said,

If this writer "has a point to make in telling us his story," what exactly is it? Is he saying he thinks he should have just let the raccoon go or that people are cruel or that he should have killed the raccoon quicker, or what? Maybe he's trying to say too much and got confused.

Another student responded,

I don't think the writer here is trying to make a point in the sense that he's telling us just one thing like "be nice to animals" or something like that. In fact I think one of the reasons it took him so long to write is that the story is bigger than some message. He's trying to see all the meanings in something that happened to him, and so I think his point is that there isn't just one meaning to it. I don't think he's confused. I think he's thinking.

What is your position on the question at issue in this exchange?

Roger Garrison's Assignment

You won't have any writing assignments in the ordinary sense of the term in this course. What you'll be doing is writing a dozen or more short papers over the semester and revising each paper several times before it is accepted. You'll choose your own subjects and set your own suitably spaced deadlines. Selecting a subject and aiming it at a reader are very much parts of the writing process, often the hardest parts. Further, when you pick your own topic, you have both an investment in it and a commitment to it: You have claimed a genuine interest, and you're committed to honest communicaton of that interest.

I encourage you to try to respond to a variety of problems in expression. I urge you especially to write about matters in which you have strong current interest, or about which you have genuine curiosity. Such variety invariably produces different rhetorical forms, since (in writing as in nature) form follows function. The papers you write will often require some library research, or interviewing of knowledgeable sources, or old-fashioned reporter's legwork. Your papers can turn into brief feature articles, or reports, or even memos, depending upon the audience they are addressed to.

In effect then, all the writing assignments in this course are the same: Create a self-designed task—and follow it through from choice of subject to finished piece. I *suggest* a length of 2½ to 4 double-spaced typed pages *at most*, and far less (even a single paragraph) if your subject warrants that brevity. Such compression will force you to follow the writer's classic process of focusing your subject, organizing it tightly, writing it economically—and learning to shut up when you're through.

❧ A Trail of Tiny Stars   *by Karen Tocher*

---

1   A dear friend once told me that when life seems hopeless and you're feeling depressed, then get close to the elements. Last night, deep inside of me, a storm was brewing—and I exploded. Oh, the tears, the anger, and the overwhelming feeling of sadness and loneliness. The wine I drank—too much—was just fuel on the fire. But today, no wine for me. Today, I listened to the wisdom of my trusted friend, and sought to get "close to the elements." I dug my bicycle out of the cluttered barn and

ROGER H. GARRISON, who died on March 1, 1984, was Emeritus Professor of English at Westbrook College in Maine. He published numerous articles and two books on writing: A Guide to Creative Writing (1950) and How a Writer Works (1981). He was a consultant to writing teachers on nearly 100 campuses since 1960, and a consultant on community college staff development since 1962. He founded and directed the National Seminar for Master Teachers and the National Institute for Community College Writing Instructors. He was a consulting editor for Little, Brown and Company and for Harper & Row.

pedaled in the winter afternoon sunshine. How simple that bike is: no pouring of gas or oil to make a big, greasy engine run; just the strength of my legs to keep it moving. "Elemental" again.

I passed an old, iced-over swimming hole where I spent many a summer day as a child, sneaking around the Keep Out signs, then innocently stripping off my clothes and splashing naked in the cool spring water. For uncounted summer hours, I rolled my young, tanned body down huge piles of sand, and skipped smooth, flat stones on the water. No hurt and turmoil inside, then.

My bike and I went on for several miles until I came upon a wide, open field, white with fresh snow that glistened in the midday sunshine. The gurgle of a brook along the roadside stopped my pedaling. Leftover autumn leaves rustled in the February breeze.

The field was bordered by huge pine and birch trees, and an old stone wall. In the middle of the field, a bare apple tree stood alone. Its stark branches seemed to reach out to me. I put my bike down and walked out into the field. The snow crunched and the soles of my sneakers imprinted a trail of tiny stars. When I finally reached the apple tree, I stretched out on my back and looked up into the blue, gleaming sky. A dozen white seagulls dived and soared in the crystal air. Far off in the distance I heard some crows. They reminded me of the little people I care for at the day care center. "B for ball, C for crow. What does the crow say? Let me hear you!" and the children shout "CAAAAWWWW!" with big smiles on their faces.

The seagulls and crows eventually disappeared. The air was cold and still, and I lay motionless beneath the apple tree. My corduroys and denim jacket were soaked from the snow. But the sun was warm.

By now, my thoughts were as clear as the air. I crunched back over the field, climbed on my bicycle, and pedaled past farmhouse after farmhouse. Many of the farms were deteriorating, but their owners hold on to the land. They are too proud to sell out to greedy developers, who will scar the fields with suburban sprawl. I fear the death of the old farmers; for then the field where I lay in solitude today will have side-by-side houses, driveway loops, and an asphalt playground. The apple tree will either get chopped down to make room for a garage, or the neighbors will fight over the crabbed fruit.

Such thoughts sadden me, and I turn toward home. The late afternoon air bites at my cheeks. Once home, tired and stiff, I build a fire, and the wood snaps and pops and sends bright orange flames leaping up the chimney. I slam down the iron stove cover to damp the hungry fire. Then I collapse, exhausted, on the rug in front of the stove, and welcome the heat as it seeps into me and relaxes aching muscles.

I think of my trusted friend and my afternoon bicycle trip and getting close to the elements. And I silently wish with all my heart that someday my children and their children will be able to leave trails of tiny stars to the apple tree that stands alone with outstretched limbs in the vast field of glistening snow.

ROGER GARRISON'S COMMENTARY

As a teacher of writing, I am, first of all, a reader; "teacher" comes second. When I pick up a piece of writing, I am predisposed to be interested, informed, or perhaps even entertained. I need to feel immediately that my writer/guide clearly knows where we are going together. In this case, she has drawn a map of the territory I am to travel. She has placed me mentally and physically at a beginning by indicating the nature of the journey. Then, the path I am to follow is clear, with unmistakable landmarks and signposts for twists or turns. The important word is *control*. My writer/guide's control is such that my needs as a reader have been anticipated simply and sometimes subtly—and smoothly enough that I don't feel as though I am being guided at all.

The genesis of "A Trail of Tiny Stars" was personal, as is so often the case with beginning writers. Karen had suffered an abrupt, shattering loss of someone she dearly loved. The anguish, the grief, was nearly insupportable; it was smothering her life and her work as a student. "I've *got* to write about this," she said. She did: one draft after another, rambling, barely coherent, flooded with emotional words. Writing to express strong feelings is especially hard, because the temptation is to let go in highly charged language—too many adjectives, too many strained adverbial phrases or overblown images, too much attempt to interpret for the reader.

Finally, after one more draft, I said, "It seems to me that your feelings are so strong, they're getting in the way of reality. What, actually, did you *do* about this?"

"I drank too much—"

"No, I mean a deliberate act, a choice, or some experience that felt like a turning point for you."

Silence. Then, "Yes, I think so. You mean write about that?"

"Yes. Try it."

"A Trail of Tiny Stars" (again, several drafts) was Karen's solution to her problem of expression. She gave up trying to characterize her feelings with phrases like "storms of tears," "the unfairness of life," "I felt lost and empty," and "the light had gone out of my life." (Grief is an inevitable human experience, and it creates its own clichés.) Instead, she chose to relate, almost matter-of-factly, an experience that helped to settle her mind and calm her spirit. The writing is cleanly specific. The writer sketches her situation quickly in the first six sentences. She packs the "emotionalism" into two sentences (the second and third), and then, in what amounts to a narrative, she shares with her reader what she *did* in response to her feelings. *Show* is the important word, not *tell*.

On the surface, it's a simple story: a long bike ride through farmland on a clear winter afternoon. But it is the sketching of explicit details that gives the writing its accumulating strength and persuasion. The brief childhood memories; the "glistening" snow; the etched trees; the "gleaming" sky and "crystal" air; the imprint of sneaker soles ("tiny stars"), all build into coherence like a charcoal sketch, where each line or shading *suggests* more than it tells. Use of a great many adjectives is risky, but I think Karen gets away with it. It is, eventually, the sense of clean brightness that dominates, ending in a cadenced sentence (read it aloud) and a "vast field of glistening snow."

The details become almost symbols of a changed state of mind. The writer did not consciously design any symbolism—far from it. Indeed, such self-conscious "technique" would not have occurred to her. Significantly, her whole effort in the successive drafts was toward *honest* telling. Eventually, that directness came through as a brief, well-paced narrative (almost like the bike ride itself), and the reader could begin to hear an honest, human voice in these pages.

Good writing is inevitably honest writing. Every writer, beginner or not, needs what Hemingway called "a built-in crap detector." All of us, like it or not, are daily immersed in tides of phony, posturing, pretentious, tired, imprecise, slovenly language, which both suffocate and corrupt the mind. (Recently, I counted the word "great" eight times in a thirty-second TV commercial, for a "great hotdog," no less. Johann Sebastian Bach is no longer a great musician, alas; the word once reserved for giants now plugs a pickle-and-relish wiener.) Academics haven't helped honest writing much, either. If I read "outcome," "cognitive," "interact," "heuristic," or "viable" many more times, I shall throw up.

I detect nothing phony in the piece of student writing I discuss here. It may be flawed—I suppose almost any writing is flawed in some way—but as a reader, I do not doubt its sincerity. (As a teacher, however, I wonder whether the paragraph about the deteriorating farms and the housing developers strikes an irrelevant note. But—well. The student's honest environmental outrage is not entirely misplaced in the context.)

Another strength in the writing comes, I think, from the *selection* and personal significance of the details. They have what poet May Sarton calls "resonance"—after-echoes, so to speak, that suggest in the reader's mind *more* than is merely said. For example, the swimming hole contrasts a memory of childhood innocence with the present "hurt and turmoil inside"; the open, clean sweep of the snowy field and its solitary apple tree connote quiet peacefulness; the seagulls and distant crow calls underline the expansiveness of sky; the warm fire at home reflects the calming of the inner turmoil, "slam down the iron stove cover to damp the hungry fire," and the soothing of aching muscles. And in a subtle but important way, the bicycle itself—simple, self-propelled, no "big, greasy engine"—represents a regaining of self-control and self-direction in the troubled person.

I emphasize immediately, however, that Karen did *not* deliberately calculate details that would prompt the kind of reader response I have just outlined. Rather, she tried to relate honestly and clearly what was important to her during that bike journey. My interpretations are almost embarrassingly academic, though they, too, are honest: They are my own *reading* of the narrative that the writer has provided. As I suggested earlier, they are the "resonance" that capable writing nearly always sets off in a reader. Over many years of writing and teaching, my own criteria for good writing have distilled into three simple questions. The questions have complex roots. They stem from a classical education (as an undergraduate, I was marinated in Aristotle, particularly the *Poetics* and *Rhetoric*, and in Greek and Roman literature), from an ingrained Yankee practicality, from having made my living by writing, and from a lifetime of curiosity (hence, study) about the nature of communication. The questions are:

What is this writer trying to *do*?
How well does he or she do it?
Is it *worth* doing?

In essence, all writing, even poetry, is functional: It *does* something. It satisfies a reasonably intelligent, reasonably curious reader that it has accomplished what it set out to do, no matter how trivial or profound. How well the writer has done the job asks for both technical and aesthetic judgments, which are the essential elements of criticism. The *worth* of the writing is a value judgment, and it depends not only upon comparison with other, similar writings, but on the reader's experience, sensibilities, and taste.

By these criteria, "A Trail of Tiny Stars" is, in my judgment, a good piece of work. My student Karen and I are pleased to share it with you.

Study Questions

1. In a classroom discussion of Karen Tocher's "A Trail of Tiny Stars" and Roger Garrison's commentary on it, one student said,

   I think Roger Garrison is reading the writer here rather than the writing. He knows the student and that she's suffered the loss of somebody. He's seen the writing go through a number of drafts too. And he seems to think writing the paper calmed her or something. So he says the paper is honest, that it isn't phony, that it's sincere. But I can see a lot of what could be called phoniness in the paper: gurgling brooks and rustling leaves and glistening snow and crystal skies—stuff like that. Also, because I don't know the event she's talking about, I don't see what she comes to know or understand. In fact I just don't believe this all happened the way the writer says it did. I think she *did* set out to design symbolism, like how sweet and pure the apple tree is and how awful suburbs and machinery are. And it's pretty easy symbolism.

Another student responded by saying,

I don't see how any teacher can help reading the student as well as the writing, first of all. If you know that this paper is about someone trying to cope with a death, how do you keep that out of your reading of it, and *why* should you keep it out? But I don't think I need to know about the death because the subject of the paper is how the writer deals with feeling hopeless. Secondly, when you say the paper's phony, that's a question of taste. As Roger Garrison says "the *worth* of the writing is a value judgment." The paper sounds sincere to me. I think the writer uses language very well. What makes your judgment right and others' judgments wrong? And I don't see how *you* know the event *didn't* happen.

What position would you take in this controversy?

2. A student writing of Karen Tocher's "A Trail of Tiny Stars" said,

What this writer seems most interested in is expressing her feelings. Maybe if she were more concerned with trying to come to terms with her feelings, by looking at exactly why and how they changed, she'd have more. Maybe she "shuts up," as Roger Garrison says, before she should. Maybe she isn't "through" really.

How do you respond to these speculations?

3. "It may be flawed," says Roger Garrison of Karen Tocher's paper. If Karen Tocher asked you whether you think the paper needs revising, how would you respond? If you do not think the paper needs revising, what makes you say so? If you think it does, how would you suggest the writer proceed?

DONALD GRAY'S Assignment

Either tell me a story of an actual or imagined event in which you carefully choose descriptive detail and arrange events so that your story makes a clear point; or, find such a story and write a paper in which you explain how its details and arrangement of events make what you think to be the point or meaning of the story.

✍ The Gypsy

by Jean Ann (Frazer) Behney

1   The last weary Disney World visitors clambered aboard the tram and dropped heavily onto the narrow seats to await the ride from within the fantasy land's gates to their cars parked in its surrounding gravel lots.

2   I was separated from the members of my family due to the fact of nature that seven-member families do not generally find seats together. I could see the back of my father's head in the tram car ahead of mine, and, by twisting my own head around, I could distinguish the forms of my mother and sisters a couple of links behind me in the train of open cars.

3   Once our trundling trip in the deepening dusk began, I looked about interestedly to see with whom I was sharing the tram car. Most of the people around me appeared to be parts of families: fathers in bermudas and sunglasses sitting with a sticky-faced child at either side, mothers tying headscarves beneath their chins, someone's grandfather juggling an awkward assortment of camera cases, and a young couple, unabashedly holding hands between them on a seat.

4   Then I caught sight of the gypsy. He sat a bit apart from everyone else in more ways than one, for there was an empty space next to him and he seemed not to fit physically with the rest of us. I could observe him perfectly from where I sat, since he was opposite me and a few places down. As I took in his swarthy complexion, long nose, and droopy moustache with the candid curiosity of a naive sixteen-year old, I thought, "A gypsy! All he needs is a gold ring in one ear and a handkerchief around his neck!"

5   The gypsy seemed unaware of his fellow passengers. In fact, he looked only at what he held—a large, flat, circular lollipop with a smiling Mickey Mouse face on both sides. As he looked at this, he twirled it by its stick between his hands, as if he were debating about something. His

---

DONALD GRAY is Professor of English at Indiana University in Bloomington. He has written on nineteenth-century British literature and topics concerning the teaching of English, and he has edited an anthology of British Victorian poetry. He is presently the editor of *College English*.

hands were strong and sun-browned; I sensed that he had used them often and for many purposes—climbing a mountain, pitching tents, cooking meat in a frying pan over a fire. His clothes reflected the free-spiritedness of an outdoorsman, from his lovingly worn work shirt to the smooth tips of his brown boots.

I was fascinated and could not impel myself to take my eyes away from him. The woman next to me was admonishing her youngest that the balloon would pop if poked with daddy's pencil, and from the car up ahead came the sound of a child's tired wailing. I was oblivious to all this, and I did not turn to watch the pink glow of Cinderella's lit up castle fading behind us as most of the others did. As I continued to watch the gypsy, my fingers in my lap began, of their own accord, to copy his movements with the lollipop. Then I caught myself doing this, and quickly stopped. The gypsy's face was quiet, but at one point I believed he was on the verge of a smile. "He's probably thinking of where he'll travel next," I decided privately, and with some satisfaction. "Maybe to Colorado, and the mountains. With a knapsack on his back, and not a care in the world."   6

The tram halted at the first parking area and several families gathered up their postcards, balloons, and sleepy children to head for their own parked vehicles. The gypsy looked up to watch those departing, each with his or her memento of the Disney World they were leaving. I myself did not hold a souvenir. Earlier in the day I had discovered myself in one of my all too frequent dissatisfied moods and as a result, I had passed up the gift shops. As the last parent descended and walked away, both the gypsy and I watched the red balloon he carried bobbing happily above him.   7

I began to grow restless as the tram started up again, but I did not understand why. As I observed the gypsy, I started trying to imagine his day at Disney World. I could not picture him whirling in the magic tea-cup ride or eating a hot dog at a picnic table. In fact, I couldn't visualize him fitting in at Disney World at all. Suddenly, I looked at myself—looked at my blue tennis shoes and the limp ribbons in my hair—and became even more restless.   8

In another two stops, it would be my turn to descend from the tram and to rejoin my family at our station wagon. How had the gypsy come here, I wondered as I gazed at him. Once, I thought I caught him looking back at me, but then I was not sure.   9

The tram was slowing again and, all too soon for me, the gypsy stood in preparation for getting off. Anxiously, I wondered again where he was going, and if I would ever go there too. To my astonishment, the gypsy did not step down from his end of the car. He crossed to my side of it and, with a peculiar half-smile that did not reach his eyes, he put his smiling   10 lollipop into my hand. Before I could react, he had lightly stepped off the tram and was disappearing in the dark, turning not towards the rows of parked cars, but walking away from them and Disney World in the direction of the newly-risen moon.

11   When we reached our car, my little sister spied the lollipop in my hand and demanded to know where I had gotten it.

12   "A gypsy gave it to me," I muttered.

13   "Who?"

14   I began to cry.

15   "What's wrong with you?" my sister said. "If somebody gave me a big lollipop, I wouldn't cry over it."

Donald Gray's COMMENTARY

Jean Ann (Frazer) Behney's essay was written when she was a first-year student in an introductory course in the reading of fiction. I have used the assignment for which "The Gypsy" was written in other undergraduate courses in literary interpretation and in elementary and advanced composition courses. For the question is one that students need to ask again and again of the texts they write as well as of those they read: What's the point?

I offer a choice between telling and analyzing a story because some students seem to feel condescended to and unserious when they are asked just to write a story. Most students, however, choose to write their own stories rather than analyze someone else's story. I suppose that they think it is easier to write narrative than it is to analyze it, or that to write their own stories somehow makes the assignment less like doing something for English. But in the writing, and especially in the discussion and rewriting of their stories, students can learn a great deal not only about the use of detail and the organization of discourse but also about the powers and possibilities of their own practices as writers and readers.

Take, for example, "The Gypsy." The essay has two principal strengths: (1) the play between details of the ordinary and of the fantastic and (2) the arrangement of events so that the character of the story-teller and her view of the central issue in the story steadily unfold. Details of the ordinary dominate the opening of the essay: the weary tourists dropping "heavily onto the narrow seats," the clutter of bermudas, sunglasses, headscarves, cameras, and sticky-faced children. The word "fantasy" in the first sentence opens a counterpoint that begins to take hold with the young lovers holding hands and the first description of the dark complexion, long nose, and drooping moustache of the solitary man whom the writer decides is a gypsy.

Her decision is crucial. The heart of the story is a contest between her imaginings about the gypsy and the ordinary reality of the tram-car and her own life. It is the story-teller who gives the man an earring and neck-handkerchief, who sees his strong and sun-browned hands climbing mountains and pitching tents, and who provides him a knapsack and sends him off to Colorado. All that is really seen and heard in the tram-car are the admonishments of tired mothers, the wailings of tired children, the collection of postcards and balloons as families leave to head for their own cars, and, strikingly, the Mickey Mouse lollipop.

Why does the story-teller invent the gypsy? The single most effective tactic in the story is its only break from chronological sequence. In the seventh paragraph the story-teller tells us that she has been "in one of my all too frequent dissatisfied moods" all day. She imagines the gypsy as similarly restless and singular, as alien as she in Disney World. Having in this summary recollection opened her condition and her motive to our speculation, she returns to the present to recall who she really is—blue tennis shoes, limp hair ribbons, a child on her way to the family car. Then she returns the story to its straight chronological course to close with the wonderful gesture of the gift lollipop and the still more wonderful lines of her younger sister, for whom lollipops are still enough.

The obvious question with which to begin a class discussion of "The Gypsy" is "Why is she crying?" I can no longer ask that question innocently. My frequent readings and discussion of the story have persuaded me that its point is its teller's recognition that, although she longs for the autonomy and freedom of an adult, she is still a child, and worse, is seen as a child even (especially) by the gypsy. She is a Cinderella who goes to the palace on a family outing and whose prince gives her not the slipper, love, and marriage, but a Mickey Mouse lollipop. I like this girl and her eager imaginings of adulthood. I feel gently sorry for the tears that say she knows at the end how long it takes to grow up.

But I am a middle-aged parent, and my condition provides its peculiar reasons for my interpretation. If I hold back my answer to the question, students often offer quite different answers and readings. Two readings are especially frequent. Some students, straining at eighteen and nineteen to put some distance between themselves and the difficult mid-passage of their adolescence, regard the story-teller with some disdain as a foolish child, a fantasizer, even a brat. Her tears confirm her childishness, not her recognition of the difficult way to adulthood, and they are to be scorned as petulant and trivial ("What's wrong with you?"). Other students, more sympathetic, see the girl as naive. The world is more mysterious, and maybe even sinister, than she knows. What is this dark, solitary man doing on a tram-car full of families? Why is he giving lollipops to young girls? In this reading the story-teller cries in frustration. The meaning of her tears is not that she has learned something about herself and growing up, but that she understands nothing, it is all beyond her.

These disagreements are valuable because they open the way to the discussion and practice of genuine revision. "The Gypsy" could be improved by some superficial editorial revision. Some arch overwriting can be excised ("due to the fact of nature that," etc.); a few words can be reconsidered ("I *sensed* that he had used them often"); the story-teller's physical appearance can be more completely described (and how can she look at the ribbons in her own hair?). These changes probably will not add significant support to any of the three readings I have described.

The next question, then, is "How can the essay be fundamentally changed so that it heads yet more certainly to one or another of the meanings that readers find in it?" What details about the event, the place, the story-teller herself can be added to make it yet more solidly the story of self-discernment and self-discovery I think it to be? How can the sequence of events in the story be changed, or what details and events can be added or subtracted, to characterize the girl more emphatically as a petulant child, or the gypsy as more mysterious, more sinister, or just more obviously different from the man the story-teller imagines? Once the readers of the essay start thinking of themselves as the authors of its revision, changes that go beyond revisions of its details and arrangement can be considered. What might the point (or points) of the story be if it were told by someone else—by the father looking on from the next tram-car, by someone in the same car who is a stranger to both the girl and the gypsy? What might be the effect of writing the story in a colloquial voice, in the language that a sixteen-year old girl (or boy: another interesting change) would use to tell the story to a contemporary?

I intend my remarks about Ms. Behney's story to make two points. The first is that her essay is excellent because she has found details and a structure that lead me to make a complex and satisfying sense of it. The second is that, even as the story stands, other meanings are possible. Because her writing is good, like the writing other students can do, her readers are easily converted to writers who accept the invitation to change the story to fit their readings. That is the gift Ms. Behney hands to readers and writers, students and teachers, in "The Gypsy."

Study Questions

1. A student writing about "The Gypsy" and Donald Gray's commentary on it said,

> This selection really confuses me about writing and reading both. The assignment for this paper asked the students to write a story that makes a clear point.

But "The Gypsy" Donald Gray admits, could be interpreted three different ways, may have *three* different points. What I want to know is why that doesn't make the story a jumble. Secondly, Donald Gray also admits that the way he reads the story depends on his being "a middle-aged parent." Does this mean that people can make stories mean whatever they feel like depending on who they are? If so, I don't see how I'm supposed to decide what makes any writing good.

How do you respond to this statement?

2. In a classroom discussion of "The Gypsy" and Donald Gray's commentary, one student said,

I don't like the idea that a reader of a story has a right to be the author of its revisions the way Donald Gray says. When I write things, I want readers to read what I say, not what they want to make me say. Suppose this writer wanted readers to make up their own minds about what she meant. Suppose that's her point. If you go changing things you ruin what she wrote.

Another student responded by saying,

That's a cop out—letting readers make up their own minds that way. That just means that as a writer you don't have to work to control anything. Besides, Donald Gray isn't saying that readers have the right to rewrite the story. The whole point is to raise possibilities for a *writer* to consider. That's what a writing class is for. If you don't want to talk about changing anything in your writing, how are you going to get better at it? No writer should ever just stick by what they wrote.

How would you enter this conversation?

3. In another classroom discussion of "The Gypsy," a student said,

I read this story a fourth way. The way I see it is this girl isn't in a hurry to grow up or sorry to be a child. She wants to stay a child forever. The gypsy frightens her. She realizes the adult world she has to grow up into is going to make demands on her that she can't meet. I think the gypsy is a symbol of sex and that this girl knows she's terrified of it. So long as she stays a child she's safe. Her tears are tears of fear.

How do you respond to this interpretation of "The Gypsy"?

Writing Assignment 9
Telling Stories

This assignment, which asks you to write a narrative, will involve you in a process of revising as well—in a process, as the word implies, of seeing something again.

Choose something you said in one of your earlier papers that you now feel you could profitably see again, that you would like to explore more fully perhaps, or that you have some questions about, or that you think needs to be considered from additional perspectives. Use the narrative form to help you revise what you first wrote by turning your earlier writing into a story of some sort, by creating a particular scene in which particular people act and speak. Feel free to sharpen or intensify your meaning by fictionalizing things in any way you think you need to. If, for example, you spoke in your original paper as an "I," you may wish to change that "I" into a "he" or a "she"—or into several "he's" or "she's"—or the other way around. You may decide to recast an event from your childhood as an occurrence taking place in someone's adulthood, or as a conflict of old age. And so on. Be sure to turn in with this paper a copy of whatever you are revising.

Next, on a separate page, write a paragraph in which you explain what you imagine any one of the students or teachers in this chapter would say to you about your *completed narrative only*. This person does *not* know, in other words, where your narrative came from, that its origins lie in an earlier paper you wrote.

But you, as someone who *does* know that the origins of your narrative lie in an earlier paper, certainly have something more, and might well have something different, to say about your narrative than could the teacher or student you chose in the second part of this assignment. On a third page, use this knowledge about your narrative to argue what sort of person might be equipped to write "creatively"—or could have any interest in doing so.

Writing about Writing 10

The critical act can be an act of creativity, and what is created is not just an object but a sensibility.

W. E. Coles, Jr.

ALL OF THE STUDENT ESSAYS IN THIS chapter are praised in one way or another for the analyses of writing that they undertake. They are praised in somewhat different terms to be sure, but in all five instances with terms that imply certain assumptions about what a good piece of written analysis tries to do. It is possible, therefore, to read each of the five commentaries in this chapter as advice on how to write a good analysis of written discourse. "Because this teacher seems to like these things about this student's writing," a reader might reason, "these are things that this teacher thinks a good analysis of a piece of writing ought to do; these are things that this teacher would advise *me* to do in writing such an analysis."

As you will see if you turn to the writing assignment at the end of this chapter, the five student essays and commentaries here are intended to provide you with a means of evaluating, of re-seeing, a piece of your own writing, which can help you redefine what you can come to do as a writer.

DAVID BLEICH'S Assignment

Since this is the end of our year-long course on the use and perception of language and literature, this essay should present a retrospective analysis of all your work—about twenty essays of various lengths—and should draw tentative conclusions about how you have come to characteristically use language at this point in your life—the end of your freshman year in college.

[In order to understand Ms. K.'s discussion, it is not necessary to read the Flannery O'Connor story "A Good Man Is Hard to Find" or the full text of Ms. K.'s Lecture Essay #9 (though these readings *would* be necessary in order to discuss Ms. K.'s work *with* her). One should know, however, that the writing assignment of Lecture Essay #9 asked the class to write about whether and how they identified with one or more characters in the O'Connor story.]

⮬ [Untitled]   *by Ms. K.* *

1   With Lecture Essay #9 my work starts to change. It still isn't as "free" as some of my essays from last semester but it isn't like the first three essays of this semester. It contains more than just "surface" thoughts.

2   When I used the word "identified" I think a better word may have been "understood." The directions asked for identifications, though, so that's what was written. I never realized how much I really do comply in these essays. I found the fourth paragraph of this paper [Essay #9] especially interesting.

> I can identify with the mom in that I have felt tired and have had to keep on going. I have also been in positions where what I say really doesn't matter—things are done anyway. I feel like cutting down someone who bothers me, just as the kids do. I hate the feeling of someone always being there that you can't get rid of—who just bugs the hell out of you. I can also feel the loneliness and need for love that the grandma feels. And when having these feelings want to help out and feel needed—just like the grandma.

---

* [*Eds. note:* The author has chosen to remain anonymous.]

DAVID BLEICH teaches in the English Department of Indiana University. He has taught the freshman course "Studying One's Own Language" for about six years, and is now completing an analytical study based on this course, entitled *Language Analysis in the Classroom.* He is also the author of *Readings and Feelings* (1975), *Subjective Criticism* (1978), and *Utopia: The Psychology of a Cultural Fantasy* (1984).

(Am I going back to my formal style?) Do I see my mom in the position of the mother in the story? Or as the grandmother? I start off with "I can identify" which I also used to start the preceding three paragraphs. The subject of the paragraph is the identification with the mother and the grandma. The subject of each sentence in the paragraph is "I"—and it is also the first word of each sentence. Hmmm. Right after I mention being in a position where what I say really doesn't matter—I talk about my feelings of wanting to cut down someone. This appears in *this* paragraph [above] about the mother. I guess a couple of these sentence can be applied to my mom. I bet you don't have to guess which two I am referring to, Mr. Bleich. The thing is, the story refers to the grandmother as the "problem" not the mother. I give my mom some of the grandma's qualities and the grandma seems to have what some of my mother's feelings would be. So I see my mother as a combination of both the mother and the grandma that are in the story. I see myself as the mother in the story—being in a position where what I say doesn't matter and when I'm in that position I feel like cutting others down—just as the kids do. When I say "I hate the feeling of someone always being there that you can't get rid of—who just bugs the hell out of you," this is how I see the mother's attitude in the story towards the grandma. Since I just said that I am like the mom in the story and my mom is like the grandma—I guess my attitude is the same as the mother's. The next sentence then talks about how I can feel for the grandmother in the story. Or, in real life, how I can understand my mom's feelings. But looking back at the beginning of this paragraph, I said I see my mom as a combination of the grandma and the mom in the story. Has the mother's qualities of being in a reduced position and the grandma's qualities of loneliness and need of love been applied to my mom? And if I see my mom like the mom in the story in some ways—and I see myself as the mom in the story in some ways—that means I identify with my mom? I say I can feel the loneliness and need for love that the grandma feels (my mom feels). In the next sentence I say that when I have these feelings I want to "help out and feel needed—just like the grandma." I understand how my mom feels because this is the way I feel too.

This is it: when my mom puts me in a "reduced" position, I want to cut her down. I can understand her need for love and her feelings of loneliness just as I understand my own feelings of these same two emotions. When she puts me in this reduced position I know that she does it because she feels as if she were in the same position and the only way for her to feel in control is to reduce someone else. Maybe this is where my dad comes in also. With dad being in a more (what's the word I want to use?)—oh my God—*authoritative* position she feels reduced and the only way for her to feel as if she has more control is to cut down others. So my mom therefore sees *me* as authoritative?

5   Where do I go from here? I thought things were different when I came to school with my family situation—I mean being away from home and all. But I guess my attitudes really haven't changed as much as I thought they had.

6   It is interesting that all through this paper I have been talking about how much I complied in my lecture essays and in my longer papers. Now I bring up the subject of "authority." I think the usage of "I'm sure," "I know," and "I think" have something to do with how I write and feel about authority. I use these usages when I'm trying to show or be authoritative. Even if I am *not* sure and do not *know*—I might use it so that I appear more sure of myself. The use of this phrase appears only once or twice throughout the essays in the first semester—except in the essay about an understanding. By using this phrase I am asserting my beliefs.

DAVID BLEICH'S COMMENTARY

The passage by Ms. K. comes from an essay of about 4,000 words and shows Ms. K.'s successful use of three contexts for understanding her language: (1) in important past relationships, in this case, with her parents; (2) in this course with this teacher; (3) in literature and in response to literature. Each of these contexts shows Ms. K.'s use of language in connection with how she perceives herself as a growing person, and each context is connected with the other two. In a general way, these three contexts represent (1) the memory of past language use, (2) awareness of present language use, and (3) language use as it appears through active use of one's imagination.

Specifically, this excerpt is about a turning point (in Ms. K.'s sense of her language use) in the second semester—the writing of the essay on the O'Connor story—and the writing of this excerpt *produces* another turning point. The first turning point is the announcement of how Ms. K. identifies with her mother; the second is her sudden recognition of how her relationship with her father contributes to this identification. Each of these turning points is based on Ms. K.'s comprehension of a specific feature of her language. Her identification with her mother is bound up with her understanding of her language habit of "cutting down," while her sense of her likeness with her father is bound up with her way of speaking "authoritatively," which means for her, speaking with confidence that her thoughts will be taken seriously. Both "cutting down" and "authoritative" language are actually *language use strategies* that Ms. K. uses without her being directly aware that they are habits.

Her year's work in analyzing her language permitted her to see when and how these strategies came out in her use of language. Let me briefly outline some of the events that led to Ms. K.'s "authoritative" statement in paragraph 4 beginning "This is it."

In the middle of the first semester, she wrote an essay about an understanding with her father, which took place after a family quarrel, and which was achieved *without either of them articulating* what was mutually understood. Ms. K. thought that this understanding was made possible because she and her father were speaking privately and face-to-face. The combination of the precipitating event (the family quarrel) and the subsequent private chat created, in her view, a moment of mutual understanding. What she thought was mutually understood was something like "her feelings for her mother," probably best described as angry and sympathetic all at once. The precipitating event was Ms. K.'s mother's apparent "cutting down" of people at a family gathering on Father's Day some years back. By writing the essay on how she felt understood by her father, she also established a point of identification with him, which, in later work, permitted her to see that she and her father share certain writing habits, such as the use of parentheses and dashes to interpolate important thoughts in her discourse. But more importantly, this led to her identifying the larger habits of using "I know" and "I'm sure" either in order to *express* her authority or to *appear* authoritative, as she describes in the last paragraph of the excerpt reproduced here. And, in another essay analyzing her first semester's work, she noted that she used the phrase "I guess" when she is actually quite sure, but, for diplomatic reasons, feels she ought not announce that certainty.

In the excerpt above, Ms. K. relates her habit of "cutting down" to her ways of using language authoritatively by wondering and implying that her mother cuts her down because the mother sees her, Ms. K., as authoritative. This is an important realization by Ms. K. because she places two language habits into the configuration of real feelings in real relationships. She reaches this point by reflecting on how she responded to the O'Connor story, particularly on how she identified with both the mother and the grandmother. It was not until her response to the story that Ms. K. brought into discussion her hitherto unannounced but nevertheless clear knowledge about how she relates to her mother. The reading of the story and the writing of the essay motivated her to announce this knowledge; but also, her ease in class increased to such an extent that she felt confident enough to present such thoughts. The complete picture given in the excerpt could not have been drawn without Ms. K. becoming aware of the exact nature of her response to the story.

As Ms. K. describes it, her "cutting down" is a verbal reaction to feeling reduced or otherwise deprived of her due authority. She sees both the mother and the grandmother in the story as occupying positions of little authority. In the first semester, in another essay, she had described her own position in her family as one in which "what I say doesn't matter." She alludes to this belief in paragraph 3 of this excerpt as well. She implies that being denied this *authority to speak* leads to the wish to cut someone down—that is, to the desire to speak with excessive, aggressive authority. She judges that the mother in the story is denied this authority and that her own mother may also be thus denied because her father is in the more authoritative position in her family. "Cutting down" thus emerges as the verbal *taking* of authority in response to feeling that verbal authority is denied. As the child of her mother and father, Ms. K. identifies with both. The new authority of Ms. K. as an individual is her ability to announce and describe the language she uses, which shows both of these identifications: "cutting down" is the strategy that shows her identification with her mother, and the taking of verbal initiative is the strategy showing her identification with her father.

I believe that both of these issues were raised by Ms. K. about six weeks into the first semester, when she wrote in response to an assignment which asked her to describe certain language features of her instructor that she thought he (I) ought to know about. In responding to my teasing and prodding in class, Ms. K. wrote that I had a habit of "cutting people down." She said that "people" who cut others down may be doing so to build up their own egos. But then she switched to direct address and wrote, "I don't think you build your ego up by cutting [people] down." The general third person statement implies that I cut people down to build up my ego; the specific statement in direct address said that she did not think it was true of me. Before any of the material regarding her parents or her response to literature entered her work, the issues of cutting down and authority emerged in the classroom context, where my authority was being investigated. This strategy of direct address, we now see in retrospect, is not unlike her direct address to her father in the "mutual understanding" essay: Ms. K. feels that she acquires authority by addressing the authoritative figure directly. Also in retrospect, we see why my teasing and prodding in class made a strong impression on Ms. K.: it recalled a situation in her home that was problematic. In that early essay, Ms. K. used her own ethical and verbal authority appropriately by addressing me directly—and diplomatically took the sting out of her point while allowing her opinion about cutting down to stand nevertheless. Also, in using my authority as discussion leader to take Ms. K.'s essay seriously, that is, to show that what she says matters, I publicly recognized her authority and thereby helped make it possible for us to pursue the issues she raised in the rest of the course. Her disciplined pursuit of these issues led to her ability to announce and study the specific senses in which her language had raised such issues in the past.

Notice, by the way, how the habit of direct address appears in the excerpt. Ms. K. says, "I guess a couple of these sentences can be applied to my mom. I bet you don't have to guess which two I am referring to, Mr. Bleich." Well, I did not have to "guess" but I did have to think! Here we see a playful and familiar tone in the direct address, as well as the use of "I guess." Ms. K. feels quite certain of the thoughts that follow "I guess," and she also feels certain that I know what she is alluding to. So certain, that the use of "I guess" becomes an artful move in her self-presentation in the excerpt, yet a move that perpetuates the feeling of thoughtful, serious investigation, and that explicitly invokes my partnership with her in this study.

Ms. K.'s acquiring authority through direct address is related to her creating authority by using rhetorical questions, eight of which appear in the excerpt. An ordinary question directly addresses the reader or conversation partner; a rhetorical question addresses *both* the reader and the writer herself. Ms. K.'s rhetorical questions are addressed both to herself and to me. In her early work, her questions were relatively conventional, such as "What could I do?" coming in a narrative of a minor crisis. The rhetorical questions in the excerpt, however, suggest that Ms. K. was using her own inner authoritative voice to guide her thoughts, as when she asks, "Am I going back to my formal style?" The rhetorical questions also should be taken as a genuine formulation of alternatives: Is my mother like the mother in the story or like the grandmother? Notice how these questions appear both at the beginning of paragraph 3 and at the end, and notice how complex they are at the end. Merely to be able to formulate such complex rhetorical questions suggests that Ms. K. has been *motivated by the importance of the issues* she is dealing with *to acquire a new command of her language.* In fact, these questions lead to the resolution, "This is it." The substance of this resolution leads, in turn, to the climactic insight, which is *verbal:* "(what's the word I want to use?)—oh my God—*authoritative.* . . ." As she turns her attention from the mainly verbal material to the relationships she is discussing, Ms. K. concludes the paragraph with a noninterrogative, nonrhetorical question: "So my mom therefore sees *me* as authoritative?" One might expect this sentence to appear in pure propositional form, that is, without the question mark. The question mark, however, renders the conclusion suitably tentative and invites my response, thus telling me that she is leaving room for us to continue working together.

It is not merely a personal matter that Ms. K. consciously speaks to me in her essay. It is, rather, the manifestation of her awareness that her thought is proceeding in a *classroom* context. Ms. K.'s excerpt shows, I think, how she connected the authority issue of the classroom with the question of authority in her home, and how she found language to be a common factor in both. Her attention to language has temporarily re-solved (not resolved) an on-going social issue in her life: compliance and authority. Because what she says really does matter, I am using it in my essay on this occasion. Her work gained more authority than she imagined it would.

After studying her own language over a period of eight months, Ms. K. was able to identify some of its basic features, as well as the reasons these features were important to her use of language. She understood many of her characteristic usages as functions of her dealings with her parents and with her class and teacher. As a result, she was able to write out her understanding fluently, intelligently, and in a tone and style well suited to the situation. Her *sense* of her language told her both the initiatives to be taken and the constraints to be respected. I don't know if this effort adds up to "good writing" but I think it does amount to the intelligent use of language.

Study Questions

1. In a classroom discussion of Ms. K.'s paper and David Bleich's commentary on it, a student said,

   > This sounds to me like it came out of a psychiatrist's office rather than a writing class—I mean both the paper and the commentary on it. The writer here is asking this teacher to be her therapist. And all the teacher is doing is trying to psych her out. That's bad news.

   Another student responded,

   > That's awfully easy talk. I don't see the writer here asking the teacher to be her therapist at all. She's writing *to* him, but not in any way *for* him. And David Bleich is reading her sentences, not her. He's concerned with what her language suggests about her, about how that shows what kind of grasp she has on things. I don't see how you could write about anything important to you without your language showing something about you.

   What position would you take in this controversy?

2. In his commentary, what assumptions does David Bleich make about the relationship between the way people use language and the way they live their lives?

   Where do you as a user of language stand in relation to these assumptions?

3. In a paper written about Ms. K.'s paper and David Bleich's commentary on it, a student said,

> I don't think there's any question that Ms. K. has understood *something* about how she uses language and what it means that she uses the patterns in her language that she does. But I do have some questions about how *much* she understands, mainly because her essay is so unfinished, so unshaped. It reads like a set of notes or an entry in a journal. David Bleich is making a lot of connections that she ought to be making, but that I'm not sure she could make. In any case, I think this teacher ought to demand a rewrite of this paper. That's the only way anybody, particularly the student, could know for sure what Ms. K. understands and what she doesn't.

How do you respond to this statement? In your response, make clear whether or not you think David Bleich is justified in claiming Ms. K. understands what he says she does.

Wayne Booth's Assignment

[This assignment was given at the beginning of the third quarter of a year-long freshman course combining "humanities" and composition. Students have different instructors for all three quarters.]

Describe what happened to your writing during winter [second] quarter. Don't leave out your feelings about it.

☞ A Lifetime of Learning   *by Michael Fitzgerald*

1   "The biggest single obstacle to education is thinking you are already."* This is a remark that [my teacher] George Anderson made in class last quarter. It is a simple way of making a simple point; like all simple things, it is so obvious that it is often overlooked. Mr. Anderson was in the precarious position of having to praise work that by his own admission wasn't good, but was getting there. He wanted us to realize that we had a long way to go. So his statement was intended to prompt us into wanting to continue developing our abilities.

2   I think that it did. [For example], I know that I have a long way to go, but I want to get there, and I instinctively know that I improved a great deal under his tutelage. Instinct is not, however, my only reason for saying that I'm a better writer. Over break, I took a look at one of my senior year high school papers, a review of Thackeray's *Vanity Fair*. The paper was given an A— by my teacher. I was so appalled by its poorness that I refused to read any of my other papers. The papers I write now don't have that kind of effect on me. In a few years they probably will, but even so they are a vast improvement over my high school papers.

3   I say this to you because in comparing my *Vanity Fair* paper with the work I did last quarter, especially towards its end, I can see vast improvements [a little repetitive]. One of the most noticeable defects in the old paper was that I didn't follow my topic sentence throughout. Well, I

---

* [About this opening, Michael's new teacher wrote, "I guarantee that this is misquoted. Either a word is omitted after 'are' or the participle 'educated' was used (perhaps 'becoming educated' where you have 'education'? Otherwise there's nothing for 'are' to agree with."—W.C.B.]

WAYNE C. BOOTH is George M. Pullman Distinguished Service Professor at The University of Chicago. He has served as Chairman of Freshman Writing at Haverford College, Chairman of the Department of English at Earlham College, and Dean of the College at Chicago. His articles on composition include "The Rhetorical Stance" and "Boring from Within." His books include *The Rhetoric of Fiction* (1961), *Modern Dogma and the Rhetoric of Assent* (1974), and *Critical Understanding: The Powers and Limits of Pluralism* (1979).

actually didn't have a topic sentence to follow. Mark one up for this class for making me realize that topic sentences are not only useful but also are necessary (and not available at any store). And mark one up for George Anderson, who made me realize that my paragraphs needed to be focused more closely [clearly?] around my topic sentence.

This brings up major deficiency number two with my *Vanity Fair* paper: it had no direction. Trying to follow my argument would be like Hansel and Gretel trying to find their way through the Minotaur's Labyrinth. I did have some halfway decent ideas in the paper, but trying to figure out where they are [were] would require the help of a codebreaker (or the guy who wrote the paper). None of the paragraphs follow logically, and it is clear that the meaning of the word "transition" was unknown to me. It's a problem that I still have, but to a greatly lessened degree. This is so because [the reason is that] Mr. Anderson spent a lot of time nagging at me to develop paragraphs that fell into place in a logical pattern, and also related to my topic sentence.

He did more than just focus my papers as a whole and help me to begin to have paragraphs and ideas which fall in orderly succession. He also helped me to organize my sentences, in much the same way as I did my paragraphs. This instruction was a continuation of first quarter's lesson, but it sunk in a little better, no doubt because I concentrated a little more on making it work. As a result, I feel that my sentences follow each other adequately (not great, and not all the time, but . . .), and my language sticks to the point.

Sticking to the point brings out the last structural point that Mr. Anderson really tried to impress upon us: finding the right word. In my now infamous *Vanity Fair* paper, I used words that sounded very impressive. Indeed, upon re-reading I thought I was looking at a SAT question sheet! Unfrotunately, they weren't the words I needed to get my point across. I spent a lot of my time trying to work out this problem last quarter, because I finally started to realize just how much difference the right word can make. And if the sentences make sense [this doesn't follow] and follow each other in rational fashion, then of course the paper will hold together much better.

I do feel that my sentence structure has improved, and along with it the way I express my opinions. The materials we read for class were good because they were stimulating; I was pleasantly surprised at discovering that poetry isn't something to line bird cages with. Incredibly enough (for me), I enjoyed the papers I wrote about poems the most of all my papers. Because I enjoyed the readings, I worked harder at my writing, in order to be better able to express myself. By keeping Mr. Anderson's adage in mind, I hope to continue to improve my writing.

WAYNE BOOTH'S COMMENTARY

The temptation is, of course, to choose one of the best papers of the year, a polished product of revision after revision, making both the student-author and the teacher look good: that penetrating analysis of "Fra Lippo Lippi," perhaps, or that extraordinary comparison of Thucydides' account of the Spartan invasion of Plataea with the Soviet occupation, in 1940, of Estonia. The truth is that the final products of my instruction would be quite useless here. Revised three or four times in the light of my characteristically incisive yet stimulating and *always* intelligible comments, they are invariably so very good that they would make any reader of this book suspicious: "*That* was written by a freshman? Without help? Not bloody likely!"

"A Lifetime of Learning" is not that kind of freshman paper. Michael Fitzgerald wrote it at the beginning of his third quarter. The essay is printed here in the exact form of Michael's submitted draft, unrevised (Grade: A−). In resubmitting it to me, as a possible choice for this book, Michael made a few tentative corrections, which I have placed in brackets.

I am of course tempted to begin by dramatizing the paper's faults. Will my readers think I don't *see* them, that I allow my students to commit awkward shifts of tense, clumsy repetitions, misspellings, solecisms like "the most," and what not? Perhaps—the anxieties continue—the essay is even more faulty than I realize. Maybe I have been fooled into admiring it by my knowledge of Michael's progress through the year. If I did not know him, would I be more troubled than I am by his air of self-congratulation and by his over-simplified view of what he needs to know to write well?

Putting all that self-protective apology aside, I want to praise this paper for virtues that might well be overlooked. They will not serve on all occasions; there is no such thing as good writing suitable for all occasions. I would not submit Michael's paper as a candidate for the annual prize in creative writing, or as an effective weighing of issues, pro and con. But its qualities will serve you well in responding to most college assignments, and they are especially useful when you are asked, as Michael was in effect asked, to take a bunch of commonplaces and turn them into something interesting.

The assignment requires students to do something with matters of common knowledge—the commonplaces of their instruction. Michael accepts the invitation by choosing to list the lessons pretty much as they were taught to him: Find something interesting to say (when you enjoy the difficult readings, you work hard at the writing—par. 7); focus on that something by developing and following a clear topic (par. 3); polish your paragraphs and sentences (pars. 4 and 5); use clear and graceful transitions among *all* the elements (almost buried in par. 4); find the right words (par. 6)—and you'll have a good paper!

As mere list, such truisms promise dullness. But of course the art of writing well is more often needed precisely when platitudes threaten. We can get along without that art, to a degree, when we have something genuinely original to say; people will listen to original thought through almost any amount of noise. But write an interesting paper on how you learned to write? Try it.

We teachers are too much inclined, I think, to suggest to you students that you must find something new to say if you are to please us. Yet we know the painful truth that we ourselves usually have nothing really new to say, and that what rescues us—if anything does—is skill in finding new garb for old ideas. In all education, but in the humanities especially, the arts of preserving and vivifying the old are even more important than the search for novelty.

The obvious temptation to anyone trying to write to a teacher about writing is to pile up platitudes comforting to the profession: "Yes indeedy, you devoted folks are teaching us faithful charges really well." Michael has not entirely resisted that temptation. But he does succeed in demonstrating that the commonplaces have become significant to him, partly by achieving some freshness in his descriptions but mainly by the way he *exhibits* the points that he claims to have *learned.*

I am especially impressed by Michael's way of illustrating coherence by insisting that every one of his sentences *show* its connections with the before and after. If someone were to cut his essay into isolated sentences and scatter them, the original order could easily be reconstructed from clues in the sentences themselves. This virtue may seem rather workaday, as compared with some of the qualities you have been asked to master. Readers tend not to notice it *as* a virtue, when it is present. But when it is missing, we notice the confusions and annoyances that result for us as readers.

Consider how Michael has worked for coherence in par. 5.

> He did *more than just focus . . . and help. . . .* He *also. . . . This* instruction . . . *it . . . a little better . . . a little more . . . it. . . . As a result . . .*

The natural flow here may seem a bit prosaic. But if it were missing we would know that something was seriously wrong. For example, Michael might have written the paragraph like this:

> The focusing of my papers as a whole and of building paragraphs and ideas that fall in orderly succession was not all that Mr. Anderson taught. Sentences ought to be organized carefully. In my first quarter we had had some instruction about good syntax. My concentration was higher in the second quarter, and *so* I was more open to hearing the message. Effort to make everything follow everything else is really paying off now.

That rewriting is not as bad as Michael himself might have made it in his first weeks of the year because I have preserved its single subject. But I have only one specific connective, as compared with Michael's nine, and the result is that in my paragraph the reader's mind has to shift gears continually, starting in false directions and then running back to start over, once the true connection has been discovered. (I am not suggesting that if he had managed to pack in fifteen connectives the essay would have been even better.)

Similarly, the point about finding the right word is in itself as old as the ancient Greeks, and Michael's statement about it is not in any sense original or flashy. But to me the simple diction of the essay is impressive—especially since it comes from a student who, as he says, was formerly inclined to show off with inappropriate polysyllables. His first papers in the fall were indeed stilted, pretentious, packed with jargon. Here again he may have moved too far, for some readers, in the opposite direction. But I like his "getting there," rather than, say, "moving vigorously and intelligently in the right direction"; his "or the guy who wrote the paper" rather than, say, "or, on the other hand, the author who composed the pretentious message"; his "sticks to the point" (repeated, without shame) rather than "maintains a consistency of argument from beginning to end"; his "nagging" rather than "steadily insisting from week to week throughout the quarter."

I'm even more impressed by signs of Michael's having learned some pointers that he doesn't even mention. His first papers of the year were not just stilted in vocabulary; they were impersonal, abstract, and full of passives. He never hazarded a metaphor, and he seldom offered examples.

Here he is highly personal, as the assignment implicitly requested, using the first person, the active voice and active verbs rather than dodges like "the present writer," passive constructions, and abstract nouns. His heavy use of "I" and "me" would not do in some kinds of writing. But in an essay about personal views, every reader will want to meet a *person*. Michael shows considerable skill in making his personal pronouns do some solid work in establishing his character (or what we sometimes call "ethos"). For example, the "Incredibly enough (for me) . . ." in par. 7, tells the reader (the teacher, who is known to love poetry) that though the honest, hard-working author used to be a clod who hated poetry, he has finally seen the light—thanks to good instruction.

The new Michael does not mention his new interest in risking metaphoric touches: Hansel and Gretel in the labyrinth, and "a code-breaker" (par. 4); the "SAT question sheet" (par. 6); "not available at any store" (par. 3). Nor does he mention the uses of humor. His first papers were utterly solemn. Here he is still no Woody Allen, but he comes through as someone who can joke about himself. The jokes are mild ("Well, I actually didn't have a topic sentence to follow" [par. 3]), but they help to support the one characteristic that his ethos absolutely must include if his paper is to work at all: a genuine humility about where he is now in his quest for an education.

Perhaps the nicest touch of the whole paper is the persuasive moment when Michael imagines himself into a future where his present paper will appall him by its "poorness" (par. 2). That is precisely the right example of what it means *not* to think you are educated already. The result of such moments (note also in par. 5, "not great, and not all the time, but . . .") is that when we come to the concluding sentence, in itself drab enough, we cannot doubt the author's claim to know his own ignorance. He is on his way.

Study Questions

1. "If someone were to cut his essay into isolated sentences and scatter them," says Wayne Booth of Michael Fitzgerald's paper, "the original order could easily be reconstructed from clues in the sentences themselves."

   Test this assertion by doing exactly that with the sentences of Michael Fitzgerald's paper. (Just for fun, try as hard as you can to come up with some order for the sentences other than the original one.) Do this same thing with one of your own papers.

   On the basis of your experiment with the two papers, how would you address the following questions: What exactly is "coherence" in writing a matter of, and why do people praise it so highly?

2. In a classroom discussion of Michael Fitzgerald's paper and Wayne Booth's commentary on it, a student said,

   > I don't see that this writer has "a genuine humility" at all. I think he's trying to snow his teacher without getting caught at it. He says he "enjoyed" writing papers about poems "most of all," but he doesn't show it. He only says that he now thinks poetry "isn't something to line bird cages with" because he knows English teachers like to hear that kind of thing. He drags up his old high school paper on *Vanity Fair* and how it got an A but was really garbage, because he knows English teachers like to hear that kind of thing too. He used to be a lousy writer but now he's a good one, thanks to his teachers, of course. I think that's a con.

   How do you respond to such a statement?

3. Make a list of Wayne Booth's criticisms of Michael Fitzgerald's paper. Imagine Michael Fitzgerald's presenting you with the list you have just made and saying something like this to you: "I'd like to rewrite my paper in order to make it something that wouldn't be open to these criticisms. Can you help me?"

   What advice would you give Michael Fitzgerald?

   What does the kind of advice you'd offer tell you about what this student knows and what he needs to learn as a writer?

Andrea Lunsford's Assignment

During the last several weeks, we have concentrated on style and on studying and comparing our own processes of writing: We have read excerpts from the work of Joseph Williams, Edward P. J. Corbett, Richard Lanham, and Donald Murray; we have practiced identifying stylistic features in the prose of others; and we have argued over what makes a particular style effective and over how stylistic characteristics relate to meaning. Your job in this assignment: to practice some stylistic analysis on your own.

As usual, this assignment sheet provides only a starting point and a framework. You can and should shape the assignment to fit your own goals and interests. I suggest that you begin thinking about the assignment by deciding whose style you will analyze (your own, a classmate's, or another writer's) and using the style profile to help you gather data. In addition to the information you can collect by using the profile, you may want to consult Corbett's chapter on style in *Classical Rhetoric for the Modern Student* and to note Williams's discussion of various types of modifiers in *Style*. As you gather your data, try to identify any "favorite" sentence patterns or other stylistic features the writer uses, always asking yourself how these stylistic features relate to the overall effect or meaning of the piece in question.

Style Profile*

Content Words

1. Number of nouns or noun substitutes
2. Number of pronouns
3. Number of verbs (percentage of active and passive as well)
4. Number of adjectives and adverbs

Sentence Patterns

1. Number of fragments
2. Number of run-ons
3. Number of simple, compound, complex, and compound-complex sentences
4. Number of dependent or subordinate clauses
5. Longest sentence; shortest sentence; average sentence length

---

* For help in getting started; *not* to be slavishly filled in!

ANDREA A. LUNSFORD is currently Associate Professor of English and Coordinator of Composition at the University of British Columbia. She has published numerous articles on the teaching of writing and on the history of rhetoric, is coauthor of *Four Worlds of Writing* (1981), coeditor of *Essays on Classical Rhetoric and Modern Discourse* (1984), and reviser with Richard Altick of *Preface to Critical Reading* (6th ed., 1984). An historical study, *The Rhetorical Works of Alexander Bain*, and a textbook, *The Thinking Writer*, are forthcoming.

6. Sentence openers: number of subject openers, dependent clause openers, prepositional phrase openers, coordinate conjunction openers—others?
7. Number of sentences that are statements, questions, commands, or exclamations (count each kind separately)

Paragraph Patterns

1. Longest paragraph; shortest paragraph; average paragraph length
2. Methods of development
3. Relationships among or between paragraphs (can you identify "chunks" or units of a piece rather than paragraphs?)

Diction

1. Use of figures of speech (see Corbett)
2. Types of nouns: choose one paragraph and list the nouns. Then try to generalize: are the nouns predominantly polysyllabic or monosyllabic, concrete or abstract, common or jargon, Latinate or Anglo Saxon, etc.?
3. Types of verbs: you already have the percentage of passive versus active verbs. How many of the verbs are some form of the verb 'to be'? How could you characterize the verbs: strong? image-creating? or the opposite?

Again as usual, we will meet in our seminar groups to discuss this assignment and to brainstorm about possible approaches to it.

Don't forget to attach your ongoing Process Journal to the end of your finished essay: The journal describes what you did during prewriting; the number and kinds of drafts you wrote; the time required to complete the essay and the circumstances under which you worked; the major strengths and weaknesses of the essay; and improvements you would like to see made in your next essay.

๛ How Maurice Sendak's Style Influenced My Own Writing for Children

by Joan Buchanan

Audience: Members of my English Composition Seminar Group.

My interest in writing for children led me to undertake a stylistic analysis of Maurice Sendak's writing in the illustrated book *Where the Wild Things Are.* Although I carried out a thorough analysis of Sendak's style, for this essay I am limiting my discussion to sentence lengths, sentence rhythms, word arrangements, and word usage. I found that several of these features have influenced my own writing for children, particularly in an illustrated story, *It's a Good Thing,* I have been working on recently.

2   Sendak's very long sentences, composed of many independent clauses joined by coordinating conjunctions, are one of his most distinguishing stylistic characteristics. The first two hundred words of Sendak's story contain twenty-one coordinating conjunctions, most of them "and." Sendak uses this large number of "and's" to join one clause to the next, forming long compound and compound-complex sentences. His average sentence length is forty words (surprising for a children's writer); his shortest is nine and his longest is 75. In the sample I studied, Sendak uses *only* compound or compound-complex sentences.

3   Such multiple coordinate clauses and the repetition of "and" create a rhythm that steadily gathers momentum. For example: "the walls became the world all around and an ocean tumbled by with a private boat for Max and he sailed off through night and day and in and out of weeks and almost over a year to where the wild things are."[1] Sendak's use of anaphora, which Edward P. J. Corbett [in *Classical Rhetoric for the Modern Student*] defines as "the repetition of the same word or group of words at the beginnings of successive clauses," adds to this rhythm. In Sendak's sample, six repetitions of "wild things" spread throughout eight clauses contribute to the crescendo of the metrical rhythm.

4   Sendak's simple and very direct word arrangement and usage also add an imperative sense to the rhythm. Although he uses seven coordinating conjunctions between compound verbs, the rest of his word arrangement follows the common subject-verb-object (when an object is present) order, the simplest complete sentence structure. He also uses familiar, Anglo-Saxon words and descriptive, active verbs, verbs such as "tamed," "roared," and "gnashed," rather than an excess of "to be" verbs common in much writing for children. Imperatives in his dialogue, such as "Be Still!" and "Now Stop!" punctuate the rhythm of the long sentences and add to the excitement.

5   As an aspiring writer, I am looking for new techniques to "steal" from other writers. Well aware of Sendak's major stylistic characteristics, I have begun experimenting with using some of them. An average sentence in my story *It's a Good Thing* contains about nine words, the length of Sendak's shortest sentence. Although I have three sentences over 25 words long, I use many short sentences and fragments such as "But 'oops!" and "She wasn't hurt." However, in my long sentences (the longest is 38 words), I join action verb phrases with coordinating conjunctions in a manner similar to Sendak's. For example: "Elizabeth tugged her out as quick as a wink and grabbed her little sister's hand and ran and ran along the forest path, along the beach and up the hill—home." I also make use of word repetition, but whereas Sendak's repetition is spread throughout an entire passage, I like to repeat words in

[1] Maurice Sendak, *Where the Wild Things Are* (New York: Harper & Row, 1963), pp. 12–16.

succession and separate them with commas, as in "Down, down, down the hill."

By using word repetition, some coordinate structures, and lots of imperatives in the dialogue (such as "Watch out!" and "Stop!"), I hope to produce the same kind of exciting rhythm that Sendak creates in a sentence like "And when he came to the place where the wild things are they roared their terrible roars and gnashed their terrible teeth and rolled their terrible eyes and showed their terrible claws till Max said 'BE STILL!' and tamed them with the magic trick of staring into all their yellow eyes without blinking once and they were frightened and called him the most wild thing of all and made him king of all wild things" (pp. 18–22). It is debatable whether I have achieved this kind of rhythm, however, especially since I resort to using many more "to be" verbs than does Sendak: "The tide was coming in fast. Elizabeth looked down at her feet. The water was touching her toes." 6

Stylistic features, of course, cannot really be studied in isolation. Sendak's strong, active verbs and multiple coordinate clauses reinforce the meaning of the passage by emphasizing rushing movement and by creating vivid images, images that are further enhanced by the pictures. I have also tried to use style to reinforce meaning, but in my story I use style to contrast two different characters. Elizabeth, the older, dreamier sister, speaks in lyrical dialogue and longer sentences: "If I were a giant, I'd eat cotton candy clouds for breakfast. I'd tear off little pieces to give to my friends." In contrast, Missy (the younger, more practical sister) speaks in short, staccato sentences: "Hurry Elizabeth! Run! The tide is coming in!" 7

I have learned a great deal by carefully studying Maurice Sendak's style. I admire his use of verbs and the direct word order of his sentences. I am not as enthusiastic, however, about his almost constant use of long strings of coordinate clauses. Since children learn a lot by listening, they may not develop an intuitive sense of sentence closure and arrangement if they are exposed only to coordinate structures. So while I have tried to borrow *some* of Sendak's stylistic features and use them to good effect in my own stories, I have not indiscriminately adopted all of his major stylistic features. Instead, I am trying to develop my own unique style. 8

[Joan's story was subsequently accepted for publication by Annick Press of Toronto. It appeared in late Spring, 1984.—A.A.L.]

Andrea Lunsford's COMMENTARY

Though Joan's essay is certainly not flawless (the organization, for instance, could be tightened up in paragraphs 4 and 5, and the transition from paragraph 6 to 7 is abrupt), it is an excellent one in my book. In the first place, the paper demonstrates that a student can improve upon an assignment by responding to it in an original way. As the assignment sheet points out, the assignment provides "only a starting point" for students to modify in order to reflect their own writing interests. Such assignments, I believe, tell students that I value writing as a way of discovering their own voices and as a way of pursuing actively their own goals. Because Joan wants to write children's books, she adapted the assignment to help her achieve that end. Other students, of course, take other approaches; three English as a Second Language students, for instance, intent on passing an upcoming proficiency exam, chose to analyze the style of three superior "Pass" essays and write up detailed plans for passing the test. The ideal assignment, for me, is one that allows students, à la Robert Frost, to "move easy in harness."

Joan's essay, in particular, demonstrates that genuine learning has taken place as a result of her dip into stylistic analysis. She has learned what techniques she favors—and why she favors them. In doing so, she has met my demand for an attempt at such analysis; but more important, she has solved a problem she set for herself: "How can I improve my writing for children?" In answering this question, Joan moves beyond gathering and classifying data (no mean trick in itself since that task demanded mastery of a fairly extensive grammatical vocabulary) to draw conclusions from the data and to act on those conclusions in her own writing. (I should note that space limitations prevent our including Joan's prewriting materials. These materials indicate that she used the style profile sheet as a flexible instrument to help her answer questions she was interested in answering. For example, though she began analyzing paragraph structure, she realized that she was not interested in working on her own children's story paragraph patterns; hence she dropped that line of investigation. These materials also graphically demonstrate what all writers know to be true: In thinking through a problem, we almost always generate much more material than we would ever want to use in a finished essay. So in a sense this "finished product" cannot by itself reflect one area of excellence in Joan's writing process: the ability to choose those data most pertinent to her goals and to abandon the rest.)

Another excellent feature of Joan's essay is her experimental use of sentence patterns that she had read about in her textbooks, ones that we had been discussing in class but that were not at all mandated in the assignment. The use of the "interrupted" pattern in the last sentence of paragraph 1 is one example; and the final modifier in the second sentence of paragraph 7 is another. This last sentence demonstrates that Joan has grasped the basic concepts of resumptive[1] and summative[2] modifiers discussed in Williams's *Style* and shows that she is willing to take a chance at using such newly recognized patterns. Much research on the development of writing abilities suggests that taking risks is a necessary element in improving writing. Put most simply, writers who stick with safe, tried-and-true simple sentences that follow a standard subject-verb-complement pattern may produce correct writing, but they will not *improve* their writing. Only by taking a gamble, by stretching to use more complex and elaborate syntactic patterns can students find forms that will complement the maturity of their thoughts and hence lead to genuine improvement. Thus I believe Joan is to be congratulated for taking such a risk and should be encouraged to take more. The long opening sentence of paragraph 6 is one that particularly troubled Joan, and she can be justifiably proud of the result, which demonstrates her ability to use parallelism, an explanatory parenthesis, and a long quotation from Sendak's story in what is a smooth, easy-to-read sentence.

Yet another excellent feature of Joan's essay is her willingness to speculate, albeit tentatively, about the purposes of writing. Her statement in the conclusion (that children may not develop an intuitive sense of sentence arrangement if they are exposed only to coordinate structures) is not developed or elaborated on, and hence could be seen as a flaw. But because it represents a reaching forward, a leap toward new knowledge created through her own "dialogue between self and soul," I prefer to view this feature as a strength that should encourage Joan to pursue her line of thought further.

Space restrictions also prevented us from including Joan's Process Journal (described in the assignment sheet), yet her own perceptions of strengths and weaknesses in this essay are revealing. Her major strength she sees as her analysis of the samples: her ability to recognize various clauses, word groups, figures of speech, and so on. After carefully reviewing her prewriting materials, I agreed that this was indeed a strength. She goes on to say that her major weakness is "not being able to draw more general conclusions about style and its effects." This comment indicates to me that Joan is at least partially aware that she is reaching out towards new conclusions in that last paragraph, and this comment further determined me to encourage her in that direction.

Although Joan's essay stands as a finished product in one sense, a

---

[1] Williams defines a *resumptive modifier* as one which repeats a key noun, verb, or adjective and then resumes the line of thought, elaborating on what went before. Example: "For several years, CBS created and developed situation *comedies* that were the best American TV had to offer, *comedies* such as 'The Mary Tyler Moore Show' and 'All in the Family,' *comedies* that sparkled with wit and invention" (*Style*, p. 85).

[2] With a *summative modifier*, Williams explains, the writer ends a part of a sentence with a comma, sums up in a noun or noun phrase what has just been said, and then continues with a modifying phrase or clause. Example: "Scientists have finally unraveled the mysteries of the human gene, *a discovery that* may lead to the control of such dread diseases as cancer and birth defects" (*Style*, p. 86).

product for which she earned a mark in our class, in another, more important sense, it is but one link in a chain of writing that Joan is working to forge. Perhaps this characteristic is a subtle but persuasive answer to the question "What makes writing good?" Surely good writing, in one sense, is that writing which serves not as an end but as a beginning, as an invitation to new thoughts, new learning, and new writing.

Study Questions

1. Joan Buchanan's "statement in the conclusion (that children may not develop an intuitive sense of sentence arrangement if they are exposed only to coordinate structures) is not developed or elaborated on," says Andrea Lunsford, "and hence could be seen as a flaw." But because this remark "represents a reaching forward, a leap toward new knowledge," Andrea Lunsford prefers "to view this feature as a strength," an attempt on the part of a particular student writer to overcome what the student herself has called her "major weakness" as a writer: "not being able to draw more general conclusions about style and its effects."

   Suppose you were to tell Joan Buchanan how she might develop or elaborate on the statement she makes in her conclusion. What would you suggest that she do?

   What might be the result of her efforts so far as you are concerned?

2. A student writing about Joan Buchanan's paper and Andrea Lunsford's commentary on it said,

   > I have to admit that when I first read what Joan Buchanan says in her analysis of the rhythms of Maurice Sendak's writing I said to myself, "Fine for her; she's got a children's book being published. But what's this got to offer *me* as a writer? *I'm* not interested in writing books for children." But then I saw that paying attention to how prose rhythms can contribute to meaning, whether in a children's story or not, could do me a lot of good as a writer of things other than books for children.

   How might you explain and defend this position?

   You too are a writer. How does your explanation and defense of the preceding statement apply to your own writing?

3. Andrea Lunsford praises Joan Buchanan's "experimental use of sentence patterns," seeing them as evidence that the student "is willing to take a chance," that she is "taking risks."

   How might a student's use of other than his or her ordinary sentence patterns be seen as a "risk"?

   Do you think all students should be encouraged to take such risks? Some students? No students? Make your reasons for your position clear.

JOSEPH WILLIAMS'S Assignment

Compare and contrast the first two speeches in Thucydides' *History*.

[The College of The University of Chicago requires all students to take a series of year-long Common Core courses, one each in the physical sciences, the biological sciences, the social sciences, and the humanities. For a variety of historical reasons, the humanities course has taken on the job of teaching writing as well as the job of teaching the skills of close reading and careful interpretation. Since this course is not a writing course as such, the papers are almost all based on an analysis of texts ranging from Lincoln's Second Inaugural Address to *King Lear* to Thucydides' *History of the Peloponnesian War*.

The situation the students in my course had to address in their papers was this. Shortly before the outbreak of the Peloponnesian War (ca. 434 B.C.), the Corinthians and the Corcyraeans, two city states in what is now Greece, were in conflict over their claim to the colony of Epidamnus, located on the coast of what is now the Adriatic, and therefore an important city because, with its powerful navy, it controlled the coasting passage to Sicily. Both sides went to Athens to plead their cases and to ask for Athenian assistance in asserting their opposing claims to what they believed were their rights to Epidamnus. All three parties—the Corinthians, the Corcyraeans, and the Athenians—knew that a general war between the Athenians and the Spartans was approaching, and that the Corinthians would ally themselves with the Spartans. The Corcyraeans were historically neutral, but decided to ask the Athenians for help against the Corinthians.

Now it is important to understand that Thucydides probably did not hear all the speeches that he incorporated in his history. He says as much at the end of his first chapter, claiming that if he did not hear the speeches himself, he created what would have been appropriate to the situation. Therefore, when I asked the class to compare and contrast the speeches, I wanted them to be able to distinguish between the speeches as real speeches, reflecting what real speakers thought, and as speeches invented by Thucydides to help us understand what Thucydides *the writer* wanted us to believe about the speakers. Then I wanted them to infer Thucydides' view of the Athenians by examining the appeals each side made and the appeal Thucydides had the Athenians accept. It is a delicate but crucial distinction about texts that is very hard for first-year students confronting the humanities seriously, often for the first time, to grasp. Their failure to grasp it results in their merely summarizing what is in a text as opposed to analyzing and evaluating what an author was up to in writing the text.

JOSEPH WILLIAMS is in the English department at The University of Chicago. He teaches first-year students in the required core humanities sequence, undergraduate writing and linguistic courses, graduate courses in language and discourse analysis, and in recent years has with two of his colleagues created and offered writing seminars for law firms, corporations, and the federal government. He is principally interested in the way readers respond to language and discourse, and is currently completing a work on discourse theory.

But I had a second objective: A large part of my particular course (as opposed to most of the other courses) is to make my students understand what counts in an essay as a point worth making in the humanities. Too often, when we give students assignments such as "Compare and contrast X and Y," "Analyze X," "Write a paper in which you categorize X," they do just that, and nothing more. And so we tell them that they didn't "go far enough," that they "didn't *do* anything with their subject." They compare and contrast, but make no point in doing so. They analyze a subject (usually summarizing it) but articulate no good reason for so doing. They make no worthwhile claim as a result of their having compared and contrasted, analyzed, discussed, categorized, and defined. They do exactly what we tell them to do, but nothing more. In other classes, faculty respond to this failure to make a point as a sense of aimlessness in a paper, as a lack of focus, or even as a failure of organization. But quite regularly, it really is more a simple failure to understand that a writer constructs a paper to address an important issue, and that the writer has to make a point that is important to people other than him or herself. The point has to be one that readers at the university level will take seriously.

And so part of what we talk about in class is how to take an assignment as vague and ill-formed (and as common) as "Compare and contrast the first two speeches in Thucydides' *History*" and then do more than compare and contrast, how to go beyond the given of the assignment to something more significant. We talk about why a claim like "The Corcyraeans and the Corinthians are alike in some ways and different in others" will not count as a point worth making; why we have to learn how the knowledge that they are different is knowledge worth having; why not knowing in particular how they differ will prevent us from understanding what Thucydides was up to. Most of my students get as far as "The Corinthians appeal basically to the past, to history and traditional obligations, while the Corcyraeans appeal basically to the future." But of course that tells us nothing about *why* Thucydides created speeches for the speakers in just that way: What did he want us to infer from the fact that one side appealed to traditional values and the other to immediate self-interest, particularly in light of the fact that the Athenians sided with the Corcyraeans, the side that appealed to the future, to self-interest?]

◦℘ Thucydides: The Historian as Creative Artist

by Greg Shaefer

As a historian of the Peloponnesian War, Thucydides could not possibly record everything. He had to discriminate, or decide, what was worth noting and what was insignificant. Thus, the actual Peloponnesian War and Thucydides' history are not one and the same. We must satisfy ourselves then with not understanding the war itself but rather understanding Thucydides. The speeches throughout his history lead to much of this understanding, for Thucydides probably constructed them entirely himself to express the probable points of view of their speakers and to anticipate the actual historical events that followed them. In particular, an examination of the pair of speeches made by the Corinthians and the Corcyraeans enables us to learn from Thucydides their interests, as he saw them. From their interests, in turn, we learn of Thucydides' perception of Athenian interests which played such an important role in the direction of the Peloponnesian war.

Thucydides chose to include in his history the conflict between Corcyra and Corinth, for, as he says: "it served as pretext for the present war" (p. 66). In fact, the war between Corcyra and Corinth was in effect a small-scale Peloponnesian war. Corinth, a city-state of the Peloponnese, reflects Lacedaemon, while Corcyra is characteristic of Athens. These similarities are important with respect to the nature and outcome of the speeches for in both, Corinth and Corcyra are appealing to Athens. Clearly Corcyra, being similar to Athens, has an advantage. Thucydides implies this in his construction of the speeches. 2

Thucydides tells us that the main concern of the Corcyraeans was to form an alliance with Athens. Unlike Corinth who was a member of the Peloponnesian league, Corcyra had no allies; thus she "decided to repair to Athens" (p. 19). In presenting the nature of their appeals, Thucydides has the Corcyraeans make use of several devices. First, they briefly appeal to justice and try to convince Athens that Corcyra is a "victim of the injustice of others" (p. 20), namely Corinth, their parent state. However, this is a twisted argument, for the Corcyraeans fail to mention that they themselves treated their own colony, Epidamnus, unjustly and that this was the main cause of the war with Corinth. Nonetheless, they use this argument to evoke Athenian sympathy for themselves, pointing out that they have no allies to assist them in their "just" cause while Corinth has many from which to obtain ships and money. 3

Thucydides has the Corcyraeans devote far more time to a less specious device—one which proved to be strongly efficacious. They appeal to the Athenians' desire for power and wealth by showing that Athens and Corcyra have the same self-interests. It is here that Thucydides gives us some insight into the nature of these two city-states. Not only are both wealthy and proud; both are also considerable naval powers. Corcyra says to the Athenians: "You may search all history without finding many instances of a power that comes in quest of assistance being in a position to give . . . as much safety and honour as she will receive" (p. 20). This point will be effective with the Athenians because Athens is well aware of its strained relations with Lacedaemon and realizes the possibility of a war in the near future. Corcyra plays upon this impending war, telling 4 the Athenians that it is inevitable. She says: "it will be urged that it is only in the case of a war that we shall be found useful" and "if any of you imagine that that war is far off, he is grievously mistaken" (p. 20). Further, Thucydides has Corcyra remind Athens that there are but three naval powers in Hellas—Athens, Corcyra, and Corinth, and she warns the Athenians: "if you allow . . . Corinth to secure us for herself, you will have to hold the sea against the united fleets of Corcyra and Peloponnese" (p. 23).

5   Thucydides thus has the Corcyraeans assert that an alliance would be beneficial to both Corcyra, in her present war against Corinth, and to Athens, in a probable future war with Lacedaemon. Athens would be acting against her own interests (not to mention Corcyra's) if she rejected Corcyra's offer of alliance. Corcyra thus says to the Athenians: "You must also remember that your decision is for Athens no less than for Corcyra" (p. 22). Indeed, the largest part of their speech is devoted to an appeal to Athenian self-interest, not to their sense of justice.

6   Thucydides also expresses his understanding of the Corinthian cast of mind through the way he has them present their speech. They, of course, try to dissuade Athens from forming an alliance with Corcyra. But unlike the Corcyraeans, Thucydides has the Corinthians emphasize justice and old obligations. Not only do they refute Corcyra's claim to justice on the basis of history, they assert their own righteousness by telling the Athenians that: "the attitude of our colony towards us has always been one of estrangement, and is now one of hostility" (p. 24). The Corinthians remind Athens that as entitled by Hellenic law, they have a right to punish their own allies and that when Athens had trouble with her own colonies in the past, Corinth did not interfere.

7   Thus Thucydides has the Corinthians emphasize the past. When Athens was in need and had many enemies, the Corinthians assisted them in their efforts: "When you were in want of ships of war for the war against the Aegintians . . . Corinth supplied you with twenty vessels. That good turn . . . enabled you to conquer Aegina" (p. 26). So they insist "do unto us as we have done unto you." The Corinthians do not emphasize the future. They say that "the coming of war . . . is still uncertain." Corinth even suggests that Athens resolve past conflicts by making amends with Lacedaemon.

8   But Corinth's reliance on justice, tradition, and old obligations proved unsuccessful. The Athenians sided with the Corcyraeans. Thucydides writes that the Athenians, after considering the two speeches, decided on an alliance with Corcyra "for it began now to be felt that the coming of the Peloponnesian war was only a question of time" (p. 27). Of course, it is Thucydides' intention to inform us that "the growth of

the power of Athens, and the alarm which this inspired in Lacedaemon, made war inevitable" (p. 14).

By presenting this pair of speeches then, Thucydides gives us insight into the nature of the Corcyraeans and the Corinthians. The Corcyraeans are looking to the future; the Corinthians seem to be concerned with the past. But by having the two speeches differ in these ways, Thucydides also tells us something about the Athenians. Because the Athenians agree with the Corcyraeans, he wants us to infer that Athenian philosophy is self-centered; their interests revolve around power and wealth. The Corinthian argument failed because for an imperial power like Athens, justice is not a very strong controlling force. Thucydides, an Athenian himself, concedes that justice doesn't promote Athenian interests. Athens with all its power can direct its empire contrary to all justice. The Athenians were "not so superior to human nature" (p. 45) as to reject the alliance; they acted in their best interests. And by showing this, Thucydides is setting the stage for the war that followed. As long as Athens understood their true self-interest, they succeeded. But when they began to put individual self-interest ahead of their true self-interest, they began to decline.   9

And in this, Thucydides is saying again that the events of history are a consequence of human nature. And since as Thucydides frequently says, the most important aspect of human nature is individual self-interest, history will repeat itself because human nature never changes.   10

JOSEPH WILLIAMS'S COMMENTARY

Greg Shaefer wrote this paper in about the fifth week of the first quarter of his college career and in it comes close to fulfilling both of the objectives I had in making the assignment. I gave it an A. Greg largely dealt with the speeches not as historical events but as artistic creations, and thereby showed a recognition that at least one subject proper for an analytical essay about a text in a humanities class is the consciousness of its writer's not merely reporting a world in language, but creating it; and that a paper on a subject such as this has no reason to exist unless the writer can point out why we should be interested in understanding why Thucydides created the world in the way that he did.

From the very first paragraph, Greg focused not on summarizing what the Corcyraeans and Corinthians said, but on what Thucydides *had* them say. He is a bit heavy-handed in making the distinction, but the niceties of voice, of style and rhetorical tact, are not what I am interested in in the fifth week of my students' academic careers; I am interested in their ability to distance themselves from a text and see the author at work constructing it, and then to find a reason why we should be conscious of what that author was up to.

At the end of the first paragraph, that position where the writer must finally commit him or herself to the direction of the paper, Greg writes a sentence that fits with the generally sophisticated distinctions he is unsophisticatedly making. He knows the point he wants to make: If we understand that Thucydides put in the mouths of the Corinthians an appeal to the past, to traditional values, to ancient obligations, and that the Athenians reject these arguments in favor of the Corcyraean argument in favor of self-interest, present gain, and future security, then we understand something about the Athenian cast of mind—oriented to the future, ready to break with the past, not interested in issues of obligation and justice but of profit and self-interest. But Greg does not give away the game too early in the paper; he is capable of delaying rhetorical closure. He claims only that if we follow the distinctions that he is going to make, we will understand something much larger: We will understand (and here, I think, he lets the *central* issue slip away from him a bit) how those Athenian interests influenced the course of the war. I would have much preferred a slightly different argument: that we would understand how *Thucydides* wants us to understand how he, Thucydides, understood the course of the war. It is a distinction that Greg makes much clearer in the last paragraph.

The second paragraph is the weakest of the paper. It is badly written and not especially well focused. But it serves the purpose of setting the context for the Corcyraean speech.

In the third paragraph, Greg begins to discuss what Thucydides was up to, but notice that he cannot consistently sustain his focus on Thucydides. He begins with the author at work: "Thucydides has the Corcyraeans make use of several devices." But then he slips back into language that makes it sound as if he is writing about flesh and blood historical speakers. By the end of the paragraph, he begins treating the rhetoric of the speeches as if it reflected historical fact. Rather than describe how Thucydides was creating speeches to put in the mouths of the Corcyraeans, he tells us what the Corcyraeans were doing.

Greg begins the fourth paragraph in the same way, but in the third sentence gets control of his topic again, Thucydides instead of the speeches or the war: "It is here that Thucydides gives us some insight into the nature of these two city-states." After a few sentences that again seem to represent the history of the event rather than its representation, Greg returns to the theme of Thucydides (Thucydides shows us how the Corcyraeans are able to "assert that an alliance would be beneficial to both . . .") and ends with an appropriate quotation.

Greg turns in the sixth paragraph to the Corinthian speech, summarizing the speech generally from the speaker's point of view. But then in the seventh paragraph, he gets back to his point—to the point Thucydides wants to make: Where Thucydides had the Corcyraeans appeal to the future, he has the Corinthians appeal to the past.

And in the ninth paragraph Greg pulls it all together and makes the point that he has been carefully preparing: by creating two speeches with very different appeals, Thucydides was able to suggest that Athens had a particular cast of mind, a cast of mind that, *according to Thucydides*, crucially influenced the outcome of the Peloponnesian War. (Several years later, the Athenians were finally too entranced by self-interest in their mounting of the disastrous Sicilian expedition and invasion, in which they lost almost everything.) And then Greg goes on to make an even larger point: By creating a pair of contrasting speeches, Thucydides could also lay the groundwork for his most significant point—history inevitably repeats itself because human nature does not change.

Greg's conclusion is very sophisticated. He makes an important point about how a history is written, and about the hand of the historian in the narrative. But he locates that point in the context of a larger point that goes to the heart of history itself, *according to Thucydides*.

Ordinarily, my students are unable to make these distinctions until considerably later in the course. Some never do. They go on summarizing stories, poems, and histories, unable to get behind the shoulder of the author and to watch him at work in creating the particular form of the text in light of some informing intention. And very few of my students at this point in their careers are able to argue a point crucial to understanding the text.

There are a number of things I don't like about the paper. The style tends to be a bit wooden in places:

> . . . an examination of the pair of speeches made by the Corinthians and the Corcyraeans enables us to learn from Thucydides their interests, as he saw them.

I would have preferred:

> . . . if we examine the speeches of the Corcyraeans and the Corinthians, we can learn how Thucydides perceived their interests.

But again, at this point, I am less concerned with style than with intention. And in fact, Greg generally did avoid the heavy abstraction, the pervasive passives and nominalizations, in which so many bright young students struggling towards the expression of complex ideas find themselves enmeshed.

And I wish that he had chosen a more sophisticated form of organization. First he deals with the first speech, that of the Corcyraeans; then with the second, that of the Corinthians. I wish he had tried to isolate comparable features of the speeches and then done a running, analytical comparison. I wish that he had been able to handle the exposition a bit more lightly. I wish that my graduate students were able to do all these things.

My evaluation of this paper as a considerable success *at this point in the course, in the fifth week,* is a direct consequence of the objectives I have constructed for the course. My first objective is to get my students to understand the difference between writing simply about the *content* of a text and writing about the *construction* of the text. I set this as my first objective because I spend a considerable amount of time discussing with them the deliberate design, the conscious construction of *their* texts. My second objective is to get them to understand that writing is a social act, that when they write an essay—for whatever course—they will be expected to make a worthwhile point, that unless they can put forward some claim that is worth defending, worth supporting, worth spending perhaps several thousand words on, they can expect to be accused of writing papers that are aimless and disorganized.

We will in a few weeks (recall this is the fifth week of the course) get to issues of voice and style, to ways to edit out the heavy academic tone. I hope that the problems of punctuation and spelling will clear up. But at this point, it is a question of first things first. One of the first things for me is to have a reason for writing, a point worth making. The other is to extricate oneself from the content, the surface meaning of the text, and see it instead as something deliberately constructed by *someone.* If we look hard at the text and think hard about it, we can find evidence of its creation and thereby come closer to understanding what stood behind the act of creation.

That, I believe, is the objective in studying the humanities. It is also the objective in teaching writing—the conscious design of a discourse to achieve a significant intention.

Study Questions

1. A student writing about Joseph Williams's commentary on Greg Shaefer's paper and about the explanation of the writing assignment to which it was addressed said,

> I wonder whether it's fair for a teacher to insist as Joseph Williams does that the writer of a student paper "has to make a point that is important to people other than him or herself," has to make a point "worth defending, worth supporting." Why can't the student talk about what's important to her to talk about? How

can the student be made responsible for what "readers at the university level will take seriously"? Isn't this really a way of saying that students have to say what their teachers want them to say?

How do you respond to this observation?

2. Many instructors and many textbooks advise students to make the very first sentence of an essay the topic sentence, a sentence that explicitly announces the subject and point of the essay as a whole. Yet Greg Shaefer's paper moves *toward* his point rather than away from it, a movement that is praised by Joseph Williams, who says that "Greg does not give away the game too early in the paper; he is capable of delaying rhetorical closure."

Devise a topic or thesis sentence for Greg Shaefer's essay, one in which you make the point of the essay as fully and as explicitly as you can. If you were to begin Greg Shaefer's paper with the sentence you have devised, what sorts of changes would you have to make in the rest of the paper?

How would you respond to someone who told you that it was a good idea to begin all essays with an explicit thesis statement?

3. In a paper written about Joseph Williams's remarks on Thucydides, a student said,

> What Joseph Williams argues Thucydides does as a writer has a lot of implications about what I do as a writer. When I write about something that "happened," I'm writing about what I *believe* happened. That's all. This means as a writer I "make up" what I'm writing about. I can make the past anything I want it to be. As a writer the only "truth" I have to be concerned about is how well my words say what I feel.

How do you respond to this statement?

RICHARD YOUNG'S Assignment

Analyzing and Formulating Problems

> To recognize a problem which can be solved and is worth solving is . . . a discovery
> in its own right.
>
> Michael Polanyi, Personal Knowledge

> The most difficult portion of any inquiry is its initiation.
>
> F. S. C. Northrop, The Logic of the
Sciences and the Humanities

In this assignment we will be concerned with analyzing and formulating problems—the earliest phase in the process of original inquiry. Problems are usually thought of as undesirable conditions in the world around us that we somehow need to get rid of. Here, however, we treat a problem as a useful psychological event, as an interpretation that we collaborate with the world in producing and that marks a point at which our minds are ready to grow.

It is difficult to ignore some problems; they can be so intrusive we often can think of nothing else. But here we are primarily concerned with a more reticent sort of problematic experience that begins with a vague sense that something is strange, curious, anomalous, puzzling, unexpected, or particularly interesting: for example, the uneasiness we feel when we sense that an argument we are reading may be flawed, or the uncomfortable reaction we have to the disapproving glance of a friend. Because our reactions may be quite subtle, we often ignore them. But if we let them fade away in our minds, we lose opportunities for what may be original and valuable inquiries and for cultivating a rich intellectual life.

If we study almost anything closely and think about it, some feature of it is likely to strike us as problematic in one way or another. Here, for example, is a poem that is sufficiently complex to stimulate problems of various sorts for the thoughtful reader:

Counting the Mad

This one was put in a jacket,
This one was sent home,
This one was given bread and meat
But would eat none,
And this one cried No No No No
All day long.

This one looked at the window
As though it were a wall,
This one saw things that were not there,

RICHARD YOUNG is Professor of English Literature and Rhetoric at Carnegie-Mellon University. He has published extensively on the theory and practice of rhetorical invention, tagmemic rhetoric, and the teaching of writing, including a writing text, *Rhetoric: Discovery and Change* (1970), with Alton Becker and Kenneth Pike that provides the rationale for the assignment in this collection.

This one things that were,
And this one cried No No No No
All day long.

This one thought himself a bird,
This one a dog,
And this one thought himself a man,
An ordinary man,
And cried and cried No No No No
All day long.   *Donald Justice**

If, as you study the poem, something strikes you as strange and worth looking into further, try to analyze and formulate it as a problem. That is, try to move from a *feeling* that something is unusual about the poem to a *conscious understanding* of what it is that produces the feeling. You can often improve the efficiency and effectiveness of your effort to formulate a problem if you use a simple heuristic procedure: First, look for an inconsistency in your experience of the poem (for example, between something you expected to find and what you did in fact find, or between two beliefs, both of which you are committed to). Then state the inconsistency in a way that clearly reveals what is clashing with what: x conflicts with y; or x, however y. Note that at least one of the two statements that articulate the inconsistency is going to be some sort of belief that you hold, or an expectation or desire based on a belief. Finally, try to state what needs to be learned (or done) in order to eliminate the inconsistency or at least make it acceptable; it helps to state this as a question. A well-formulated problem includes both the inconsistency and the question that grows out of it.

Remember that you are writing this for yourself, to position yourself to begin an inquiry; you need not be concerned here with explaining the problem to anyone else. The emphasis in this assignment is on careful thinking and clear and precise use of language. If you need more than three of four sentences to state the problem, you probably should think more about the sources of your reaction. If you don't formulate your problem the first time in a way that satisfies you (and you probably won't), try again. It's not as easy to do well as it may seem. Save all your drafts, even if you are unhappy with them; looking back over them often helps you see more clearly what you are after.

---

๑ [Untitled]   *by William Younger, Jr.*

Version 1:

"Counting the Mad" is a puzzling poem. The poem is obviously similar in   1
form with the toe-pulling nursery rhyme "This Little Piggy Went to
Market." Instead of describing this little piggy, the poet talks about "this

---

one." Yet aside from form, there is no apparent relationship with the nursery rhyme. I wish to understand what the poet means when he says "this one." His meaning is abstruse. It is not even clear whether he is describing one person or more. Further inquiry should be focused on the subject "this one." What does the poet mean by "this one"?

Version 2:

2   "Counting the Mad" is a puzzling poem. The poem is obviously similar in form with the toe-pulling nursery rhyme "This Little Piggy Went to Market." Yet there is no apparent reason for the structural parallel. The poem and nursery rhyme differ greatly in content, audience, and meaning. Why is "This Little Piggy Went to Market" echoed in the poem "Counting the Mad"?

Richard Young's COMMENTARY

The assignment asks the student, Bill Younger, to use writing not as a means for transferring information to someone else but as a means for creating knowledge, in this case knowledge of a problem that has begun to emerge in his mind. Writing is usually thought of as a way of communicating with others, but here the student is his own audience. Writing becomes part of an original inquiry—supplementing, reinforcing, prompting what is going on in the mind as it probes for meanings it does not yet apprehend. Evaluating writing as a kind of ancillary thinking requires somewhat different standards for judgment than evaluating writing as an instrument for public communication.

Why do I admire what Bill has written? I admire it because it is a genuine problem for him and because he has formulated it well; but I also admire it because he went about the task with intelligence and skill. As an example of what I mean, compare Version 1 with Version 2. Version 1 is his first effort, or more likely an early effort, at moving from a feeling that something about the poem is strange to a clear and conscious understanding of that strangeness. The statement is, however, deficient because the answer to the question "What does the poet mean by 'this one'?" would not eliminate his puzzlement. The obvious answer (that is, "this human being") is not responsive to the source of Bill's puzzlement, which seems to be some general incongruity between the nursery rhyme and the subject of the poem. Since the puzzlement remains, he has asked the wrong question. Comparing the first problem statement to the second version, clearly a more satisfying one, we become aware of an extremely important point about original thinking: that is, we seldom do it well the first time. Bill and the rest of us as well move toward our goal by a series of what we hope are increasingly intelligent mistakes. If we do not understand that this is the case, even with the best thinkers and writers, we may become discouraged too soon and give up, convinced that we are incapable of either good thinking or good writing. Revising, then, not tidying up what has first come to mind or to paper—revisioning, re-seeing—is essential to effective thinking and writing. One impressive feature of Bill's work is that he demonstrates that he really understands the nature of revision. When revising Version 1, he did more than tinker with the language while leaving the ideas unchanged; he rethought the problem and in doing so captured what had eluded him earlier.

This is not to say that what we end up with, when it finally comes, is always glowing with its own perfection; it may in fact not be the best possible formulation of the problem. It does not have to be; it must, though, be sufficient for the purpose of initiating an effective inquiry. It is not uncommon to backtrack and reformulate the problem even after the inquiry is well underway. But the inquiry is likely to be more effective, certainly less time-consuming, if the problem is well formulated early on.

We can be reasonably precise about the features of a well-formulated problem. One feature that must be present, and stated with considerable precision, is the source of the difficulty. The source will be an awareness of an incompatibility between a belief or value and something we are experiencing, or a clash between two beliefs, or a mismatch between what we expect or desire to find and what we do in fact find. Our first awareness of such inconsistencies, however, usually comes as a feeling, often a vague and subtle one, that something is not as it should be. John Dewey appropriately called this experience a "felt difficulty"; it is at first, he says, "merely an emotional quality of the whole situation." If the felt difficulty feels important enough to us, it may well be the beginning of a sustained inquiry. But to put ourselves in a position to think about the felt difficulty clearly and effectively, we must coax it into consciousness—which is another way of saying we must give it a linguistic shape.

And here we can see another reason why Bill's work is impressive: that is, he does appear to capture the inconsistency that puzzles him.

> The poem is obviously similar in form with the toe-pulling nursery rhyme "This Little Piggy Went to Market." Yet there is no apparent reason for the structural parallel. The poem and nursery rhyme differ greatly in content, audience, and meaning.

And he puts it in a form that is clear, simple, and precise—important characteristics since this statement will serve as the point of departure for an extended inquiry.

If we want to tell someone about a problem we have, we may state an inconsistency of the sort we have been discussing ("I want to go down-town today, but I have to study for an exam." "I believe in obeying the law, but I admire Gandhi's civil disobedience." "I always believed that animals were structured symmetrically, but the scales on this side of the fish are different from the scales on the other side.") Sometimes we may state the problem as a question: "How does . . . ? Who is . . . ? Why are . . . ? Where is . . . ? What is . . . ?" However, it is important to understand that the two kinds of statements—inconsistencies and questions—are not alternative ways of saying the same thing. In the process of inquiry, the inconsistency is prior to the question; it tells us what question is to be asked. To put it another way, the question derives from the inconsistency, as can be seen in the student's problem statement, "Why is 'This Little Piggy Went to Market' echoed in the poem 'Counting the Mad'?" This question will guide the inquiry: it enables Bill to know what information is relevant to the solution and what is irrelevant; and it lets him know when he has finished the inquiry. It should be even more apparent now why the inconsistency needs to be stated precisely. Not only is it what prompts us to ask the question that will guide the inquiry, but precisely stated, it also enables us to see what question needs to be asked.

Still another reason I admire what Bill has done—a more controversial reason, for some people, than those I have discussed so far—is that he made skillful use of the heuristic procedure described in the assignment. A heuristic is a kind of rule of thumb, an effective guessing procedure, the function of which is to reduce the number of trials and errors necessary for reaching a goal. Heuristic procedures come from an effort to articulate what it is we know when we say we know how to do something; the heuristic in this assignment is an effort to articulate what we know when we say we know how to formulate a problem. Usually we can reach our intellectual goals by muddling through; heuristics are intended to help us do better (more quickly, more precisely, more promptly) what we usually can do without their aid. They are particularly valuable, however, in new, complex, and perplexing situations, such as the often difficult and discriminating process of analyzing and formulating a problem.

If we look at Bill's two problem statements closely, we can see that he is not only probing his experience of puzzlement for some sort of inconsistency, he is using the language patterns called for by the heuristic (the antithetical clauses and the derived question) to coax the inconsistency into consciousness. Notice that the same patterns are used in both versions; however, in the first version he does not quite have hold of the inconsistency he is looking for, and that is probably why he asks an unproductive question. He needs one more try before he gets something that satisfies him. The language patterns are not the result of his conscious understanding of the experience; they are a tool that helps him achieve understanding. Many people object to the use of heuristics because they confuse them with rigid rules for doing something, like the rules for doing multiplication problems. Such rules are routine, mechanical, and, hence, easily learned; their use requires little knowledge and skill. (The simplicity and rigidity of the rules is what makes pocket calculators possible.) Heuristics, however, are more difficult to learn; they require for effective use not only a substantial body of information relevant to the subject at hand, but imagination, intellectual flexibility, and skill. Rules bind us in unvarying procedures, any deviation from which produces an error. Heuristics guide our abilities in useful directions; to borrow a metaphor from Robert Frost, effective use of heuristics requires "moving easy in harness"—a subtle skill, but one that this student has learned.

Eliminating the difficulty is the principal goal of any inquiry; it is also the principal test of whether the problem has been formulated well. Consider the student's question again: Why is the nursery rhyme echoed in the poem? A reasonable answer (not the only one surely but the one Bill finally worked out) was that Donald Justice wants the reader to recall the happiness, simplicity, and innocence of the infant; the harsh world of the adult is introduced against this background of childhood memories and moods as a way of intensifying our sense of the tragedy of human life. Such an answer transforms a puzzling inconsistency into an intelligible and effective poetic strategy. The question is answered; the difficulty is eliminated.

I admire this student's work, then, not only because he has produced an interesting, well-formulated problem but because he has clearly gone about the task intelligently. John Holt once remarked that intelligence is not something that can be measured and assigned a number but is rather an effective style of behaving, especially in new, strange, and perplexing situations. What we see in Bill Younger's work is good style.

Study Questions

1. In a classroom discussion of William Younger's paper and Richard Young's commentary on it, one student said,

> The thing that bothers me about this technique is that the question the student asks about the poem is the most *obvious* question to ask, but the answer to it doesn't get him to the meaning of the poem. Why does Justice vary the refrain the way he does in the third stanza of the poem? That's the key question to ask, I think. That's what explains the use of the nursery rhyme. Maybe it's not the

first question the student ought to ask, but when he asks the question he does, one he can then go on to answer, maybe he never sees that there's a more important question he never touches. He hasn't gotten to the meaning of the poem at all until he deals with what Justice means by "An ordinary man," but I don't know whether the student knows that.

Another student responded,

> "Obvious question" to whom? "Key question" for whom? "Meaning of the poem" for whom? I think you're doing exactly what Richard Young in his first paragraph implies causes trouble about problems. You're seeing the problem of this poem as separate from the psychology of the student. This student is looking for a place to start for *himself*. His question is only the first one he asks, not the only one he asks. How do you know he won't get to what you call "the meaning of the poem" his own way?

What position would you take in this controversy?

2. "Remember," says Richard Young to his students in his writing assignment, "that you are writing this for yourself, to position yourself to begin an inquiry; you need not be concerned here with explaining the problem to anyone else."

   Suppose William Younger wished to make his problem the basis for a paper in which he concerned himself primarily with explaining that problem to others. What changes would you suggest he make in what he has written in order to make others understand and accept what he is talking about?

3. In his writing assignment and commentary, Richard Young describes a heuristic, a kind of intellectual tool that is designed to improve the efficiency and effectiveness of an effort to formulate a problem. In his discussion, however, Richard Young says little about when to *use* the heuristic.

   What kind of writing situations can you imagine in which using a heuristic might be helpful to you as a writer?

   What kinds of writing situations can you imagine in which using a heuristic might *not* be helpful to you as a writer, in which deferring or suspending judgment might be preferable to pushing through to an interpretation of the sort that William Younger develops?

   Judging from your responses to these two questions, what can you say about when it might be helpful to a writer to use a heuristic?

Writing Assignment 10
Writing about Writing

For this assignment, select from among the commentaries in this chapter one that you think you can turn into advice that will be helpful to you in writing an analysis of a piece of your writing. Write a paragraph that will make clear what advice you have drawn from this commentary. If you feel that making a list first will help you to write your paragraph, by all means feel free to start your thinking that way. But what really matters here, what your paragraph should explain, is what you make your list *mean* to you.

Next, on a separate page, write a paper in which you use this advice to analyze the *first* paper you wrote for this course. Try to look at that first paper as though it were done—as in a sense it was—by someone else. Who is the speaker in that paper? What kind of a writer do you see before you? Judging from the evidence in the paper, what would you say are the strengths and weaknesses of this writer? What does this writer seem to know about how to make sentences, about how to make sentences into paragraphs? What would you say this writer has to learn about writing?

Be sure to turn in a copy of your first paper along with your analysis of it.

Locating the Self

11

The question "Who am I?" obsesses the mind and all human activity provides answers, ever changing, uncertain, risky. Grammatically it would seem that "I" am a user of prepositions. "I" see something as above or below, to the left or to the right, before or after, but the thing itself ever eludes me. And "I" myself turn out to be a maker of patterns, of orders, a constructor of worlds.

Theodore Baird

ALL FIVE OF THE STUDENT ESSAYS IN this chapter make particularly clear that whatever an interesting essay of definition may involve, it always involves more than someone's simply looking something up in a dictionary—or for that matter anywhere else. Although Lindsay Lankford depends on a common understanding of a phrase like "to write a letter," you will not find anything like her interpretation of letter writing under these words in *Webster's New World Dictionary*, for instance. The "excerpts and essays all concerned in one way or another with 'ambition' " did not provide Ellen Chafee with her paper. George Humphrey did not get his definition of "University" from a college catalog. You cannot look *yourself* up in the dictionary. You cannot create a definition of anything that is worth attempting to define simply by quoting someone else.

The student papers and teachers' commentaries of this chapter are offered as a way of helping you to explore the activity of defining in order to draw your own conclusions about what the activity of defining can do for you.

WILLIAM COLES'S Assignment

We [Robert Francis and Robert Frost] looked at Gibson's poem "David" the last line of which, "Of course, we tell him what we can," Frost had always especially admired. "Would make a good motto over an educational institution," he remarked. "In place of VERITAS."

Robert Francis

What *is* the proper metaphor with which to define a university so far as you are concerned?

Is your university for you a trade school, a mill, a country club?

Or is it, in the terms of one writer we read, a kind of key ring, or that which dispenses pictures to guide you in fitting the jigsaw pieces of the world together?

How do you like "nest of adversaries" as a metaphor? Remember that one? How about "group of collaborators," as another writer put it?

Any others you can think of? A prison? Real Life? An Ivory Tower?

✎ [Untitled]

by George Humphrey

1   Next to this desk at which I write is a couch where my wife is sleeping. She is nineteen. So am I. The couch is old, with large stuffed pillows and a rounded stuffed back. It is covered with a dirty red, rough material. The wooden legs are curved and scratched. The couch reminds me of one my grandmother used to have, except hers had small lace doilies on the arms. Ours does not.

2   Out of the window above the couch I can see the back of the Medical School, a corner of the old Dental School, and the University power plant. The windows of the power plant have a blue-green tint to them, and it looks as though the machinery behind them is under water. The buildings do not look much like Ivory Towers. From here, now, they look like a factory.

3   A factory. I remember when my parents came to visit us a few weeks ago my father, who is an engineer, was very interested in the power plant. He said that the next time he came he would like to go over and "check it out."

4   "I'll just tell them my son is a student here and I'd like to see what kind of a set up you've got for him."

WILLIAM ELIOT COLES, JR. is currently Professor of English and formerly Director of Composition at the University of Pittsburgh. He has published numerous articles and several books on the teaching of writing: *Composing* (1974), *Teaching Composing: Writing as a Self-Creating Process* (1974); *The Plural I* (1978); and *Composing II* (1981). For four summers (1977–1980) he directed NEH seminars entitled "Teaching Writing: Theories and Practices."

My mother, on the other hand, was more interested in the garden in front of the Museum of Art. She also likes the couch. 5

"Well," we said, "it's comfortable, anyway." 6

The Rapid Transit runs past the window of our apartment; so, as I look out at the power plant, I can see the lighted cars running by. Every ten minutes. 7

When I look out the window over my desk I see two pear trees and a small garden. There is no trace of the University, and, in the ten minutes between trains, our apartment could be in the country, instead of University Circle. But the Rapid goes by, and my attention is drawn past my wife and the couch to the University in the other window. 8

Last year I lived in the dorms. I remember looking out the window of my room on the sixth floor of Clarke Tower. I could see the dorm parking lot and a few houses on the other side. Nothing from there looked much like a university: it looked like a regular city block. 9

I used to have conversations about D. H. Lawrence with a friend in the elevator. It started one day when I noticed a copy of *The Rainbow* under his arm, and he noticed a copy under mine. The conversations did not last long—just long enough for the elevator to get from the 6th floor to the lobby, but now the only time I see my friend is in a class we have together. We say hello, but that is about all we say. 10

My wife has started to read Lawrence, though, and I talk with her about him. 11

Sometimes in our apartment we're conscious of the Rapid going by; sometimes we're not. 12

William Coles's COMMENTARY

Like most teachers of writing, I'd be reluctant to specify any one student paper as the best I've ever received, but I have no trouble at all singling out the piece of student writing that has meant more to me than any other I've ever read. Meant and means. This is partly a matter, undoubtedly, of my unfaded sense of the rhetorical scene of the paper. We were almost at the end of a freshman writing course, one I was concluding by having students examine various ways of defining a university—almost at the end of a course, and that same spring, 1970, twenty-five miles from Kent State (as the bullet flies), almost at what felt like the end of everything else as well. It's partly a matter of what I remember of the writer of the paper too—what he had come from and through in his work for the course for one thing; the boy himself for another: filament-thin, fierce, graceless, as improbably gladdening as a crocus in the snow. And above all I remember the silence that followed my reading the paper aloud in class, deep enough in that time of that place to still the waters it seemed, to winnow heaven from earth.

So I had better begin by admitting that part of what makes George Humphrey's paper excellent for me, just for me as a reader, is connected with the incantatory power it has to chant me not back to but into a present relationship with what I'm in constant danger of forgetting is the most important thing I know as a teacher of writing: that language can be used to create possibilities for living. By anybody. Anywhere. Anytime.

There are two ways, however, in which I'd say the excellence of the paper lies beyond the exclusivity of my experience with it. "Writing properly pursued," says Richard Lanham, "does not make you better. It makes you more alive"—and part of why I praise the paper just as a piece of writing is the power it has to suggest to readers that this is one thing the writing of it must in some measure have done for its writer. But even more important to me is the power the paper has, and as no more than an ordering of words in the context of a particular assignment, to compel *readers* to become as alive in their terms as the writer is in his. This is the main thing I wish to praise, and I do so well aware that as an arrangement of words, the paper is not completely within the writer's control, may even be read as seriously flawed.

Much of what the writer does *is* I think controlled, marvelously, not the least of which is the very subtle, very complicated way he goes about doing what at first he seems to have avoided altogether: addressing the assignment. By describing the effects of a university education as he does, in and with the terms of his own life, the writer makes the paper *itself* the metaphor defining what for him a university "is." A university, at least as I read this writer, as both a time of and the agency for change, as an occasion for growing up, is nowhere. Devisedly and necessarily, it is a place that isn't one. But for a university student, in whom memory and desire mingle, who holds in the same mind what are discrete if not disparate things outside the mind, a university is *a* nowhere at the same time. It is a no-place that in being between worlds, the old ones undead, the new ones not quite born, is nevertheless where someone who chooses to become a university student must be in order to make of the hellos and goodbyes demanded of him, the claims of the past and the pressures of the future, somewhere to live. To lose can be to gain as a university student, but to gain is also to have to lose.

Hence the couch tying the writer to his past even as it emphasizes his separation from it. Hence the friend who in never exactly having been made one is both more and less than gone. Hence the parents, clumsily conventional, remote, touching, exasperating, whose desire to protect and endorse can at least be decently acknowledged, honored, even in its situational irrelevance (". . . that the days of thy life may be long" [*Exodus* 20:12]). Hence the wife, there with him ("we said," "we're conscious"), but sleeping, the embodiment of the subject of *The Rainbow* (once only a book for a course?), who has begun, even if she has only just begun, to read Lawrence. Hence the conflicting attitudes toward marriage—as frightening ("She is nineteen. So am I"), an ineluctable impingement on the writer's student world ("Next to this desk at which I write . . ."); but as thrilling too ("*my* wife"), a precarious refuge ("our apartment"), that which is impinged *upon* by the student world demanding the writer's focus ("my attention is drawn past my wife and the couch to the University in the other window"). Hence the writer's seeing of the university as "power plant," the way to a life of one's own (maybe?), symbolized (perhaps?) by the gardens, the two pear trees, an apartment in the country—a vision that at the same time is qualified by the writer's sense of the university as "factory" also, its real power drowned ("under water"), the life launched from it as but another version of ordinariness ("regular city block") and routine ("every ten minutes"). World folds into world and back again as perspective melts into perspective ("Sometimes in our apartment we're conscious of the Rapid going by; sometimes we're not."). Life at a university is life on a Möbius strip, where all opposites meet even as they are held from joining. The proper metaphor for a university then, this writer suggests, is whatever meaning a university student can make at any given moment of the many kinds of self-consciousness a university is designed to promote.

I think.

Because I'm not sure that the university as a unique kind of no-place, as a language-learning center, for example, is as explicitly and firmly at the heart of things in this paper as I'd like to imagine it is. Some of the parallels and oppositions I see the possibilities for I think are calculated and controlled by the writer, but not all of them are. The writer's handling of the couch, for example, I feel sure of; but does his recurrent reference to the Rapid Transit mean what I think it does? How about those two pear trees? The writer's use of *The Rainbow?* His description of the power plant?

The paper is obscure then, an example, perhaps, of disparate experience insufficiently amalgamated, of a new whole unsuccessfully formed?

Maybe.

That is if I refuse to acknowledge what I know full well is often the consequence of someone's trying as bravely as does this student to put and hold together not just too much with too little, but all he knows with all he has.

Or is *that* argument simply my way of refusing to admit that I'm a sucker for this paper, a sentimentalist, someone who poses as a reader in order to do a writer's work for him? I know I push myself as a reader of this paper, that I have to in order to read it at all, but do I push myself too far, over the line into irresponsibility?

Again, the answer would have to be maybe, maybe so.

Except that I still have to deal with what there is in the paper that generates my impulse to do the writer's work for him to begin with. Is it the form of the paper, for instance, which one would have to invent a terminology even to describe? The explosion of tone into multiple meanings—"Well," we said, "it's comfortable, anyway"—that is moment by moment so beautifully sure? Those crystalline images? The exquisite timing of the repetitions? The disciplined struggle to be fair—"but that is about all we say"—felt as a capacity to revere? The bone-clean, bedrock spareness of the prose throughout? Some unnameable combination of such things?

I push myself as a reader of this paper all right, but I don't believe I make something out of nothing with it—any more than I do when I worry the puns in *Hamlet*, in lots of Conrad, in Wallace Stevens, in lots and lots of Ezra Pound. Literature, and that's what I think we have here, is sometimes like that. Indeed, that I am pushed by this paper, have been for years, to the edge of irresponsibility, to becoming as a reader what I never figured I'd have to become as a reader of student writing—not better, but more alive—is precisely why I call it excellent.

The paper is an anomaly. I want to make clear that I understand this. I do not believe it should be used as a model for students to imitate. It is not an example of what I think any writing classroom ought to teach students to do. But for me it is a paper worth sharing with students and explaining as an enactment of what I have to see the teaching of writing as being about, as having the possibility of involving, if I am to keep going as a teacher at all. "Give me a sentence," says Thoreau, "which no intelligence can understand. There must be a kind of life and palpitation to it, and under its words a kind of blood must circulate forever." Dangerous and dreadful this would be to teach as a doctrine surely, in any writing classroom, but without being informed by an awareness of what the sentences point to, no real writing classroom can be.

Study Questions

1. "Dangerous and dreadful this would be to teach as a doctrine," says William Coles specifically of what he quotes from Thoreau, but by implication of the position he takes on the student paper he discusses as well. What is this "doctrine"? In what senses might it be "dangerous and dreadful" if taught in a writing classroom?

But William Coles also suggests that the teaching of writing ought somehow to be informed by what this doctrine "points to." What does it "point to" exactly?

What do you think it would be like to be a student in a writing class that was informed by what the doctrine "points to"? Would you want to be a student in such a class? Why?

2. How do you describe the form of George Humphrey's paper? Use whatever terms you feel you need to help you explain how the paper is shaped, how it moves from paragraph to paragraph, what holds the paper together.

Now look again at William Coles's remark about the form of George Humphrey's paper: "one would have to invent a terminology even to describe [it]."

On the basis of your experience describing the form of this student's paper, why would you say that William Coles's remark is accurate or inaccurate?

3. In a classroom discussion of George Humphrey's paper and William Coles's commentary on it, a student said,

> I think what William Coles does is to read the *student* and what he calls the rhetorical scene of the paper rather than the actual paper. Without his explanation of the context of the paper, I'm not sure I could figure out what the paper was about even, what all those details add up to. If the writer of this paper has enough control to write sentences as good as some of them are, doesn't he have enough control to have made himself a lot clearer than he has—and doesn't a teacher have a responsibility to insist on that? But William Coles doesn't say anywhere that he thinks the paper needs rewriting or that he asked the student to rewrite it. Maybe he is, as he says, a "sucker" for this student's paper. I think he certainly lets him get away with more than he should have.

How do you respond to this statement?

Rebecca Faery's Assignment

[There were no specific assignments given in this course. We followed the workshop model and agreed at the beginning that class members would write and submit their work on a regular basis. At the end of the term, each student was to submit for a grade a portfolio of at least twenty-five typed pages, in which each piece of writing was to have been at least once discussed in our workshop and subsequently revised. This essay was the fourth or fifth that Lindsay Lankford wrote for the course.]

ॐ On Writing Letters

by Lindsay Lankford

1　My post office box is empty today, as it is almost every day. To peer inside is always an afterthought, seldom rewarded. Once a month, though, I'm assured of mail. C & P Telephone Company loves me, and sends me nice long bills, each call marked in minutes and money owed. These bills, and the stubs in my checkbook from their payment, are all that remain of past communications. The telephone, however, is fast and easy to use. Letters can take days, sometimes weeks to reach their destination. Furthermore, writing letters involves a great deal of time and effort; yet letters have some very real advantages.

2　I spent a year in Paris and quickly discovered that transatlantic phone calls were not within my budget. So I was left with that most archaic mode of communication, the letter. And I loved it. Every Sunday morning was devoted to my weekly letter home, a letter which often took all morning. I'd go through the whole week in memory, and re-live it. I'd go to the *tabac*, and remember how pleased I was when the little man with his dirty black apron complimented my slowly improving French. Or I'd be in the Jeu de Paume, and feel again the excitement I felt when I finally learned to love Cezanne. I'd recall how bitterly and miserably cold I was last Thursday, and how really good the coffee tasted in that cafe near Sacre Coeur. I'd remember walking out of Notre Dame at seven p.m., after an hour of warm and rich Vivaldi, and finding Paris dusted with snow, glinting and sparkling in the streetlights. Or summer nights in the Latin Quarter, drinking *vin ordinaire* in outdoor cafes, talking too much

REBECCA BLEVINS FAERY is Coordinator of Writing at Hollins College, a private, liberal arts women's college in Virginia, where she teaches writing and directs the Writing Center. She was a Fellow of the NEH-Iowa Institute on Writing in 1980. She has published poems, essays, and reviews in various books and periodicals, including a section in *Courses for Change in Writing* (1984), the volume of curricular materials developed at the Institute on Writing.

about Life and Art and the Future, subjects that are always and can only be discussed after too much wine.

My Sunday letters were the times when I put these vignettes together, and made my memories concrete and coherent. Mama has kept these letters for me, in a manila folder in the top drawer of her Louis XV desk. And whenever I want them, whenever I want to remember, they are there for me. For although I addressed them to Mama and Daddy, they were always written essentially to myself. Mama and Daddy saw Europe through my eyes, with my perceptions and impressions. My letters were unselfconscious and utterly honest, for the time and space lag between letters made intimacy easier. My parents learned more about me from a year of letters than they had in nineteen years of personal interaction. 3

I loved their letters to me, too. They were never filled with earth-shattering news, but they revealed a lot. Actually, most people's lives are dull; it's the way they perceive their lives that is interesting. My sister Allison lives in the Negev Desert, in a tiny trailer. Her world consists of her husband, their two small children, and very little else. Her letters were always wrinkled, smeared with something sticky, covered in crayons and written over extended periods of time. They were a mess: descriptions of the gingerbread village Allison had made for the Christmas party, their plans for moving back to the States, Lauren's latest word, and details of Elizabeth's third birthday party. Allison's letters were disjointed, but ebullient. Living on an army base in the Israeli desert would seem a barren existence, yet Allison's letters describe a busy and happy, if somewhat chaotic, life. 4

I saw Mama's world through her letters. With her eyes and her words, I saw the spring I was missing in Birmingham, how bright the azaleas were, how she'd never seen so many dogwoods in bloom. I realized how acute her perceptions are, how she notices the little details. She wrote of the garden, of the ever-growing, never-ending crop of green beans. Of the squirrel without a tail, how well he had adapted. From her letters, I knew how empty the house felt when Daddy was away on business, and then how cozy it was when he returned and they made great pots of seafood gumbo together. Mama's sphere is small: her house, her friends and her husband. Yet her letters taught me that her deep awareness of her world gave it its richness. 5

Daddy didn't write much, but his few letters were remarkable for what they revealed. Daddy is sixty-two and still passionate about learning. Daddy, who had one year of French in college and that forty years ago, wrote to me in French. My mental image of Daddy in his office, surrounded by French dictionary and grammar book, is very precious. I treasure the idea of Daddy as the student, instead of the one who knows 6 all. And what Daddy can't say in English, he can write in French: *Je t'aime* ended every letter.

7   My post office box is empty today, and very likely to remain so tomorrow. For we've all slipped back into old patterns, old ways of communicating. Sometimes, we still find time to send little notes, notes written in haste and without much pleasure. These new letters are little more than abbreviations of the details we once vividly described. I think we all miss our old letters, although we neither discuss nor write them anymore. The barriers are back up. We're careful again, wary of the reckless revelations we once shared. The physical distances between us are less now; cautiously, we distance ourselves in spirit.

8   I've still got those old letters. They are priceless to me. For writing deals harshly with the banal, the superficial. The things we say to each other can seldom survive on paper. The things we dare to write are those we really mean.

Rebecca Faery's COMMENTARY

As soon as I read the first paragraph of this essay, I knew I was reading something very good, something that represented a breakthrough for the writer. Not that I had a particular reason to expect anything special; Lindsay's earlier pieces had been competent and interesting, but somehow slight. I remembered as I read this one, though, that during the past weeks she had been listening with quiet intensity to everything we had said in class. And we had been talking about writing, what it really is and what it can do.

It was the spring of 1982, and I was teaching a course in advanced expository writing. I did, and do, take the term "expository" to mean something at once broad and specific: The "explaining" or "setting forth" implied in the word can cover almost any subject, as long as it covers something in particular (though its particular subject may be different from what is suggested on the surface). I am most attracted by the idea of exposition as an act that, at best, *exposes* or *reveals* the truth about something. The course was, then, taking as its subject and activity the whole universe of nonfiction prose. We were operating as a writers' workshop, with the class members submitting essays in various stages of completion for review and reaction from all of us. There were no specific assignments, just an understanding that everybody would be writing and submitting regularly. We had spent those first weeks of the course considering what an essay was, what it had been historically as a literary form, how it was being used now by writers who valued the form and knew how to make something of it, and what its possibilities were. I hoped that reading essays of many kinds on many subjects by many writers (we were using a reader as a supplement to the course) would get their creative juices flowing, stimulate them to move beyond the cautious academic essays most of them were used to writing, invite them to get involved in trying the essay form out, trying it on, seeing what they could make of it for themselves.

Most of all, though, I had been trying to suggest that writing is not so much a performance, something made for someone else to judge, as it is a way of creating meaning, a way of discovering the truth about the world. A way, in fact, of creating a world for ourselves in which we can live with a minimum of confusion. I wanted them to understand that we do this with language all the time, but that with written language, we do it in a way that allows us to reflect upon our experiences and integrate those experiences into the world that we are imaginatively constructing every day. Perhaps best of all, with written language we can share in and contribute to the experience of others, and thus we enter into our culture, the shared world-view of all who speak our language.

It was this understanding of the nature of written language that I saw in Lindsay's piece as soon as I started reading it. It is a piece of writing about writing, a "meta-text," if you will. In her essay she explores what writing means for her, and implicitly for all of us, in terms of sharpening memory, of shaping and reshaping experience, of building and managing connections with other people, and of minimizing the chaos of life by imposing on it form and order, sense and meaning.

The first image in the essay is a very powerful one: a piece about writing letters opens with an empty post office box. No, not quite empty—a telephone bill turns up once a month, a reminder that neglecting letters and substituting the telephone is a costly habit in more ways than one. By the time the image of the empty post box is repeated near the end of the essay, it has become a powerful metaphor for a significant absence in the writer's life. The world of letters is a world of beauty, pleasure, and love: Paris sparkling in the snow, music and art, good talk over wine, families who risk real intimacy, food and flowers, and gardens where things grow in abundance. The world without letters is represented by an empty box.

"Actually," says Lindsay, "most people's lives are dull; it's the way they perceive their lives that is interesting." And in this essay, we have examples of exactly that perceptive transformation, in the letters of the sister and the mother, who both live within the woman's traditional "small sphere": for Allison, it is a home with a husband and two children in the Israeli desert; for the mother, it is again home, husband, friends, kitchen, garden. But in both women's letters, we're told, their lives take on color and energy, even adventure. In the act of being recorded, their lives are transformed and invested with meaning. For Lindsay, her mother and sister transcend the narrowness of their lives with the words they use to portray them. The women's "deep awareness" of their world "[gives] it its richness." Her father, too, escapes a masculine cliché when he writes; the "I love you" which he cannot speak in words is written in the French he labors to use for his daughter's sake. It is a labor inspired by a passion for learning, yet he learns more than French. His lesson is learning of an elemental kind. By contrast, in the world of no letters it is the telephone company which "loves" Lindsay and sends her "nice long bills, each call marked in minutes and money owed."

We see, then, the three family members all confined by custom and convention, each of whom manages in the act of writing letters to escape the apparent limits of her or his situation. Lindsay, on the other hand, is not confined; quite the opposite. Sprung from her parental home, from her familiar college, from her native land and native tongue, she struggles to hold on to her identity even as she is building a new one. Her letters home are a lifeline to both selves, the Birmingham girl and the young woman of nineteen in Paris, living away from home in all the senses of the word, and standing on the threshold of adulthood. She writes to her family, but she knows she writes also to herself. Those luxurious Sunday mornings spent on the letters are her chance, as James Britton puts it, to step back from being a participant in her life and become a spectator of it. In re-seeing her week's activities and experiences and in choosing language to shape and record them, she gives her life a form and order which make it possible for her to incorporate her own life within her view of the world and to lay claim to the self she is in the process of becoming.

That, Lindsay tells us, is what writing letters meant to her during that year in Paris. But what did writing this essay do for her, and what does it do for us who read it? It's pretty clear, I think, that this is not just a record of the role letters played in her life in that Paris year. It is, rather, a nostalgic recollection of a world which was transformed for her through writing; and it is, moreover, a call to the reader to reconsider the possibilities that writing holds for each of us. She makes a graceful transition in this piece of writing from the personal to the universal, from a narrative of experience to a comment on the role of written language in human lives. It is a mature transition, made possible once again by her role as spectator to the letter-writing that she and her family engaged in while she was away. We learn from the narrative that those long weekly letters she wrote enabled her to relive and assimilate her experiences in a great city far from home; we learn that writing this essay has allowed her to learn something very important about the experience of writing the letters. We read her poignant comments about the world without writing in view of what we know of the world now lost to her: "The barriers are back up. We're careful again, wary of the reckless revelations we once shared. The physical distances between us are less now; cautiously, we distance ourselves in spirit." And we experience, I think, the flash of recognition which unites us with her. Yes, we say. That's true. That *is* what we, all we human beings, really do. Thus we are able to re-see, to re-evaluate, our own experience in light of what Lindsay tells us about hers. We as readers are changed by the reading.

Writing, this essay suggests, calls forth from writer and readers an honesty and openness which may not always be comfortable: "For writing deals harshly with the banal, the superficial." The very fact of language prompts writers and readers to refine our perceptions, to dismiss the deceptive or irrelevant, and to move ever closer to what is real. We are compensated for our effort, though, by the grace which language exhibits in the hands of one who cares about it. Clearly Lindsay is one of those who cares about it. She has used in this essay all the properties of well-managed words which delight us as we read. The truth she reaches for may be a harsh one, because she passes an unmerciful judgment on our era, which has dispensed with the practice of writing as a way of developing a picture of the world and of forming connections and relationships which make people feel at home in it and not alone. The way she discovers that truth with words, though, is lovely to watch. The essay moves out of the language of the everyday world and into that of literature; it has rhythm, rhetorical repetition, and symmetry; in it objects become images, which become metaphors. It has a powerful climactic order and a dramatic sense of closure. It is, in short, an achievement of the writer's craft which I admire very much.

I think after reading Lindsay's essay our picture of the world has changed in response to the picture she offers us. I know that reading it makes me nostalgic for an era I never knew, when letter-writing was a practiced art among large numbers of people. It invites me to reflect on the consequences, for those people, of taking the time to make a world with words, and on the consequences, for our time, of so few people spending such time. Could the habit of writing to and for ourselves and others lessen our sense of chaos and alienation? Maybe. It might be worth a try.

Study Questions

1. A student writing about Lindsay Lankford's "On Writing Letters" and Rebecca Faery's commentary on it said,

> It's ironic to me that Lindsay Lankford and Rebecca Faery both write about a form of communication, letter writing, in a way that makes clear how writing is a lot more than just a form of communication.

How would you explain this remark to someone who did not understand it? What do both Lindsay Lankford and Rebecca Faery say about writing to make clear that it is "more than just a form of communication"?

What's the point of seeing writing as "more than just a form of communication," particularly writing as obviously directed to someone as is a letter?

2. Though "no specific assignments" were given in the course for which Lindsay Lankford wrote her paper, suppose you were told that, in other composition courses she teaches, Rebecca Faery does make use of specific writing assignments. What kinds of writing assigments might she use to promote the understanding of writing that she praises Lindsay Lankford for displaying? What sorts of questions would she ask? What would she hope that addressing those questions might do for her students?

3. In a classroom discussion of Lindsay Lankford's "On Writing Letters" and Rebecca Faery's commentary on it, a student said,

> You know, you could use these two essays to make a really good argument not just about how writing is *different* from talking, but about how in and with writing you can do things you can't do just with talk.

By means of specific reference to both Lindsay Lankford's paper and Rebecca Faery's commentary on it, make the strongest possible argument you can for this student's assertion.

What is your position with the argument you've just made?

[I commissioned a freshman student, Lili Velez, to work with me on a project designed specifically for *What Makes Writing Good*. First, I asked her to look through her freshman composition textbook, *Writing in the Arts and Sciences*, to find a question that she would like to use as a starting point for a 1,000-word example of discursive prose addressed to the wide audience of freshman readers who would one day read the anthology. She and I decided that the finished essay ought to reflect what she had learned after studying for a year in Beaver College's writing-across-the-curriculum program.

Lili began with this assignment: Without actually concerning yourself with the answer to the following question, work out a list of subordinate questions and a strategy for developing an answer—"Can we know what is evil and what is good?" From that starting point Lili worked for several weeks on writing expressively in her journal, checking the *Oxford English Dictionary* for definitions of key terms (*know, evil, good*), drafting, and redrafting. Lili and I had many conferences, several by long-distance telephone after she left campus for summer vacation. She wrote a self-analysis of several drafts and asked friends at home to write peer responses. What you see here has evolved from the original question and focuses on the nature and purpose of a broad range of philosophic questions like: Why should we ask such questions? Should these questions stay in the philosophy class, where they usually appear, or should we examine them in the dormitories and dining rooms of our lives?

Lili does not believe that she has finished the assignment. I have tried to convince her that no assignment is ever finished; it is merely abandoned, sometimes to public notice.]

❧ Examinations Outside the Classroom

by Lili Velez

We panic, we pack, we get to college, and then panic again, moaning, "I wish I had known I'd need this!" "This" could be anything from that extra pillow to the answers to a high school test on *Hamlet*, or it might be something more abstract, like how to deal with issues we never thought we would encounter outside a classroom. For example, when a philoso-

---

ELAINE P. MAIMON directs the program in writing across the curriculum, which she initiated at Beaver College, where she is also Professor of English and Associate Dean. With four colleagues representing a variety of disciplines, she has written two composition textbooks, *Writing in the Arts and Sciences* (1981) and *Readings in the Arts and Sciences* (1984). She has contributed a chapter entitled "Maps and Genres" to *Literature and Composition: Bridging the Gap* (1983). As a member of the NEH National Board of Consultants, she has advised many colleges and universities on writing and the humanities.

337

phy professor asks us to examine what is evil and what is good, that's okay; we're getting graded on it. But do we ask such questions in the cafeteria? In the dormitory? At home? Who needs to ponder academic questions outside of class? It's an invasion of our private lives. I thought so until a question followed me home and shook up my ideas on what belonged in the classroom and what I should never be without.

2   It was in English 102, in small group discussion of my friend, Donna's paper, which was about whether fighting was a natural tendency for humans, as it is in other animals that live in groups. What had prompted her to write on this topic was her previous paper supporting the Nuclear Freeze. She wanted to know why humans were always competing in such destructive ways. As Donna was telling us how her drafts of the paper were going, she stopped mid-sentence. If, she reasoned, violent tendencies were instinctive, then there was nothing to be done about them, since no one had ever succeeded in changing human nature. This argument sounded perfectly logical to us. What was wrong? Donna explained, horrified, that she had just provided a great way to rationalize murder.

3   "Donna, you ought to be a lawyer," joked my roommate Heather, breaking the stunned silence. "I always hated logic," muttered another student. I felt very uncomfortable. My uneasiness lasted into lunch, when Heather and I discussed how ironic it was that Donna's two papers contradicted one another. Still, the incident haunted me.

4   I thought of my own paper on the Nuclear Freeze. I had managed to write it without any nasty surprises, but how? Both pro-Freeze people and their opponents used logic to support their claims that the world would be destroyed if the other course were taken. I didn't base my argument on the logic of either position. I said I would rather fry while trying to get rid of nuclear arsenals than be destroyed because we let the arms race continue. According to my convictions—or, if I may use that dreaded term, my ethical philosophy—the former manner of death was more moral.

5   There was the trick! I'd treated the issue as an ethical question, not as a political or logical debate. By examining the question in terms of good and evil, I was able to make a decision with minimal risk of leaving embarrassing loopholes. When I mentioned my discovery to my friends, they pointed out that human nature and the Nuclear Freeze were "big issues" that would naturally fit the artificial world of ethical thinking. But I began to see that ethical questions also lurked in the most mundane experiences. I started noticing that the question, "Should I eat dinner?" was a front for considering that if my father's unemployment checks have already paid for the cafeteria food, is it right to go order pizza?

6   I'm not saying I whip out my classnotes from a 4-credit philosophy

course or Kant's *Critique of Pure Reason* to decide whether or not to attempt the cafeteria's egg rolls. Nor do I want Plato lectures in freshman orientation. But with all the uncertainties of college life, I want to examine my choices in all situations, and the principles behind those choices, so that I don't get shocked anymore the way I did in English when I wasn't looking hard enough at someone's argument.

When Donna said, "Gee, this is the perfect excuse for murder," it was a revelation. Looking back on this incident, I realize that if I don't strip issues down to questions of good and evil, I may never know—never be aware of—what I've done until someone discovers it's the perfect excuse for heaven-knows-what. Flipping through my journals, I see dozens of everyday instances which require the philosophical art of examination: Should I review my friend's paper or rewrite it? Should I major in what I excel at or what will help me get a job? When one roommate wants to work until 2:00 a.m. and my other roommate and I have an 8:30 exam, is it right to throw the nightowl in the lounge so we can sleep? 7

Nobody can ignore these questions. We have to live with our decisions. It's not a matter of knowing for sure what is evil and what is good, but of examining all sides to make certain we haven't created any "perfect excuses." Ethical philosophy ranks high on the list of things I never thought I'd need, and it was discouraging at first to realize what I had reserved as homework was lurking in "real-life" incidents. But from all my writing and thinking about real-life and abstract questions, I know one thing for certain about evil, good, and innocuous decisions. Ethical philosophy isn't an intellectual frill, it's part of the survival kit. 8

ELAINE MAIMON'S COMMENTARY

What makes good writing good? Thinking and taking risks. Lili had to think hard about a fundamental question of the human condition. She also had to think hard about all of you, that group of absent strangers who might one day read and criticize her essay. That's where the risk-taking comes in. All of you have much greater power over Lili than any composition teacher ever had over you. A teacher can do no worse than give you an F. You can stop reading and annihilate the writer through your lack of attention. Or you can finish reading the essay, because a teacher assigned you to do so, and then see no point in it or judge Lili harshly without ever meeting her.

Lili's essay is good because she has something to say and the courage to say it to a real group of readers. *Purpose* and *audience*: you, like Lili, have probably heard those words many times from your own composition teachers. Lili's purpose is to engage your attention in something important to her—the idea that classroom questions spill out of the classroom into the corridors and commons. But she has to make that point in a way that will not offend you. Nor does she want to sound like a snob or a grind. She wants to engage you in conversation, to make you say something back to her. If her writing makes you feel like getting into the conversation, it is good writing.

If you happen to be taking a course in philosophy, you might be willing to think and write about evil and good for the fifty minutes of the class session. In fact, your philosophy instructor might ask you to write a contemplative piece responding to Lili's original question, "Can we know what is evil and what is good?" In fulfilling such an assignment you would be obliged to write an analysis covering the following areas: an explanation of the problem and why it is a problem; a formulation of criteria for an acceptable solution; and a defense of the solution. In short, you would be applying the philosophic method. Your finished paper would present a carefully reasoned argument, connected by logical transitions (*therefore, such as, so, because, since, accordingly, for, so it follows that*). If you regarded the assignment as nothing more than busy work for a grade, the exercise would be sterile and formalistic. If, however, you saw the philosopher's methodology as a way of trying on the role of philosopher, a role played by Plato, Aristotle, Descartes, Hume, and other brilliant participants in the conversation of civilization, then you would learn a great deal about philosophy and about yourself.

Lili was not writing her paper in a philosophy class, nor could we be sure that any of you would be taking a philosophy course. Our preoccupying problem became how in the world we could interest you in a question of ethical philosophy outside the context of a philosophy class. Lili feared breaking in on you unawares, after you had just returned from soccer practice or from a beer party, and asking you to consider whether we can know what is evil and what is good. She did not want to preach, and she did not want you to groan. As she and I discussed the problem and as she wrote draft after draft, the real topic of the paper emerged: Why should academic assignments hold any interest for student writers beyond the immediate purpose of passing college courses? Lili and I saw that our question was central to the goal of the Beaver College writing program, which is designed to help students explore the various conversational roles within the liberal arts: philosopher, anthropologist, literary critic, biologist. By learning to speak in many tongues, students may be able to find their own voice as educated citizens.

Lili's writing is good for another reason. As her teacher, I learned a great deal from the collaboration in which she and I engaged. Lili maintained ownership of her essay even when, in my panic over the fast-approaching publication deadline, my comments became more directive than I hope I would ever have allowed them to become in a classroom. For example, I suggested a new title, which Lili tactfully—but firmly—rejected. Lili has offered suggestions and posed questions about drafts of my contribution to this chapter, and I have profited from her advice. Both of us have learned that what makes writing good is conversation freely engaged in by those who understand that civilization is defined by thoughtful—sometimes contemplative—written exchange.

Study Questions

1. A student writing about Lili Velez's "Examinations Outside the Classroom," said,

    > I have a feeling that something is being evaded in this writer's argument, or maybe it's that the problem she's dealing with isn't the problem. Good and evil, right and wrong, can be involved in issues outside the classroom. O.K. But anybody who can read a newspaper knows that. Where I stand on things like the Nuclear Freeze and abortion depends on my convictions. Of course, but that's obvious too. What I have trouble with is this writer's suggesting that simply because you see a thing in terms of good and evil, that you can then "make a decision with minimal risk of leaving embarrassing loopholes." I don't think you can throw logic out the window that way. She says, "I would rather fry while trying to get rid of nuclear arsenals than be destroyed because we let the arms race continue." But what if somebody else says, "I would rather fry while trying to create nuclear arsenals than be destroyed because we let the Russians develop the power to blow us to pieces without trying to stop them." Both positions I guess are ethical, but they've both got "embarrassing loopholes" too, logical loopholes. "Ethical philosophy" is a term that covers up as much as it covers in this essay.

    How do you respond to this statement?

2. "Lili," says Elaine Maimon, "does not believe that she has finished the assignment. I have tried to convince her that no assignment is ever finished; it is merely abandoned, sometimes to public notice."

    Do you agree that no assignment is ever finished? If so, what makes you say so?

    If you disagree, what are your criteria for deciding when an assignment is finished?

3. In a classroom discussion of Lili Velez's paper and Elaine Maimon's commentary on it, a student said,

I don't understand why Elaine Maimon doesn't speak of the importance of things like word choice and grammar and punctuation and organization to good writing. "Thinking and taking risks." Having "something to say and the courage to say it to a real group of readers." It's things like that she says make writing good. But can't you have all those things and have bad writing too?

Another student, drawing specifically upon what Elaine Maimon says in her commentary, argued that she does indeed talk about the importance of "things like word choice and grammar and punctuation and organization to good writing."

How might you support the latter argument?

What is your position on these two points of view on how to talk about what makes writing good?

This is your last long assignment, and so you will have a week rather than the usual three or four days to do it in. Attached are about thirty pages of excerpts and essays, all concerned in one way or another with "ambition." Since we are coming to the end of a course in which our question has always been "What is a historian?" you might try here to write a history of ambition in the last century, and if you do so, feel free to use the ambitions you have, or that others in your generation and preceding generations have had. But you may be more comfortable simply asking "Where do I see myself in relation to these authors on the subject of ambition?" Do not feel compelled to use all the authors, especially if, in trying to do so, you find yourself only performing a dazzling but uninteresting piece of jugglery. As always, the negative goal is to avoid distortion, of yourself or your materials; as always, the positive goal is to make relations that enable you to feel both fresh and precise.

[Included in the materials were Virginia Woolf's "Professions for Women," part of Thoreau's "Where I Lived and What I Lived For," excerpts from autobiographies by Andrew Carnegie and by an early union organizer, Pauline Newman, and some pages from Joseph Epstein's recent book on ambition, in which that trait is praised and its apparent decline in America is lamented.]

❧ [Untitled]   by Ellen Chafee

Ambition in all these selections has much to do with Van Gogh's statement: "If you hear a voice within you saying, 'You are not a painter', then by all means paint, boy, and that voice will be silenced only by working." The voice does not have to come from within, and need not be a voice at all; it can be circumstances. Woolf fights off the Angel of the House, and worry about "what men will say of a woman who speaks the truth about her passions." Carnegie and Newman fight their way out of poverty, Carnegie by getting rich and Newman by working to build the union. Thoreau fought off entering any career, and in the process his ambition became "searching for simplicity of life and elevation of purpose."

There is, then, a struggle related to or implicit in ambition. Carnegie and Newman come to similar conclusions about their impoverished beginnings. Newman feels that though "conditions were dreadful in those

ROGER SALE is Professor of English at the University of Washington. He is the author of *On Writing* (1970); he has taught courses in composition, and courses and workshops in the teaching of composition, at Washington and elsewhere for almost thirty years.

days . . . there was something that is lacking today and I think it was the devotion and the belief. We believed in what we were doing. We fought and we bled and we died. Today they don't have to." Carnegie believes that "to abolish honest, industrious, self-denying poverty would be to destroy the soil upon which mankind produces the virtues which enable our race to reach still higher civilization than it now possesses." I'm sure that if you had talked to either Carnegie or Newman back when one was bleeding and dying and the other living in "honest, industrious, self-denying poverty," neither would have been so enthusiastic. It is not the poverty they want to praise, but the struggle out of it. I wonder if they would have struggled so hard if they had known that upon reaching success they would look back on the struggle itself as being equally or more satisfying than the success.

3   Ambition implies a desire for something, which usually means a struggle to get that something. Inherent in ambition is a strange contradictory relation between wanting something and wanting a lot of resistance while getting it. We don't talk about people who reach for what they know they can have as ambitious. We wouldn't call Virginia Woolf or Henry Thoreau ambitious if Woolf had used her beauty to catch a rich handsome husband, or if Thoreau had entered a business and made a killing. We might say they were "successful," but the distance traveled doesn't warrant the name "ambition."

4   Joseph Epstein criticizes "the educated" (certainly Thoreau and Woolf fall into this category) for claiming "to have given up on ambition as an ideal" when "they have perhaps most benefited from ambition—if not always their own then that of their parents and grandparents." Epstein has a point; educated people are usually from well-to-do families that didn't have to make the money, but someone did, or from not so well-to-do families that sacrificed a lot for their children's education. Beneficiaries of this ambition and these sacrifices have no business pooh-poohing it. On the other hand, what would Epstein say about Thoreau? He turned his back on his Harvard education and refused to follow his parents' wish that he go into business or a profession. That could be taken to mean he had given up on "ambition as an ideal," but actually Thoreau opened himself up to having a real ambition, a real struggle for his life. Woolf does the same. She was well-suited to marry as her "profession." She was beautiful, and from a good family. But instead of becoming an Angel of the House, Woolf made a career of fighting that Angel. You can't say Thoreau and Woolf were not ambitious because they were not ambitious for wealth or because they did not have the constant needling of poverty to ensure their struggle that Carnegie and Newman had.

I fall into the category of Woolf, Thoreau, and "the educated." My ambition will never result in a rags-to-riches story. But I have tried to avoid easy ways out. My first paper for this class was about my decision to attend an integrated public school against my parents' wishes. In that paper I wrote: "I felt as a child I was disqualified from having any real adventures by my nice home, my loving parents, my quiet neighborhood. This grew into a feeling that my environment was sterile, lacking some sort of rigor that was essential for truly growing up." I wanted what Carnegie and Newman had, for the same reaon that, after they were no longer poor, they were glad they had it. 5

The same issue arose when I went to college. I went to Dartmouth, and left because I felt disqualified from having any real adventures; the environment was sterile. Two years later I ended up at the University of Washington, which is both a continuation of my desire to leave a sterile environment, and a giving in. UW is not a country club disguised as a school, but it is school, and school is where I am expected to be right now. There is nothing new in that. 6

What is new, and what I was trying to say in my paper #11, is that writing in school has become for me something important, important enough that I have sacrificed my image of myself as a good student for it. I struggle at writing as I struggle at nothing else in school. I am scared to say that my ambition is to be a writer, but I know I want to write well and that if, in the long run, I fail at it, I'm going to be really disappointed. Writing for me now has the taste of risk, not sterile, but real adventures. 7

Roger Sale's COMMENTARY

Most of the students who tried in this assignment to confront, as Ellen Chafee did, the passages I'd given them, ended up with some common denominator, something all the writers "have in common." Toss the excerpts, blend them, puree them, until ambition is only a word one finds in a dictionary and until what is said about it is mostly a dictionary definition.

What I like first, then, about Chafee's paper is that each writer is considered individually without the general subject being lost. The first fruit of that consideration is the third paragraph, her generalizations about wanting something but also "wanting a lot of resistance while getting it." I see two things taking place here, both of which, if not central to discovering "what makes writing good," are central to good writing in this context. First, there is a willingness to generalize in order to understand similarities among differences, and second, there is a willingness to generalize *early*, to treat a generalization as a working hypothesis in order to then plunge back, equipped with a miner's helmet and light, into particulars. Generalizations treated always and simply as conclusions tend to be fatuous; generalizations used to initiate thinking can often be exciting.

When writers generalize this way, they must, sooner or later, discuss the context of their generalization and the culture they have inherited and are creating. "We wouldn't call Virginia Woolf or Henry Thoreau ambitious if Woolf had used her beauty to catch a rich handsome husband, or if Thoreau had entered a business and made a killing." The moment she accepts that proposition, Chafee has work ahead of her—not just in replying to "Why wouldn't we?" which she can do easily by distinguishing between ambition and success, but in describing their ambition so as to make clear her own.

When anyone tries to locate similarities between the writer and the "big" figures in the culture, the result all too often is either a simplified "I can relate to"/"I cannot relate to" this or that, or a balloon of belief or conviction into which both writer and the big figure rise and disappear: "Like Milton, I believe. . ." or "Mill was right when he said . . . for I have seen in my own experience that . . ." Culture is degraded when it is treated only as a springboard. Yet how else can she treat her own relatively untested and modest ambitions in the arena offered by these writers? First, by making no effort to compare anything in her life to the struggles out of poverty undertaken by Andrew Carnegie and Pauline Newman. Second, though it is in the company of Woolf and Thoreau that Chafee wants to put herself, by not staring at the ambitions of Woolf or Thoreau, much less at their achievements; to do that would be like staring at the sun. Rather, take Joseph Epstein's reasonable but inadequate statement about these people, who have "given up on ambition as an ideal," and use it to support her earlier generalizations, which distinguish ambition and success.

As she describes her desire, first to go to an integrated school, then to leave Dartmouth, then to be a writer in ways she is unsure she knows how to be, Chafee thus neither diminishes nor falsely exalts her experience. Her own experiences are illuminated as examples of ambition when they might otherwise seem to be the obvious gestures of an upper middle class person trying to be slightly, and obviously, different. To be able to generalize in this way is to be able to join the company of Woolf and Thoreau without the least bit overvaluing what she herself has done or wishes to do.

Having thus said that I see Chafee's success as the result of her handling of generalizations, I should hasten to add that this ability is not one that can be learned or mastered. Chafee had, in fact, confessed to me a couple of days before the paper was due that the assignment was tying her into knots. Having little to suggest, and wanting to suggest no more than a little, I said: "You are good at reading authors hard. Concentrate on doing that, and maybe the rest will come." She *is* good at reading authors hard, that is, reading their words carefully, though in this case the result is nothing like careful literary analysis. The result is a trust, not in my judgment, not even in her ability, but in her authors; they can sustain her inquiry, they can point a way to go. Many writers, not feeling that trust, look at authors, especially authors long dead, either through the long end of a telescope ("You are so far away I can barely make you out") or else as a patch of roses and dense weeds ("If I can just hack away at this, reduce it all to a couple of arguments and assumptions, I may kill the roses, but I will also get rid of the weeds").

I cannot say where such trust comes from, but I know that it does not arrive at birth, and that it is accompanied by hard work and more than occasional failure. In Chafee's case, I think it also helps that she has had a more than occasional success; writing has the right taste of risk for her because it is not weighted with the heavy load of constantly feeling unable. From what she calls her sterile environment she has gained the ability as well as the desire to leave it, or so I surmise. But that trust seems an important ingredient in any good writing. To be able to say "I *can* make a relation between my self and the other, the 'out there,' the subject," is to begin to know that in a piece of writing both the self and the subject can live, and, in small ways or large, as they never have before.

Study Questions

1. In a classroom discussion of Ellen Chafee's paper, a student said,

   > What I like about this paper is that at a couple of places in it the writer seems about to give herself an easy way out of thinking. She *looks* like she's going to oversimplify or settle for uncomplicated distinctions. But in what follows she comes back on herself, almost as though she refuses to sell out.

   Show how it is possible to support this claim about Ellen Chafee's paper.

   Explain why you believe or do not believe that it is legitimate to evaluate Ellen Chafee's paper from such a perspective.

2. Judging from Roger Sale's writing assignment as well as from his commentary on Ellen Chafee's paper, how do you think he would respond to the question "How and why are readings important in a writing course?"

Explain why you would or would not agree with Roger Sale's response as you have imagined it?

3. In a paper written about Ellen Chafee's essay and Roger Sale's commentary on it, a student said,

> Roger Sale seems to feel that how a writer handles generalizations is crucial to whether the writing is good. But he goes on to say that Ellen Chafee's ability to handle them successfully "is not one that can be learned or mastered." What I want to know is where this leaves me as a writer who would like to use generalizations better than I do. What am I supposed to do? According to Roger Sale? According to anybody else?

How do you respond to this student's questions?

JAMES VOPAT'S Assignment

[This writing assignment came towards the end of a course that focused on *Working* by Studs Terkel.]

Throughout the interviews that compose Terkel's book, individuals speak of the loss of human potential, the physical and psychological violence that they endure in their everyday working situations. Your writing assignment, then, is to define *degradation* in Studs Terkel's *Working*.

❧ [Untitled]
by Peggy Bloxam

I cannot write this paper. I have sat here and rotisseried all kinds of ideas, from the most banal and animalistic to those of pristine morality and naivete. It's all bullshit, because I just don't know what to think about work and degradation. But I can tell you this—writing this paper has been a degrading experience. Explaining why so will give you my personal viewpoint (whose value is definitely questionable, but at least not bullshit) and may give me a larger perspective that I will not mind calling my own in this mess of Franken-ideas I have created. If you feel like throwing this aside right now, please do. If I thought I had the choice to stop writing it, I would.

I guess I really shouldn't say that writing this paper is degrading. I drink soda after soda. I light cigarette after cigarette. I move from my room to the study room and back again. I am trapped. I think that the really degrading thing is the knowledge that I will be punished because of a personal limitation. I'm not wilfully refusing to write. I just can't do it. God knows I would if I could. But the fact that I usually can produce will be overlooked and I will be punished as if I did something wrong. My punishment will be a lower grade and a continuation of my anxiety until I can produce a paper. I am going to be punished because my will and ability does not happen to match what is expected of me.

There's another thing, too, that kind of relates to what I just said. There are other things that I could be doing that would not be frustrating. I have other work to do that I know would get done if I did it. But I am forced to sit here and be essentially unproductive because this paper is due soon and I don't want to be punished unfairly. I am being forced to

JAMES B. VOPAT is currently Associate Professor of English at Carroll College. In addition to being coeditor of this book, he has published numerous articles on the teaching and evaluation of writing—most notably "Uptaught Rethought" and "Going APE" (both in *College English*), and "Guilty Secrets of an ETS Grader" (in *The Washington Monthly*).

be something that I don't want or have to be—unproductive. It's unnatural and therefore degrading for me to be unproductive. It's not *me.*

4 Speaking of unfair punishment—that's a very interesting concept. I find that justified punishment is kind of uplifting. It seems right and almost comforting that I get caught when I do something wrong on purpose. If I know it's wrong and I do it anyway I am denying my true self. Because I am not the kind of person who likes to do wrong things. So basically, justified punishment is punishing me for not being myself, and that seems fair enough. On the other hand, unjustified punishment is degrading because it is punishing me for being myself. It may punish my limits or my morals or my hopes, and those are things that I don't think anyone has the right to mess with as long as they hurt no one. They belong to me and I am responsible for them.

5 One last point. I don't want to write about work and degradation. I don't feel that I am ready or experienced enough to voice an opinion on degradation that I must be responsible for. But I have no choice. Someone has chosen "degradation" as a topic, and that choice becomes my limitation. I'd rather set my own limitations. Also, by being forced to voice an opinion before I am clear on all aspects of the topic I run the risk of being false to myself. I have already gone against my personal ethics by accepting this chosen topic as my limitation. I could do it again by choosing an opinion that does not reflect me, either because I didn't know all the facts or because I just wanted to get the damned thing done. Since I *know* that I'm not being myself in writing this paper, I feel that I should be punished. But chances are that I won't be, and that's degrading, too. It's like others can't tell what is really me. It's a loss of identity, another loss of self.

6 So. Trying to write this paper is degrading. I think that why I find it so can be applied to what the people of *Working* say about their jobs.

7 There are a lot of different voices in the pages of *Working.* Some are angry, some whining, some indifferent, and some are cynical. But they all have something in common, no matter how they voice it. These people have all had experiences that they felt were degrading in their work situations. These experiences seem to result in one or more of three things that are unmistakeably degrading:

1. a lowering of personal moral and intellectual standards
2. a limiting of potential ability and usefulness
3. punishment of manifestations of an individual will

8 The receptionist blushes at first when she must tell lies over the phone. After a time it doesn't bother her any more. The strip miner says that he doesn't like tearing up what took eons to lay down, but he does it anyway. A woman writer/producer continually "toes the line of the good

nigger" although she hates herself for destroying her self-esteem. And I go ahead and pass judgment on a topic I feel inexperienced in because my class demands it. In another case, where no one demanded an opinion, I'd keep my mouth shut. These people all feel degraded, and no wonder. They are lowering their moral and intellectual standards to meet the demands of a job. In a sense, they are denying their true selves and imposing over it a false self that meets requirements set by their circumstances.

The telephone operator is not allowed to talk to people who are lonely and in need of someone. The receptionist is no longer able to communicate with people outside of her job. The spot-welder can't help the guy next to him who just got hurt because he'll screw up the rest of the assembly line. I sit and stare at a piece of paper when I could be writing a paper for a different class. These are degrading circumstances because they are limiting the real potential of the worker. Here, too, a false self possessing characteristics totally divorced from those of the real self has taken over.   9

The telephone operator gets written up if she spends too much time talking to a patron. The actor who contradicts a "bigwig" loses friends and jobs. The young farm worker who steals some blankets simply to keep warm must return them sterilized and pressed. And I will be punished because I was not able to write a paper on degradation when I was supposed to. People are *punished* for being *themselves!* It's wild.   10

Why does working so often result in the degradation of loss of self? The answer, I think, is inherent in the contradiction between the purpose of the job and the worker's complexity as an individual. Most jobs involve providing a service to a large number of people or things; some very simple function. Therefore jobs tend to require maximum speed and efficiency or simple things like smoothing ruffled feathers or being a shill for a product all day.   11

But people were not made to be efficient robots or shills all day. We are more complex than that. We have egos and imaginations, so we fight being shills and daydream on the assembly line. We feel a responsibility and kinship toward the people we deal with on the job, so we screw up the line to help the guy who's hurt and joke with the person on the phone. I guess I mean that jobs today don't reflect the human condition. They are too simple for us to deal with as complete human beings. To cope with the anxiety and tension that this discrepancy causes, we sacrifice little bits of our personality and allow the job to graft on one of its own characteristics. The worker essentially accepts the morals of the service or function he is filling. That really is degrading, especially when the function of the job is highly impersonal.   12

I guess that this is what degradation is all about to me, and to many of   13 the people found in *Working*. The final indignity is the loss of self, or personality, of choice, and the acceptance of morals, limits, and expectations that reflect the demands of the job and not the potential and choice of the individual.

JAMES VOPAT'S COMMENTARY

As I walk up the steps of Old Main, a student walks by me in the middle of a complaint. "Every time I think of that test," she says to her companion, "I get sick to my stomach, and my knees start to shake." I wonder if this nausea and quaking doesn't demonstrate a problem common to any testing situation, and whether most writing assignments, including those so generously given out in introductory college writing courses, are not, in fact, testing situations. College Writing has, I remind myself, a style all its own. Such writing is usually safe and competent, an introduction-body-conclusion mechanism aimed at the correct answer. And what, I continue to wonder, is my role in this?

I am wondering about these things because I am about to teach "I cannot write this paper" in the same English course it had been written for five years before. It occurs to me that reading this paper has changed my way of looking at the teaching of writing and at my role as a teacher. For that reason it provides sufficient motivation for me to continue to teach writing—although perhaps not what passes for College Writing.

A major—I would say *the* major—difficulty facing the teacher of writing is the fact that students have already formed their own definitions of writing. That the historical as well as the present context of this definition is often negative and punitive significantly limits what can happen in the writing classroom. For the great majority of students, writing has been and continues to be the occasion of error and defeat; an academic playing field littered with penalty flags and no chance of a touchdown.

It is not the essay but the essay test that students have come to fear. And no wonder. A recent study by a professor of education at the University of Indiana found that not only will various teachers grade an essay differently, but a person who reads the same essay on two different occasions will give it two different scores. The Indiana study concluded with the following advice to the would-be writer of the essay test: "If you know the instructor thinks you are a good student, but the answer escapes you, write it somewhat illegibly." Enter the absurd world of Freshman English.

"I cannot write this paper" marked the first time I had really seen how writing could be placed in a systematic context of punishment, and that is the principal reason it remains so significant to me. I distribute copies of the essay to members of my class, and I read it aloud. From its opening line, the paper establishes itself as representative of an entire genre of papers that most English teachers would rather ignore: those two or three papers each semester written by students who strike out boldly with an embittered description of the hardships involved—the frustration, the blank page, the accidental unfairness of deadlines and grades. No representative of this genre, however, has expressed that frustration as concretely as do the opening paragraphs here. One person's choice becomes another person's limitation—how is that for a working definition of College Writing? Writing is a loss of identity, another loss of self—how is that for an overview of the history of Rhetoric?

I ask the students how they would evaluate "I cannot write this paper." If they were the teacher, how would they respond to the writer? One of the students observes that Peggy Bloxam "didn't do the assignment." I ask what he, as the teacher, would say, and he answers, "I like the paper personally, but as a teacher, I must note that you didn't respond to the assignment." Another student objects that the paper "does deal with degradation on a real level," but I am struck by the previous student's definition of the writing teacher: someone who judges on the basis of his expectations, someone, that is, who is caught in the trap of his own writing assignment.

I am interested in whether it is possible to make a writing assignment that is completely free of degradation. I am also interested in whether the more answer-oriented the writing is, the more degrading the context of the writing experience becomes. Does the college student see her experience with writing mainly as a failure on her part to measure up to some predetermined objectives? How close does the college writing teacher actually come to requiring the student to merely fill in the blanks? "I cannot write this paper" makes me as a teacher want to reconsider the purpose behind my writing assignments.

Another student mentions how frequently "I" is used on the first page, and how it disappears towards the conclusion. Peggy Bloxam has predicted this movement beyond the personal level in the opening paragraph: "Explaining why . . . may give me a larger perspective that I will not mind calling my own." This is my idea of political writing: seeing the implications of experience, the "I" as both personal and representative. The writer is also the worker; the "I" literally becomes part of the "we." "I cannot write this paper" is emphatically not a paper that begins and ends by stating the same dulled position. It is a paper that moves forward to an end that is not predictable. As its sentences spiral into the meaning of their implications, the "I" is subsumed by "people" and "we." This sense of the writer and writing as part of a larger whole is particularly important.

"I cannot write this paper" is writing that defines itself by its unconventionality: It does not have a three-part structure, and it is not particularly respectful of rules. It is writing that does not treat the idea, the writer, the teacher, or the act of writing itself in the expected College Writing way. This paper makes "one last point," for example, before it begins to address the assigned question. The writer proves that she cares about this assignment in the very process of declaring that she doesn't care. For, in an opening paragraph remarkable for the energy behind its choice of words, she goads the reader: "If you feel like throwing this aside right now, please do." She works at establishing an immediate and active relationship with the reader, acknowledging that he may choose to read or not read, and that his decision matters. One of the more generous definitions of writing involves the desire to affect an audience.

The unconventionality of the paper extends to its style. "I cannot write this paper" is decidedly not a series of right answers related through someone else's style. That the writer is selecting words and rhythms is apparent from the outset. Sentence structure itself is used to create mood: "I drink soda after soda. I light cigarette after cigarette." Here, the halting, repetitious frustration is not only stated but, through the cadence of the words, experienced. Incomplete sentences suddenly seem very complete. "So."—with its combined sense of fate, resignation, and determination to subdue the writing assignment, this sentence is the turning point of the paper. Genuine style is always a risk because it strives not to be ordinary. Only here, at this precise moment in this particular paper, will *rotisserie* be forged into a verb. *Rotisseried* did not exist until this opening paragraph. Similarly, "banal," "animalistic," "pristine," "bullshit," and "Franken-ideas" demonstrate the extent to which the writer has committed herself to writing an original paper. Whether we agree with Peggy's argument or not, we will certainly remember it.

"I cannot write this paper" unrelentingly examines the complexity of its idea. The connection between writing and punishment becomes more complicated with each paragraph until there is no ready conclusion. This paper is not exactly a case of writing to discover; it is more like writing in pursuit. The writer shows a determination to somehow triumph by the very means that threatened to lead to degradation, to express a personal viewpoint while giving "a larger perspective that I will not mind calling my own in this mess of Franken-ideas I have created." What the writer achieves is a redefinition of the writing assignment. When the writer takes control of the writing context, the risk of degradation diminishes. As for the central question of punishment as the motivation for writing—the responsibility for that distortion of the teacher's goal must surely lie within the cultural context of the writing situation. That, in the writing classroom, this responsibility individualizes to the teacher is a problem that deserves attention and some serious adjustments.

And so we come back to the role of the writing teacher: this well-meaning individual caught between the never-never lands of providing an incentive to write *and* evaluating the quality of the writing. More than one student laughed when I read, "Someone has chosen 'degradation' as a topic, and that choice becomes my limitation." I am that "someone." Each writing assignment is a working paradigm for writing instruction, a working definition of teacher, student, writing, and evaluation. Is the writing assignment itself a means of degradation? Often writing assignments do contain hidden catches and predestined expectations. The teacher knows the "right" answer, and all the students have to do is repeat it back. Is there a connection between the degree to which the teacher already knows the answer to the writing question and the potential level of degradation involved in the student "discovering" that fated answer?

"I cannot write this paper" makes me realize how limited my own definitions of writing are. A grade—whether low or high—seems, each time I read the paper, a very insufficient means of evaluation. In fact, my initial reading of the paper prompted me to stop giving letter grades on individual student papers altogether. Instead, I decided to rely on comments and the assumption that all written work for any course is but part of one semester-long writing sequence: All writing is work in process. "I cannot write this paper" changed, and continues to change, the way I view the quality of the writing context and my role in it. As the makers of the writing assignments and the givers of the grades, we are also "not made to be efficient robots or shills all day."

Study Questions

1. In a classroom discussion of Peggy Bloxam's paper, the following exchange took place. One student said,

> The whole first half of this paper really puts me off, the whininess of it. The writer's got "degrading" defined as her having to do anything she doesn't happen to feel like doing, and so when she's in a situation, like college, where she's going to have to pay if she does just what she feels like doing, she calls that "unjustified punishment." If she feels that way, why did she come to college? Suppose somebody in college doesn't take a calculus test because he doesn't "feel that [he's] ready or experienced enough to voice an opinion" about it and then fails the course. Is that "unjustified punishment"? How can the writer define "personal ethics" the way she does and see college as anything other than a sell out? She's just afraid to put herself in a position to learn anything.

Another student responded,

> If this student were afraid to put herself into a position to learn, she wouldn't have written the paper she did. If she were just whining, she wouldn't have written anything for the assignment at all. Also, I think the writer *uses* the first half of her paper to write the second. She deals with the problem of defining "degradation" in Terkel by defining it for herself first. I think she's doing exactly what a college student should be expected to do. She's making what she's studying in college her individual concern.

What position would you take in this controversy?

2. James Vopat says that reading Peggy Bloxam's paper caused him to "stop giving letter grades on individual student papers altogether." Instead he "decided to rely on comments." He does not, however, say what comment he wrote on Peggy Bloxam's paper.

Judging from what he says in his commentary, what do you think James Vopat might have written on Peggy Bloxam's paper?

How useful do you think such a comment would be to Peggy Bloxam as a writer?

3. A student, writing about Peggy Bloxam's paper and James Vopat's commentary, said,

> I think I'd be a little more convinced than I am that Peggy Bloxam's paper "is not a series of right answers related through the use of someone else's style" if her statements about the relationship of people to institutions weren't so repetitive and if I hadn't heard so many of them before. Do people really lose their individuality ("the final indignity is the loss of self") as easily as she says? And I think I knew that "people were not made to be efficient robots or shills all day. We are more complex than that." Wouldn't this paper be improved if this writer worked to eliminate some of her clichés?

How would you respond to this statement?

Writing Assignment 11
Locating the Self

For some weeks now we have been talking both generally and specifically about what makes writing good within a context of what it may be considered good for. Your assignment for this paper is to write an essay defining what *you* would call good writing.

In deciding on a point of view from which to address this assignment, you might find it helpful to bear in mind that, since all writing may be seen, in a sense, as an act of definition, there are as many ways to write a definition of good writing as there are writers to do it. It is entirely possible, for instance, to define good writing by discussing an example of it—or by creating what you would call an example of it.

Once you have written your definition of good writing, imagine someone asking you the value of your having done so. How do you respond? Are you now confident that you'll know good writing when you see it? Are you now more able yourself to produce it? Or what exactly is your position?

Synthesis

12

Writing Assignment 12

Synthesis[*]

This is the last paper you'll write for this course. It's an opportunity for you to review the work you've done this term in order to assess yourself as a writer. Where did you start? What did you move through? Where do you see yourself now? What are your hopes for the future?

The question you will be concerned with in this paper, you will notice, is one that you have touched on in other papers you have written this term: in your analysis of your first paper for Writing Assignment 10, for example; in your definition of good writing for Writing Assignment 11; and perhaps in others as well. In this paper, however, you are being asked to describe your *development* as a writer over a period of time in order to examine how you got to where you are now, in order to see how best to move on. Things you said in earlier papers may certainly be *made* relevant to your understanding of this development, but "made" is the important word here. The relevance is one you will have to create. For you are not just taking an inventory in writing this paper, making a list of your strengths and weaknesses; you are not just setting goals for yourself as a writer. Rather you will be talking about your strengths and weaknesses as a means of seeing where you can go as a writer and what you will have to do to get there. Without some sense of what your development as a writer can mean to you, such an analysis is not worth making; the story of your created "I" is not worth the telling.

A list of some sort will be a helpful first step in writing this paper (and please turn in this list with your paper). You'll also need to refer to specific examples in

---

[*] We are indebted to Laura Dice of the University of Pittsburgh for the yearbook analogy and Pirsig quotation in this assignment.

specific papers in order to be able to locate and identify the points of your transformation as a writer. You might consider the difference between early and late papers, both in what they are like and how you wrote them. Judging from what you wrote at different points in the course, what kind of reader of student essays and teachers' commentaries were you? How did you change? You might consider how you coped with different kinds of writing situations, how well you organized your thoughts for this paper or that one, what you learned about thinking and writing from doing so. You might consider the voice in your papers, how careful you were to prepare and revise, how conscious you were of various writing processes, how much you might have changed the way you approach writing tasks. Make a list first. You can concern yourself with what you will make of it later.

But a list is not going to tell you what is significant about any changes you notice. What do the changes mean? Which ones are important to talk about and which ones aren't? When looking through an old photograph album, or a yearbook, you could make a list of the things that were different about the way you looked then as compared to now. But your list cannot tell you the *meaning* of the changes, whether longer or shorter hair is an acknowledgment of peer pressure or a reaction against it, for example. Whether your taste in clothes has changed because styles have changed, or because you have. Whether your holding your head at different angles means nothing or everything.

Robert M. Pirsig in *Zen and the Art of Motorcycle Maintenance* talks about this kind of assessment:

> Now, in getting that screw out [of a side cover] you aren't interested in what it *is*. What it *is* has ceased to be a category of thought and is a continuing direct experience. . . . You are interested in what it does and why it's doing it. You will ask functional questions. Associated with your questions will be a subliminal quality discrimination.

In doing this paper, try to ask the kinds of questions that can lead to a *conscious* "quality discrimination." Of your own. For yourself.

1 2 3 4 5 6 7 8 9 0